*

AMERICAN WRITERS SERIES
*
HARRY HAYDEN CLARK

General Editor

*

AMERICAN WRITERS SERIES

*Volumes of representative selections, prepared by American
scholars under the general editorship of Harry H. Clark,
University of Wisconsin*

*

(Ready by September, 1934)

RALPH WALDO EMERSON
Frederic I. Carpenter, Harvard University

ALEXANDER HAMILTON and THOMAS JEFFERSON
Frederick C. Prescott, Cornell University

NATHANIEL HAWTHORNE
Austin Warren, Boston University

WASHINGTON IRVING
Henry A. Pochmann, Mississippi State College

HENRY WADSWORTH LONGFELLOW
Odell Shepard, Trinity College

MARK TWAIN
Fred L. Pattee, Rollins College

EDGAR ALLAN POE
Margaret Alterton, University of Iowa

HENRY DAVID THOREAU
Bartholow Crawford, University of Iowa

WALT WHITMAN
Floyd Stovall, University of Texas

(Ready early in 1935)

WILLIAM CULLEN BRYANT
Tremaine McDowell, University of Minnesota

JAMES FENIMORE COOPER
Robert Spiller, Swarthmore College

OLIVER WENDELL HOLMES
Robert Shafer, University of Cincinnati

JAMES RUSSELL LOWELL
*Norman Foerster, University of Iowa
and Harry H. Clark, University of Wisconsin*

THOMAS PAINE
Harry H. Clark, University of Wisconsin

JOHN GREENLEAF WHITTIER
Harry H. Clark, University of Wisconsin

*Pen drawing by Kerr Eby, after
a painting by John Trumbull*

ALEXANDER HAMILTON

ÆT. 45

Alexander Hamilton

AND

Thomas Jefferson

REPRESENTATIVE SELECTIONS, WITH
INTRODUCTION, BIBLIOGRAPHY, AND NOTES

BY

FREDERICK C. PRESCOTT

Professor of English
Cornell University

AWS

AMERICAN BOOK COMPANY

New York   Cincinnati   Chicago
Boston   Atlanta

150369

PREFACE

The arrangement of the extracts, in general chronological, has been modified in the case of Jefferson's *Autobiography* and *Anas*, from which the extracts are included (with slight exception) under the years to which they refer.

As far as possible the extracts—letters, papers, addresses, etc.—are printed entire. In order, however, to represent the writers most adequately within the prescribed space it has been necessary to make some omissions (marked by . . .). Fewer essays from the *Federalist* have been included than would have been desirable were not this work already available in many forms. Author's notes are printed at the bottom of the pages, as they occur; editor's notes at the end of the volume. A few of the less important author's notes have been omitted.

The text has been modernized in spelling and punctuation, but otherwise, it is hoped, represents as accurately as is possible the originals. The extracts from Hamilton's *Farmer Refuted* and from Jefferson's *Summary View* and *Autobiography* have been compared with the earliest editions. The text of the extracts from Hamilton is that of the best edition—by H. C. Lodge, nine volumes, 1885–1886. For permission to make this use the editor is grateful to the publishers, G. P. Putnam's Sons. He is also indebted to Professors H. H. Clark and Gilbert Chinard for valued assistance.

F. C. P.

CONTENTS

Contents

INTRODUCTION

The inclusion of Hamilton and Jefferson in a series devoted to American literature may at first seem questionable. Neither of these men was a writer of books. Jefferson indeed made "Notes on Virginia," not intending them for publication, which have probably been more often reprinted than any other work produced in the South; and, like Franklin, he left at his death an incomplete "Autobiography," which is of the highest interest. But during a long career he wrote surprisingly little over his own name, and indeed he prided himself on not writing for the press. Hamilton has the air of a man too busy to write books even if he had wished. In general both men, like Franklin, wrote only in the course of business. But both had to write much, and both are now represented by a generous number of volumes. Those of Hamilton include his official papers, his political speeches and essays—among them, in the *Federalist*, a work of the first rank—and his letters, which are almost entirely political in subject. Those of Jefferson, besides the two notable works mentioned, include his official papers—among them his draft for the Declaration of Independence and his inaugural addresses—and a great number of letters, on a wide range of subjects, which are among the most interesting America has produced. Men of this kind—like Franklin and Lincoln—practical in their purpose and too intent on their subject-matter to ornament it, often attain a directness and naturalness not given to professed men of letters. At any rate, both these men wrote well—Hamilton with an orderly clearness and masterful confidence, perhaps sometimes betrayed by rapidity; Jefferson with a happy combination of the slight formality and slight negligence proper to a Virginia gentleman, and, as John Adams remarked, with "a peculiar felicity of expression." Not so much the style as the substance of these volumes, however, gives them their value. Probably no two men had, and continue to have, greater influence on American life and thought; and this influence was exerted—largely by Hamilton, perhaps mainly by Jefferson—through their writings. The purpose of this book is to represent, so far as space will permit, the thought of these two men.

ALEXANDER HAMILTON

I. POLITICAL APPRENTICE

Hamilton's interests of public concern were mainly political. His work as a lawyer was secondary; that as a financier and economist, as will appear, was subordinate to his political activity. We are here concerned, therefore, primarily with the development of his political theory and its applications.

When the outbreak of the Revolution converted Hamilton, at the age of nineteen, from a student to a soldier, his political views, as in spite of his precocity we might expect, were drawn not so much from his own mind as from his reading and from the revolutionary atmosphere of the time. A memorandum kept in 1776 contains a list of books indicating the quality of his reading. This ranges from "Orations—Demosthenes," through many works political and financial—"Lex Mercatoria" and "Hobbes's Dialogues"—to "Smith's History of New York"; and is followed by serious notes and reflections. If we may trust his own statement, he had at first "strong prejudices" on the loyalist side—perhaps a significant admission—but was won over by "the superior force of the arguments in favor of the American claims." [1]

What were the theories of government, inherited by Hamilton

[1] "Advertisement" to *The Farmer Refuted*, in *Works*, I, 52 (compare, however, H. J. Ford, *Hamilton*, p. 27). Unless otherwise indicated, all references are to *Works of Hamilton*, edited by H. C. Lodge, 9 vols., 1885–1886.

and his contemporaries, between which they might choose to find "arguments" fitted to support their "claims"? When Englishmen gave up the notion of rule by divine right, they attempted to solve their political difficulties by suiting government rationally to human needs. Reviving ideas that had come down to them from antiquity and the middle ages—the state of nature, the law of nature, natural rights, the social compact— they gave them new and vigorous discussion. From this emerged, in the seventeenth and eighteenth centuries, three main tendencies in government: first, the notion of an enlightened absolutism; secondly, that of a limited and responsible rule under a constitution; and finally, that of a democracy. The first is best represented by Hobbes in his *Leviathan* (1651). Having a poor opinion of men and believing them moved solely by their passions, Hobbes pictured them in a state of nature as equal and free indeed, but miserable indeed also—constantly at war, and their life "poor, nasty, brutish, and short." To escape anarchy they surrendered their natural rights to a sovereign, making an indefeasible contract. Henceforth the duty of the sovereign, after vigorously protecting his own sovereignty, was to promote the welfare of the people; the duty of the subject was entire obedience. This doctrine sets up a benevolent, but absolute and paternal government. Though Hobbes contemplates a monarchical sovereign, there is nothing in his theory to prevent the sovereign being an absolute parliament or congress. This theory was obviously not one to attract the American revolutionists; but in considering Hamilton we must keep it in mind and later revert to it.

Locke, who developed the second theory in his *Two Treatises on Government* (1690), and who fathered the ideas prevailing in the eighteenth century, had a better opinion of mankind. In a state of nature men lived tolerably, but finding it convenient in order to protect a certain precious portion of their natural rights—particularly that of property—they contracted to form a government, which, however, derived its powers from their consent. Not merely a theorist but also an apologist for the revolution of 1689, Locke took care to include in his theory the principle that if government disregarded the people's welfare, the contract was thereby broken and government dissolved. The third, the democratic theory, most Americans were not yet quite ready for. This of Locke, however, suited them exactly. Having lived under pioneer conditions, they were familiar with equality, freedom, and "natural rights"; they could interpret their charters as "social compacts"; and they were governed mainly by laws made with their own consent. Above all, they could use the arguments by which Locke had justified one revolution to justify another. "If," says Locke, "a long train of abuses, prevarications, and artifices, all tending the same way, make the design [of tyranny] visible to the people . . . it is not to be wondered at that they should then rouse themselves."[2] This theory supplied "the glittering generalities that became the political gospel of the American revolutionists."[3] And with these "generalities" Hamilton, at first at any rate, was very much impressed. Later, with greater experience, he developed quite different views, as, if we take up his writings, we shall see.

As in 1774 the people of the New York colony were dividing themselves into Whigs and Tories, the "no-trade agreement," recently adopted by Congress, was warmly debated. A forcible pamphlet, by "A Westchester Farmer,"[4] attacking it, called forth many replies, among them *A Full Vindication of the Measures of Congress* (1774) and *The Farmer Refuted* (1775), from the pen of Hamilton, a student at King's College. These pamphlets, which exhibit their immaturity in a jocosity which

[2] *Two Treatises on Government*, Book II, sec. 225. The theories of Hobbes and Locke are conveniently summarized, with interesting criticism, in W. Graham, *English Political Philosophy*, pp. 1–87.

[3] E. Channing, *History of the United States*, III, 10.

[4] *Free Thoughts on the Proceedings of the Continental Congress*, now known to be by Samuel Seabury.

fortunately he later abandoned, were able enough to give him reputation as the "Defender of Congress"; and being the only public expression of his political views before 1781, they deserve some examination. "All men," he declares in the first, "have one common original; they participate in one common nature, and consequently have one common right. . . . The pretensions of Parliament are contradictory to the law of nature, subversive of the British Constitution, and destructive of the faith of the most solemn compacts."[5] Presently, however, he proceeds from abstract right to more realistic argument, and with some show of the information and thoroughness which are the sources of his later strength, he examines the consequences of interrupted trade. Here very early he hit upon one of his important ideas. One of these consequences will be the extension of American manufactures; and "if, by the necessity of the thing, manufactures should once be established . . . they will pave the way still more to the future grandeur and glory of America; and by lessening its need for external commerce, will render it still securer against the encroachments of tyranny."[6] This is almost a brief summary of the argument of his famous "Report on Manufactures."

The Farmer Refuted, though later by only a few weeks, marks a striking advance; its careful examination of colonial rights under the charters, for example, exhibits the research and acumen which made Hamilton a great lawyer. It is most interesting, however, as showing a conflict in his mind between what might roughly be called Lockian and Hobbesian principles. He begins by rehearsing the familiar arguments, appealing "more especially" to "the law of nature, and that *supreme law* of every society—*its own happiness.*" He presently finds "the fundamental source of all the errors" of his opponent in "a total ignorance of the natural rights of mankind." Curiously, he detects a "strong similitude" between his opponent's low

[5] *Works,* I, 6.　　　　　　[6] *Works,* I, 18.

notions of man in the natural state and "those maintained by Mr. Hobbes." But after all, "the sacred rights of mankind are not to be rummaged for among old parchments or musty records. They are written, as with a sunbeam, in the whole volume of human nature, by the hand of divinity itself; and can never be erased or obscured by mortal power." [7] Hamilton, however, was perhaps not as much of an anti-Hobbesian as he supposed. Elsewhere in this pamphlet, writing with less revolutionary enthusiasm but perhaps greater sincerity, he appears more realistic. Arguing shrewdly concerning the relations of the colonies to Europe, he finds these governed by anything but altruism. Americans cannot trust to the good will of England, which already discovers "a jealousy of our dawning splendor"; for "jealousy is a predominant passion of human nature." He cites from Hume, who held Hobbes's low opinion of human nature, a passage which perhaps colored all his later views. "Political writers," he quotes Hume as saying, "have established it as a maxim that, in contriving any system of government . . . *every man* ought to be supposed a *knave;* and to have no other end but *private interest.* By this interest we must govern him; and, by means of it, *make him coöperate to public good,* notwithstanding his insatiable avarice and ambition." [8] If such, politically, are the motives of mankind, it is vain to trust to the wisdom or justice of the British Parliament. "A fondness for power is implanted in most men, and it is natural to abuse it when acquired." Such abuse can be met only by forcible resistance. Natural rights are very fine, Hamilton now seems to say,

[7] *Works*, I, 108. Printed in capitals in the original. Though not perhaps entirely characteristic, this is used as title-page motto in the Lodge edition.

[8] See Selections following, p. 8. The passage will be found in Hume, *Essays* (London, 1767), I, 37. For Hamilton's considerable debt to Hume see Bein, *Die Staatsidee Hamiltons*, p. 165. Though there is not definite evidence as to the extent of Hamilton's reading, he was clearly less well read than Adams and Jefferson. He sought in books not so much new ideas as effective quotations and arguments from authority.

but they belong to those who can obtain and defend them. Here, then, there are two strains of thought, two attitudes toward human nature and human rights, confused and unreconciled; the thought is not yet integrated. The second, as we shall see, indicates the direction in which Hamilton's thought eventually moved. We may note further that Hamilton closes by acknowledging himself, perhaps only formally, "a warm advocate for limited monarchy, and an unfeigned well-wisher of the royal family." However, in proposing that, though sovereignty should remain in a common monarch, coördinate legislatures should be provided for his English and American dominions, he is advocating the very principle of decentralization, or states' rights, which he spent his later life in combating. But experience, "the parent of wisdom," will clarify his views.

II. POLITICAL THEORIST

Thoughtful Americans of the 1770's realized, as Hamilton was wise enough to do very early, that the forces behind the Revolution might break down not only British domination but the ties of ordered government at home; that the prevailing notions of "natural right" and "consent of the people," carried too far, would lead to disintegration and anarchy. "The same state of the passions," Hamilton writes in 1775, "which fits the multitude . . . for opposition to tyranny and oppression, very naturally leads them to contempt and disregard of all authority. . . . When the minds [of the unthinking populace] are loosened from their attachment to ancient establishments and courses they . . . are apt more or less to run into anarchy." [9] Troops, he recommends, should be stationed in New York to preserve order. Realization of this danger grew stronger with experience, and experience came rapidly. When in 1777, barely turned twenty, Hamilton was made an aide to Washington, he found himself in a position with many advantages. He was

[9] Letter to Jay, April 26, 1775, in A. M. Hamilton, *Intimate Life*, p. 25.

thrown into the very midst of momentous affairs, he was in intimate relations with the wisest statesman of his time, and he probably soon knew more about continental affairs than any one else, save Washington himself. He continued his study of finance and administration, not merely in books but in events. He matured his character and his views.

He soon found that men who had had too much of English government were determined to have as little as possible of their own. The jealousy of the states had been transferred from Parliament to a Congress, which, weak in its personnel, half legislative and half administrative in its functions, full of corruption and divergent interests, could act only on sufferance and was growing more and more inefficient.[10] The result was failure in recruitment and supply, and disintegration of the finances. In 1780 he says of the army: "It is now a mob rather than an army; without clothing, without provision, without morals, without discipline."[11] Nothing could have been more distressing to one of orderly temperament. Seeing these evils meant with Hamilton devising a remedy—even though he were as yet powerless to apply it. As usual he sought the underlying causes, and found one of these in a direction to which he had given much attention. "It is by introducing order into our finances—by restoring public credit—not by gaining battles, that we are finally to gain our object."[12] He devotes two notable letters to this subject. The first, probably of 1779, contains this characteristic sentence: "A great source of error in disquisitions of this nature is the judging of events by abstract calculations; which, though geometrically true, are false as they relate to the concerns of beings governed more by passion and prejudice, than by an enlightened sense of their interests."[13] Henceforth

[10] See, for example, his letter to Clinton, Selections following, p. 13.
[11] See Selections following, p. 24.

[12] *Works*, III, 84.

[13] *Ibid.*, III, 69. Without date, address, or signature, this letter has puzzled biographers; see Sumner, *Hamilton*, p. 107, and Ford, *Hamilton*, p. 84.

than one which will be able to usurp the powers of the people."
The danger is "that the common sovereign will not have power
sufficient to unite the different members together, and direct
the common forces to the interest and happiness of the whole."
The goal, then, is national strength and unity. Congress, therefore, should "consider themselves vested with full power *to
preserve the republic from harm*,"—that is, Congress should assume all powers necessary to the ends of government. If this be
considered too bold, it should call a convention which may grant
these powers. Those necessary he carefully enumerates, and,
be it noted, they are, with minor exceptions, those granted
under the Constitution in 1787. Let Congress, he concludes,
assume an air of authority and confidence, for "men are governed by opinion; this opinion is as much influenced by appearances as by realities."

As a step toward action Hamilton attempted to place these
ideas before the public in a series of papers, significantly entitled the *Continentalist*. "The extreme jealousy of power . . .
attendant on all popular revolutions" has fatally reduced the
authority of Congress. But "in a government framed for
durable liberty, not less regard must be paid to giving the magistrate a proper degree of authority to make and execute the laws
with rigor, than to guard against encroachments upon the
rights of the community; as too much power leads to despotism,
too little leads to anarchy, and both eventually to the ruin of the
people." [17] In a federation, like the United States, the real
danger is anarchy—with state discord and foreign interference.
The only safety is in a strong central government. The government must have the "power of the purse," for "power without
revenue . . . is a name"; and the power of regulating trade, for
trade will not regulate itself and a regulation national in scope is
necessary. [18] From the contemptible actuality—"a number of

[17] See Selections following, p. 35.
[18] *Continentalist*, No. IV, *Works*, I, 248–9. Hamilton has already

Hamilton is to be influenced mainly by practical considerations. After careful review of actual conditions he proposes a national bank, the earliest known project of that character in America. In the second letter, of the following year, to Robert Morris, he deals more fully with the finances. Utilizing the experience of other countries and then carefully calculating the possibilities of taxation, he concludes that the government must borrow, and he again proposes, as an instrument, a national bank, with a detailed plan for its establishment. "A national debt," he says, in words later turned against him, "if it is not excessive, will be a national blessing."[14] His purpose, however, is not merely financial but also political, for he adds: "It will be a powerful cement of our Union."[15]

Another letter, to James Duane, written between the dates of those just mentioned, ranking among the most significant of his papers, makes a landmark in the development of his theory.[16] In this he is seeking "the defects of the present system, and the changes necessary to save us from ruin." One defect is "want of method and energy in the administration" due to the lack of "a proper executive." The revolutionary jealousy of strength in administration has trusted everything to the legislature. This might be remedied by separating the executive functions, and assigning them to single responsible ministers—of war, finance, etc. But "the fundamental defect is want of power in Congress," arising partly from "an excess of liberty in the states," partly from timidity and want of vigor in Congress itself. "Nothing appears more evident to me," he says, "than that we run much greater risk of having a weak and disunited federal government,

[14] Compare from Report on Public Credit (1790): "The creation of debt should always be accompanied with the means of extinguishment." —*Works*, II, 100.

[15] *Ibid.*, III, 124. Sumner, a student of finance, after noting that the bank scheme "contained financial fallacies which . . . he never conquered," remarks: "It is the statesmanship of it which is grand, not the finance."— *Hamilton*, p. 114.

[16] See Selections following, p. 18.

petty states, with the appearance only of union, jarring, jealous, and perverse, without any determined direction, fluctuating and unhappy at home, weak and insignificant in the eyes of other nations"—from this he turns, in his often quoted conclusion, to the "noble and magnificent perspective of a great Federal Republic, closely linked in the pursuit of a common interest, tranquil and prosperous at home, and respectable abroad." [19] Hamilton is already an architect of government; he has devised his essential plan, if not all of his specifications; he has, by publishing it, taken a step toward its adoption. He is in fact prepared to become one of the builders of the nation he has already in imagination conceived. In other words these papers, of 1779 to 1781, contain or imply the essential principles in Hamilton's political theory. His appeal is no longer to the abstractions of "natural right," but to "experience and reason"; he is no longer troubled by confusion and conflict; and he now speaks with entire conviction and confidence. From this time, 1781, his principles develop but they do not change.

The student of Hamilton is impressed by a remarkable agreement between his political thought, in its maturity, and his personal character. Life, career, and thought were unusually integrated. He was ambitious, as Washington said after long intimacy,—adding, however, that his ambition was "of that laudable kind that prompts a man to excel in whatever he takes in hand." [20] He found it easy to excel, for he had, within his range, extraordinary ability. He had concentration of purpose and of will, which accounted largely for his strength; and this accorded with his idea of strength and unity in a sovereign state. He had courage and tireless energy; it was natural for

adopted a theory of government interference and protection, later developed in his "Report on Manufactures." He here interprets Hume's "Jealousy of Trade" as not unfavorable to his view. His argument that the consumer does not pay the duty, now timeworn, appears here; see *Works*, I, 260.

[19] *Ibid.*, I, 273.
[20] To Adams, in *Works*, ed. J. C. Hamilton, VI, 360.

him to conceive an equally bold and energetic government. He was scrupulously honest; and he had a strong sense of governmental and international obligation. He had a passion for order, and easily mastered details by ordering them; he was by temperament the foe of anarchy and the friend of ordered government. He was a born organizer and executive; and he was fond of comparing efficient government to a machine smoothly running under the control of its engineer. Coming to New York an alien and alone, he had neither the strength nor the weakness of local ties and sentimental attachments. He was thus fitted to take "continental" views. Though he was not without patriotism, and though he found in the new world a field favorable to his ambition and invention, he would perhaps have been equally at home had his lot fallen in another age or country—in the England of Pitt or the France of Colbert. He perhaps cared less for the people of his adopted country than for his appointed task of providing them with an efficient government. "His sympathies," says a friendly biographer, "were always aristocratic, and he was born with a reverence for tradition." [21] He thought accordingly that government should be in the right hands, and that its conduct should command an honor and respect akin to that due to right behavior in a private gentleman. Though inventive and no slave of the past, he was fond of appealing to history, and especially to experience. He was a realist, not a visionary or a romantic,—not, in his own words, among those "enthusiasts who expect to see the halcyon scenes of the poetic or fabulous age realized in America." His deficiencies appear only when he is compared with the greatest men; he lacked the serene wisdom of Washington, the sympathy and humanity of Lincoln, and these deficiencies affected his policy.

As the Revolution closed Hamilton saw clearly not only the national need and the remedy, as we have seen, but also the

[21] Oliver, *Hamilton*, p. 27.

difficulties, which were great. "Peace made," he wrote in 1782 to his friend Laurens, "a new scene opens. The object then will be to make our independence a blessing. To do this we must secure our Union on solid foundations—a herculean task—and to effect which mountains of prejudice must be leveled." To Washington he wrote a year later: "The centrifugal is much stronger than the centripetal force in these States; the seeds of disunion much more numerous than those of union." [22] For five more years he saw the country slipping deeper into anarchy, into bankruptcy in its finances and reputation. Entering Congress in 1782 he had experience with its disability; he urged measures for strengthening the government, but had to abandon them, he says, for "lack of support." In a *Vindication of Congress* (1783), he found the fault not in the personnel but in the system. "In these circumstances" he urged that all should unite "to direct the attention of the people to the true source of the public disorders—the want of an *efficient general government*." [23]

At last came an opportunity for effective action. Sent in 1786 as delegate to the Annapolis Convention, he framed an address which was unanimously adopted, recommending that Commissioners be appointed by the States to meet at Philadelphia, to devise such "provisions as shall appear to them necessary to render the Constitution of the Federal Government *adequate to the exigencies* of the Union." He was presently chosen as delegate to the Convention of 1787.

The problem confronting this famous body was formidable, —to provide a government. It was natural to seek precedents; for men of English race—provided they were not experimentalists or visionaries—to seek them in the English constitution. This had on the whole secured both stability and freedom; and this had already served as model for the colonial governments. Evidently, however, it must be modified to suit their purposes. Having got rid of one king, most of them did not

[22] See Selections following, p. 37.   [23] *Works*, I, 315.

wish another. They must transform their monarchical model into a republic. They knew, indeed, that modern examples of republican government had not met with reassuring success; they could not know that their own experiment would eventually furnish the most notable one. All was project and experiment. The essential question, however, was how far they should go in modifying their English model by the introduction of republican and democratic principles. The whole problem was further complicated by the difficulty of adjusting the relations of the already existing state governments to the proposed central one.

Though for well-known reasons Hamilton's share in the convention was not large, it discloses very interesting developments in his theory. He at once placed his views before the convention in a speech, submitting at the same time a draft for a constitution, and from time to time he made other speeches.[24] Closed doors permitted him to express himself with the greatest frankness. In a word, he favored, first, as near an approach as possible to the English model; secondly, as complete a subordination as possible of the states to the federal government. His speech, however, must be briefly examined.

The only solution, he believes, is "one General Government" with "complete sovereignty," for "two sovereignties cannot exist within the same limits." [25] Two objections indeed arise: first, the expense of such an all-embracing government,—which, however, will not be too great if the burden of the state governments is largely removed; and, secondly, the size of the country; he despairs of extending republican government over so great a territory.[26] He hesitates about proposing any other

[24] The draft is preserved; the speeches only in his rough notes and in abbreviated reports by Madison and Yates. All the material is conveniently collected in _Works_, I, 331–400.

[25] It has been pointed out that this was proved by the Civil War.

[26] He is here adopting—or utilizing—Montesquieu's principle; see _Esprit des Lois_, Book VIII, sec. xiv.

form, but in his private opinion he has "no scruple in declaring that the British government is the best in the world"; and he "doubts whether anything short of it will do for America." In the words of Necker: "It is the only government which unites public strength with individual security." In every community there will be a natural division into the *few* and the *many*. Each of these interests should have power, and they should be separated, one checking the other. The people should have their voice in an Assembly; but the voice of the people is not the voice of God; "the people are turbulent and changing. They seldom judge or determine right." Give, therefore, the few a distinct permanent share in government. The English House of Lords "is a most noble institution," a barrier against "pernicious innovation" attempted by either Crown or Commons. And so with the executive: you cannot have a good executive on the democratic plan; nothing short of the excellency of the British executive can be efficient. Accordingly he proposes an Assembly to be elected by the people for three years; a Senate and an Executive to be elected by electors chosen by the people, to hold office during life. Will this be a truly republican government? Yes, if all officers are chosen by the people, or by a process of election originating with the people. To give the general government full sovereignty the states must be, not extinguished indeed, but completely subordinated—reduced to "corporations for local purposes."

Hamilton then did not propose a monarchy or an oligarchy, though in his balanced constitution he gave great weight to the principles which those features in the English system represent. It should be especially noted, indeed, that he proposed an assembly chosen by universal manhood suffrage—an unheard-of innovation in that day when a property qualification was everywhere a requirement. In general, however, the provisions of his proposed constitution look toward unity, strength, stability, and conservatism.

It has been said by defenders of Hamilton against the charge of "monarchical principles" that he was here advocating a system beyond that in which he really believed, merely to counteract tendencies in an opposite direction. His record both before and after the Convention, indeed in the Convention itself, does not bear this out. He was perfectly frank and explicit. "He acknowledged himself not to think favorably of a republican government, but addressed his remarks to those who did think favorably of it, in order to prevail on them to tone their government as high as possible." He recalls the prevalent opinion that a republican form of government is dependent on the virtue of its citizens;[27] and finds the prospect not reassuring. "The science of policy," he says, "is the knowledge of human nature. . . . Take mankind as they are, and what are they governed by? Their passions. There may in every government be a few choice spirits, who may act from more worthy motives. . . . Our prevailing passions are ambition and interest; and it will ever be the duty of a wise government to avail itself of the passions, in order to make them subservient to the public good." The English system, in its wisdom, recognizes and profits by the evil in human nature. Hume, he says, "pronounced that all the influence on the side of the crown which went under the name of corruption, was an essential part of the weight which maintained the equilibrium of the constitution."[28]

In these speeches of 1787 Hamilton probably expressed more definitely and frankly than anywhere else his true policy of government. When, however, as he expected, the Convention adopted what seemed to him a weaker plan, he was too wise and too magnanimous to withhold his support. "No man's ideas," he said, "were more remote from the plan than his own

---

[27] From Montesquieu, *Esprit des Lois*, Book III, sec. iii.
[28] Compare Hume, "Of the Independency of Parliament," in *Essays* (London, 1767), I, 40.

were known to be; but is it possible to deliberate between anarchy and convulsion on the one side and the chance of good to be expected on the other?" He urged that all delegates should sign, and when the Constitution was submitted he became its most effective supporter.

The *Federalist* was so entirely conceived and planned, and so largely written by Hamilton, that it will always be thought of as his work. Of the compromise constitution now submitted, however, he must be regarded not as the author, but as the highly effective, if not quite whole-hearted advocate. An expression in the first number is significant: "My motives must remain in the depository of my own breast. My arguments will be open to all. . . . They shall at least be offered in a spirit which will not disgrace the cause of truth." [29] It is not hard in the *Federalist* to detect shiftings of position for the sake of more effective advocacy. Hamilton could now find, for instance, along with depravity, "other qualities in human nature which justify a certain portion of esteem and confidence." [30] There was thus some hope even for a republic. Though he had before and probably still believed in "complete sovereignty," he could now turn a defect into a virtue: "the vigilance and weight" of the states will serve as an effective check against federal usurpations. [31]

Fortunately, however, he could on the whole support the Constitution with sincerity. If a compromise, it was a compromise in the right direction, and the country had gone a long way toward meeting his views. In 1776 the leaders were intent on "dissolving bands"; now on forming at least a "*more* perfect union." The *Federalist*, therefore, carries over indeed, but does not dwell upon the ideas of '76—natural rights, the social compact, the necessary-evil theory of government; its argument

[29] See Selections following, p. 45.

[30] *Federalist*, ed. P. L. Ford, No. 55.

[31] *Federalist*, No. 51; Speech on the Compromises of the Constitution, *Works*, I, 436.

is little related to them.[32] Much more conspicuous is the idea that "the citizens of America have too much discernment to be argued into anarchy. . . . Experience has wrought a deep and solemn conviction in the public mind that greater energy of government is essential to the welfare of the community."[33] The problem indeed is the perennial one,—of combining "stability and energy in government with the inviolable attention due to liberty and to the republican form."[34] Liberty will not suffer, however, under a government deriving ultimately from the people, and provided with a most effective system of checks and balances. Even a Bill of Rights is unnecessary. It is the other principle of strength that is in danger of being slighted. Hamilton has been forced to compromise on the Constitution, but he has by no means modified his views.

In brief, his argument rests ultimately on principles with which we are now familiar. He has no use for "the reveries of those political doctors whose sagacity disdains the admonitions of experimental instruction."[35] Experience has abundantly shown that the selfishness of man inevitably brings dissension and aggression—between individuals, states, nations. Let us not think that human nature has improved—even in an American republic. Alike to avoid domestic strife and foreign attack, a firm government is necessary; and only a government having powers adequate to its ends will ensure national stability and permanence. "These powers ought to exist without limitation, because it is impossible to foresee or define the extent and variety of national exigencies, or the correspondent extent and variety of the means which may be necessary to satisfy them."[36] It is the plain duty, then, of the American people to ratify and establish such an authoritative government, and to give it their support. Only by so doing can they secure true freedom, threatened alike by tyranny on the one hand and anarchy on the other. Thus would Hamilton reconcile two apparently opposed

[32] See, for example, Nos. 2, 23, 43.
[33] No. 26.   [34] No. 37.   [35] No. 28.   [36] No. 23.

principles; true liberty comes only from submission to a just, self-constituted authority. Thus might becomes right, because might secures right. The antagonisms are reconciled in the more inclusive conception of political justice.

Though the *Federalist* papers are said to have been written hurriedly—"in the cabin of a Hudson River sloop; by the dim candle of a country inn"—they represent Hamilton at his best. Their style has become classical in the sense that it has served as a model for later writings on the Constitution and for opinions of the Supreme Court. In no sense a man of letters, Hamilton made his way in life largely through the use of his pen. His boyish description of a West Indian hurricane won him an education; his reply to the "Westchester Farmer" led to a military secretaryship under Washington. Writing in this capacity countless letters, he learned even under pressure to write well. His skill was widely recognized. His friend Laurens thought he held the pen of Junius; his opponents, Callender and Jefferson, considered him the Burke of America, the "Colossus" of the Federalist party. To natural gift he added industry. He was tireless in investigating his subject, in seeking its governing principles, in tracing these principles in their remotest applications; and he could support his conclusions with complete confidence. If in the letters of Publius or Camillus his elaboration is sometimes excessive, he always carries his reader along by his logic, lucidity, and force.

Though too busy to formulate a theory, he occasionally indicated his notions of style. "Our communications," he says in 1796, "should be *calm, reasoning,* and *serious,* showing steady resolution more than feeling, having force in the idea rather than in the expression." And again, "Energy without asperity seems best to comport with the dignity of a national language."[37]

[37] *Works,* VIII, 430; J. C. Hamilton, *Life,* VI, 5. "Hamilton," says Chancellor Kent, "generally spoke with great earnestness and energy, and with considerable and sometimes vehement gesture. His language was clear, nervous, and classical. He went to the foundation and reason of every doctrine he examined."—A. M. Hamilton, *Intimate Life,* p. 93.

He is here speaking of public communications, in which he is ordinarily severe,—without humor, figure, or ornament. In private letters he could be graceful. Hawthorne notes of one of these: "It gives the impression of high breeding and courtesy, as little to be mistaken as if we could see the writer's manner and hear his cultivated accents. . . . There is likewise a rare vigor of expression and pregnancy of meaning, such as only a man of habitual energy of thought could have conveyed into so common-place a thing as an introductory letter."[38]

Hamilton's style cannot be highly individual, else it would have given a clue to the authorship of the disputed letters in the *Federalist*. It approaches a common or standard style— formal but earnest and business-like—in which the statesmen of the period seem naturally to have expressed themselves. In the political writers of the Revolution and early Republic, who thought independently and maturely, and who felt too strongly to be insincere, America may be said to have come of age and to have made its first substantial contribution to literature. Among these Hamilton holds high rank.

III. SECRETARY OF THE TREASURY

In the writings already examined, particularly in those on the Constitution in 1787, we have Hamilton's political theory developed in virtual maturity and completeness; in the future it is only elaborated and applied. His work was now not to plan government but to execute it. Concerned here with his thought, we may therefore pass somewhat rapidly over the less formative, though more eventful, portion of his career. Appointed in 1789 Secretary of the Treasury, he found himself in a position of great influence. Having the support of Washington and of Congress, he became the directing mind in the new administration. For the first and only time he was in power,

[38]*Works of Hawthorne*, Riverside edition, XII, 102.

with practically a free hand to realize his notions of government. His business was to make the paper constitution work, —at the outset, and in the right way; in Madison's phrase, to *administration* it into efficiency; in his own words, to provide "additional buttresses to the Constitution, a fabric which can hardly be stationary, and which will retrograde if it cannot be made to advance." [39] The task suited his love of power, his sense of public duty, his joy in difficulty to be overcome.

Wise politicians, he had noted in one of his earliest memoranda, ought to "march at the head of affairs," and "produce the *event*." [40] How then produce the event? He had, if possible, to contrive measures which should be immediately and strikingly effective, and at the same time provide a basis for permanent development. The exigencies of the moment, however, were decisive. To restore the public credit was the first step toward buttressing the national government.

The measures Hamilton adopted, all directed to this one purpose, may be very briefly noted. In his Report on Public Credit (1790) he advocated full payment of public debts,— including those incurred by the States "as the sacred price of liberty." He would thus "cement the Union" by establishing the national credit, and by enlisting the support of all holders of public securities. [41] In his Report on a National Bank (1790) he revived, in new form, the project of his Letter to Morris of 1781. [42] He remembered how an English government, after a revolution, had chartered the Bank of England, in order to solve its financial difficulties, and at the same time to solidify the Whig mercantile interest in its support. By incorporating a similar syndicate he could accomplish the same purposes. He must of

[39] *Works*, VIII, 540.

[40] Quoted from Demosthenes; in *Works*, ed. J. C. Hamilton, I, 6.

[41] As early as 1779 he had thought of this device; a bank, he then said, "will make it the *immediate* interest of the moneyed man to coöperate with Government in its support."—*Works*, III, 73.

[42] *Ibid.*, III, 100.

course draw upon the "implied powers"; he had long since seen that only thus was it possible to meet the needs of government.[43] In his famous Report on Manufactures (1791) he proposed government aid to "infant industries," in order to assure in war a "national supply," to establish economic along with political independence, and in general to develop the national resources. Contemplating a wise central management of the whole American estate, he foresaw local swallowed up by national interests in a country self-contained and self-sufficient.

In urging government interference to this end Hamilton was pursuing an economic policy entirely parallel to his political one. In both one notes a kinship with seventeenth-century thought. The old theory of mercantilism, favoring national regulation of trade, had in European countries gradually given way to one more in accord with modern ideas. In the economy of a state, as in other sciences, human and physical, philosophers had traced laws—the laws of nature and of reason; of God also, for "neither men nor governments *make* them nor *can* make them. They recognize them as conforming to the supreme reason which governs the universe." [44] The true political economy, then, was to trust to nature's laws and abandon all foolish human interference. This philosophic position was reënforced by the growing power of the mercantile classes, now ready to profit by freedom. Thus was developed, first in France by the physiocrats, then in England by Adam Smith, the doctrine of *laissez faire*. Though before writing his report Hamilton had carefully read the *Wealth of Nations*, he was as little inclined, either by temperament or by his realistic view of American conditions, to adopt this abstract doctrine of economics as he was any of its congeners in politics. Here again he would trust not to a providential operation of the "laws of nature,"

---

[43] The idea of implied powers comes in as early as the Letter to Duane; see Selections following, p. 19.

[44] See H. S. Randall, *The Growth of Modern Thought*, p. 323.

but to the well-considered policy of a paternal government.[45]

Especially in connection with these measures, all financial in character, there is danger of a misleading "economic interpretation of history,"—of finding their key in an economic purpose. A recent writer makes Hamilton the protagonist in a great struggle between capitalism and agrarianism, coolly devising a system favoring the privileged classes to which he belonged at the expense of the common people whom he despised.[46] Mixed and human as his motives may have been, this view does not on the whole accord with his expressions, with his habit of thought, with the habit of thought of his time. He had indeed a keen sense of property rights; he might even have subscribed to Locke's dictum that "government has no other end but the preservation of property." His measures were on their face economic, and had large economic consequences in which he was by no means uninterested. Could he have foreseen the tremendous economic development of which he was laying the foundations he would doubtless have gloried in it. As far as the two can be separated, however, his ends both seemed to him, and actually were, political. He knew nothing of the modern science of *economics*, with its forces determining political events. Like other statesmen of his time he had read and thought upon *political* economy,—that is, on the business side of a political state. His interest was in business only as furthering the interests of the state.

A typical example may be found in the much discussed assumption of the state debts. For this there was little economic motive, the national government having quite debts enough of its own without assuming others. The true motive was political: "If all the public creditors receive their dues from one source . . .

---

[45] See note 26 (p. 409), on the Report on Manufactures.
[46] Parrington, *The Colonial Mind*, p. 294; compare Sumner, *Hamilton*, p. 213.

their interest will be the same. And having the same interests, they will unite in the support of the fiscal arrangements of the government."[47] Furthermore, this measure would replace state by national tax-gatherers, and bring his government to every door. The final argument for every measure is the old one: "It will be a powerful cement for our Union."

To hold him responsible for building up Northern capitalism would be like holding his democratic states' rights opponents guilty of building up the slavery capitalism of the South. The true issue was not between capitalistic and agrarian interests, not even between aristocratic and democratic control, though both these conflicts were involved in the problem. The issue for Hamilton was where the older critics placed it: between ordered government and the disintegrating forces unloosed by the Revolution. He would increase national authority by drawing on every available source of interest or good will. He favored capitalism as a centralizing, opposed agrarianism as a decentralizing influence. It was blindness to ignore classes. One might temporarily suffer; another, employed as an instrument, might be temporarily advantaged. In the long run, he believed, his policy would benefit both, and the wise statesman considers the permanent welfare of the whole. Individuals, classes, interests, states, must be duly organized, according to their character and weight, into an ordered government.

Familiar now with Hamilton's principles, we shall have no difficulty with his foreign policy, directed to the same ends. The new American sovereignty, the first outside Europe, must be not merely recognized, but established and adjusted in its international relations. His ultimate purpose had been stated in the *Federalist.* "Let the thirteen States, bound together in a strict and indissoluble Union, concur in erecting one great

---

[47] *Works*, II, 65. In his "Defence of the Funding System" (1795), it is true, he does not mention this, emphasizing fairness and practicability.— *Ibid.*, VII, 423.

American system, superior to the control of all transatlantic force or influence, and able to dictate the terms of the connection between the old and the new world."[48] The key, at the outset, lay in non-interference and neutrality: "peace and trade with all nations, ... political connection with none."[49] Any other policy would be expensive, interfere with the development of the Constitution, and make the United States a football in the European struggle for empire. The new nation, still weak, must indeed proceed cautiously, for "America, if she attains to greatness, must *creep* to it."[50] Its policy, however, must be entirely realistic. It must of course observe international obligation; but within the bounds of honesty and justice, it must be directed neither by friendship nor enmity, but solely by national interest.[51]

The outbreak of European war in 1793 turned Hamilton's attention, with that of the country, sharply to international affairs. Peace and independence were threatened by both England and France. Hamilton, however, had only to apply, amid great difficulties and so far as conditions would permit, his established principles. American welfare should be the only guide. Gratitude to France and resentment against England, though natural fruits of the Revolution, are alike childish in foreign policy.[52] "I would *mete* the same measure to both of them, though it should even furnish the extraordinary spectacle of a nation at war with two nations at war with each other." And again, with the significant word underlined: "We are laboring hard to establish in this country principles more and more *national*, and free from all foreign ingredients, so that we may be neither 'Greeks nor Trojans,' but truly Americans."[53]

[48] No. 11.   [49] *Works*, IV, 366.   [50] *Works*, VIII, 543.
[51] The domestic measures, already considered, partly served this purpose; the fiscal measures by securing independence, the protection of manufactures by securing commercial equilibrium with England.

[52] Jefferson and Madison "have a womanish attachment to France and a womanish resentment against Great Britain"; see Selections following, p. 119.   [53] *Works*, VIII, 490, 436.

The proclamation of neutrality of April, 1793, probably the most important action of Washington's administration in foreign affairs, had Hamilton's entire support. It will hardly do to give him credit for thus establishing the Monroe principle, which, going beyond neutrality, undertook to exclude the "system" of the Holy Alliance from every "portion of this hemisphere"; this point Hamilton was never called upon to decide. His whole policy, however, was permanently embodied in Washington's Farewell Address, which he had a large share in preparing; here, it might be said, he joined Washington in warning the country against weakening the Union, against factional divisions, and against foreign entanglements.

After his resignation from the Treasury in 1795, as has been frequently noted, there was a lowering of Hamilton's behavior. He gave up to party, even to intrigue, what was meant for mankind. There is a corresponding loosening of his principles,— at least misapplication or exaggeration of them. The hidden forces of democracy, now marching against him, like Birnam Wood on Dunsinane; the poison of French revolutionary doctrines, covering the earth like a miasma,—these were enemies beyond the weapons which even Hamilton carried. One notes a change of tone. Already as he addresses the "pretended republicans" of the Whiskey Rebellion, in 1794, his firmness seems verging on a truculence which suggests alarm: "It is our intention," he says, "to begin by securing obedience to our authority, from those who have been bold enough to set it at defiance." [54] These "pretended republicans" were only too closely related to those of France. From the beginning Hamilton had looked with suspicion on the French Revolution,— on its "mere speculatists" and "philosophic politicians." [55] As it ran its course his feeling grew to foreboding, horror, detestation. In 1793 he thought the revolutionists butchers, atheists,

[54] *Works*, VI, 25.
[55] See letter to Lafayette, Selections following, p. 99.

and fanatics.[56] In 1798, with the "despots of France" waging war against us, he was moved to solemn warning and adjuration: "Reverence to the Supreme Governor of the Universe enjoins us not to bow the knee to the modern Titans who erect their impious crests against him and vainly imagine they can subvert his eternal throne."[57]

Now forsaking his previous policy of neutrality, he urged on a war with France which events soon proved avoidable. The motives of this change should be weighed carefully by the student of his statesmanship. He hoped to defend American shores against the enemies of liberty, religion, and ordered government. He probably hoped at last to discipline the people, concentrate the federal power, and discomfit its democratic enemies. It is even said that, forming ambitious plans of conquest, he hoped to lead an army into Louisiana and Mexico, and after acquiring by arms what was later got by purchase, to "return laurel-crowned, at the head of his victorious legion, to become the first citizen of America."[58] He is thus represented as approaching in grandiose ambition, though not perhaps in perfidy, that final antagonist whom he so often styled the Cæsar or the Catiline of the Republic. That this view can be held, with or without conclusive evidence, by competent historians is significant.

In this connection we may note Hamilton's only memorable references to education and religion—in two letters to Bayard of Delaware. In the first, anxious to find a president for Columbia College, he states the requirements: "That he be a gentleman in his manners, as well as a sound and polite scholar," and so forth,—and lastly, "that his politics be of the right sort." In the second he proposes, as a cure for what he somewhere calls "Godwinism," the founding of a "Christian Constitu-

[56] *Works*, ed. J. C. Hamilton, V, 566.
[57] See Selections following, p. 161.
[58] Morison and Commager, *The Growth of the American Republic*, p. 258; compare letter to Miranda, *Works*, VIII, 506.

tional Society . . . its objects to be: 1st. The support of the Christian Religion; 2d. The support of the Constitution of the United States." [59] These letters, which both turn shortly to politics, show, among other things, the narrowness of his effective thought and its exclusively political character.

In a letter written near the end of his career Hamilton struck an unusual note of despondency. "Mine," he says, "is an odd destiny. Perhaps no man in the United States has sacrificed or done more for the present Constitution than myself; and contrary to all my anticipations of its fate, as you know from the very beginning, I am still laboring to prop the frail and worthless fabric. . . . Every day proves to me more and more that this American world was not made for me. . . . The time may ere long arrive," he adds, "when the minds of men will be prepared to make an effort to *recover* the Constitution, but . . . we must wait a while." [60]

Hamilton was clearly undervaluing his own labors. If he seemed to fail, it was because he had gone too fast and had neglected elements of the problem which to the country seemed essential. In the further development of the Constitution it was necessary to go back and pick up principles which were the result of hard-won victories in the pre-constitutional period— local and individual rights, democratic participation in government—principles which he had passed over but which must now be incorporated with his work. He lacked sympathy and experience with the people, and underestimated their power. His character was, so to speak, completed in that of Lincoln, who, with equal devotion to the Union, had the humane understanding to give it a broader base. This lack perhaps led Woodrow Wilson to say that he was a great statesman, not a great American. The verdict is a harsh one, considering his great services to America—services too well known to be recounted

[59] See *Works*, VIII, 560, 598.
[60] Feb. 27, 1802; see Selections following, p. 172.

here. The essential idea animating and quickening his political activity throughout was that of a strong, united, and permanent American nation. "In a time when American nationality meant nothing, he alone grasped the great conception in all its fulness, and gave all he had of will and intellect to make its realization possible." [61]

Hamilton's ideal conception of government was never realized, but it has perhaps made some contribution to the general theory of politics. By a recent writer it has been identified with that of Hobbes—the "leviathan state." [62] With this indeed it has something in common—in its outlook, even in its principles. Hamilton believed in an undivided and indefeasible sovereignty, and in the subject's duty of disciplined obedience. He believed it the duty of the sovereign jealously to protect its own sovereignty, and to provide for the subject's welfare by well considered and strictly enforced laws. He believed in a wise and benevolent paternal government. Not, however, in an absolute one. Taking over the conception of the strong state as he found it in Hobbes and elsewhere, he modified it to suit his own purposes, by adapting it to American conditions, by attempting to make it at once strong and responsible. He clearly added to it a new element in combining it with universal manhood suffrage. He took care to introduce also other principles of representation and carefully devised safeguards on the popular will. Thus he sought to make his state not only powerful and permanent, but balanced and responsible—indeed the more permanent because balanced and responsible. He attempted to reconcile apparently conflicting, but, as he thought, essential principles by turning the leviathan state into a republic. Though not in its fulness realized, his conception has influenced the political thought not only of America but of Europe. [63]

[61] Lodge, *Hamilton*, p. 282.
[62] Parrington, *The Colonial Mind*, pp. 292, 300.
[63] On the influence in England and Germany, see Bein, *Die Staatsidee Hamiltons*, p. 163.

Thomas Jefferson

I. REVOLUTIONIST

Jefferson is remarkable for his breadth. As his letters show, he was alive to almost every interest of his time—agriculture, literature and language, music, architecture, religion, and science in many fields—as well as public affairs. Though famous as a statesman, he is perhaps best thought of as a Virginia gentleman of scholarship and culture, master of the mansion and model plantation of Monticello, where in his library or on his farm, he spent "philosophic evenings and rural days." From this ideal retreat, however, he was frequently called by his sense of duty and the pressure of events, to take his share of public life. He was indeed always fond of political theory, he wrote his most vigorous letters on that subject, and he had a gift for practical politics. We must deal first and principally with this major interest. Nowhere given final or systematic treatment, his political thought must be gathered from many letters and papers, dealing with particular conditions or events. Covering an unusually long career, in which he was now observer and theorist and again responsible officer of government, it naturally contains some shifts and discrepancies. On the whole, however, it is strikingly consistent, showing no change in fundamental principles. These principles will be most clearly understood if we trace them in their early development.

Very early in life Jefferson must have adopted the new ideas which during the eighteenth century were gradually transforming the thought of America, as of the world. Highly important here is the change in religious outlook. Man, it now came to be felt, was not after all fatally involved in Adam's fall; he was not naturally depraved, but naturally good. His salvation was a matter more of this world than of the world to come; it was to be accomplished, not by a miracle of divine grace, but by a natural improvement, through his own supreme faculty of reason.[64]   No change of thought could be more momentous. In a general, if not in a strictly religious sense, Jefferson early adopted the new view. He believed that man is good—just, honest, and honorable—and that he is "perfectible to a degree of which we cannot as yet form any conception." Here obviously he differed *in toto* from Hamilton, who, in a political sense at least, held firmly to natural depravity. Hamilton's view led him inevitably to a *machtpolitik;* Jefferson's, as we shall see, made him throughout a champion of the people.[65]

Jefferson turned from the practice of law to take part in the Revolution. He had been not a mere practitioner, but a close student of law, "bold in the pursuit of knowledge," as is shown by a laborious digest of his early reading, recently published in part.[66] This, with other evidence, shows that he read, pen in hand, not only English law, from Alfred to Blackstone, but works of Voltaire, Helvétius, and Montesquieu; as he undoubtedly did also the standard English treatises on government—Harrington, Milton, Hobbes, Locke,—"whose little book on government is perfect as far as it goes"[67]—and Sidney. By this study, covering legal rights, colonial self-government, and comparative constitutions,[68] he formed or confirmed his views. When, for example, in his copy of Sidney's *Discourses on Government*, he marked, among other sentences, "Just governments are established for the good of the governed,"[69] he

[64] The view of the New England transcendentalists (upon whom Jefferson had some influence), except that they took *reason* in quite a different sense.

[65] It has seemed best in this Introduction to avoid the common method of extended contrast between the two men—which may easily become rhetorical or misleading. After mastering their thought the reader may make intelligent comparisons.

[66] *The Commonplace Book*, edited, with an instructive introduction, by G. Chinard, 1926.

[67] *Writings*, ed. by A. E. Bergh, 1903 (to which subsequent notes refer), VIII, 31.

[68] See, for example, *Commonplace Book*, secs. 708, 729–757.

[69] See Hirst, *Jefferson*, p. 510.

was doubtless noting not a discovery but an agreement. In any case, nothing can be more certain than that he formed his political theory, not merely out of his own head, but after research in the best sources.

Though Jefferson's debt to these sources cannot here be examined, he clearly derived from them two strains of thought—one theoretical or philosophical, the other more strictly legal—which stand out in his early writing and activity. In the first place, from Locke and other liberal writers he adopted the doctrines of natural rights, popular will, and justice of rebellion, which he shared with his compatriots; in the second place, he found in the constitutional history of England a basis, more his own and more juristic, for his revolutionary position. In going over this history he concluded that Englishmen had enjoyed their true common-law rights only during the Anglo-Saxon period, these rights having been after the Norman Conquest gradually abridged or overlaid by royal and ecclesiastical encroachments. It was for Americans, then, to go back and reclaim their Saxon liberties. Though these two strains of thought—one rational and modern, the other legal and conservative—are at first sight opposed, they were in Jefferson's mind identified. He had only to imagine "our Saxon ancestors" living in a state of nature to find Saxon liberties and natural liberties coming to the same thing. In other words, natural rights being reasonable rights—that is, such rights as appealed to Thomas Jefferson and other equally reasonable men—it made little difference whether one sought these in abstract reason or in a period reasonably discoverable in English history at which they seemed to have been enjoyed. At any rate, common-law rights and natural rights reënforced each other.

Jefferson's expressions in the Revolution employ this double argument. After asserting in behalf of the freeholders of his own county that the privileges of self-government "are the common rights of mankind," he drafted instructions to the Virginia delegation to Congress in 1774, which, though not adopted, were widely read as "A Summary View of the Rights of British North America." Here he finds Parliament encroaching "upon the rights which God, and the law, have given equally to all." Among these are the good old rights of expatriation and conquest. Our Saxon ancestors exercised the "right nature has given to all men, of going in quest of new habitations," and in their new home they were independent of their mother country. A similar right and freedom belong to Americans. Again, these ancestors possessed the lands they thus occupied as free holdings, until Norman lawyers found means to saddle them with feudal burdens. Americans likewise hold their lands, not from the king, but by simple natural right. This appeal to Saxon liberties would doubtless have appeared peculiarly technical to George III, had it ever reached him,—as it evidently did to the Virginia convention.

Perhaps in drafting a Declaration of Independence for Congress two years later Jefferson thought best to take less novel ground. "Not to find out new principles, or new arguments, never before thought of ... but to place before mankind the common sense of the subject in terms so plain and firm as to command their assent," was now his object. This Declaration "was intended to be an expression of the American mind," resting its authority "on the harmonizing sentiments of the day, whether expressed in conversation, in letters, printed essays, or in the elementary books of public right, as Aristotle, Cicero, Locke, Sidney, etc." [70] Jefferson was only giving imperishable expression to the common thought. In the Declaration again, however, appears the double appeal—first, to abstract and then to legal rights. The well-known sentences of the second paragraph lay a philosophical foundation, finding in Locke, or other

[70] To Henry Lee, *Writings*, XVI, 118. Compare: "I did not consider it any part of my charge to invent new ideas altogether," etc.—*Ibid.*, XV, 462.

equally familiar source, the principles of equality, inalienable right, consent of the governed, and just rebellion. The later paragraphs show that a long train of illegal "abuses and usurpations" is reducing the people "under an absolute despotism." Denied the rights they have inherited both as men and as Englishmen, they justly "dissolve their political bands." Though Jefferson is here voicing the common mind, he is also stating ideas basic to his entire later theory, as we shall see. He never ceased to believe that men are created equal.

Returning to Virginia, now an independent state, Jefferson undertook, as a member of its first legislature, to cleanse the law, following the principles we have just noticed. Assuming as the legal basis for the state the common law—the *lex non scripta* of the Saxons—the problem was to free this law from obvious "feudal and unnatural" corruptions. On November 1, 1776, he introduced the first of his reformatory measures—a bill to abolish entails, and a little later he proposed another to abolish inheritance by primogeniture,—his objects being to distribute the land more widely in free holdings and to do away with the aristocracy of birth and wealth. Other measures provided for easy naturalization, on the principle of expatriation as a natural right, and for the reduction of unreasonable criminal punishments.

Of his efforts to secure religious freedom in Virginia Jefferson was especially proud. His approach to this subject may be taken as typical. As he explains in his *Notes on Virginia*,[71] the Virginia convention, in its Bill of Rights, "declared it to be a truth, and a natural right, that the exercise of religion should be free." Taking a first step, the same body, now sitting as the Assembly, in October, 1776, "repealed all *Acts of Parliament* which had rendered criminal the maintaining of any opinions in matters of religion." "Statutory oppressions being thus wiped away," there was still left, however, the common law, under which

[71] See Selections following, pp. 237 ff.

heresy was a capital offence. Here Jefferson found in his study of English history excrescence and corruption. The prefixing of four chapters of the Jewish law to the laws of Alfred was an "awkward monkish fabrication"; the introduction of the "whole Bible and Testament in a lump" into the common law was a fraud of the clergy; the ten commandments had never been made part of the law even by legislative enactment.[72] The common law, therefore, in its purity, had no concern with religion. By such legal argument Jefferson could support his bill for Establishing Religious Freedom. When he came to drafting the bill, however—evidently distrusting an appeal to the public so technical in nature—he resorted to "natural" grounds. "Almighty God," he says, "has created the mind free"; constraint is "sinful and tyrannical"; "the rights here asserted are of the natural rights of mankind." The legal gives place to the abstract argument.

Jefferson had earlier, in the legislature of 1769, made an effort "for the permission of the emancipation of the slaves"; but "during the regal government nothing liberal could expect success." Now, in 1778, he carried through a bill to prevent their future importation, and he prepared an amendment to the bill on the subject of slaves, providing for their freedom and deportation. He found, however, "that the public mind would not yet bear this proposition."[73] On this subject too he had made notes in his *Commonplace Book*, but whereas Montesquieu, as there digested, apparently rejects slavery as inexpedient or dangerous,[74] Jefferson opposes it on the broad ground of natural freedom. "Can the liberties of the nation be thought secure," he says, "when we have removed their only firm basis, a conviction in the minds of the people that these liberties are of the gift of God? . . . I tremble for my country when I reflect that God is

---

[72] *Commonplace Book*, pp. 359–363.
[73] *Autobiography, Writings*, I, 4, 56, 72.
[74] *Commonplace Book*, pp. 277–279.

just." [75] He continued to work for emancipation until his death. [76]

A final measure, to which Jefferson gave the strongest support, was the bill providing for a universal system of education. For this his argument was primarily political. "Every government degenerates when trusted to the rulers of the people alone. The people themselves, therefore, are its only safe depositories. And to render even them safe, their minds must be improved to a certain degree." [77] Though the bill was defeated or nullified, Jefferson continued to support the principle of general education, and, as we shall see, met at last some degree of success. By the measures we have just noticed, all introduced or furthered by Jefferson, a foundation was laid in Virginia, as he hoped, "for a government truly republican."

The *Notes on Virginia*, written in 1781–2, throw much light on Jefferson's political views, mainly, however, by way of developing or justifying ideas involved in the measures we have just considered, some of which were still pending as he wrote. One passage, however, is particularly notable. In 1781 the legislature, amid the distresses of the Revolution, was on the point of turning over the state government to a dictator. This betrayal called forth an outburst perhaps more impassioned than can be found elsewhere in Jefferson's writings. "The very thought alone was treason against the people; was treason against mankind in general; as riveting forever the chains which bow down their necks, by giving to their oppressors a proof, which they would have trumpeted through the universe, of the imbecility of republican government." [78] Having entered the Revolutionary contest "from a pure love of liberty," having made every sacrifice to preserve the "inalienable rights," Jefferson could not bear to see these frittered away by the Ameri-

[75] *Notes on Virginia;* see Selections following, p. 243.
[76] See, for example, a letter of 1825, *Writings*, XVI, 120.
[77] *Notes on Virginia;* see Selections following, p. 235.
[78] See Selections following, p. 231.

cans themselves. This indeed was the golden opportunity for establishing liberty on a firm basis. "From the conclusion of this war we shall be going down hill. . . . The shackles which shall not be knocked off at the conclusion of this war will remain on us long, will be made heavier and heavier, till our rights shall revive or expire in a convulsion." [79]

II. MINISTER TO FRANCE

A comparison of the *Notes on Virginia* with later writings shows that when they were composed,—that is, before the close of the Revolution—Jefferson's main political principles were permanently formed. Going now, however, to France to serve as minister there until 1789, he was to observe, if not to take some part in, another revolution even more momentous. This experience inevitably had some influence on his political outlook. Already opposed to monarchy and absolutism, he found in France under the old régime a terrible warning and example—a corrupt court and aristocracy, supported by a standing army, controlling religious belief and the press, and through privilege entailing endless misery on the people—in short, "the worst government on earth." "If anybody thinks that kings, nobles, or priests are good conservators of the public happiness," he writes after living two years in Paris, "send them here. It is the best school in the universe to cure them of that folly." [80] There was, however, a saving remnant. The American Revolution, he writes in 1788, had awakened the thinking part of the French nation; and thus a liberal party, comprehending all the honesty of the kingdom, had been formed; revolutionary sentiments had spread, had even become "the mode," attracting people of fashion. [81] To this party the famous author

---

[79] *Notes on Virginia;* see Selections following, p. 241.
[80] See Selections following, p. 257.
[81] To Washington, *Writings*, VII, 227; *Autobiography*, I, 103.

of the Declaration of Independence, supplying the place of Dr. Franklin, became an oracle. With the group, republican in sentiment, gathering about his old friend Lafayette—Brissot de Warville, Dupont de Nemours, Condorcet, and others, both gentlemen and ladies—he had frequent association and correspondence. He also read the radical and revolutionary works of these and other Frenchmen, which led up to the revolution of 1789.[82] That coming from America upon this vigorous group Jefferson should have learned nothing new in government would be strange; yet it is safe to say that he taught much more than he learned.

Here, however, as we are on debatable ground, some attention is necessary. The traditional view later promulgated by the Federalists, was that Jefferson, after associating during his stay in Paris with "that vile hag, Philosophy," returned to America to teach anarchy and atheism; and indeed something like this view, stated less opprobriously, has been advanced by his friends and by competent writers.[83] The question is, how far his principles were modified by his stay in France. On this point we have his own later statement. "I had left France," he says, "in the first year of its revolution, in the fervor of natural rights, and the zeal for reformation. My conscientious devotion to these rights could not be heightened, but it had been aroused and excited by daily exercise."[84] His letters of this time show that it was indeed excited. "My God!" he exclaims after being in France for eight months, "how little do my countrymen know what precious blessings they are in possession of, and which no other people on earth enjoy."[85] As the Revolution develops his expression becomes even more vigorous. Hearing

[82] For a careful and documented account see Vossler, *Die Amerikanischen Revolutionsideale*, pp. 105–111. The absence of any evidence showing that Jefferson read or was influenced by Rousseau, whose *Contrat Social* appeared in 1762, is remarkable.

[83] This is the thesis of Vossler, in the work just cited.

[84] *The Anas*, Selections following, p. 297.

[85] To Monroe, April 15, 1785, *Writings*, ed. Ford, IV, 59.

of Shays's rebellion, he cries: "What signify a few lives lost in a century or two? The tree of liberty must be refreshed from time to time, with the blood of patriots and tyrants."[86] "Our young Republic," he writes, must "besiege the throne of heaven with eternal prayers, to extirpate from creation this class of human lions, tigers, and mammoths called Kings; from whom, let him perish who does not say, 'Good Lord, deliver us.'"[87] In 1789 he prophesies the success of the French revolution. "Nor will it end with this country. Hers is but the first chapter of the history of European liberty."[88] In Paris, it is argued, Jefferson begins to write like a Jacobin. He had come to France, however, no friend of kings, and he denounces them no more passionately than he had denounced a dictator for Virginia in 1781.

Reverting to the two strains of thought which we found in Jefferson's early writings, we may notice, as time goes on, a disposition to appeal less to history and legal rights, more to reason and natural rights. This tendency, which we have already encountered in the Act for Establishing Religious Freedom, perhaps becomes more marked during the stay in France. "The writings published on this occasion [the meeting of the States General, 1789] are, some of them," he says, "very valuable; because, unfettered by the prejudices under which the English labor, they give a full scope to reason, and strike out truths, as yet unperceived and unacknowledged on the other side of the Channel."[89] The bitter hostility toward America which he found in England even after 1783 and the backwardness of its government, contrasted with the sympathy of the new France, might be expected to turn him away from the legal and toward the rational approach to political problems. He now propounds the "principle that the earth belongs to the living and not to the dead," and advocates taking "reason for

---

[86] To Smith, *Writings*, VI, 373.
[87] To Humphreys, *ibid.*, VI, 279.
[88] To Diodati, August 3, 1789.
[89] *Writings*, VII, 321.

our guide instead of English precedents." [90] We may attribute the change partly to French influence, partly also to greater experience, especially in finding how little legal reasonings appealed to the multitude; but at any rate, we should remember that already in the *Notes on Virginia* Jefferson had declared "reason and free inquiry to be the only effectual agents against error," and that his temperament had always impelled him to make reason his guide of life. If Jefferson was corrupted by "philosophy," it must have been before he went to France.

In his advice to the French reformers Jefferson was no extremist. They should repair rather than overthrow their government, following, temporarily at least, the English model; they should allow the people to do no more than vote and sit on juries, a counsel not savoring of Rousseauism; they were not yet ready for self-government, or even for a free press; they should attempt only what the established habits of the people were ripe for, or they might lose all. His advice throughout was practical and moderate. On the whole, then, we may conclude that Jefferson left France, as he had entered it, a friend of the rights of man, but not a rabid revolutionist. [91]

The conservatism of Jefferson, usually too little noted, comes out also in his attitude toward the Constitution in 1787, adopted while he was in France. He had, of course, approved the republicanism of the Confederation,—"with all its imperfections" finding it among governments "the best existing, or that ever did exist." [92] While Adams thought Congress "not a legislative but a diplomatic assembly," Jefferson considered it a true legislature, superior in its field to the states. No one, however, was better situated to see its imperfections, at least in

[90] See Selections following, p. 271.
[91] The opinion of Chinard, who is fitted to judge on this point: "I do not see that his prolonged sojourn in France modified to any extent the conclusions he had already reached independently in the *Notes on Virginia.*" —*Jefferson*, p. 215.
[92] To Carrington, *Writings*, VI, 227.

foreign affairs, than the minister to France. When, therefore, the new Constitution was submitted to him he gave it hearty approval, objecting only to the reëligibility of the president and the omission of a bill of rights to safeguard the sacred freedoms of religion and of the press—objections that were later sustained by the popular will. Jefferson returned to republican America with confident hopes of the new government; and was soon to declare that his inclination would never permit him again to cross the Atlantic.

III. STATESMAN AND PRESIDENT

When in March, 1790, Jefferson arrived in New York to become our first Secretary of State, he found, he says, "a state of things which of all I had ever contemplated, I the least expected." All the ideas he had considered American were now outmoded. Reactionary, succeeding to revolutionary, impulses, had carried through a conservative reformation of the government, and created, in New York at least, a new political atmosphere. The welcome of the principal citizens and the "courtesies of their dinner parties" placed him, he says, "at once in their familiar society." Between the society he had just been frequenting in Paris and this the contrast was complete. He had left France "in the fervor of natural rights"; he found New York now directing its sympathies, along with its commerce, back toward England, and expressing "a preference for kingly over republican government." [93] He found the patriots of '76 replaced by a colonial aristocracy attempting to be more English than the English; and even Washington giving up the easy hospitality of Virginia for a "court" and "levees" in the grand style. Had his work of twenty years gone for nothing? This condition was bitterly disappointing—even alarming. He was not reassured as he watched the development of the new administration. The Constitution was in the hands of the new order

[93] See Jefferson's account in the *Anas*, Selections following, pp. 297 ff.

and a brilliant Secretary of the Treasury was establishing a financial system calculated, as he thought, to puzzle the popular understanding and corrupt the legislature!

During ten years Jefferson watched this perversion, as he regarded it, of American government,—and clung to his original principles. He was as unwilling as when he wrote the *Notes on Virginia* to give to an oligarchy or a monarchy what belonged to the people.[94] During this period indeed his fears, along with party and personal hostility, led him far, as opponents have thought, toward exaggeration and fanaticism. In his celebrated *Anas*—private memoranda made during this period—he recorded every instance in which his opponents, especially his most notable one, had doubted the permanence of the republic, or spoken of the Constitution as a "shilly-shally thing," or toasted George the Third. In May, 1792, he wrote to Washington complaining that a "corrupt squadron" in Congress were infringing the rights of the states and consolidating the powers of the government in order to prepare the way for a monarchy.[95] When Washington replied that "there might be *desires*, but he did not believe there were *designs*" to overturn the government, he was evidently not reassured. As late as 1798 he not only recorded as "a very remarkable fact," hearing that such a conspiracy was formed before the Constitution was adopted,[96] but he saw another actually threatening. On the Alien and Sedition laws he wrote: "If this goes down, we shall immediately see attempted another act of Congress, declaring that the President shall continue in office during life. . . . At least this may be the aim of the Oliverians, while Monk and the Cavaliers . . . may be playing their game for the restoration of his most gracious Majesty, George the Third."[97]

[94] Compare Selections following, p. 229.
[95] *Writings*, VIII, 344.   [96] *Anas, ibid.,* I, 418.
[97] *Ibid.,* X, 62. Jefferson probably refers to the followers of Adams and Hamilton respectively. Chinard, noting that this very usurpation happened in France, says: "But France had Bonaparte, while neither Adams

Throughout, however, he clung to the idea that the safety and strength, as well as the authority of government depended on the consent of the governed. "It was by the sober sense of our citizens that we were safely and steadily conducted from monarchy to republicanism, and it is by the same agency alone that we can be kept from falling back." [98] To oppose a despotic central government based on "feudal" class distinctions, and to protect the rights of the people, not merely those of the states themselves, he stood out against the pernicious doctrine of "implied powers," opposed the Bank scheme as unconstitutional, and tried to nullify the flagrancy of the Alien and Sedition Acts through the Kentucky Resolutions.

This issue in domestic politics was sharpened by a parallel one in foreign affairs. Jefferson watched the progress, as he had the beginning, of the revolution in France, with anxiety, convinced that the cause of liberty in America depended upon its outcome. His Americanism was clearly uppermost; his concern was always for the American rather than the French republic. The success of the French Revolution, he says in a typical letter, "will ensure the progress of liberty in Europe, and its preservation here. The failure of that would have been a powerful argument with those who wish to introduce a king, lords, and commons here." [99] "I shall rely that the great mass of our own community is untainted with these heresies. . . . On this," he says, "I build my hopes that we have not labored in vain." Even the excesses of 1792 did not shake him: "Was ever such a prize won with so little innocent blood? . . . Were there but an Adam and an Eve left in every country, and left

nor Washington ever had the inclination or the power to bring about such a change in America." Hamilton indeed may have had the inclination, hardly the power. Jefferson's suspicions were not therefore "absolutely groundless."—*Jefferson*, p. 344.

[98] To Campbell, September 1, 1797, *Writings*, IX, 421.

[99] To Pendleton, 1791, *Writings*, ed. Ford, V, 358. Compare Selections following, p. 328.

free, it would be better than it now is." [100]   When, following the
execution of Louis XVI, war between France and the Coalition
appeared clearly as a struggle between opposing theories of
government, and the sympathies of his opponents, with their
commercial interests, turned sharply toward England, he was
glad to see "all the old spirit of 1776 rekindling from Boston
to Charleston." Placing American interests uppermost, he
supported Washington's Proclamation of Neutrality in 1793,
and the dismissal of Genet; but he found the outcome unfortunate. "The Anglomen and monocrats had so artfully confounded the cause of France with that of freedom that both
went down in the same scale." Throughout his view was liberal:
the French Revolution was a warning not against anarchy but
against monarchy; the Napoleonic *coup d'état* showed not the
weakness of a republic but the danger of a standing army; and
the whole affair exhibited, for the thousandth time in history,
the evils of despotism.

In 1789, in considering the Constitution, Jefferson had dis-
claimed party: "I am not of the party of the federalists; but I
am much further from that of the anti-federalists." When,
however, two years later, the issue having changed, a party
calling itself Federalist began bending the Constitution toward
a despotism, it was again time for organized resistance. Finding his opponents strongly entrenched, he was too wise to
attempt meeting them on their own ground. For ten years
his policy had on the whole to be one of watchful waiting.
Gradually, however, he formed, or found forming about him,
a political party. "The body of the American people," he wrote
in 1799, "is substantially Republican, but . . . they have been
the dupes of artful manœuvres and made for a moment to be
willing instruments in forging chains for themselves." [101]   At
last he saw his opponents bringing about their own ruin, and

[100] *Writings*, IX, 10.
[101] From a letter quoted in Chinard, *Jefferson*, p. 356.

the people awakening from their evil dream. "The revolution of 1800," he said, "was as real a revolution in the principles of our government as that of 1776 was in its form." [102]

Federalist perversions having now been rejected by the people, Jefferson hoped to restore the government to its original purity. "The storm through which we have passed," he wrote two days after his inauguration, "has been tremendous indeed. The tough sides of our Argosy have been thoroughly tried. . . . We shall put her on her republican tack, and she will now show by the beauty of her motion the skill of her builders." [103] He was temperamentally inclined to conciliation, and always prone to believe that his own reason could not fail eventually to become the reason of others. Thinking that now, after the decisive election of 1800, all, "excepting the ardent monarchists," were "agreed in the ancient Whig principles," [104] he looked forward to a "perfect consolidation" and "era of good feeling." Assuming office with republican simplicity, he made harmony his "key note": "We are all republicans; we are all federalists." He went on in his Inaugural Address to a statement of "the essential principles of our government, and consequently of those which ought to shape its administration,"—a statement which might have been written by Washington, and was calculated to attract Washington's followers. His purpose, therefore, was to return to Washington's "essential principles," and on this basis to banish party feeling. That his hopes were not entirely vain appeared in 1805 when he was overwhelmingly reëlected, with the support even of John Adams.

IV. POLITICAL THEORIST

When at the end of his second term he refused to stand again, and, after forty years of public service, retired for good to

---

[102] *Writings*, XV, 212. [103] *Ibid.*, X, 217.
[104] See Selections following, p. 337.

Monticello, he found himself at last free to elaborate his political theory, solely in accordance with "reason and pure Americanism." We may now attempt, therefore, if only in briefest outline, a general statement of his principles, particularly as they appear in his later writings.

In Jefferson's theory, as in his character, there are some conflicts to be resolved. Inheriting on the one side from a rough and vigorous frontiersman, with "a character not unlike that of Daniel Boone," and on the other from one of the gentle families of Virginia, educated partly in the wilderness, partly in the formal society of Williamsburg, he combined the independence and democracy of the frontier with the cultivation of an eighteenth-century gentleman. He has been called the most aristocratic of democrats. He sincerely loved the people, but he looked down upon them—as Monticello looks down upon the plain. Not without his enthusiasms, he had the outlook, with something of the shallowness, of eighteenth-century rationalism. Though he believed "with Condorcet, that man's mind is perfectible to a degree of which we cannot as yet form any conception," he was never blind to the weaknesses of mankind. He was well read in history and had himself seen a good deal of it transacted, but he was inclined to find it a record of mistakes to be avoided.[105] "I like the dreams of the future," he wrote to Adams, "better than the history of the past." He is held up on the one hand as a dreamer and idealist; on the other as a good farmer, a skillful diplomat, and an astute politician. In politics he was both philosopher and practical statesman; and he set one as a watch on the other. Playing, so to speak, a double part and inviting the charge of duplicity, he could advocate in private letters what he believed theoretically wise, in public utterances what he found practicable or what he recognized as the popular will—a will to which even wisdom must submit. In his politics

---

[105] "Forty years of experience in government is worth a century of book reading."—_Writings_, XV, 40.

discrepancies appear, giving rise to sharp differences of opinion. He has been represented as the founder of a party, as the friend of French ideas, as the champion of states' rights, as the originator of doctrines—nullification and secession—hostile to our government. On the other hand, it is shown that he could place country above party, advocate alliance with England against France, favor union and paternal government, construe the Constitution loosely to suit his purpose, and oppose secession as a national danger. Some of these difficulties may be resolved if we attempt to get at his fundamental principles.

Though these principles drew freely upon Locke and other liberal writers, and paralleled those of Rousseau, they must be regarded as original, and in some respects distinctively American. They might be called the principles of a cultivated frontiersman. They are based on a belief in the common man as an absolute value, an end in himself, irrespective of his birth or standing in society. "All men are created equal"; the truth is "self-evident"; equal not in their minds or possessions, but in their natural rights and duties—before the law and in the sight of God. Moreover, taken on the average, men in a free society —in the lower walks of life quite as surely as in the upper—are honest, just, and reasonable; and hence capable of self-government.[106] No aspect of Jefferson's theory will be found inconsistent with these fundamental principles.

It should be noted at once, however, that Jefferson was the friend but not the flatterer of the plain people; he recognized superiority in intelligence, learning, and insight, and its worth to society. "There is a natural aristocracy among men," he says, and the grounds for this are not wealth and birth, but

---

[106] "I cannot act as if all men were unfaithful because some are so. . . . I had rather be the victim of occasional infidelities, than relinquish my general confidence in the honesty of man."—*Writings*, XIV, 43. With greater attainments the upper classes are more greedy and unscrupulous, always contriving "to nestle themselves into the places of power and profit."—IX, 307.

talents and virtue. "This natural aristocracy I consider as the most precious gift of nature. . . . That form of government is the best which provides the most effectually for a pure selection of these natural *aristoi* into the offices of government." [107] He did not believe in government by the ignorant or irresponsible, or in mob rule.

All men, however, have natural rights. These apparently divide into two classes: first rights, like those of free thought and speech, "which can be fully exercised without the aid of exterior assistance," and which are never given up; secondly, rights like that of property, which require protection, and must therefore be entrusted to society for that purpose. Both classes, however, are in strictness inalienable; if delegated they may at any time be resumed.[108] For these rights, as we have seen, Jefferson in his earlier reasoning found a double foundation—in law and in nature. Now, apparently discarding the legal basis, he seeks them solely in "nature" and "reason." [109] He is thus left dangerously free, as occasion arises, to treat any right appealing to his own reason—the right to unoccupied territory, to free use of the ocean—as a natural one. The natural rights on which he most insists, however, are those then generally recognized,—for instance in the Declaration of Independence and the Bill of Rights.

The correlative feature in his theory must not be overlooked. Born not only an individual but also a member of society, man "has no natural right in opposition to his social duties"; [110] and "no man has a natural right to commit aggression on the equal rights of another." [111] An enlightened self-interest will recognize not only the individual right but the no less cogent social

---

[107] See letter to Adams, Selections following, p. 375.

[108] "The idea is quite unfounded, that on entering into society we give up any natural right."—See Selections following, p. 389.

[109] "This narrow notion [of common law rights] was a favorite in the first moment of rallying to our rights against Great Britain. . . . The truth is, that we brought with us the *rights of men*."—*Writings*, XIII, 165.

[110] *Ibid.*, XVI, 282.   [111] See Selections following, p. 389.

demand; and the laws will enforce both equally. In a just society there will be equality of service and privilege; under a just government equality of taxation and military service, along with equality of protection and representation.

The people, equal in their rights, taken together form a political society or nation. In this national society lies the principle of political life and continuity. "I consider the source of authority with us to be the Nation. Their will, declared through its proper organ, is valid, till revoked by their will." [112] The popular will is supreme,—above all government; it can change government at any time to suit its object. And "the only orthodox object of the institution of government is to secure the greatest degree of happiness possible to the general mass of those associated under it." [113] Government is instituted by a political contract, which in Jefferson's mind is not a legal fiction; at least if a primitive contract, in the sense of Hobbes, is to be conjectured, this is supplemented by an actual contract, or series of contracts, by which government is definitely established. The Constitution, with its restrictive Bill of Rights, is such a contract—which must be construed according to its exact terms, like any other legal document.

The government thus set up of course rests entirely on the consent of the governed. "Every government degenerates when trusted to the rulers of the people alone. The people themselves, therefore, are its only safe depositories." [114] This fundamental idea is reiterated in many forms. The will of the people may exert itself in two ways. If in the extreme case they find their will denied by government and have no other recourse, they are justified in rebellion. Indeed a little rebellion, now and then, may even be "a good thing, and as necessary in the political world as storms are in the physical." Even the evils of an insurrection "will not weigh against the incon-

[112] *Writings*, VIII, 301.   [113] *Ibid.*, XIII, 135.
[114] *Notes on Virginia;* see Selections following, p. 235.

veniences of a government of force, such as are monarchies and aristocracies." [115]   Ordinarily, however, the will of the people can be asserted peaceably, through the ballot box, by means of frequent elections. This will is taken to be that of a majority, for "the _lex majoris partis_ is the fundamental law of every society of individuals of equal rights. . . . This law once disregarded, no other remains but that of force." [116]   The people must have constant control not only of their immediate government, but over the original contract,—that is, over the Constitution, about which there is nothing sacred or unchangeable. In order that each new generation may live unfettered by the old, it should have its opportunity to renew or modify the fundamental law, say every nineteen or twenty years. [117]   In this complete and constant control by the people, in Jefferson's opinion, lies the novelty of his theory—at any rate of the American experiment: "Our countrymen, first in modern times, have taken the ground of government founded on the will of the people." [118]   This is the principle extolled by Lincoln and given final statement in the Gettysburg Address.

Jefferson inclines to the necessary-evil theory of government. Possibly a society would be happiest without government, like that of the Indians; next best would be a pure democracy; but both these are "inconsistent with any great degree of population." Ordinarily the solution is a republic,—a government being republican "in proportion as every member composing it has his equal voice in the direction of its concerns—not indeed in person, which would be impracticable beyond the limits of a city, or small township,—but by representatives chosen by him-

[115] _Writings_, VI, 155; see Selections following, p. 280. Expressions to this effect are numerous, but only in connection with Shays's Rebellion, during Jefferson's stay in France.

[116] _Ibid._, XV, 127. Note, however, the qualification in the First Inaugural: the will of the majority must be "reasonable," and the "minority possess their equal rights, which equal laws must protect."

[117] This, according to the "mortality tables," being the life of a generation.—_Ibid._, XV, 42.   [118] _Ibid._, VIII, 291.

self, and responsible to him at short periods." [119]   In brief, a republic is a representative democracy.

To the common people, however, should be entrusted only those functions and offices "to the exercise of which they are competent,"—the lowest offices, jury duty, the choosing of representatives. They are "the most honest and safe, although not the most wise depository of the public interests." [120] Apparently, however, they can be trusted to select from the *aristoi* those best fitted for the higher offices, for which training and skill are necessary.

There are "two hooks," Jefferson said, on which the success of a republican government depends. The first is education; "no other sure foundation can be devised for the preservation of freedom and happiness." The second is local government. He recommended dividing the country into small units or "wards," modeled on the New England towns, each having charge of its local concerns as a pure democracy. These would be combined in the larger divisions—in turn into counties, states, and federal government—a series of larger and larger republics. The ideal political system would be one in which each of the governments in the ascending series should retain such rights as it could protect unaided, and send on to the next higher in the series those others of wider concern that were beyond its competence. That system would be most safe and free in which government should be kept nearest to the people—that is, toward the lower rather than the higher units in this hierarchy. Jefferson's concern for states' rights was only one form of his concern for local rights— or rather for the rights of the people, the rights of man, which should be the first concern of all government.

A republican system in this ideal form, or even in any form, was not necessarily best for all the peoples of the world. Though Jefferson had little of the proselytizing spirit of the French and Russian revolutions, and had no thought of imposing the

[119] *Ibid.*, XV, 33.   [120] *Ibid.*, XVI, 73.

American solution on other countries, he was interested in the cause of human liberty everywhere and hoped America would become "a standing monument and example for the aim and imitation of the people of other countries." This did not mean, however, that the republican form could be adopted, at any rate immediately, by the peoples of Europe and South America; for some of them indeed a monarchy might still be best. "The excellence of every government is its adaptation to the state of those to be governed by it." [121] A free government must be based on the virtue of its citizens. Fortunately in America the conditions were favorable, and would remain so as long as agriculture was the principal pursuit. "Those who labor in the earth are the chosen people of God," and they are the most valuable citizens. Living in Virginia as a farmer among farmers,[122] and finding there an ideal society, he conceived the future America as a nation of farmers, living a free and wholesome life on their own soil. He was dismayed by the growth of cities, which, with their factories and commerce, their ignorance and corruption, he viewed as "pestilential to the morals, the health, and the liberties of man." As this growth continued, he was forced to recognize it and to speak in his Inaugural Address of "agriculture, and of commerce its handmaid"—even, a little later, of "agriculture, manufactures, commerce, and navigation, the four pillars of our prosperity." But he continued to the end to cherish the vision of an agricultural society.

For this reason he has sometimes been interpreted as the leader of an agrarian party, as the proponent of a policy favorable, in an economic sense, to the agricultural class.[123] This view is narrow and misleading—involving indeed a misunderstand-

[121] See Selections following, p. 385.

[122] "When I first entered on the stage of public life . . . I came to a resolution never . . . to wear any other character than that of a farmer."— *Writings*, IX, 44.

[123] The view of Beard, *Economic Origins of Jeffersonian Democracy* (Chap. XIV); and of Nock, *Jefferson*—who explains him as the champion of the "producer."

ing of his character and thought. Though his policy had, or if pursued, might have had, important economic consequences, with these he was little concerned. The idea of even indirectly putting money into the pockets of a class, his own class, would have had for him more than a touch of dishonesty and vulgarity —if he had ever considered it. He was concerned not with economic, but with social and particularly with political consequences. He "favored" the class of farmers, just as he "favored" next to it the class of sailors, not in order that the government might benefit them, but in order that they might benefit society,—that is, because they were naturally virtuous citizens. He "was solely interested in protecting and preserving a certain pattern of civilization which was essentially an agricultural pattern—the only safe foundation for the political and private virtues of vital importance in a democracy." [124]

This political position merges interestingly into Jefferson's foreign policy, of which the main principle was announced at the close of the Revolution: peace and friendship with every nation. He always wished for peace if it could be "preserved, *salve fide et honore*," and thought war "the greatest scourge of mankind." It might be better, he speculates at this time (1781), to give up commerce and "abandon the ocean altogether"; this would "make us invulnerable to Europe"; "turn all our citizens to the cultivation of the earth"; and remove many occasions for war. Since the people have willed to be commercial, however, "their servants are in duty bound to calculate all their measures on this datum." [125] Henceforward, therefore, his policy is one of free trade and political isolation, as finally expressed in the well known: "Peace, commerce, and honest friendship with all

---

[124] Chinard, *Jefferson*, p. 328.
[125] See *Notes on Virginia*, Selections following, p. 244; and, for the extreme statement of this doctrine, *Writings*, V, 183; also a letter of 1805 in which Jefferson, while president, modifies his views in the light of "the wonderful changes which have taken place since 1781, when the *Notes on Virginia* were written."—XI, 55.

nations—entangling alliances with none." This policy involves not only a complete non-participation in the "throes and
convulsions of the ancient world," but the exclusion of all
European interference in the politics of the new. As early as
1790, while Secretary of State, he "intimates" to the British
ministry that "we cannot be indifferent to enterprises of this
kind." [126]   He comes gradually to believe "that America should
separate herself from the system of Europe, and establish one
of her own,"—a republican system, which he sees gradually
spreading to "cover the whole northern, if not the southern
continent." Thus his expressions over many years anticipate
the important letter to the President, in which he embodies the
principles of the Monroe Doctrine some six weeks before it was
officially promulgated.[127]

V. SAGE OF MONTICELLO

If most space is here devoted to Jefferson's political ideas, it
is because through these he has exerted his chief influence—
especially if, as he evidently intended, we connect with these
his advocacy of education and religious freedom. We must not,
however, overlook his many other interests. He was happiest
when he left the political world for his labors at Monticello—as
farmer, builder, and student. He was one of the earliest scientific farmers, studying soils, rotation of crops, improvements in
machinery, and economy of labor; and he made his farm a model
to his state. He was particularly fond of planting and gardening.
"No occupation," he said, "is so delightful to me as the culture
of the earth, and no culture comparable to that of the garden."
He brought to this country "exotics of distinguished usefulness"—the upland rice, the cork oak; and sent abroad in exchange the American pecan. Year after year he received from
his "good old friend Thonin, of the Jardin des Plantes at Paris"

[126] Instructions to G. Morris, *Ibid.*, VIII, 85.
[127] See Selections following, p. 399.

boxes of seeds for distribution to American gardens. "The greatest service which can be rendered any country is to add an useful plant to its culture." Thus gardening, like everything else he undertook, became a matter not only of amusement but of intelligent pursuit, and led naturally to a scientific study of botany, as his farmer's observations of the weather led to the study of meteorology.

"Nature intended me," he wrote shortly after he gave up the presidency, "for the tranquil pursuits of science, by rendering them my supreme delight." He was not only an accomplished botanist and meteorologist, but intelligently interested in zoölogy, ethnology, and astronomy; and he was skilled in mathematics, all his life employing the calculus. He thought chemistry "big with future discoveries." Since most of his scientific work is now superseded it is perhaps most important to notice that he had a good share of the modern scientist's mind and temper—curiosity, observation, accuracy, and refusal to conclude without evidence. For example, he doubted Buffon's theory that animals are larger in the old world than in the new, and that the greater moisture of the new is unfavorable to size. He diligently collected specimens to disprove the first point, and secured from Franklin some data showing Philadelphia less moist than London and Paris. Eventually evidence might decide the matter. "In the meantime," he says, "doubt is wisdom." And again: "It is always better to have no ideas than false ones; to believe nothing than to believe what is wrong." [128]

Jefferson was disposed, however, to take a practical and utilitarian view of science. He was little interested in metaphysics, much in practical invention—while on his travels carefully observing the steam engines, grist mills, and screw propellers that he thought might be of benefit to America. In this as in other matters, indeed, the improvement of American conditions always seems uppermost. He thought science had for

[128] *Writings*, VII, 74.

its main objects "the freedom and happiness of man," and was "more important in a republican than in any other government."

His interest in the fine arts was similarly practical and patriotic. His notes in France on "Objects of Attention for an American" are illuminating. "Painting, Statuary. Too expensive for the state of wealth among us. It would be useless therefore ... for us to make ourselves connoisseurs in those arts. They are worth seeing, but not studying. . . . Architecture worth great attention. As we double our numbers every twenty years, we must double our houses. . . . It is desirable to introduce taste into an art which shows so much." [129] In architecture he showed himself capable of enthusiasm. In a well-known letter from Nîmes, he told of "gazing whole hours at the Maison Quarrée, like a lover at his mistress"; and he presently sent home a model and plan of it for reproduction in the capitol at Richmond, following them up with untiring injunctions until his plan was carried out.

After his return he remodelled Monticello, having supplemented his early study of Palladio by French and Roman examples. His architectural drawings, discovered in 1911, show his artistic invention and beautiful draughtsmanship. [130] In Jefferson the Marquis de Chastellux found "the first American who has consulted the fine arts to find out how to shelter himself from the weather." To his skill Monticello and the University of Virginia are enduring monuments.

This fondness for the most useful of the fine arts goes along with his practical taste in literature. In youth indeed, as his

[129] *Ibid.*, XVII, 292.

[130] "In the pervasive classical revival common to Europe and America, of which Jefferson's work forms a part, it will be found that his position was not always derivative and secondary, in comparison to European standards, but that in certain respects he anticipated corresponding buildings in other countries, and in some other directions gave to American architecture an original direction."—Kimball, *Thomas Jefferson, Architect*, p. 14. This work reproduces Jefferson's drawings.

notes show,[131] he was fond of poetry. While in France he wrote an essay, remarkably sound for its time, on English prosody; and some of his early critical observations show true insight.[132] In 1801 he complained that his "relish" for poetry had deserted him: "I cannot read even Virgil with pleasure." [133] All his life, however, he was a reader, indeed a close student, of the classics, allowing scarcely a day to pass without its portion.[134] He urged the study of Latin and Greek as useful, but here as in architecture, he could rise nobly above utility: "To read the Latin and Greek authors in their original is a sublime luxury; and I deem luxury in science to be at least as justifiable as in architecture, painting, gardening, or the other arts." He was particularly interested in language, devoting long hours to Greek pronunciation, instruction in Anglo-Saxon, the Indian languages, "reformed" spelling, and the like. If his conclusions sometimes seem "sensible" rather than profound, they at least show him intelligent, painstaking, and tireless, as in every subject he undertook.

Jefferson's views on language and style were naturally liberal and forward-looking. Of grammar he says, "The scanty foundation, laid in at school, has carried me through a life of much hasty writing, more indebted for style to reading and memory, than to the rules." He would "readily sacrifice the niceties of syntax to euphony and strength. It is by boldly neglecting the rigorisms of grammar that Tacitus has made himself the strongest writer in the world." "I am no friend," he says, "to what is called *purism*, but a zealous one to the *neology* which has introduced these two words without any authority from the

---

[131] See the *Literary Bible of Thomas Jefferson*, edited by G. Chinard, containing favorite passages from Greek, Latin, and English poets—which, however, seem selected for their teaching rather than their pure poetry.

[132] See, for example, the letter to Skipwith, Selections following, p. 183.

[133] "As we advance in life these things fall off one by one, and I suspect we are left at last with only Homer and Virgil, perhaps with Homer alone."—*Writings*, XVIII, 448.

[134] Rayner, *Jefferson*, p. 22.

dictionary. I consider one as destroying the verve and beauty of the language, while the other improves both and adds to its copiousness." [135] He is sure that a new "American dialect," formed to express new experiences, will not debase but enrich the language. He finds in the Greeks and Romans "the purest models which exist of fine composition." Of English writers Robertson, Sterne, Addison, and Hume are "of the first merit." [136] He contrasts interestingly the styles of Paine and Bolingbroke. "No writer has exceeded Paine in ease and familiarity of style, in perspicuity of expression, happiness of elucidation, and in simple and unassuming language. . . . Lord Bolingbroke's, on the other hand, is a style of the highest order. The lofty, rhythmical, full-flowing eloquence of Cicero. Periods of just measure, their members proportioned, their close full and round."

In his letters Jefferson is easy and familiar—sometimes prolix, but often concise and expressive. Like Paine he struck out political aphorisms which have become current in our speech. In his more formal public utterances he could attain the "periods of just measure"; the First Inaugural is an example. In the Declaration of Independence he is at his best. Seldom have man and occasion more fortunately met. Avoiding the pitfalls into which a less discerning mind might have fallen—of homeliness on the one hand, of passion or pathos on the other—he struck the clear high tone just fitted to that time of firm purpose and high hope. The substance of the famous document loses nothing in its expression.

Believing that education was the chief means of "ameliorating the condition, promoting the virtue, and advancing the happiness of man," he made it a major and a lifelong interest. "Enlighten the people," he said, "and tyranny and oppressions of

---

[135] See *Writings*, XIII, 339; XV, 414; XIII, 340; X, 146.
[136] *Ibid.*, XV, 353. Of Hume, however: "The charms of his style and matter have made tories of all England, and doubtful republicans here."

body and mind will vanish like spirits at dawn of day." [137] After carrying in mind over forty years his early and abortive bill for the diffusion of knowledge, he revived it in 1817 as a comprehensive plan for education in Virginia.[138] This provided for the establishment in each county of elementary schools; in nine larger districts of as many "colleges," or secondary schools; and "in a central and healthy part of the state an University wherein all the branches of useful sciences may be taught." To the founding of this University of Virginia Jefferson gave the last years of his life. As its Rector he raised money, planned the buildings, secured materials, partly from abroad, and supervised the construction. Realizing, better than many founders, that buildings do not constitute a University, he tried to make it a model not only in its architecture, but in the character and learning of its professors and in its modern system of instruction. Though space here is wanting for his fruitful innovations in university education, we may note two characteristic features.[139] In selecting a professor of law, he wrote Madison, "we must be rigorously attentive to his political principles." Before the Revolution Virginia lawyers were all Whigs, but they had now begun to "slide into toryism." Through a good appointment the "vestal flame" of republicanism might be "kept alive." If Jefferson here falls disappointingly short of the true idea of a university, he made up by providing for full religious freedom. Though he did not object to the sectarian instruction of his students apart from their regular studies, and provided "ethical lectures developing those moral obligations in which all sects agree," he would have no professorship of divinity, nor any religious requirement of either professor or student. Thus for the first time, education was freed of church control and secularized. In this respect, as in others, he furnished a model for

[137] See Selections following, p. 388.
[138] For this "Plan" see *Writings*, XVII, 417.
[139] Honeywell, *The Educational Work of Jefferson*, is a careful study of this subject.

the great system of state universities which has played so large a part in the training of American democracy.

To Jefferson's religion undue attention has been given, because it was long a matter of illiberal and partisan controversy, —his opponents calling him "atheist" and "infidel," his friends "a public professor of the Christian religion." Objectively considered, his religious views, as far as they can be ascertained, do not appear very unusual in his time, or very valuable. Certainly he was not a great religious, as he was a great political, leader. It is not generally noted that he was formally an Episcopalian—baptized, married, and buried according to the rites of that church, and frequently attending its services, prayer-book in hand.[140] About his private views he was always very reticent, insisting that "religion is a matter which lies solely between man and his God,"—its evidence before the world to be sought only in man's life: "if that has been *honest and dutiful* to society, the religion which has regulated it cannot be a bad one." This position was partly a matter of principle, freedom of opinion being one of the natural rights strictly inalienable and under no circumstances given up to society.[141] Any religious profession or even discussion might lead to interference, at least to contention, which he always avoided. Sometimes, in his later life, he wrote frankly on the subject to intimate friends. It is safe to say that never after reaching maturity did he accept the doctrines of orthodox Christianity, that he believed throughout in God as the Creator of the Universe, that he was thus a typical eighteenth-century deist, and that toward the end he was willing to call himself, as the nineteenth-century equivalent, a unitarian. He would have been unwilling, however, to spell this word with a capital or to associate himself with a Unitarian denomination. "I never submitted the whole system of my opinions," he says,

---

[140] Randall, *Jefferson*, III, 555.
[141] His grandson writes: "Of his peculiar religious views his family knows no more than the world."—*Ibid.*, p. 561.

"to the creed of any party of men whatever, in religion ... or in anything else, where I was capable to thinking for myself." [142] To one inquirer he writes, "I am of a sect by myself, as far as I know." [143] Again he took a practical view, considering "religion a supplement to law in the government of man," [144] and clearly valuing it for its ethical rather than its spiritual content. Little concerned with the "life to come," he found that religion best which furnished the best guide to human conduct. In one of his most interesting letters on religion he took "a comparative view of the ethics of the enlightened nations of antiquity," and awarded to Jesus the highest place as an ethical teacher. "His moral doctrines ... were more pure and perfect than those of the most correct of the philosophers, and greatly more so than those of the Jews; and they went far beyond both in inculcating universal philanthropy ... gathering all into one family, under the bonds of love, charity, peace, common wants and common aids." [145] He could say therefore: "I am a Christian, in the only sense in which he wished anyone to be, sincerely attached to his doctrines, in preference to all others." In order to have the Christian teaching before him, without its "corruptions," he extracted from the Gospels the "Life and Morals of Jesus of Nazareth," ranging the essential texts in parallel columns—Greek, Latin, French, and English. [146]. His great service, however, was not to religion, but to religious freedom. Throughout his life—from his proposed draft for the Virginia Constitution in 1776 to his latest letter—he strove to establish this principle.

Ten days before his death he had to decline an invitation to take part in celebrating the fiftieth anniversary of Independence.

---

[142] See Selections following, p. 292.

[143] See Selections following, p. 393.

[144] *Writings*, XVI, 19. In his library classification he ranged religion under jurisprudence.—Honeywell, *Educational Work of Jefferson*, p. 213.

[145] See letter to Rush, Selections following, p. 343.

[146] The so-called "Jefferson Bible,"—photographically reproduced in *Writings*, XX.

"May it be to the world," he wrote, "what I believe it will be (to some parts sooner, to others later, but finally to all), the signal for arousing men to burst the chains under which monkish ignorance and superstition had persuaded them to bind themselves, and to assume the blessings and security of self-government."

SELECTED BIBLIOGRAPHIES

ALEXANDER HAMILTON

Adams, J. T., editor. *Jeffersonian Principles and Hamiltonian Principles*. Boston: 1922. (Extracts from the writings, with Introductions.)

Atherton, G. *The Conqueror*. New York: 1902. (A novel covering Hamilton's life, based on careful study of the sources and some fresh investigations.)

Atherton, G., editor. *A Few of Hamilton's Letters*. New York: 1903. (New letters.)

Bassett, J. S. *The Federalist System, 1789-1801*. New York: 1906. (American Nation series. Deals with "the establishment of the government under the Constitution . . . chiefly due to Hamilton.")

Bassett, J. S., editor. *Selections from the Federalist*. New York: 1921. (Inexpensive, with good introduction. The *Federalist* is also in Everyman's Library.)

Bein, A. *Die Staatsidee Alexander Hamiltons in ihrer Entstehung und Entwicklung*. München and Berlin: 1927. (Excellent on Hamilton's thought in its development to 1789. A "Literatur-verzeichnis" of value.)

Beveridge, A. J. *Life of John Marshall*. Boston: 1916–1919. 4 vols. (A history of the period, valuable for both Hamilton and Jefferson.)

Bourne, E. G. "The Authorship of the *Federalist*," *American Historical Review*, II, 443–460. (Criticizes ascriptions of P. L. Ford in his introduction to the *Federalist*.)

Bourne, E. G. "Alexander Hamilton and Adam Smith," *Quarterly Journal of Economics*, VIII, 328 (1894). (Shows, in parallel columns, use of the *Wealth of Nations* in the Report on Manufactures.)

Cole, A. H., editor. *Industrial and Commercial Correspondence of Alexander Hamilton, Anticipating his Report on Manu-*

factures. Chicago: 1928. (Shows Hamilton's careful investigation and use of material.)

Coleman, W. *A Collection of Facts and Documents Relative to the Death of Alexander Hamilton.* New York: 1804. Reprinted, Boston: 1904. (Collects contemporary documents.)

Culbertson, W. S. *Alexander Hamilton.* New Haven: 1911. (Useful, particularly on the economic side.)

Dunbar, C. F. "Financial Precedents Followed by Hamilton," *Quarterly Journal of Economics*, III, 32–59 (1888). (Shows clear precedents, mainly English.)

Dunbar, L. B. *A Study of "Monarchical Tendencies" in the United States from 1776 to 1801.* Urbana, Illinois: 1922. (Treats Hamilton briefly.)

Fiske, J. "Alexander Hamilton and the Federalist Party"; "Thomas Jefferson, the Conservative Reformer," in *Essays Historical and Literary.* New York: 1902. (Readable summaries.)

Ford, H. J. *Alexander Hamilton.* New York: 1931. (Intelligent biography, with some fresh and interesting interpretations.)

Ford, H. J. *Washington and his Colleagues.* New Haven: 1920. (Treats Hamilton as the "Master Builder.")

Ford, P. L. *Bibliotheca Hamiltoniana: a List of Books Written by or relating to Alexander Hamilton.* New York: 1886.

Ford, P. L. *American Historical Review*, II, 675–687 (1897). (Replies to the argument of E. G. Bourne, q. v.)

Ford, P. L., editor. *The Federalist . . . with Notes, Illustrative Documents, and Index.* New York: 1898. (The most useful edition; well indexed.)

Hamilton, A. McL. *The Intimate Life of Alexander Hamilton.* New York: 1910. (By Hamilton's grandson. New material, especially concerning the private life.)

Hamilton, J. C. *History of the Republic . . . as Traced in the Writings of Alexander Hamilton.* New York: 1857–1860. 6 vols. (An expansion and continuation of the *Life*, next entry, which extends only to 1787.)

Hamilton, J. C. *The Life of Alexander Hamilton.* New York:

1834. 2 vols. (By Hamilton's son; partisan, but basic and indispensable for its factual material.)

Hamilton, J. C., editor. *The Works of Alexander Hamilton.* New York: 1851. 7 vols. (The first collected edition; some material not in the Lodge edition; still useful.)

Lodge, H. C. *Alexander Hamilton.* Boston: 1882. (American Statesmen series. A well-informed account, by a former senator from Massachusetts of Hamiltonian principles.)

Lodge, H. C., editor. *The Works of Alexander Hamilton.* New York: 1885–1886. 9 vols. [Also in 12 vols. New York: 1904.] (The best editions.)

Merriam, C. E. *A History of American Political Theories.* New York: 1926. (Contains good summaries of the systems of Hamilton and Jefferson.)

Morse, A. D. "Alexander Hamilton," *Political Science Quarterly,* V, 1–23 (1890). (Excellent summary of Hamilton's thought.)

Morse, J. T., Jr. *The Life of Alexander Hamilton.* Boston: 1876. 2 vols. (Favorable, but attempts justice to opponents.)

Munro, W. B. "Hamilton and the Economic Supremacy of the Federal Government," in *The Makers of the Unwritten Constitution.* New York: 1930. (Hamilton demonstrated that the "Constitution could be given an expansive quality by legislation.")

Oliver, F. S. *Alexander Hamilton.* London: 1906. (An Englishman writes "frankly from the standpoint of Hamilton." One-sided, often perverse, but suggestive. Applies Hamilton's principles to British imperial policy.)

Parrington, V. L. *The Colonial Mind.* New York: 1927. (Well written and penetrating. Inclines to an economic interpretation. Treats Hamilton with less than justice; Jefferson sympathetically.)

Riethmiller, C. J. *The Life and Times of Alexander Hamilton.* London: 1864. (An Englishman relates the work of Hamilton to the issues of the Civil War, during which the book was written, and to English policy.)

Shea, G. *The Life and Epoch of Alexander Hamilton.* Third

edition. Boston: 1881. (After celebrating Hamilton as "the founder of Empire," deals with his early life, to 1776.)

Sumner, W. G. *Alexander Hamilton.* New York: 1890. (Treats Hamilton's financial measures in the light of contemporary conditions, from the standpoint of a free-trader; finds them frequently unsound.)

Vandenburg, A. H. *The Greatest American, Alexander Hamilton* "with a Symposium of Opinions by Distinguished Americans." New York: 1922. (The "symposium" has some value.)

(Many books in each list of course deal with both Hamilton and Jefferson,—in particular, besides the biographies, those by J. T. Adams, J. S. Bassett, C. A. Beard, A. J. Beveridge, C. G. Bowers, H. J. Ford, C. E. Merriam, and V. L. Parrington. See also A. Nevins on Hamilton and D. Malone on Jefferson in *Dictionary of American Biography;* and F. S. Philbrick on both in *Encyclopædia Britannica,* 14th edition.)

Thomas Jefferson

Adams, Henry. *History of the United States . . . during the First and Second Administrations of Thomas Jefferson.* New York: 1889–1890. 4 vols. (Well written and authoritative; slightly unsympathetic in treatment of Jefferson.)

Adams, H. B. *Thomas Jefferson and the University of Virginia.* Washington: 1888. (U. S. Bureau of Education Circular of Information, No. 1. Authoritative.)

Arrowood, C. F. *Thomas Jefferson and Education in a Republic.* New York: 1930. ("Aims to present, in his own words . . . an account of the contributions of Thomas Jefferson to the progress of education.")

Beard, C. A. *Economic Origins of Jeffersonian Democracy.* New York: 1915. (Chap. XIV gives Jefferson's policy an economic interpretation.)

Becker, C. *The Declaration of Independence.* New York: 1922. (Excellent, especially on trains of thought leading up to the Declaration.)

Bergh, A. L., editor. *The Writings of Thomas Jefferson.* Washington: 1903. 20 vols. (The fullest collection; valuable facsimiles; text very untrustworthy. Vol. XX contains a bibliography of 73 pages.)

Bowers, C. G. *Jefferson and Hamilton.* Boston: 1925. (A vivacious treatment of the Hamilton-Jefferson conflict, making "liberal use of the newspapers of the period." Aiming at "complete justice to both," its sympathy is clearly with Jefferson.)

Channing, E. *The Jeffersonian System, 1801–1811.* New York: 1906. (Excellent for this period.)

Chinard, G. *Honest John Adams.* Boston: 1933. (Relevant to both Hamilton and Jefferson.)

Chinard, G. *Jefferson et les Idéologues.* Baltimore and Paris: 1925. (The influence of Destutt de Tracy and other French liberals on Jefferson.)

Chinard, G. *Thomas Jefferson, the Apostle of Americanism.* Boston: 1929. (The best biography; sympathetic, sound, and well documented.)

Chinard, G., editor. *The Commonplace Book of Thomas Jefferson.* Baltimore and Paris: 1926. (Jefferson's notes on early reading afford "a repertory of his ideas on government." Valuable introduction.)

Chinard, G., editor. *The Literary Bible of Thomas Jefferson.* Baltimore and Paris: 1928. (Jefferson's selections from the philosophers and poets, with introduction.)

Dodd, W. E. "Thomas Jefferson," in *Statesmen of the Old South.* New York: 1911. (Treats Jefferson in relation to Virginia politics and the South.)

Fisher, G. P. "Jefferson and the Social Compact Theory," *Yale Review,* II, 403–417 (1894). (Traces sources.)

Foley, J. P., editor. *The Jeffersonian Cyclopedia.* New York: 1900. (A useful compilation of extracts on many topics arranged alphabetically.)

Ford, P. L., editor. *The Writings of Thomas Jefferson.* New York: 1892–1894. 10 vols. (Best text. Vol. I contains a list of Jefferson's printed works.)

Ford, W. C., editor. *Thomas Jefferson Correspondence;* printed from the originals in the collection of William K. Bixby. Boston: 1916. (Letters not in the collected editions.)

Friedenwald, H. *The Declaration of Independence.* New York: 1904. (Traces forces leading up to the Declaration.)

Gould, W. D. "The Religious Opinions of Thomas Jefferson," in *Mississippi Valley Historical Review,* XX, 191–209 (1933). (Based on unpublished material in Library of Congress.)

Hazelton, J. H. *The Declaration of Independence.* New York: 1906. (The fullest treatment.)

Hirst, F. W. *Life and Letters of Thomas Jefferson.* New York: 1926. (An Englishman's view. Sympathetic, readable, and well-informed.)

Honeywell, R. J. *The Educational Work of Thomas Jefferson.* Cambridge: 1931. (Harvard Studies in Education, vol. 16. Best on this subject.)

Johnson, A. *Jefferson and his Colleagues.* New Haven: 1921. (In Chronicles of America. A readable account of Jefferson's presidency.)

Kimball, S. F. *Thomas Jefferson, Architect.* Boston: 1916. (Jefferson's development and influence as architect. Numerous architectural drawings.)

Morse, J. T. *Thomas Jefferson.* Boston: 1883. (American Statesmen series. Lacks sympathy and understanding.)

Muzzey, D. S. *Thomas Jefferson.* New York: 1918. (Good brief biography.)

Nock, A. J. *Jefferson.* New York: 1926. ("A study in conduct and character." Inclines to economic interpretation.)

Parton, J. *Life of Thomas Jefferson.* Boston: 1874. (Needs some correction; still readable.)

Randall, H. S. *Life of Thomas Jefferson.* New York: 1858. 3 vols. (The official biography; painstaking, copious, partisan, but the most important source of information.)

Randolph, S. N. *The Domestic Life of Thomas Jefferson.* New York: 1871. (Material concerning Jefferson's private life not elsewhere available.)

Randolph, T. J., editor. *Memoirs, Correspondence, and Mis-*

cellanies. Charlottesville, Virginia: 1829. 4 vols. (The earliest collection, containing the Autobiography, Anas, etc.)

Rayner, B. L. *The Life, Writings, and Opinions of Thomas Jefferson with Selections of . . . his . . . Correspondence.* New York: 1832.

Riley, I. W. "Virginia and Jefferson," in *American Philosophy, the Early Schools.* New York: 1907. (Summarizes views on religion and philosophy,—"an eclecticism of a pronounced deistic type.")

Schouler, J. *Thomas Jefferson.* New York: 1893. (Brief and judicious.)

Sears, L. M. *Jefferson and the Embargo.* Durham, N. C.: 1927. (The best study of this subject.)

Tucker, G. *The Life of Thomas Jefferson.* Philadelphia: 1837. 2 vols. (The first important life; by a friend of Jefferson; draws on local sources.)

Vossler, O. *Die Amerikanischen Revolutionsideale in ihrem verhältnis zu den Europäischen; untersucht an Thomas Jefferson.* München and Berlin: 1929. (Attempts to show that Jefferson's views were profoundly modified by his stay in France and other European influences.)

Washington, H. A., editor. *Writings of Thomas Jefferson.* Washington: 1853–1854. 9 vols. (An early collection, still valuable.)

Wayland, J. W. "The Poetical Tastes of Thomas Jefferson," *Sewanee Review,* XVIII, 283 (1910).

Williams, J. S. *Thomas Jefferson.* New York: 1913. (By a former Democratic senator from Mississippi. Very favorable, but documented and valuable.)

Wilstach, P. *Jefferson and Monticello.* New York: 1926. (Interesting on Jefferson at home.)

CHRONOLOGICAL TABLES

ALEXANDER HAMILTON

1757. January 11, Hamilton born in the island of Nevis.
1772. Arrives in New York.
1773. Enters King's (Columbia) College.
1774. Publishes *A Full Vindication*.
1775. Publishes *The Farmer Refuted*.
1776. Appointed Captain of a company of artillery.
1777. Joins Washington's staff, as military secretary.
1780. Marries Elizabeth Schuyler.
1781. Begins the *Continentalist*.
1782. Admitted to the bar. Enters Congress.
1786. Represents New York at the Annapolis Convention.
1787. Delegate to the Constitutional Convention.
1787. October 27. Begins the *Federalist*.
1789. September. Appointed Secretary of the Treasury.
1790. January 14. Makes first Report on Public Credit.
1793. Writes letters of "Pacificus."
1795. Resigns Secretaryship and returns to law.
1798. Appointed Inspector-General, with rank of Major-General.
1804. July 11. Shot by Burr in a duel.
1804. July 12. Dies in New York.

THOMAS JEFFERSON

1743. April 13. Jefferson born at Shadwell, Albemarle County, Virginia.
1760. Enters William and Mary College.
1767. Admitted to the bar.
1769. Elected to the House of Burgesses.
1772. Marries Martha Wayles Skelton.
1775. Attends the Continental Congress.
1776. June 11. Appointed on a Committee to draft the Declaration of Independence.

1776. Member of the Virginia Assembly.
1779. Elected Governor of Virginia. Reëlected, 1780; resigned, 1781.
1783. Member of Congress.
1784. Elected minister to France. Arrives in Paris, August 11.
1789. October. Leaves France.
1790. February 14. Accepts Secretaryship of State.
1793. December 31. Resigns Secretaryship.
1797. Becomes Vice-President.
1798. Drafts the Kentucky Resolutions.
1801. Becomes President of the United States.
1803. Louisiana treaty ratified.
1807. Signs Embargo Act.
1809. Retires to Monticello.
1826. July 4. Dies at Monticello.

*

Selections from
ALEXANDER HAMILTON

*

ALEXANDER HAMILTON

1. TO EDWARD STEVENS[1]

[AMBITION IS PREVALENT]

St. Croix, November 11, 1769.

This just serves to acknowledge receipt of yours per Capt. Lowndes, which was delivered me yesterday. The truth of Capt. Lightbowen and Lowndes' information is now verified by the presence of your father and sister, for whose safe arrival I pray; and that they may convey that satisfaction to your soul that must naturally flow from the sight of absent friends in health; and shall, for news this way, refer you to them. As to what you say respecting your having soon the happiness of seeing us all, I wish for an accomplishment of your hopes, provided they are concomitant with your welfare; otherwise not; though I doubt whether I shall be present or not, for, to confess my weakness, Ned, my ambition is prevalent, so that I contemn the grovelling condition of a clerk or the like, to which my fortune, etc., condemns me, and would willingly risk my life, though not my character, to exalt my station. I am confident, Ned, that my youth excludes me from any hopes of immediate preferment; nor do I desire it; but I mean to prepare the way for futurity. I am no philosopher, you see, and may justly be said to build castles in the air; my folly makes me ashamed, and I beg you'll conceal it; yet, Neddy, we have seen such schemes successful when the projector is constant. I shall conclude saying, I wish there was a war.

P. S.—I this moment received yours by William Smith, and am pleased to see you give such close application to study.

---

[1] Superior figures throughout the text refer to correspondingly numbered notes at the end of the volume, pp. 405 ff.

3

2. *From* THE FARMER REFUTED [2]

[AMERICAN RIGHTS INVADED]

FEBRUARY 5, 1775.

. . . I shall, for the present, pass over to that part of your pamphlet in which you endeavor to establish the supremacy of the British Parliament over America. After a proper *éclaircissement* of this point, I shall draw such inferences as will sap the foundation of every thing you have offered.

The first thing that presents itself is a wish, that "*I* had, explicitly, declared to the public my ideas of the *natural rights* of mankind. Man, in a state of nature (you say), may be considered as perfectly free from all restraints of *law* and *government;* and, then, the weak must submit to the strong."

I shall, henceforth, begin to make some allowance for that enmity you have discovered to the *natural rights* of mankind. For, though ignorance of them, in this enlightened age, cannot be admitted as a sufficient excuse for you; yet it ought, in some measure, to extenuate your guilt. If you will follow my advice, there still may be hopes of your reformation. Apply yourself, without delay, to the study of the law of nature. I would recommend to your perusal, Grotius, Puffendorf, Locke, Montesquieu, and Burlemaqui. I might mention other excellent writers on this subject; but if you attend, diligently, to these, you will not require any others.

There is so strong a similitude between your political principles and those maintained by Mr. Hobbes, that, in judging from them, a person might very easily *mistake* you for a disciple of his. His opinion was exactly coincident with yours, relative to man in a state of nature. He held, as you do, that he was then perfectly free from all restraint of *law* and *government*. Moral obligation, according to him, is derived from the introduction of civil society; and there is no virtue but what is purely artificial, the mere contrivance of politicians for the maintenance of social intercourse. But the reason he ran into this absurd and impious doctrine was, that he disbelieved the existence of an intelligent superintending principle, who is the governor, and will be the final judge, of the universe.

As you sometimes swear *by Him that made you*, I conclude your sentiment does not correspond with His in that which is the basis of the doctrine you both agree in; and this makes it impossible to imagine whence this congruity between you arises. To grant that there is a Supreme Intelligence who rules the world and has established laws to regulate the actions of His creatures, and still to assert that man, in a state of nature, may be considered as perfectly free from all restraints of *law* and *government*, appear, to a common understanding, altogether irreconcilable.

Good and wise men, in all ages, have embraced a very dissimilar theory. They have supposed that the Deity, from the relations we stand in to Himself and to each other, has constituted an eternal and immutable law, which is indispensably obligatory upon all mankind, prior to any human institution whatever.

This is what is called the law of nature, "which, being coeval with mankind, and dictated by God himself, is, of course, superior in obligation to any other. It is binding over all the globe, in all countries, and at all times. No human laws are of any validity, if contrary to this; and such of them as are valid derive all their authority, mediately or immediately, from this original."—BLACKSTONE.[3]

Upon this law depend the natural rights of mankind; the Supreme Being gave existence to man, together with the means of preserving and beautifying that existence. He endowed him with rational faculties, by the help of which to discern and pursue such things as were consistent with his duty and interest; and invested him with an inviolable right to personal liberty and personal safety.

Hence, in a state of nature, no man had any *moral* power to deprive another of his life, limbs, property, or liberty; nor the least authority to command or exact obedience from him, except that which arose from the ties of consanguinity.

Hence, also, the origin of all civil government, justly established, must be a voluntary compact between the rulers and the ruled, and must be liable to such limitations as are necessary for the security of the *absolute rights* of the latter; for what original title can any man, or set of men, have to govern others, except their own consent? To usurp dominion over a people in their own despite, or to grasp at a more extensive power than they are willing to intrust, is to violate that law of nature which gives every man a right to his personal liberty, and can therefore confer no obligation to obedience.

"The principal aim of society is to protect individuals in the enjoyment of those absolute rights which were vested in them by the immutable laws of nature, but which could not be preserved in peace without that mutual assistance and intercourse which is gained by the institution of friendly and social communities. Hence it follows, that the first and primary end of human laws is to maintain and regulate these *absolute rights* of individuals."—Blackstone.

If we examine the pretensions of Parliament by this criterion, which is evidently a good one, we shall presently detect their injustice. First, they are subversive of our natural liberty, because an authority is assumed over us which we by no means assent to. And, secondly, they divest us of that moral security for our lives and properties, which we are entitled to, and which it is the primary end of society to bestow. For such security can never exist while we have no part in making the laws that are to bind us, and while it may be the interest of our uncontrolled legislators to oppress us as much as possible.

To deny these principles will be not less absurd than to deny the plainest axioms. I shall not, therefore, attempt any further illustration of them. . . .

The most valid reasons can be assigned for our allegiance to the king of Great Britain, but not one of the least force or plausibility for our subjection to parliamentary decrees.

We hold our lands in America by virtue of charters from British monarchs, and are under no obligations to the Lords or Commons for them. Our title is similar, and equal, to that by which they possess their lands; and the king is the legal fountain of both. This is one grand source of our obligation to allegiance. . . .

But what merits still more serious attention is this: there seems to be already a jealousy of our dawning splendor. It is looked upon as portentous of approaching independence. This, we have reason to believe, is one of the principal incitements to the present rigorous and unconstitutional proceedings against us. And though it may have chiefly originated in the calumnies of designing men, yet it does not entirely depend upon adventitious or partial causes, but is also founded in the circumstances of our country and situation. The boundless extent of territory we possess, the wholesome temperament of our climate, the luxuriance and fertility of our soil, the variety of our products, the rapidity of our population, the industry of our countrymen, and the commodiousness of our ports, naturally lead to a suspicion of independence, and would always have an influence pernicious to us. Jealousy is a predominant passion of human nature, and is a source of the greatest evils. Whenever it takes place between rulers and their subjects, it proves the bane of civil society.

The experience of past ages may inform us, that when the circumstances of a people render them distressed their rulers generally recur to severe, cruel, and oppressive measures. Instead of endeavoring to establish their authority in the *affection* of their subjects, they think they have no security but in their *fear*. They do not aim at gaining their fidelity and obedience by making them flourishing, prosperous, and happy, but by rendering them abject and dispirited. They think it necessary to intimidate and awe them to make every accession to their own power, and to impair the people's as much as possible.

One great engine to effect this in America would be a large standing army, maintained out of our own pockets, to be at the devotion of our oppressors. This would be introduced under pretense of defending us, but, in fact, to make our bondage and misery complete.

We might soon expect the martial law, universally prevalent to the abolition of trials by juries, the *habeas corpus* act, and every other bulwark of personal safety, in order to overawe the honest assertors of their country's cause. A numerous train of *court dependents* would be created and supported at our expense. The value of all our possessions, by a complication of extorsive methods, would be gradually depreciated till it became a mere shadow.

This will be called too high-wrought a picture, a phantom of my own deluded imagination. The highest eulogies will be lavished on the wisdom and justice of the British nation. But deplorable is the condition of that people who have nothing else than the wisdom and justice of another to depend upon.

"Political writers," says a celebrated author,* "have established it as a maxim, that, in contriving any system of government, and fixing the several checks and controls of the constitution, *every man* ought to be supposed a *knave*, and to have no other end, in all his actions, but *private interest*. By this interest we must govern him, and by means of it *make him co-operate to public good*, notwithstanding his insatiable avarice and ambition. Without this we shall in vain boast of the advantages of *any constitution*, and shall find, in the end, that we have no security for our liberties and possessions except the *good-will* of our rulers; that is, we should have *no security at all*.

"It is therefore a just *political* maxim, that *every man must be supposed a knave*. Though, at the same time, it appears somewhat strange, that a maxim should be true in politics which is false in fact. But to satisfy us on this head, we may consider that men are generally more honest in a private than in a public capacity, and will go greater lengths to serve a party than when their own private interest is alone concerned. Honor is a great check upon mankind. But where a considerable body of men act together, this check is in a great measure removed, since a man is sure to be approved by his own party for what promotes the common interest, and he soon learns to despise the clamors of adversaries. To this we may add, that every court or senate is determined by the greater number of voices; so that, if self-interest influences only the majority (as it will

* Hume, Vol. I, Essay V.[4]

always do), the whole senate follows the allurements of this separate interest, and acts as if it contained not one member who had any regard to public interest and liberty." What additional force do these observations acquire when applied to the dominion of one community over another!

From what has been said, it is plain that we are without those checks upon the representatives of Great Britain which alone can make them answer the end of their appointment with respect to us; which is the preservation of the rights and the advancement of the happiness of the governed. The direct and inevitable consequence is, *they have no right to govern us*. . . .

3. TO THE COMMITTEE OF THE NEW YORK CONVENTION

[TREATMENT OF NEW YORK LOYALISTS]

HEADQUARTERS, MORRISTOWN, April 20, 1777.

GENTLEMEN:

The disposition of the convention, with respect to the disaffected among you, is highly commendable, and justified by every principle of equity and policy. The necessity of exemplary punishment throughout the States is become evident beyond a doubt, and it were to be wished every one of the thirteen would imitate the judicious conduct of New York. Lenity and forbearance have been tried too long to no purpose: it is high time to discard what the clearest experience has shown to be ineffectual.

But in dispensing punishment, the utmost care and caution ought to be used. The power of doing it, or even of bringing the guilty to trial, should be placed in hands that know well how to use it. I believe it would be a prudent rule to meddle with none but those whose crimes are supported by very sufficient evidence, and are of a pretty deep dye. The apprehending innocent persons, or those whose offences are of so slender a nature as to make it prudent to dismiss them, furnishes an occasion of triumph, and a foundation for a species of animadversion which is very injurious to the public cause. Persons so apprehended generally return home worse than they were, and by expatiating on their sufferings, first excite the pity towards themselves, and afterwards the abhorrence towards their persecutors, of those with whom they converse. I believe it would also be in general a good rule either to pardon offenders entirely, or to inflict capital and severe punishments. The advice given by a certain general to his son, when the latter had the Roman army in his power, was certainly very politic: he advised him either to destroy them utterly, or to dismiss them with every mark of honor and respect. By the first method, says he, you disable the Romans from being your enemies; by the last, you make them your friends. So with respect to the Tories; I would either disable them from doing us any injury, or I would endeavor to gain their friendship by clemency. Inflicting trifling punishments only embitters the minds of those on whom they fall, and increases their disposition to do mischief without taking away the power of doing it.

I shall communicate your additional resolve to the General and consult him on what you mention, and shall let you know his opinion in my next: mine, however, is that those who appear to be of such a character as to be susceptible of reformation, should be employed; but it is a delicate point.

As to news, the most material is, that from intelligence received from Rhode Island, it appears the enemy are abandoning it. This is a preparatory step to the intended operations of the enemy.

The other day we surprised a lieutenant's guard, took sixteen prisoners, and killed three or four.

In a private letter from Philadelphia I am informed that a treaty of a very particular nature is on the point of being concluded between the Court of France and the States of America. There is a prospect of opening a trade with Sweden. I hear Mr. Morris, of Philadelphia, has a vessel arrived from thence.

4. TO GOUVERNEUR MORRIS

[SUGGESTIONS FOR A NEW YORK GOVERNMENT]

HEADQUARTERS, MORRISTOWN, May 19, 1777.

DEAR SIR:

I this moment received the favor of your letter of the 16th instant.

I partly agree and partly disagree with you respecting the deficiencies of your Constitution. That there is a want of vigor in the executive, I believe, will be found true. To determine the qualifications proper for the chief executive magistrate requires the deliberate wisdom of a select assembly, and cannot be safely lodged with the people at large. That instability is inherent in the nature of popular governments I think very disputable; unstable democracy, is an epithet frequently in the mouths of politicians; but I believe that from a strict examination of the matter—from the records of history, it will be found that the fluctuations of governments in which the popular principle has borne a considerable sway, have proceeded from its being compounded with other principles;—and from its being made to operate in an improper channel. Compound governments, though they may be harmonious in the beginning, will introduce distinct interests, and these interests will clash, throw the State into convulsions, and produce a change or dissolution. When the deliberative or judicial powers are vested wholly or partly in the collective body of the people, you must expect error, confusion, and instability. But a representative democracy, where the right of election is well secured and regulated, and the exercise of the legislative, executive, and judiciary authorities is vested in select persons, chosen really and not nominally by the people, will, in my opinion, be most likely to be happy, regular, and durable.[5] That the complexity of your Legislature will occasion delay and dilatoriness, is evident, and I fear may be attended with a much greater evil;—as expedition is not very material in making laws, especially when the government is well digested and matured by time. The evil I mean is, that in time your Senate, from the very name, and from the mere circumstance of its being a separate member of the Legislature, will be liable to degenerate into a body purely aristocratical.

And I think the danger of an abuse of power from a simple legislature, would not be very great in a government where the equality and fulness of popular representation is so wisely provided for as in yours. On the whole, though I think there are the defects intimated, I think your government far the best that we have yet seen, and capable of giving long and substantial happiness to the people. Objections to it should be suggested with great caution and reserve.

Nothing particular in the military line. The enemy still in the Jerseys, though they have been some time sending away their stores, baggage, etc., and are raising new works of defence. All this may be preparatory to an evacuation at all events, and they may be only intended to pave the way for a retreat, in case of an attack or any accident.

Advices from the West Indies, that have an appearance of authenticity, mention a French vessel bound for the continent, being taken by the British frigate Perseus, and carried into Dominique; and a remonstrance being made by the Governor of Martinique, threatening reprisals in case of a detention. Nay, some accounts say he has actually seized all the English vessels in the harbor of Martinique, and imprisoned their seamen till restitution shall be made. If these accounts be true, they are important, and may be considered as an earnest of more general hostility.

Perhaps your next favor will find me at Boundbrook. Headquarters will soon be moved there. Our family seem desirous of cultivating a closer acquaintance with the enemy than we have had the pleasure of for some time past.

Relying on your punctuality in favoring me with any important intelligence your way, I am likely to lose a beaver hat, which was staked against the truth of the report of the stores at St. John's being destroyed. If you forget me in future, I will certainly excommunicate you.

5. TO GEORGE CLINTON

[WEAKNESS OF THE CONTINENTAL CONGRESS]

HEADQUARTERS, February 13, 1778.

DEAR SIR:

I did myself the honor of writing to you immediately after my arrival at headquarters, in answer to two letters I found here from you.

There is a matter which often obtrudes itself upon my mind, and which requires the attention of every person of sense and prudence among us—I mean a degeneracy of representation in the great council of America. It is a melancholy truth, sir, the effects of which we daily see and feel, that there is not so much wisdom in a certain body as there ought to be, and as the success of our affairs absolutely demands. Many members of it are, no doubt, men in every respect fit for the trust, but this cannot be said of it as a body. Folly, caprice, a want of foresight, comprehension, and dignity characterize the general tenor of their action. Of this, I dare say, you are sensible, though you have not, perhaps, so many opportunities of knowing it as I have. Their conduct, with respect to the army especially, is feeble, indecisive, and improvident—insomuch that we are reduced to a more terrible situation than you can conceive. False and contracted views of economy have prevented them, though repeatedly urged to it, from making that provision for officers which was requisite to interest them in the service, which has produced such carelessness and indifference to the service as is subversive to every officer-like quality. They have disgusted the army by repeated instances of the most whimsical favoritism in their promotions, and by an absurd prodigality of rank to foreigners and to the meanest staff of the army. They have not been able to summon resolution enough to withstand the impudent importunity and vain boasting of foreign pretenders, but have manifested such a ductility and inconsistency in their proceedings as will warrant the charge of suffering themselves to be bullied by every petty rascal who comes armed with ostentatious pretensions of military merit and experience. Would you believe it, sir, it is become almost proverbial in the mouths of the French officers and other foreigners, that they have nothing more to do to obtain whatever they please than to assume a high tone and assert their own merit with confidence and perseverance? These things wound my feelings as a Republican more than I can express, and in some degree make me contemptible in my own eyes.

By injudicious changes and arrangements in the middle of a campaign, they have exposed the army frequently to temporary want, and to the danger of dissolution from absolute famine. At this very day there are complaints from the whole line of having been three or four days without provisions; desertions have been immense, and strong features of mutiny begin to show themselves. It is indeed to be wondered at that the soldiery have manifested so unparalleled a degree of patience as they have. If effectual measures are not speedily adopted I know not how we shall keep the army together or make another campaign.

I omit saying any thing of the want of clothing for the army. It may be disputed whether more could have been done than has been done.

If you look into their conduct in the civil line you will equally discover a deficiency of energy, dignity, and extensiveness of views; but of this you can better judge than myself, and it is unnecessary to particularize.

America once had a representation that would do honor to any age or nation. The present falling off is very alarming and dangerous. What is the cause? or how is it to be remedied?— are questions that the welfare of these States requires should be well attended to. The great men who composed our first council; are they dead, have they deserted the cause, or what has become of them? Very few are dead and still fewer have deserted the cause; they are all, except the few who still remain in Congress, either in the field or in the civil offices of their respective States; for the greater part are engaged in the latter. The only remedy then is to take them out of these employments and return them to the place where their presence is infinitely more important.

Each State, in order to promote its own external government and prosperity, has selected its best members to fill the offices within itself, and conduct its own affairs. Men have been fonder of the emoluments and conveniences of being employed at home; and local attachment falsely operating has made them more provident for the particular interests of the State to which they belonged, than for the common interests of the Confederacy. This is a most pernicious mistake and must be corrected. However important it is to give form and efficiency to your interior constitutions and police, it is infinitely more important to have a wise general council; otherwise a failure of the measures of the Union will overwhelm all your labors for the advancement of your particular good, and ruin the common cause. You should not beggar the councils of the United States to enrich the administration of the several members. Realize to yourself the consequence of having a Congress despised at home and abroad. How can the common force be exerted if the power of collecting it be put in weak, foolish, and unsteady hands? How can we hope for success in our European negotiations, if the nations of Europe have no confidence in the wisdom and vigor of the great Continental Government? This is the object on which their eyes are fixed; hence it is, America will derive its importance or insignificance in their estimation.

Arguments to you, sir, need not be multiplied to enforce the necessity of having a good general council; neither do I think we shall very widely differ as to the fact that the present is very far from being such.

The sentiments I have advanced are not fit for the vulgar ear; and circumstanced as I am now, I should with caution utter them except to those in whom I may place an entire confidence. But it is time that men of weight and understanding should take the alarm, and excite each other to a proper remedy. For my part, my insignificance allows me to do nothing more than to hint my apprehensions to those of that description who are pleased to favor me with their confidence. In this view I write to you.

As far as I can judge, the remarks I have made do not apply to your State nearly so much as to the other twelve. You have a Duane, a Morris, and, may I not add, a Duer? But why do you not send your Jay, and your R. R. Livingston? I wish General Schuyler was either explicitly in the army or in Congress. For yourself, sir, though I mean no compliments, you must not be spared from where you are.

But the design of this letter is not so much that you may use your influence in improving or enlarging your own representation, as in discreetly giving the alarm to other States through the medium of your confidential friends. Indeed, sir, it is necessary there should be a change. America will shake to its centre if there is not.

You and I had some conversation when I had the pleasure of seeing you last, with respect to the existence of a certain faction. Since I saw you I have discovered such convincing traits of the monster that I cannot doubt its reality in the most extensive sense. I dare say you have heard enough to settle the matter in your own mind. I believe it unmasked its batteries too soon, and begins to hide its head; but, as I imagine it will only change the storm to a sap, all the true and sensible friends to their country, and of course to a certain great man, ought to be upon the watch to counterplot the secret machinations of his enemies. Have you heard any thing of Conway's history?[6] He is one of the vermin bred in the entrails of this chimera dire and there does not exist a more villainous calumniator and incendiary. He is gone to Albany on a certain expedition.

6. TO MISS LIVINGSTON

[A GRACEFUL REFUSAL]

HEADQUARTERS, March 18, 1779.

I can hardly forgive an application to my humanity to induce me to exert my influence in an affair in which ladies are concerned, and especially when you are of the party.[7] Had you appealed to my friendship or to my gallantry, it would have been irresistible. I should have thought myself bound to have set prudence and policy at defiance, and even to have attacked wind-mills in your ladyship's service. I am not sure but my imagination would have gone so far as to have fancied New York an enchanted castle—the three ladies so many fair damsels ravished from their friends and held in captivity by the spells of some wicked magician—General Clinton, a huge giant, placed as keeper of the gates—and myself, a valorous knight, destined to be their champion and deliverer.

But when, instead of availing yourself of so much better titles, you appealed to the cold, general principle of humanity, I confess I felt myself mortified, and determined, by way of revenge, to mortify you in turn. I resolved to show you that all the eloquence of your fine pen could not tempt our Fabius to do wrong; and, avoiding any representation of my own, I put your letter into his hands and let it speak for itself. I knew, indeed, this would expose his resolution to a severer trial than it could experience in any other way, and I was not without my fears for the event, but if it should decide against you, I anticipated the triumph of letting you see your influence had failed. I congratulated myself on the success of my scheme; for, though there was a harder struggle upon the occasion between inclination and duty, than it would be for his honor to tell; yet he at last had the courage to determine that, as he could not indulge the ladies with consistency and propriety, he would not run the risk of being charged with a breach of both. This he desired me to tell you, though, to be sure, it was done in a different manner, interlarded with many assurances of his great desire to oblige you, and of his regret that he could not do it in the present case, with a deal of stuff of the same kind, which I have too good an opinion of your understanding to repeat. I shall, therefore, only tell you that whether the Governor and the General are more honest or more perverse than other people, they have a very odd knack of thinking alike; and it happens in the present case that they both equally disapprove the intercourse you mention, and have taken pains to discourage it. I shall leave you to make your own reflections upon this, with only one more observation, which is that the ladies for whom you apply would have every claim to be gratified, were it not that it would operate as a bad precedent. But, before I conclude, it will be necessary to explain one point. This refusal supposes that the ladies mean only to make a visit and return to New York. If it should be their intention to remain with us, the case will be altered. There will be no rule against their coming out, and they will be an acquisition. But this is subject to two provisos—1st, that they are not found guilty of treason or any misdemeanor punishable by the laws of the State, in which case the General can have no power to protect them; and, 2dly, that the ladies on our side do not apprehend any inconvenience from increasing their number. Trifling apart, there is nothing could give me greater pleasure than to have been able to serve Miss Livingston and her friends on this occasion, but circumstances really did not permit it. I am persuaded she has too just an opinion of the General's politeness not to be convinced that he would be happy to do any thing which his public character would justify in an affair so interesting to the tender feelings of so many ladies. The delicacy of her own ideas will easily comprehend the delicacy of his situation;—she knows the esteem of her friend,   A. HAMILTON.

The General and Mrs. Washington present their compliments.

7. TO JAMES DUANE [8]

[DEFECTS OF THE CONFEDERATION AND REMEDIES]

LIBERTY POLE, September 3, 1780.

DEAR SIR:

Agreeably to your request, and my promise, I sit down to give you my ideas of the defects of our present system, and the changes necessary to save us from ruin. They may, perhaps, be the reveries of a projector, rather than the sober views of a politician. You will judge of them, and make what use you please of them.

The fundamental defect is a want of power in Congress. It

is hardly worth while to show in what this consists, as it seems to be universally acknowledged; or to point out how it has happened, as the only question is how to remedy it. It may, however, be said, that it has originated from three causes: an excess of the spirit of liberty, which has made the particular States show a jealousy of all power not in their own hands,—and this jealousy has led them to exercise a right of judging in the last resort of the measures recommended by Congress, and of acting according to their own opinions of their propriety, or necessity; a diffidence, in Congress, of their own powers, by which they have been timid and indecisive in their resolutions, constantly making concessions to the States, till they have scarcely left themselves the shadow of power; a want of sufficient means at their disposal to answer the public exigencies, and of vigor to draw forth those means, which have occasioned them to depend on the States individually to fulfil their engagements with the army,—the consequence of which has been to ruin their influence and credit with the army, to establish its dependence on each State separately, rather than *on them*—that is, rather than on the whole collectively.

It may be pleaded that Congress had never any definite powers granted them, and of course could exercise none, could do nothing more than recommend. The manner in which Congress was appointed would warrant, and the public good required that they should have considered themselves as vested with full power *to preserve the republic from harm*. They have done many of the highest acts of sovereignty, which were always cheerfully submitted to: The declaration of independence, the declaration of war, the levying of an army, creating a navy, emitting money, making alliances with foreign powers, appointing a dictator, etc. All these implications of a complete sovereignty were never disputed, and ought to have been a standard for the whole conduct of administration. Undefined powers are discretionary powers, limited only by the object for which they were given; in the present case the independence and freedom of America.[9] The Confederation made no difference, for as it has not been generally adopted, it had no operation. But from what I recollect of it, Congress have even descended from the authority which the spirit of that act gives them, while the particular States have no further attended to it than as it suited their pretensions and convenience. It would take too much time to enter into particular instances, each of which separately might appear inconsiderable, but united are of serious import. I only mean to remark, not to censure.

But the Confederation itself is defective, and requires to be altered. It is neither fit for war nor peace. The idea of an uncontrollable sovereignty in each State over its internal police will defeat the other powers given to Congress, and make our union feeble and precarious. There are instances without number where acts, necessary for the general good, and which rise out of the powers given to Congress, must interfere with the internal police of the States; and there are as many instances in which the particular States, by arrangements of internal police, can effectually, though indirectly, counteract the arrangements of Congress. You have already had examples of this, for which I refer you to your own memory.

The Confederation gives the States, individually, too much influence in the affairs of the army. They should have nothing to do with it. The entire formation and disposal of our military forces ought to belong to Congress. It is an essential cement of the union; and it ought to be the policy of Congress to destroy all ideas of State attachments in the army, and make it look up wholly to them. For this purpose all appointments, promotions, and provisions, whatsoever, ought to be made by them. It may be apprehended that this may be dangerous to liberty. But nothing appears more evident to me than that we run much greater risk of having a weak and disunited federal government, than one which will be able to usurp upon the rights of the people.

Already some of the lines of the army would obey their States in opposition to Congress, notwithstanding the pains we have taken to preserve the unity of the army. If anything would hinder this it would be the personal influence of the General—a melancholy and mortifying consideration.

The forms of our State constitutions must always give them great weight in our affairs, and will make it too difficult to bend them to the pursuit of a common interest, too easy to oppose whatever they do not like, and to form partial combinations subversive of the general one. There is a wide difference between our situation and that of an empire under one simple form of government, distributed into counties, provinces, or districts, which have no Legislatures, but merely magistratical bodies to execute the laws of a common sovereign. Here the danger is that the sovereign will have too much power, and oppress the parts of which it is composed.[10] In our case, that of an empire composed of confederated States, each with a government completely organized within itself, having all the means to draw its subjects to a close dependence on itself, the danger is directly the reverse. It is that the common sovereign will not have power sufficient to unite the different members together, and direct the common forces to the interest and happiness of the whole.

The leagues among the old Grecian republics are a proof of this. They were continually at war with each other, and for want of union fell a prey to their neighbors. They frequently held general councils; but their resolutions were no further observed than as they suited the interests and inclinations of all the parties, and at length they sank entirely into contempt.

The Swiss Cantons are another proof of the doctrine. They have had wars with each other, which would have been fatal to them, had not the different powers in their neighborhood been too jealous of one another, and too equally matched, to suffer either to take advantage of their quarrels. That they have remained so long united at all, is to be attributed to their weakness, to their poverty, and to the causes just mentioned. These ties will not exist in America; a little time hence some of the States will be powerful empires; and we are so remote from other nations, that we shall have all the leisure and opportunity we can wish to cut each other's throats.

The Germanic corps might also be cited as an example in favor of the position.

The United Provinces may be thought to be one against it. But the family of the Stadtholders, whose authority is interwoven with the whole government, has been a strong link of union between them. Their physical necessities, and the habits founded upon them, have contributed to it. Each province is too inconsiderable, by itself, to undertake anything. An analysis of their present constitutions would show that they have many ties which would not exist in ours, and that they are by no means a proper model for us.

Our own experience should satisfy us. We have felt the difficulty of drawing out the resources of the country, and inducing the States to combine in equal exertions for the common cause.

The ill success of our last attempt is striking. Some have done a great deal; others little, or scarcely anything. The disputes about boundaries, etc., testify how flattering a prospect we have of future tranquillity, if we do not frame, in time, a confederacy capable of deciding the differences and compelling the obedience of the respective members.

The Confederation, too, gives the power of the purse too entirely to the State Legislatures. It should provide perpetual funds, in the disposal of Congress, by a land tax, poll tax, or the like. All imposts upon commerce ought to be laid by Congress, and appropriated to their use. For, without certain revenues, a government can have no power. That power which holds the purse-strings absolutely, must rule. This seems to be a medium which, without making Congress altogether independent, will tend to give reality to its authority.

Another defect in our system is want of method and energy in the administration. This has partly resulted from the other defect; but in a great degree from prejudice, and the want of a proper executive. Congress have kept the power too much in their own hands, and have meddled too much with details of every sort. Congress is, properly, a deliberative corps, and it forgets itself when it attempts to play the executive. It is impossible such a body, numerous as it is, and constantly fluctuating, can ever act with sufficient decision or with system. Two-thirds of the members, one half the time, cannot know what has gone before them, or what connection the subject in hand has to what has been transacted on former occasions. The members who have been more permanent, will only give information that promotes the side they espouse in the present case, and will as often mislead as enlighten. The variety of business must distract, and the proneness of every assembly to debate must at all times delay.

Lately, Congress, convinced of these inconveniences, have gone into the measure of appointing Boards. But this is, in my opinion, a bad plan.

A single man in each department of the administration would be greatly preferable. It would give us a chance of more knowledge, more activity, more responsibility, and, of course, more zeal and attention. Boards partake of a part of the inconveniences of larger assemblies. Their decisions are slower, their energy less, their responsibility more diffused. They will not have the same abilities and knowledge as an administration by single men. Men of the first pretensions will not so readily engage in them, because they will be less conspicuous, of less importance, have less opportunity of distinguishing themselves. The members of Boards will take less pains to inform themselves and arrive to eminence, because they have fewer motives to do it. All these reasons conspire to give a preference to the plan of vesting the great executive departments of the State in the hands of individuals. As these men will be, of course, at all times under the direction of Congress, we shall blend the advantages of a monarchy and republic in our constitution.

A question has been made, whether single men could be found to undertake these offices. I think they could, because there would be then everything to excite the ambition of candidates. But, in order to effect this, Congress, by their manner of appointing them, and the line of duty marked out, must show that they are in earnest in making these officers officers of real trust and importance.

I fear a little vanity has stood in the way of these arrangements, as though they would lessen the importance of Congress and leave them nothing to do. But they would have precisely the same rights and powers as heretofore, happily disencumbered of the detail. They would have to inspect the conduct of their ministers, deliberate upon their plans, originate others for the public good; only observing this rule—that they ought to consult their ministers, and get all the information and advice they could from them, before they entered into any new measures or made changes in the old.

A third defect is the fluctuating constitution of our army. This has been a pregnant source of evil; all our military misfortunes, three-fourths of our civil embarrassments, are to be ascribed to it. The General has so fully enumerated the mischiefs of it, in a letter of 20 August, 1780, to Congress, that I could only repeat what he has said, and will therefore refer you to that letter.

The imperfect and unequal provision made for the army is a fourth defect, which you will find delineated in the same letter. Without a speedy change the army must dissolve. It is now a mob, rather than an army; without clothing, without pay, without provision, without morals, without discipline. We begin to hate the country for its neglect of us. The country begin to hate us for our oppressions of them. Congress have long been jealous of us. We have now lost all confidence in them, and give the worst construction to all they do. Held together by the slenderest ties, we are ripening for a dissolution.

The present mode of supplying the army, by State purchases, is not one of the least considerable defects of our system. It is too precarious a dependence, because the States will never be sufficiently impressed with our necessities. Each will make its own ease a primary object, the supply of the army a secondary one. The variety of channels through which the business is transacted will multiply the number of persons employed and the opportunities of embezzling public money. From the popular spirit on which most of the governments turn, the State agents will be men of less character and ability, nor will there be so rigid a responsibility among them as there might easily be among those in the employ of the Continent; of course, not so much diligence, care, or economy. Very little of the money raised in the several States will go into the Continental treasury, on pretence that it is all exhausted in providing the quotas of supplies; and the public will be without funds for the other demands of government. The expense will be ultimately much greater and the advantages much smaller. We actually feel the insufficiency of this plan, and have reason to dread under it a ruinous extremity of want.

These are the principal defects in the present system that now occur to me. There are many inferior ones in the organization of particular departments, and many errors of administration, which might be pointed out, but the task would be troublesome and tedious; and if we had once remedied those I have mentioned, the others would not be attended with much difficulty.

I shall now propose the remedies which appear to me applicable to our circumstances, and necessary to extricate our affairs from their present deplorable situation.

The first step must be to give Congress powers competent to the public exigencies. This may happen in two ways: one by resuming and exercising the discretionary powers I suppose to have been originally vested in them for the safety of the States, and resting their conduct on the candor of their countrymen and the necessity of the conjuncture; the other, by calling immediately a Convention of all the States, with full authority to conclude finally upon a General Confederation, stating to them beforehand, explicitly, the evils arising from a want of power in Congress, and the impossibility of supporting the contest on its present footing, that the delegates may come possessed of proper sentiments as well as proper authority to give efficacy to the meeting. Their commission should include a right of vesting Congress with the whole, or a proportion, of the unoccupied lands, to be employed for the purpose of raising a revenue; reserving the jurisdiction to the States by whom they are granted.

The first plan, I expect, will be thought too bold an expedient by the generality of Congress; and, indeed, their practice hitherto has so riveted the opinion of their want of power, that the success of this experiment may very well be doubted.

I see no objection to the other mode that has any weight in competition with the reasons for it. The Convention should assemble the first of November next. The sooner the better. Our disorders are too violent to admit of a common or lingering remedy. The reasons for which I require them to be vested with plenipotentiary authority are that the business may suffer no delay in the execution, and may, in reality, come to effect. A Convention may agree upon a Confederation; the States individually hardly ever will. We must have one at all events, and a vigorous one, if we mean to succeed in the contest and be happy hereafter. As I said before, to engage the States to comply with this mode Congress ought to confess to them, plainly and unanimously, the impracticability of supporting our affairs on the present footing and without a solid coercive union. I ask that the Convention should have a power of vesting the whole, or a part, of the unoccupied lands in Congress; because it is necessary that body should have some property as a fund for the arrangements of finance; and I know of no other kind that can be given them.

The Confederation, in my opinion, should give Congress complete sovereignty, except as to that part of internal police which relates to the rights of property and life among individuals, and to raising money by internal taxes. It is necessary that every thing belonging to this should be regulated by the State Legislatures. Congress should have complete sovereignty in all that relates to war, peace, trade, finance; and to the management of foreign affairs; the right of declaring war; of raising armies, officering, paying them, directing their motions in every respect; of equipping fleets, and doing the same with them; of building fortifications, arsenals, magazines, etc., etc.; of making peace on such conditions as they think proper; of regulating trade, determining with what countries it shall be carried on; granting indulgences; laying prohibitions on all the articles of export or import; imposing duties; granting bounties and premiums for raising, exporting or importing, and applying to their own use, the product of these duties—only giving credit to the States on whom they are raised in the general account of revenues and expenses; instituting Admiralty Courts, etc.; of coining money; establishing banks on such terms, and with such privileges as they think proper; appropriating funds, and doing whatever else relates to the operations of finance; transacting every thing with foreign nations; making alliances, offensive and defensive, treaties of commerce, etc., etc.

The Confederation should provide certain perpetual revenues, productive and easy of collection; a land tax, poll tax, or the like; which, together with the duties on trade, and the unlocated lands, would give Congress a substantial existence, and a stable foundation for their schemes of finance. What more supplies were necessary should be occasionally demanded of the States, in the present mode of quotas.

The second step I would recommend is, that Congress should instantly appoint the following great officers of State: A Secretary of Foreign Affairs, a President of War, a President of Marine, a Financier, a President of Trade. Instead of this last, a Board of Trade may be preferable, as the regulations of trade are slow and gradual, and require prudence and experience more than other qualities, for which Boards are very well adapted. . . .

I have only skimmed the surface of the different subjects I have introduced. Should the plans recommended come into contemplation in earnest, and you desire my further thoughts, I will endeavor to give them more form and particularity. I am persuaded a solid confederation, a permanent army, and a reasonable prospect of subsisting it, would give us treble consideration in Europe, and produce a peace this winter.

If a Convention is called, the minds of all the States and the people ought to be prepared to receive its determinations by sensible and popular writings, which should conform to the views of Congress.[11] There are epochs in human affairs when *novelty* even is useful. If a general opinion prevails that the old way is bad, whether true or false, and this obstructs or relaxes the operations of the public service, a change is necessary, if it be but for the sake of change. This is exactly the case now. It is a universal sentiment that our present system is a bad one, and that things do not go right on this account. The measure of a Convention would revive the hopes of the people and give a new direction to their passions, which may be improved in carrying points of substantial utility. The Eastern States have already pointed out this mode to Congress; they ought to take the hint and anticipate the others.

And, in future, my dear sir, two things let me recommend as fundamental rules for the conduct of Congress: to attach the army to them by every motive; to maintain an air of authority (not domineering) in all their measures with the States. The manner in which a thing is done has more influence than is commonly imagined. Men are governed by opinion; this opinion is as much influenced by appearances as by realities. If a government appears to be confident of its own powers, it is the surest way to inspire the same confidence in others. If it is diffident, it may be certain there will be a still greater diffidence in others; and that its authority will not only be distrusted, controverted, but contemned.

I wish, too, Congress would always consider that a kindness consists as much in the manner as in the thing. The best things done hesitatingly and with an ill grace lose their effect, and produce disgust rather than satisfaction or gratitude. In what Congress have at any time done for the army, they have commonly been too late. They have seemed to yield to importunity rather than to sentiments of justice or to a regard to the accommodation of their troops. An attention to this idea is of more importance than it may be thought. I, who have seen all the workings and progress of the present discontents, am convinced that a want of this has not been among the most inconsiderable causes.

You will perceive, my dear sir, this letter is hastily written and with a confidential freedom; not as to a member of Congress whose feelings may be sore at the prevailing clamors, but as to a friend who is in a situation to remedy public disorders, who wishes for nothing so much as truth, and who is desirous of information even from those less capable of judging than himself. I have not even time to correct and copy, and only enough to add that I am, very truly and affectionately, dear sir,

Your most obedient servant.

8. TO JAMES DUANE

[GATES' DEFEAT]

September 6, 1780.

MY DEAR SIR:

The letter accompanying this has lain by two or three days for want of an opportunity. I have heard since of Gates' defeat: a very good comment on the necessity of changing our system.[12] His passion for militia, I fancy, will be a little cured, and he will cease to think them the best bulwark of American liberty. What think you of the conduct of this great man? I am his enemy personally, for unjust and unprovoked attacks upon my character; therefore what I say of him ought to be received as from an enemy, and have no more weight than as it is consistent with fact and common sense. But did ever any one hear of such a disposition or such a flight? His best troops placed on the side strongest by nature, his worst on that weakest by nature, and his attack made with these. 'T is impossible to give a more complete picture of military absurdity. It is equally against the maxims of war and common sense. We see the consequences. His left ran away, and left his right uncovered. His right wing turned on the left has in all probability been cut off. Though, in truth, the General seems to have known very little what became of his army.

Had he placed his militia on his right, supported by the morass, and his Continental troops on his left, where it seems he was most vulnerable, his right would have been more secure, and his left would have opposed the enemy; and instead of going backward when he ordered to attack, would have gone forward. The reverse of what has happened might have happened.

But was there ever an instance of a general running away,

as Gates has done, from his whole army? And was there ever so precipitate a flight? One hundred and eighty miles in three days and a half. It does admirable credit to the activity of a man at his time of life. But it disgraces the general and the soldier. I always believed him to be very far short of a Hector, or a Ulysses. All the world, I think, will begin to agree with me.

But what will be done by Congress? Will he be changed or not? If he is changed, for God's sake overcome prejudice, and send Greene. You know my opinion of him. I stake my reputation on the events, give him but fair play.

But, above all things, let us have, without delay, a vigorous government, and a well constituted army for the war.

9. TO JOHN LAURENS[13]

[EXECUTION AND CHARACTER OF ANDRÉ]

October, 1780.

... André was, without loss of time, conducted to the head-quarters of the army, where he was immediately brought before a Board of General Officers, to prevent all possibility of misrepresentation, or cavil on the part of the enemy. The Board reported that he ought to be considered as a spy, and, according to the laws of nations, to suffer death, which was executed two days after.

Never, perhaps, did a man suffer death with more justice, or deserve it less. The first step he took after his capture was to write a letter to General Washington, conceived in terms of dignity without insolence, and apology without meanness. The scope of it was to vindicate himself from the imputation of having assumed a mean character for treacherous or interested purposes; asserting that he had been involuntarily an impostor; that contrary to his intention, which was to meet a person for intelligence on neutral ground, he had been betrayed within our posts, and forced into the vile condition of an enemy in disguise; soliciting only that, to whatever rigor policy might devote him, a decency of treatment might be observed, due to a person who, though unfortunate, had been guilty of nothing dishonorable. His request was granted in its full extent; for, in the whole progress of the affair, he was treated with the most scrupulous delicacy. When brought before the Board of Officers he met with every mark of indulgence, and was required to answer no interrogatory which could even embarrass his feelings. On his part, while he carefully concealed every thing that might involve others, he frankly confessed all the facts relating to himself; and, upon his confession, without the trouble of examining a witness, the Board made their report. The members of it were not more impressed with the candor and firmness, mixed with a becoming sensibility, which he displayed, than he was penetrated with their liberality and politeness. He acknowledged the generosity of the behavior towards him in every respect, but particularly in this, in the strongest terms of manly gratitude. In a conversation with a gentleman who visited him after his trial, he said he flattered himself he had never been illiberal; but if there were any remains of prejudice in his mind, his present experience must obliterate them.

In one of the visits I made to him (and I saw him several times during his confinement), he begged me to be the bearer of a request to the General, for permission to send an open letter to Sir Henry Clinton. "I foresee my fate," said he, "and though I pretend not to play the hero, or to be indifferent about life, yet I am reconciled to whatever may happen, conscious that misfortune, not guilt, has brought it upon me. There is only one thing that disturbs my tranquillity. Sir Henry Clinton has been too good to me; he has been lavish of his kindness. I am bound to him by too many obligations, and love him too well, to bear the thought that he should reproach himself, or that others should reproach him, on the supposition of my having conceived myself obliged, by his instructions, to run the risk I did. I would not for the world leave a sting in his mind that should embitter his future days." He could scarce finish the sentence, bursting into tears in spite of his efforts to suppress them, and with difficulty collected himself enough afterwards to add, "I wish to be permitted to assure him I did not act under this impression, but submitted to a necessity imposed upon me, as contrary to my own inclination as to his orders." His request was readily complied with, and he wrote the letter annexed, with which I dare say you will be as much pleased as I am, both for the diction and sentiment.

When his sentence was announced to him he remarked that since it was his lot to die, there was still a choice in the mode, which would make a material difference in his feelings, and he would be happy, if possible, to be indulged with a professional death. He made a second application, by letter, in concise but persuasive terms. It was thought this indulgence, being incompatible with the customs of war, could not be granted, and it was therefore determined, in both cases, to evade an answer, to spare him the sensations which a certain knowledge of the intended mode would inflict.

In going to the place of execution, he bowed familiarly as he went along, to all those with whom he had been acquainted in his confinement. A smile of complacency expressed the serene fortitude of his mind. Arrived at the fatal spot, he asked, with some emotion, "Must I then die in this manner?" He was told that it had been unavoidable. "I am reconciled to my fate," said he, "but not to the mode." Soon, however, recollecting himself, he added: "It will be but a momentary pang," and, springing upon the cart, performed the last offices to himself, with a composure that excited the admiration and melted the hearts of the beholders. Upon being told that the final moment was at hand, and asked if he had any thing to say, he answered: "Nothing but to request you will witness to the world that I die like a brave man." Among the extraordinary circumstances that attended him, in the midst of his enemies, he died universally esteemed and universally regretted.

There was something singularly interesting in the character and fortunes of André. To an excellent understanding, well improved by education and travel, he united a peculiar elegance of mind and manners, and the advantage of a pleasing person. 'T is said he possessed a pretty taste for the fine arts, and had himself attained some proficiency in poetry, music, and painting. His knowledge appeared without ostentation, and embellished by a diffidence that rarely accompanies so many talents and accomplishments; which left you to suppose more than appeared. His sentiments were elevated, and inspired esteem; they had a softness that conciliated affection. His elocution was handsome; his address easy, polite, and insinuating. By his merit he had acquired the unlimited confidence of his general, and was making a rapid progress in military rank and reputation. But in the height of his career, flushed with new hopes from the execution of a project, the most beneficial to his party that could be devised, he was at once precipitated from the summit of prosperity, and saw all the expectations of his ambition blasted, and himself ruined. . . .

10. THE CONTINENTALIST (I) [14]

[WANT OF POWER IN CONGRESS]

It would be the extreme of vanity in us not to be sensible that we began this revolution with very vague and confined notions of the practical business of government. To the greater part of us it was a novelty; of those who under the former constitution had had opportunities of acquiring experience, a large proportion adhered to the opposite side, and the remainder can only be supposed to have possessed ideas adapted to the narrow colonial sphere in which they had been accustomed to move, not of that enlarged kind suited to the government of an independent nation.

There were, no doubt, exceptions to these observations,— men in all respects qualified for conducting the public affairs with skill and advantage. But their number was small; they were not always brought forward in our councils; and when they were, their influence was too commonly borne down by the prevailing torrent of ignorance and prejudice.

On a retrospect, however, of our transactions, under the disadvantages with which we commenced, it is perhaps more to be wondered at that we have done so well than that we have not done better. There are, indeed, some traits in our conduct as conspicuous for sound policy as others for magnanimity. But, on the other hand, it must also be confessed, there have been many false steps, many chimerical projects and utopian speculations, in the management of our civil as well as of our military affairs. A part of these were the natural effects of the spirit of the times, dictated by our situation. An extreme jealousy of power is the attendant on all popular revolutions, and has seldom been without its evils. It is to this source we are to trace many of the fatal mistakes which have so deeply endangered the common cause; particularly that defect which will be the object of these remarks—a want of power in Congress.

The present Congress, respectable for abilities and integrity, by experience convinced of the necessity of change, are preparing several important articles, to be submitted to the respective States, for augmenting the powers of the Confederation. But though there is hardly at this time a man of information in America who will not acknowledge, as a general proposition, that in its present form it is unequal either to a vigorous prosecution of the war or to the preservation of the Union in peace; yet when the principle comes to be applied to practice, there seems not to be the same agreement in the modes of remedying the defect; and it is to be feared, from a disposition which appeared in some of the States on a late occasion, that the salutary intentions of Congress may meet with more delay and opposition than the critical posture of the States will justify.

It will be attempted to show, in a course of papers, what ought to be done, and the mischiefs of a contrary policy.

In the first stages of the controversy, it was excusable to err. Good intentions, rather than great skill, were to have been expected from us. But we have now had sufficient time for reflection, and experience as ample as unfortunate, to rectify our errors. To persist in them becomes disgraceful, and even criminal, and belies that character of good sense, and a quick discernment of our interests, which, in spite of our mistakes, we have been hitherto allowed. It will prove that our sagacity is limited to interests of inferior moment, and that we are incapable of those enlightened and liberal views necessary to make us a great and a flourishing people.

History is full of examples where, in contests for liberty, a jealousy of power has either defeated the attempts to recover or preserve it, in the first instance, or has afterward subverted it by clogging government with too great precautions for its felicity, or by leaving too wide a door for sedition and popular licentiousness. In a government framed for durable liberty, not less regard must be paid to giving the magistrate a proper degree of authority to make and execute the laws with rigor, than to guard against encroachments upon the rights of the community. As too much power leads to despotism, too little leads to anarchy, and both, eventually, to the ruin of the people. These are maxims well known, but never sufficiently attended to, in adjusting the frames of governments. Some momentary interest or passion is sure to give a wrong bias, and pervert the most favorable opportunities.

No friend to order or to rational liberty can read without pain and disgust the history of the Commonwealths of Greece. Generally speaking, they were a constant scene of the alternate tyranny of one part of the people over the other, or of a few usurping demagogues over the whole. Most of them had been originally governed by kings, whose despotism (the natural disease of monarchy) had obliged their subjects to murder, expel, depose, or reduce them to a nominal existence, and institute popular governments. In these governments, that of Sparta excepted, the jealousy of power hindered the people from trusting out of their own hands a competent authority to maintain the repose and stability of the Commonwealth; whence originated the frequent revolutions and civil broils with which they were distracted. This, and the want of a solid federal union to restrain the ambition and rivalship of the different cities, after a rapid succession of bloody wars, ended in their total loss of liberty, and subjugation to foreign powers.

In comparison of our governments with those of the ancient

republics, we must, without hesitation, give the preference to our own; because every power with us is exercised by representation, not in tumultuary assemblies of the collective body of the people, where the art or impudence of the *Orator* or *Tribune*, rather than the utility or justice of the measure, could seldom fail to govern. Yet, whatever may be the advantage on our side in such a comparison, men who estimate the value of institutions, not from prejudices of the moment, but from experience and reason, must be persuaded that the same *jealousy* of *power* has prevented our reaping all the advantages from the examples of other nations which we ought to have done, and has rendered our constitutions in many respects feeble and imperfect.

Perhaps the evil is not very great in respect to our State constitutions; for, notwithstanding their imperfections, they may for some time be made to operate in such a manner as to answer the purposes of the common defence and the maintenance of order; and they seem to have, in themselves, and in the progress of society among us, the seeds of improvement.

But this is not the case with respect to the Federal Government; if it is too weak at first, it will continually grow weaker. The ambition and local interests of the respective members will be constantly undermining and usurping upon its prerogatives till it comes to a dissolution, if a partial combination of some of the more powerful ones does not bring it to a more *speedy* and *violent end.*

II. TO JOHN LAURENS

[A NEW SCENE OPENS]

August 15, 1782.

I received with great pleasure, my dear Laurens, the letter which you wrote me in —— last. Your wishes in one respect are gratified. This State has pretty unanimously elected me to Congress. My time of service commences in November. It is not probable it will result in what you mention. I hope it is too late. We have great reason to flatter ourselves. Peace on our own terms is upon the carpet. The making it is in good hands. It is said your father is exchanged for Cornwallis, and gone to Paris to meet the other commissioners, and that Granville, on the part of England, has made a second trip there; in the last instance, vested with plenipotentiary powers.

I fear there may be obstacles, but I hope they may be surmounted.

Peace made, my dear friend, a new scene opens. The object then will be to make our independence a blessing. To do this we must secure our Union on solid foundations—a herculean task,—and to effect which, mountains of prejudice must be levelled! It requires all the virtue and all the abilities of the country. Quit your sword, my friend; put on the toga. Come to Congress. We know each other's sentiments; our views are the same. We have fought side by side to make America free; let us hand in hand struggle to make her happy. Remember me to General Greene with all the warmth of sincere attachment. Yours forever.

12. TO GEORGE WASHINGTON

[CONGRATULATION]

PHILADELPHIA, March 24, 1783.

SIR:

Your Excellency will, before this reaches you, have received a letter from the Marquis de Lafayette, informing you that the preliminaries of peace between all the belligerent powers have been concluded. I congratulate your Excellency on this happy conclusion of your labors. It now only remains to make solid establishments within, to perpetuate our Union, to prevent our being a ball in the hands of European powers, bandied against each other at their pleasure; in fine, to make our independence truly a blessing. This, it is to be lamented, will be an arduous work; for, to borrow a figure from mechanics, the centrifugal is much stronger than the centripetal force in these States,—the seeds of disunion much more numerous than those of union.

I will add that your Excellency's exertions are as essential to accomplish this end as they have been to establish independence. I will upon a future occasion open myself upon this subject.

Your conduct in the affair of the officers is highly pleasing here. The measures of the army are such as I could have wished them, and will add new lustre to their character as well as strengthen the hands of Congress.

13. *From* LETTERS FROM PHOCION (II)[15]

[JUSTIFYING THE REVOLUTION]

1784.

. . . I shall now, with a few general reflections, conclude.

Those who are at present entrusted with power, in all these infant republics, hold the most sacred deposit that ever was confided to human hands. 'T is with governments as with individuals; first impressions and early habits give a lasting bias to the temper and character. Our governments, hitherto, have no habits. How important to the happiness, not of America alone, but of mankind, that they should acquire good ones!

If we set out with justice, moderation, liberality, and a scrupulous regard to the Constitution, the government will acquire a spirit and tone productive of permanent blessings to the community. If, on the contrary, the public councils are guided by humor, passion, and prejudice; if from resentment to individuals, or a dread of partial inconveniences, the Constitution is slighted, or explained away, upon every frivolous pretext, the future spirit of government will be feeble, distracted, and arbitrary. The rights of the subject will be the sport of every party vicissitude. There will be no settled rule of conduct, but every thing will fluctuate with the alternate prevalency of contending factions.

The world has its eye upon America. The noble struggle we have made in the cause of liberty has occasioned a kind of revolution in human sentiment. The influence of our example has penetrated the gloomy regions of despotism, and has pointed the way to enquiries which may shake it to its deepest foundations. Men begin to ask, everywhere: Who is this tyrant that dares to build his greatness on our misery and degradation? What commission has he to sacrifice millions to the wanton appetites of himself and a few minions that surround his throne?

To ripen enquiry into action, it remains for us to justify the revolution by its fruits.

If the consequences prove that we really have asserted the cause of human happiness, what may not be expected from so illustrious an example? In a greater or less degree, the world will bless and imitate.

But if experience, in this instance, verifies the lesson long taught by the enemies of liberty, that the bulk of mankind are not fit to govern themselves; that they must have a master, and were only made for the rein and the spur; we shall then see the final triumph of despotism over liberty; the advocates of the latter must acknowledge it to be an *ignis fatuus*, and abandon the pursuit. With the greatest advantages for promoting it that ever a people had, we shall have betrayed the cause of human nature.

Let those in whose hands it is placed pause for a moment, and contemplate with an eye of reverence the vast trust committed to them. Let them retire into their own bosoms and examine the motives which there prevail. Let them ask themselves this solemn question: Is the sacrifice of a few mistaken or criminal individuals an object worthy of the shifts to which we are reduced, to evade the Constitution and the national engagements? Then let them review the arguments that have been offered with dispassionate candor; and if they even doubt the propriety of the measures they may be about to adopt, let them remember, that, in a doubtful case, the Constitution ought never to be hazarded without extreme necessity.

PHOCION.

14. IMPRESSIONS AS TO THE NEW CONSTITUTION [16]

[FORECASTING ITS RECEPTION]

September, 1787.

The new Constitution has in favor of its success these circumstances: A very great weight of influence of the persons who framed it, particularly in the universal popularity of General Washington. The good will of the commercial interest throughout the States, which will give all its efforts to the establishment of a government capable of regulating, protecting, and extending the commerce of the Union. The good will of most men of property in the several States, who wish a government of the Union able to protect them against domestic violence, and the depredations which the democratic spirit is apt to make on property, and who are besides anxious for the respectability of the nation. The hopes of the creditors of the United States, that a general government possessing the means of doing it, will pay the debt of the Union. A strong belief in the people at large of the insufficiency of the present Confederation to preserve the existence of the Union, and of the necessity of the Union to their safety and prosperity; of course, a strong desire of a change, and a predisposition to receive well the propositions of the convention.

Against its success is to be put the dissent of two or three important men in the convention, who will think their characters pledged to defeat the plan; the influence of many *inconsiderable* men in possession of considerable offices under the State governments, who will fear a diminution of their consequence, power, and emolument, by the establishment of the general government, and who can hope for nothing there; the influence of some *considerable* men in office, possessed of talents and popularity, who, partly from the same motives, and partly from a desire of *playing a part* in a convulsion for their own aggrandizement, will oppose the quiet adoption of the new government (some considerable men out of office, from motives of ambition, may be disposed to act the same part). Add to these causes the disinclination of the people to taxes, and of course to a strong government; the opposition of all men much in debt, who will not wish to see a government established, one object of which is to restrain the means of cheating creditors; the democratical jealousy of the people, which may be alarmed at the appearance of institutions that may seem calculated to place the power of the community in few hands, and to raise a few individuals to stations of great pre-eminence; and the influence of some foreign powers, who, from different motives, will not wish to see an energetic government established throughout the States.

In this view of the subject it is difficult to form any judgment whether the plan will be adopted or rejected. It must be essentially matter of conjecture. The present appearances and all other circumstances considered, the probability seems to be on the side of its adoption.

But the causes operating against its adoption are powerful, and there will be nothing astonishing in the contrary.

If it do not finally obtain, it is probable the discussion of the question will beget such struggles, animosities, and heats in the community, that this circumstance, conspiring with the *real necessity* of an essential change in our present situation, will produce civil war. Should this happen, whatever parties prevail, it is probable governments very different from the present in their principles will be established. A dismemberment of the Union, and monarchies in different portions of it, may be expected. It may, however, happen that no civil war will take place, but several republican confederacies be established between different combinations of the particular States.

A reunion with Great Britain, from universal disgust at a state of commotion, is not impossible, though not much to be feared. The most plausible shape of such a business would be the establishment of a son of the present monarch in the supreme government of this country, with a family compact.

If the government be adopted it is probable General Washington will be the President of the United States. This will ensure a wise choice of men to administer the government, and a good administration. A good administration will conciliate the confidence and affection of the people, and perhaps enable the government to acquire more consistency than the proposed constitution seems to promise for so great a country. It may then triumph altogether over the State governments, and reduce them to an entire subordination, dividing the larger States into smaller districts. The *organs* of the general government may also acquire additional strength.

If this should not be the case in the course of a few years, it is probable that the contests about the boundaries of power between the particular governments and the general government, and the *momentum* of the larger States in such contests, will produce a dissolution of the Union. This, after all, seems to be the most likely result.

But it is almost arrogance in so complicated a subject, depending so entirely on the incalculable fluctuations of the human passions, to attempt even a conjecture about the event.

It will be eight or nine months before any certain judgment can be formed respecting the adoption of the plan.

15. THE FEDERALIST (I) [17]

[INTRODUCTORY]

To the People of the State of New York:

After an unequivocal experience of the inefficiency of the subsisting federal government, you are called upon to deliberate on a new Constitution for the United States of America. The subject speaks its own importance; comprehending in its consequences nothing less than the existence of the UNION, the safety and welfare of the parts of which it is composed, the fate of an empire in many respects the most interesting in the world. It has been frequently remarked that it seems to have been reserved to the people of this country, by their conduct and example, to decide the important question, whether societies of men are really capable or not of establishing good government from reflection and choice, or whether they are forever destined to depend for their political constitutions on accident and force. If there be any truth in the remark, the crisis at which we are arrived may with propriety be regarded as the era in which that decision is to be made; and a wrong election of the part we shall act may, in this view, deserve to be considered as the general misfortune of mankind.

This idea will add the inducements of philanthropy to those of patriotism, to heighten the solicitude which all considerate and good men must feel for the event. Happy will it be if our choice should be directed by a judicious estimate of our true interests, unperplexed and unbiased by considerations not connected with the public good. But this is a thing more ardently to be wished than seriously to be expected. The plan offered to our deliberations affects too many particular interests, innovates upon too many local institutions, not to involve in its discussion a variety of objects foreign to its merits, and of views, passions and prejudices little favorable to the discovery of truth.

Among the most formidable of the obstacles which the new Constitution will have to encounter may readily be distinguished the obvious interest of a certain class of men in every State to resist all changes which may hazard a diminution of the power, emolument, and consequence of the offices they hold under the State establishments; and the perverted ambition of another class of men, who will either hope to aggrandize themselves by the confusions of their country, or will flatter themselves with fairer prospects of elevation from the subdivision of the empire into several partial confederacies than from its union under one government.

It is not, however, my design to dwell upon observations of this nature. I am well aware that it would be disingenuous to resolve indiscriminately the opposition of any set of men (merely because their situations might subject them to suspicion) into interested or ambitious views. Candor will oblige us to admit that even such men may be actuated by upright intentions; and it cannot be doubted that much of the opposition which has made its appearance, or may hereafter make its appearance, will spring from sources, blameless at least, if not respectable—the honest errors of minds led astray by preconceived jealousies and fears. So numerous indeed and so powerful are the causes which serve to give a false bias to the judgment, that we, upon many occasions, see wise and good men on the wrong as well as on the right side of questions of the first magnitude to society. This circumstance, if duly attended to, would furnish a lesson of moderation to those who are ever so much persuaded of their being in the right in any controversy. And a further reason for caution, in this respect, might be drawn from the reflection that we are not always sure that those who advocate the truth are influenced by purer principles than their antagonists. Ambition, avarice, personal animosity, party opposition, and many other motives not more laudable than these, are apt to operate as well upon those who support as those who oppose the right side of a question. Were there not even these inducements to moderation, nothing could be more ill-judged than that intolerant spirit which has, at all times, characterized political parties. For in politics, as in religion, it is equally absurd to aim at making proselytes by fire and sword. Heresies in either can rarely be cured by persecution.

And yet, however just these sentiments will be allowed to be, we have already sufficient indications that it will happen in this as in all former cases of great national discussion. A torrent of angry and malignant passions will be let loose. To judge from the conduct of the opposite parties, we shall be led to conclude that they will mutually hope to evince the justness of their opinions, and to increase the number of their converts by the loudness of their declamations and the bitterness of their invectives. An enlightened zeal for the energy and efficiency of government will be stigmatized as the offspring of a temper fond of despotic power and hostile to the principles of liberty. An over-scrupulous jealousy of danger to the rights of the people, which is more commonly the fault of the head than of the heart, will be represented as mere pretence and artifice, the stale bait for popularity at the expense of the public good. It will be forgotten, on the one hand, that jealousy is the usual concomitant of love, and that the noble enthusiasm of liberty is apt to be infected with a spirit of narrow and illiberal distrust. On the other hand, it will be equally forgotten that the vigor of government is essential to the security of liberty; that, in the contemplation of a sound and well-informed judgment, their interest can never be separated; and that a dangerous ambition more often lurks behind the specious mask of zeal for the rights of the people than under the forbidding appearance of zeal for the firmness and efficiency of government. History will teach us that the former has been found a much more certain road to the introduction of despotism than the latter, and that of those men who have overturned the liberties of republics, the greatest number have begun their career by paying an obsequious court to the people; commencing demagogues, and ending tyrants.

In the course of the preceding observations, I have had an eye, my fellow-citizens, to putting you upon your guard against all attempts, from whatever quarter, to influence your decision, in a matter of the utmost moment to your welfare, by any impressions other than those which may result from the evidence of truth. You will, no doubt, at the same time, have collected from the general scope of them, that they proceed from a source not unfriendly to the new Constitution. Yes, my countrymen, I own to you that, after having given it an attentive consideration, I am clearly of opinion it is your interest to adopt it. I am convinced that this is the safest course for your liberty, your dignity, and your happiness. I affect not reserves which I do not feel. I will not amuse you with an appearance of deliberation when I have decided. I frankly acknowledge to you my convictions, and I will freely lay before you the reasons on which they are founded. The consciousness of good intentions disdains ambiguity. I shall not, however, multiply professions on this head. My motives must remain in the depository of my own breast. My arguments will be open to all, and may be judged of by all. They shall at least be offered in a spirit which will not disgrace the cause of truth.

I propose, in a series of papers, to discuss the following interesting particulars:—*The utility of the UNION to your*

*political prosperity—The insufficiency of the present Confederation
to preserve that Union—The necessity of a government at least
equally energetic with the one proposed, to the attainment of this
object—The conformity of the proposed Constitution to the true
principles of republican government—Its analogy to your own
State constitution—and lastly, The additional security which its
adoption will afford to the preservation of that species of government, to liberty, and to property.*[18]

In the progress of this discussion I shall endeavor to give a
satisfactory answer to all the objections which shall have made
their appearance, that may seem to have any claim to your
attention.

It may perhaps be thought superfluous to offer arguments to
prove the utility of the UNION, a point, no doubt, deeply
engraved on the hearts of the great body of the people in every
State, and one which, it may be imagined, has no adversaries.
But the fact is, that we already hear it whispered in the private
circles of those who oppose the new Constitution, that the
thirteen States are of too great extent for any general system,
and that we must of necessity resort to separate confederacies of
distinct portions of the whole.* This doctrine will, in all probability, be gradually propagated, till it has votaries enough to
countenance an open avowal of it. For nothing can be more
evident, to those who are able to take an enlarged view of the
subject, than the alternative of an adoption of the new Constitution or a dismemberment of the Union. It will therefore be
of use to begin by examining the advantages of that Union, the
certain evils, and the probable dangers, to which every State
will be exposed from its dissolution. This shall accordingly
constitute the subject of my next address.   PUBLIUS.

*The same idea, tracing the arguments to their consequences, is held out
in several of the late publications against the new Constitution.—PUBLIUS.

16. THE FEDERALIST (VI)

[DANGERS OF INTERNAL DISSENSION]

To the People of the State of New York:

The three last numbers of this paper have been dedicated to an enumeration of the dangers to which we should be exposed, in a state of disunion, from the arms and arts of foreign nations. I shall now proceed to delineate dangers of a different and, perhaps, still more alarming kind—those which will in all probability flow from dissensions between the States themselves, and from domestic factions and convulsions. These have been already in some instances slightly anticipated; but they deserve a more particular and more full investigation.

A man must be far gone in Utopian speculations who can seriously doubt that, if these States should either be wholly disunited, or only united in partial confederacies, the subdivisions into which they might be thrown would have frequent and violent contests with each other. To presume a want of motives for such contests as an argument against their existence, would be to forget that men are ambitious, vindictive, and rapacious. To look for a continuation of harmony between a number of independent, unconnected sovereignties in the same neighborhood, would be to disregard the uniform course of human events, and to set at defiance the accumulated experience of ages.

The causes of hostility among nations are innumerable. There are some which have a general and almost constant operation upon the collective bodies of society. Of this description are the love of power or the desire of pre-eminence and dominion—the jealousy of power, or the desire of equality and safety. There are others which have a more circumscribed though an equally operative influence within their spheres. Such are the rivalships and competitions of commerce between commercial nations. And there are others, not less numerous than either of the former, which take their origin entirely in private passions; in the attachments, enmities, interests, hopes, and fears of leading individuals in the communities of which they are members. Men of this class, whether the favorites of a king or of a people, have in too many instances abused the confidence they possessed; and assuming the pretext of some public motive, have not scrupled to sacrifice the national tranquillity to personal advantage or personal gratification.

The celebrated Pericles, in compliance with the resentment of a prostitute,* at the expense of much of the blood and treasure of his countrymen, attacked, vanquished, and destroyed the city of the *Samnians*. The same man, stimulated by private pique against the *Megarensians*,† another nation of Greece, or to avoid a prosecution with which he was threatened as an accomplice in a supposed theft of the statuary Phidias,‡ or to get rid of the accusations prepared to be brought against him for dissipating the funds of the state in the purchase of popularity,§ or from a combination of all these causes, was the primitive author of that famous and fatal war, distinguished in the Grecian annals by the name of the *Peloponnesian* war; which, after various vicissitudes, intermissions, and renewals, terminated in the ruin of the Athenian commonwealth.

The ambitious cardinal, who was prime minister to Henry VIII, permitting his vanity to aspire to the triple crown,** entertained hopes of succeeding in the acquisition of that splendid prize by the influence of the Emperor Charles V. To secure the favor and interest of this enterprising and powerful monarch, he precipitated England into a war with France, contrary to the plainest dictates of policy, and at the hazard of the safety and independence, as well of the kingdom over which he presided by his counsels, as of Europe in general. For if there ever was a sovereign who bid fair to realize the project of universal monarchy, it was the Emperor Charles V, of whose intrigues Wolsey was at once the instrument and the dupe.

* Aspasia, vide *Plutarch's Life of Pericles.*—PUBLIUS.
† *Ibid.*—PUBLIUS. ‡ *Ibid.*—PUBLIUS.
§ *Ibid.* Phidias was supposed to have stolen some public gold, with the connivance of Pericles, for the embellishment of the statue of Minerva. —PUBLIUS. ** Worn by the popes.—PUBLIUS.

The influence which the bigotry of one female,* the petulance of another,† and the cabals of a third,‡ had in the contemporary policy, ferments, and pacifications, of a considerable part of Europe, are topics that have been too often descanted upon not to be generally known.

To multiply examples of the agency of personal considerations in the production of great national events, either foreign or domestic, according to their direction, would be an unnecessary waste of time. Those who have but a superficial acquaintance with the sources from which they are to be drawn, will themselves recollect a variety of instances; and those who have a tolerable knowledge of human nature will not stand in need of such lights, to form their opinion either of the reality or extent of that agency. Perhaps, however, a reference, tending to illustrate the general principle, may with propriety be made to a case which has lately happened among ourselves. If Shays had not been a *desperate debtor*, it is much to be doubted whether Massachusetts would have been plunged into a civil war.

But notwithstanding the concurring testimony of experience, in this particular, there are still to be found visionary or designing men, who stand ready to advocate the paradox of perpetual peace between the States, though dismembered and alienated from each other. The genius of republics (say they) is pacific; the spirit of commerce has a tendency to soften the manners of men, and to extinguish those inflammable humors which have so often kindled into wars. Commercial republics, like ours, will never be disposed to waste themselves in ruinous contentions with each other. They will be governed by mutual interest, and will cultivate a spirit of mutual amity and concord.

Is it not (we may ask these projectors in politics) the true interest of all nations to cultivate the same benevolent and philosophic spirit? If this be their true interest, have they in fact pursued it? Has it not, on the contrary, invariably been found that momentary passions, and immediate interests, have

* Madame de Maintenon.—PUBLIUS.
† Duchess of Marlborough.—PUBLIUS.
‡ Madame de Pompadour.—PUBLIUS.

a more active and imperious control over human conduct than general and remote considerations of policy, utility, or justice? Have republics in practice been less addicted to war than monarchies? Are not the former administered by *men* as well as the latter? Are there not aversions, predilections, rivalships, and desires of unjust acquisitions, that affect nations as well as kings? Are not popular assemblies frequently subject to the impulses of rage, resentment, jealousy, avarice, and of other irregular and violent propensities? Is it not well known that their determinations are often governed by a few individuals in whom they place confidence, and are, of course, liable to be tinctured by the passions and views of those individuals? Has commerce hitherto done anything more than change the object of war? Is not the love of wealth as domineering and enterprising a passion as that of power or glory? Have there not been as many wars founded upon commercial motives since that has become the prevailing system of nations, as were before occasioned by the cupidity of territory or dominion? Has not the spirit of commerce, in many instances, administered new incentives to the appetite, both for the one and for the other? Let experience, the least fallible guide of human opinions, be appealed to for an answer to these inquiries.

Sparta, Athens, Rome, and Carthage were all republics; two of them, Athens and Carthage, of the commercial kind. Yet were they as often engaged in wars, offensive and defensive, as the neighboring monarchies of the same times. Sparta was little better than a well-regulated camp; and Rome was never sated of carnage and conquest.

Carthage, though a commercial republic, was the aggressor in the very war that ended in her destruction. Hannibal had carried her arms into the heart of Italy, and to the gates of Rome, before Scipio, in turn, gave him an overthrow in the territories of Carthage, and made a conquest of the commonwealth.

Venice, in later times, figured more than once in wars of ambition, till, becoming an object to the other Italian states, Pope Julius II found means to accomplish that formidable league,* which gave a deadly blow to the power and pride of this haughty republic.

The provinces of Holland, till they were overwhelmed in debts and taxes, took a leading and conspicuous part in the wars of Europe. They had furious contests with England for the dominion of the sea, and were among the most persevering and most implacable of the opponents of Louis XIV.

In the government of Britain the representatives of the people compose one branch of the national legislature. Commerce has been for ages the predominant pursuit of that country. Few nations, nevertheless, have been more frequently engaged in war; and the wars in which that kingdom has been engaged have, in numerous instances, proceeded from the people.

There have been, if I may so express it, almost as many popular as royal wars. The cries of the nation and the importunities of their representatives have, upon various occasions, dragged their monarchs into war, or continued them in it, contrary to their inclinations, and sometimes contrary to the real interests of the state. In that memorable struggle for superiority between the rival houses of *Austria* and *Bourbon*, which so long kept Europe in a flame, it is well known that the antipathies of the English against the French, seconding the ambition, or rather the avarice, of a favorite leader,† protracted the war beyond the limits marked out by sound policy, and for a considerable time in opposition to the views of the court.

The wars of these two last-mentioned nations have in a great measure grown out of commercial considerations—the desire of supplanting and the fear of being supplanted, either in particular branches of traffic or in the general advantages of trade and navigation.

From this summary of what has taken place in other countries, whose situations have borne the nearest resemblance to our own, what reason can we have to confide in those reveries

---

*The League of Cambray, comprehending the Emperor, the King of France, the King of Aragon, and most of the Italian princes and states.—PUBLIUS.

† The Duke of Marlborough.—PUBLIUS.

which would seduce us into an expectation of peace and cordiality between the members of the present confederacy, in a state of separation? Have we not already seen enough of the fallacy and extravagance of those idle theories which have amused us with promises of an exemption from the imperfections, weaknesses, and evils incident to society in every shape? Is it not time to awake from the deceitful dream of a golden age, and to adopt as a practical maxim for the direction of our political conduct that we, as well as the other inhabitants of the globe, are yet remote from the happy empire of perfect wisdom and perfect virtue?

Let the point of extreme depression to which our national dignity and credit have sunk, let the inconveniences felt everywhere from a lax and ill administration of government, let the revolt of a part of the State of North Carolina, the late menacing disturbances in Pennsylvania, and the actual insurrections and rebellions in Massachusetts, declare——!

So far is the general sense of mankind from corresponding with the tenets of those who endeavor to lull asleep our apprehensions of discord and hostility between the States, in the event of disunion, that it has from long observation of the progress of society become a sort of axiom in politics, that vicinity, or nearness of situation, constitutes nations natural enemies. An intelligent writer expresses himself on this subject to this effect: "NEIGHBORING NATIONS [says he] are naturally enemies of each other, unless their common weakness forces them to league in a CONFEDERATIVE REPUBLIC, and their constitution prevents the differences that neighborhood occasions, extinguishing that secret jealousy which disposes all states to aggrandize themselves at the expense of their neighbors."* This passage, at the same time, points out the EVIL and suggests the REMEDY.   PUBLIUS.

*Vide *Principes des Négociations*, par l'Abbé de Mably.—PUBLIUS.

17. THE FEDERALIST (XV)

[DEFECTS OF THE CONFEDERATION]

To the People of the State of New York:

In the course of the preceding papers, I have endeavored, my fellow-citizens, to place before you, in a clear and convincing light, the importance of Union to your political safety and happiness. I have unfolded to you a complication of dangers to which you would be exposed, should you permit that sacred knot which binds the people of America together to be severed or dissolved by ambition or by avarice, by jealousy or by misrepresentation. In the sequel of the inquiry through which I propose to accompany you, the truths intended to be inculcated will receive further confirmation from facts and arguments hitherto unnoticed. If the road over which you will still have to pass should in some places appear to you tedious or irksome, you will recollect that you are in quest of information on a subject the most momentous which can engage the attention of a free people, that the field through which you have to travel is in itself spacious, and that the difficulties of the journey have been unnecessarily increased by the mazes with which sophistry has beset the way. It will be my aim to remove the obstacles from your progress in as compendious a manner as it can be done, without sacrificing utility to despatch.

In pursuance of the plan which I have laid down for the discussion of the subject, the point next in order to be examined is the "insufficiency of the present Confederation to the preservation of the Union." It may perhaps be asked what need there is of reasoning or proof to illustrate a position which is not either controverted or doubted, to which the understandings and feelings of all classes of men assent, and which in substance is admitted by the opponents as well as by the friends of the new Constitution. It must in truth be acknowledged that, however these may differ in other respects, they in general appear to harmonize in this sentiment, at least, that there are material imperfections in our national system, and that something is necessary to be done to rescue us from impending anarchy. The facts that support this opinion are no longer objects of speculation. They have forced themselves upon the sensibility of the people at large, and have at length extorted from those, whose mistaken policy has had the principal share in precipitating the extremity at which we are arrived, a reluctant confession of the reality of those defects in the scheme of our federal government, which have been long pointed out and regretted by the intelligent friends of the Union.

We may indeed with propriety be said to have reached almost the last stage of national humiliation. There is scarcely anything that can wound the pride or degrade the character of an independent nation which we do not experience. Are there engagements to the performance of which we are held by every tie respectable among men? These are the subjects of constant and unblushing violation. Do we owe debts to foreigners and to our own citizens contracted in a time of imminent peril for the preservation of our political existence? These remain without any proper or satisfactory provision for their discharge. Have we valuable territories and important posts in the possession of a foreign power which, by express stipulations, ought long since to have been surrendered? These are still retained, to the prejudice of our interests, not less than of our rights. Are we in a condition to resent or to repel the aggression? We have neither troops, nor treasury, nor government.* Are we even in a condition to remonstrate with dignity? The just imputations on our own faith, in respect to the same treaty, ought first to be removed. Are we entitled by nature and compact to a free participation in the navigation of the Mississippi? Spain excludes us from it. Is public credit an indispensable resource in time of public danger? We seem to have abandoned its cause as desperate and irretrievable. Is commerce of importance to national wealth? Ours is at the lowest point of declension. Is respectability in the eyes of foreign powers a safeguard against foreign encroachments? The imbecility of our government even forbids them to treat with us.

*I mean for the Union.—Publius.

Our ambassadors abroad are the mere pageants of mimic sovereignty. Is a violent and unnatural decrease in the value of land a symptom of national distress? The price of improved land in most parts of the country is much lower than can be accounted for by the quantity of waste land at market, and can only be fully explained by that want of private and public confidence which are so alarmingly prevalent among all ranks, and which have a direct tendency to depreciate property of every kind. Is private credit the friend and patron of industry? That most useful kind which relates to borrowing and lending is reduced within the narrowest limits, and this still more from an opinion of insecurity than from the scarcity of money. To shorten an enumeration of particulars which can afford neither pleasure nor instruction, it may in general be demanded, what indication is there of national disorder, poverty, and insignificance that could befall a community so peculiarly blessed with natural advantages as we are, which does not form a part of the dark catalogue of our public misfortunes?

This is the melancholy situation to which we have been brought by those very maxims and councils which would now deter us from adopting the proposed Constitution; and which, not content with having conducted us to the brink of a precipice, seem resolved to plunge us into the abyss that awaits us below. Here, my countrymen, impelled by every motive that ought to influence an enlightened people, let us make a firm stand for our safety, our tranquillity, our dignity, our reputation. Let us at last break the fatal charm which has too long seduced us from the paths of felicity and prosperity.

It is true, as has been before observed, that facts, too stubborn to be resisted, have produced a species of general assent to the abstract proposition that there exist material defects in our national system; but the usefulness of the concession, on the part of the old adversaries of federal measures, is destroyed by a strenuous opposition to a remedy, upon the only principles that can give it a chance of success. While they admit that the government of the United States is destitute of energy, they contend against conferring upon it those powers which are requisite to supply that energy. They seem still to aim at things repugnant and irreconcilable! at an augmentation of federal authority, without a diminution of State authority; at sovereignty in the Union, and complete independence in the members. They still, in fine, seem to cherish with blind devotion the political monster of an *imperium in imperio*. This renders a full display of the principal defects of the Confederation necessary, in order to show that the evils we experience do not proceed from minute or partial imperfections, but from fundamental errors in the structure of the building, which cannot be amended otherwise than by an alteration in the first principles and main pillars of the fabric.

The great and radical vice in the construction of the existing Confederation is in the principle of LEGISLATION for STATES or GOVERNMENTS, in their CORPORATE or COLLECTIVE CAPACITIES, and as contradistinguished from the INDIVIDUALS of which they consist. Though this principle does not run through all the powers delegated to the Union, yet it pervades and governs those on which the efficacy of the rest depends. Except as to the rule of apportionment, the United States has an indefinite discretion to make requisitions for men and money; but they have no authority to raise either, by regulations extending to the individual citizens of America. The consequence of this is, that though in theory their resolutions concerning those objects are laws, constitutionally binding on the members of the Union, yet in practice they are mere recommendations which the States observe or disregard at their option.

It is a singular instance of the capriciousness of the human mind, that, after all the admonitions we have had from experience on this head, there should still be found men who object to the new Constitution for deviating from a principle which has been found the bane of the old, and which is in itself evidently incompatible with the idea of GOVERNMENT; a principle, in short, which, if it is to be executed at all, must substitute the violent and sanguinary agency of the sword to the mild influence of the magistracy.

There is nothing absurd or impracticable in the idea of a league or alliance between independent nations for certain defined purposes precisely stated in a treaty regulating all the details of time, place, circumstance, and quantity; leaving nothing to future discretion; and depending for its execution on the good faith of the parties. Compacts of this kind exist among all civilized nations, subject to the usual vicissitudes of peace and war, of observance and non-observance, as the interests or passions of the contracting powers dictate. In the early part of the present century there was an epidemical rage in Europe for this species of compacts, from which the politicians of the times fondly hoped for benefits which were never realized. With a view to establishing the equilibrium of power and the peace of that part of the world, all the resources of negotiation were exhausted, and triple and quadruple alliances were formed; but they were scarcely formed before they were broken, giving an instructive but afflicting lesson to mankind, how little dependence is to be placed on treaties which have no other sanction than the obligations of good faith, and which oppose general considerations of peace and justice to the impulse of any immediate interest or passion.

If the particular States in this country are disposed to stand in a similar relation to each other, and to drop the project of a general DISCRETIONARY SUPERINTENDENCE, the scheme would indeed be pernicious, and would entail upon us all the mischiefs which have been enumerated under the first head; but it would have the merit of being, at least, consistent and practicable. Abandoning all views towards a confederate government, this would bring us to a simple alliance offensive and defensive; and would place us in a situation to be alternate friends and enemies of each other, as our mutual jealousies and rivalships, nourished by the intrigues of foreign nations, should prescribe to us.

But if we are unwilling to be placed in this perilous situation; if we still will adhere to the design of a national government, or, which is the same thing, of a superintending power, under the direction of a common council, we must resolve to incorporate into our plan those ingredients which may be considered as forming the characteristic difference between a league and a government; we must extend the authority of the Union to the persons of the citizens—the only proper objects of government.

Government implies the power of making laws. It is essential to the idea of a law, that it be attended with a sanction; or, in other words, a penalty or punishment for disobedience. If there be no penalty annexed to disobedience, the resolutions or commands which pretend to be laws will, in fact, amount to nothing more than advice or recommendation. This penalty, whatever it may be, can only be inflicted in two ways: by the agency of the courts and ministers of justice, or by military force; by the COERCION of the magistracy, or by the COERCION of arms. The first kind can evidently apply only to men; the last kind must of necessity be employed against bodies politic, or communities, or States. It is evident that there is no process of a court by which the observance of the laws can, in the last resort, be enforced. Sentences may be denounced against them for violations of their duty; but these sentences can only be carried into execution by the sword. In an association where the general authority is confined to the collective bodies of the communities that compose it, every breach of the laws must involve a state of war; and military execution must become the only instrument of civil obedience. Such a state of things can certainly not deserve the name of government, nor would any prudent man choose to commit his happiness to it.

There was a time when we were told that breaches, by the States, of the regulations of the federal authority were not to be expected; that a sense of common interest would preside over the conduct of the respective members, and would beget a full compliance with all the constitutional requisitions of the Union. This language, at the present day, would appear as wild as a great part of what we now hear from the same quarter will be thought, when we shall have received further lessons from that best oracle of wisdom, experience. It at all times betrayed an ignorance of the true springs by which human conduct is actuated, and belied the original inducements to the establishment of civil power. Why has government been instituted at all? Because the passions of men will not conform to the dictates of reason and justice, without constraint. Has it been found that bodies of men act with more rectitude or greater disinterestedness than individuals? The contrary of this has been inferred by all accurate observers of the conduct of mankind; and the inference is founded upon obvious reasons. Regard to reputation has a less active influence, when the infamy of a bad action is to be divided among a number, than when it is to fall singly upon one. A spirit of faction, which is apt to mingle its poison in the deliberations of all bodies of men, will often hurry the persons of whom they are composed into improprieties and excesses, for which they would blush in a private capacity.

In addition to all this, there is, in the nature of sovereign power, an impatience of control, that disposes those who are invested with the exercise of it, to look with an evil eye upon all external attempts to restrain or direct its operations. From this spirit it happens, that in every political association which is formed upon the principle of uniting in a common interest a number of lesser sovereignties, there will be found a kind of eccentric tendency in the subordinate or inferior orbs, by the operation of which there will be a perpetual effort in each to fly off from the common centre. This tendency is not difficult to be accounted for. It has its origin in the love of power. Power controlled or abridged is almost always the rival and enemy of that power by which it is controlled or abridged. This simple proposition will teach us how little reason there is to expect that the persons intrusted with the administration of the affairs of the particular members of a confederacy will at all times be ready, with perfect good humor, and an unbiased regard to the public weal, to execute the resolutions or decrees of the general authority. The reverse of this results from the constitution of human nature.

If, therefore, the measures of the Confederacy cannot be executed without the intervention of the particular administrations, there will be little prospect of their being executed at all. The rulers of the respective members, whether they have a constitutional right to do it or not, will undertake to judge of the propriety of the measures themselves. They will consider the conformity of the thing proposed or required to their immediate interests or aims; the momentary conveniences or inconveniences that would attend its adoption. All this will be done; and in a spirit of interested and suspicious scrutiny, without that knowledge of national circumstances and reasons of state, which is essential to a right judgment, and with that strong predilection in favor of local objects, which can hardly fail to mislead the decision. The same process must be repeated in every member of which the body is constituted; and the execution of the plans, framed by the councils of the whole, will always fluctuate on the discretion of the ill-informed and prejudiced opinion of every part. Those who have been conversant in the proceedings of popular assemblies; who have seen how difficult it often is, where there is no exterior pressure of circumstances, to bring them to harmonious resolutions on important points, will readily conceive how impossible it must be to induce a number of such assemblies, deliberating at a distance from each other, at different times, and under different impressions, long to co-operate in the same views and pursuits.

In our case, the concurrence of thirteen distinct sovereign wills is requisite, under the Confederation, to the complete execution of every important measure that proceeds from the Union. It has happened as was to have been foreseen. The measures of the Union have not been executed; the delinquencies of the States have, step by step, matured themselves to an extreme, which has, at length, arrested all the wheels of the national government, and brought them to an awful stand. Congress at this time scarcely possess the means of keeping up the forms of administration, till the States can have time to agree upon a more substantial substitute for the present shadow of a federal government. Things did not come to this desperate extremity at once. The causes which have been specified produced at first only unequal and disproportionate degrees of compliance with the requisitions of the Union. The greater deficiencies of some States furnished the pretext of example and the temptation of interest to the complying, or to the least delinquent States. Why should we do more in proportion than those who are embarked with us in the same political voyage? Why should we consent to bear more than our proper share of the common burden? These were suggestions which human selfishness could not withstand, and which even speculative men, who looked forward to remote consequences, could not, without hesitation, combat. Each State, yielding to the persuasive voice of immediate interest or convenience, has successively withdrawn its support, till the frail and tottering edifice seems ready to fall upon our heads, and to crush us beneath its ruins. PUBLIUS.

18. THE FEDERALIST (XXIII)

[NEED FOR AN ENERGETIC GOVERNMENT]

To the People of the State of New York:

The necessity of a Constitution, at least equally energetic with the one proposed, to the preservation of the Union, is the point at the examination of which we are now arrived.

This inquiry will naturally divide itself into three branches —the objects to be provided for by the federal government, the quantity of power necessary to the accomplishment of those objects, the persons upon whom that power ought to operate. Its distribution and organization will more properly claim our attention under the succeeding head.

The principal purposes to be answered by union are these— the common defence of the members; the preservation of the public peace, as well against internal convulsions as external attacks; the regulation of commerce with other nations and between the States; the superintendence of our intercourse, political and commercial, with foreign countries.

The authorities essential to the common defence are these: to raise armies; to build and equip fleets; to prescribe rules for the government of both; to direct their operations; to provide for their support. These powers ought to exist without limitation, *because it is impossible to foresee or define the extent and variety of national exigencies, or the correspondent extent and variety of the means which may be necessary to satisfy them.* The circumstances that endanger the safety of nations are infinite, and for this reason no constitutional shackles can wisely be imposed on the power to which the care of it is committed. This power ought to be co-extensive with all the possible combinations of such circumstances; and ought to be under the direction of the same councils which are appointed to preside over the common defence.

This is one of those truths which, to a correct and unprejudiced mind, carries its own evidence along with it; and may be obscured, but cannot be made plainer by argument or reasoning. It rests upon axioms as simple as they are universal; the *means* ought to be proportioned to the *end;* the persons, from whose agency the attainment of any *end* is expected, ought to possess the *means* by which it is to be attained.

Whether there ought to be a federal government entrusted with the care of the common defence, is a question in the first instance open for discussion; but the moment it is decided in the affirmative, it will follow, that that government ought to be clothed with all the powers requisite to complete execution of its trust. And unless it can be shown that the circumstances which may affect the public safety are reducible within certain determinate limits; unless the contrary of this position can be fairly and rationally disputed, it must be admitted, as a necessary consequence, that there can be no limitation of that authority which is to provide for the defence and protection of the community, in any matter essential to its efficacy—that is, in any matter essential to the *formation*, *direction*, or *support* of the NATIONAL FORCES.

Defective as the present Confederation has been proved to be, this principle appears to have been fully recognized by the framers of it; though they have not made proper or adequate provision for its exercise. Congress have an unlimited discretion to make requisitions of men and money; to govern the army and navy; to direct their operations. As their requisitions are made constitutionally binding upon the States, who are in fact under the most solemn obligation to furnish the supplies required of them, the intention evidently was, that the United States should command whatever resources were by them judged requisite to the "common defence and general welfare." It was presumed that a sense of their true interests, and a regard to the dictates of good faith, would be found sufficient pledges for the punctual performance of the duty of the members to the federal head.

The experiment has, however, demonstrated that this expectation was ill-founded and illusory; and the observations, made under the last head, will, I imagine, have sufficed to convince the impartial and discerning, that there is an absolute necessity for an entire change in the first principles of the system; that if we are in earnest about giving the Union energy and duration, we must abandon the vain project of legislating upon the States in their collective capacities; we must extend the laws of the federal government to the individual citizens of America;[19] we must discard the fallacious scheme of quotas and requisitions, as equally impracticable and unjust. The result from all this is that the Union ought to be invested with full power to levy troops; to build and equip fleets; and to raise the revenues which will be required for the formation and support of an army and navy, in the customary and ordinary modes practised in other governments.

If the circumstances of our country are such as to demand a compound instead of a simple, a confederate instead of a sole, government, the essential point which will remain to be adjusted will be to discriminate the OBJECTS, as far as it can be done, which shall appertain to the different provinces or departments of power; allowing to each the most ample authority for fulfilling the objects committed to its charge. Shall the Union be constituted the guardian of the common safety? Are fleets and armies and revenues necessary to this purpose? The government of the Union must be empowered to pass all laws, and to make all regulations which have relation to them.

The same must be the case in respect to commerce, and to every other matter to which its jurisdiction is permitted to extend. Is the administration of justice between the citizens of the same State the proper department of the local governments? These must possess all the authorities which are connected with this object, and with every other that may be allotted to their particular cognizance and direction. Not to confer in each case a degree of power commensurate to the end, would be to violate the most obvious rules of prudence and propriety, and improvidently to trust the great interests of the nation to hands which are disabled from managing them with vigor and success.

Who so likely to make suitable provisions for the public defence as that body to which the guardianship of the public safety is confided; which, as the centre of information, will best understand the extent and urgency of the dangers that threaten; as the representative of the WHOLE, will feel itself most deeply interested in the preservation of every part; which, from the responsibility implied in the duty assigned to it, will be most sensibly impressed with the necessity of proper exertions; and which, by the extension of its authority throughout the States, can alone establish uniformity and concert in the plans and measures by which the common safety is to be secured? Is there not a manifest inconsistency in devolving upon the federal government the care of the general defence, and leaving in the State governments the *effective* powers by which it is to be provided for? Is not a want of co-operation the infallible consequence of such a system? And will not weakness, disorder, an undue distribution of the burdens and calamities of war, an unnecessary and intolerable increase of expense, be its natural and inevitable concomitants? Have we not had unequivocal experience of its effects in the course of the revolution which we have just accomplished?

Every view we may take of the subject, as candid inquirers after truth, will serve to convince us, that it is both unwise and dangerous to deny the federal government an unconfined authority, as to all those objects which are intrusted to its management. It will indeed deserve the most vigilant and careful attention of the people, to see that it be modelled in such a manner as to admit of its being safely vested with the requisite powers. If any plan which has been, or may be, offered to our consideration, should not, upon a dispassionate inspection, be found to answer this description, it ought to be rejected. A government, the constitution of which renders it unfit to be trusted with all the powers which a free people *ought to delegate to any government*, would be an unsafe and improper depositary of the NATIONAL INTERESTS. Wherever THESE can with propriety be confided, the coincident powers may safely accompany them. This is the true result of all just reasoning upon the subject. And the adversaries of the plan promulgated by the convention ought to have confined themselves to showing that the internal structure of the proposed government was such as to render it unworthy of the confidence of the people. They ought not to have wandered into inflammatory declamations and unmeaning cavils about the extent of the powers. The POWERS are not too extensive for the OBJECTS of federal administration, or, in other words, for the management of our NATIONAL INTERESTS; nor can any satisfactory argument be framed to show that they are chargeable with such an excess. If it be true, as has been insinuated by some of the writers on the other side, that the difficulty arises from the nature of the thing, and that the extent of the country will not permit us to form a government in which such ample powers can safely be reposed, it would prove that we ought to contract our views, and resort to the expedient of separate confederacies, which will move within more practicable spheres. For the absurdity must continually stare us in the face of confiding to a government the direction of the most essential national interests, without daring to trust it to the authorities which are indispensable to their proper and efficient management. Let us not attempt to reconcile contradictions, but firmly embrace a rational alternative.

I trust, however, that the impracticability of one general system cannot be shown. I am greatly mistaken, if anything of weight has yet been advanced of this tendency; and I flatter myself that the observations which have been made in the course of these papers have served to place the reverse of that position in as clear a light as any matter still in the womb of time and experience can be susceptible of. This, at all events, must be evident, that the very difficulty itself, drawn from the extent of the country, is the strongest argument in favor of an energetic government; for any other can certainly never preserve the Union of so large an empire. If we embrace the tenets of those who oppose the adoption of the proposed Constitution, as the standard of our political creed, we cannot fail to verify the gloomy doctrines which predict the impracticability of a national system pervading entire limits of the present Confederacy.   PUBLIUS.

19. THE FEDERALIST (XXIV)

[PROVISION FOR NATIONAL FORCES]

To the People of the State of New York:

To the powers proposed to be conferred upon the federal government, in respect to the creation and direction of the national forces, I have met with but one specific objection, which, if I understand it right, is this—that proper provision has not been made against the existence of standing armies in time of peace; an objection which, I shall now endeavor to show, rests on weak and unsubstantial foundations.

It has indeed been brought forward in the most vague and general form, supported only by bold assertions, without the appearance of argument; without even the sanction of theoretical opinions; in contradiction to the practice of other free nations, and to the general sense of America, as expressed in most of the existing constitutions. The propriety of this remark will appear the moment it is recollected that the objection under consideration turns upon a supposed necessity of restraining the LEGISLATIVE authority of the nation, in the article of military establishments; a principle unheard of, except in one or two of our State constitutions, and rejected in all the rest.

A stranger to our politics, who was to read our newspapers at the present juncture, without having previously inspected the plan reported by the convention, would be naturally led to one of two conclusions: either that it contained a positive injunction, that standing armies should be kept up in time of peace; or that it vested in the EXECUTIVE the whole power of levying troops, without subjecting his discretion, in any shape, to the control of the legislature.

If he came afterwards to peruse the plan itself, he would be surprised to discover that neither the one nor the other was the case; that the whole power of raising armies was lodged in the *Legislature*, not in the *Executive;* that this legislature was to be a popular body, consisting of the representatives of the people periodically elected; and that instead of the provision he had supposed in favor of standing armies, there was to be found, in respect to this object, an important qualification even of the legislative discretion, in that clause which forbids the appropriation of money for the support of an army for any longer period than two years—a precaution which, upon a nearer view of it, will appear to be a great and real security against the keeping up of troops without evident necessity.

Disappointed in his first surmise, the person I have supposed would be apt to pursue his conjectures a little further. He would naturally say to himself, it is impossible that all this vehement and pathetic declamation can be without some colorable pretext. It must needs be that this people, so jealous of their liberties, have, in all the preceding models of the constitutions which they have established, inserted the most precise and rigid precautions on this point, the omission of which, in the new plan, has given birth to all this apprehension and clamor.

If, under this impression, he proceeded to pass in review the several State constitutions, how great would be his disappointment to find that *two only* of them* contained an interdiction

---

* This statement of the matter is taken from the printed collection of State constitutions. Pennsylvania and North Carolina are the two which contain the interdiction in these words: "As standing armies in time of

of standing armies in time of peace; that the other eleven had either observed a profound silence on the subject, or had in express terms admitted the right of the legislature to authorize their existence.

Still, however, he would be persuaded that there must be some plausible foundation for the cry raised on this head. He would never be able to imagine, while any source of information remained unexplored, that it was nothing more than an experiment upon the public credulity, dictated either by a deliberate intention to deceive, or by the overflowings of a zeal too intemperate to be ingenuous. It would probably occur to him, that he would be likely to find the precautions he was in search of in the primitive compact between the States. Here, at length, he would expect to meet with a solution of the enigma. No doubt, he would observe to himself, the existing Confederation must contain the most explicit provisions against military establishments in time of peace; and a departure from this model, in a favorite point, has occasioned the discontent which appears to influence these political champions.

If he should now apply himself to a careful and critical survey of the articles of Confederation, his astonishment would not only be increased, but would acquire a mixture of indignation, at the unexpected discovery that these articles, instead of containing the prohibition he looked for, and though they had, with jealous circumspection, restricted the authority of the State legislatures in this particular, had not imposed a single restraint on that of the United States. If he happened to be a man of quick sensibility, or ardent temper, he could now no

---

peace are dangerous to liberty, THEY OUGHT NOT to be kept up." This is, in truth, rather a CAUTION than a PROHIBITION. New Hampshire, Massachusetts, Delaware, and Maryland have, in each of their bills of rights, a clause to this effect: "Standing armies are dangerous to liberty, and ought not to be raised or kept up WITHOUT THE CONSENT OF THE LEGISLATURE"; which is a formal admission of the authority of the Legislature. New York has no bills of rights, and her constitution says not a word about the matter. No bills of rights appear annexed to the constitutions of the other States, except the foregoing, and their constitutions are equally silent. I am told, however, that one or two States have bills of rights which do not appear in this collection; but that those also recognize the right of the legislative authority in this respect.—PUBLIUS.

longer refrain from regarding these clamors as the dishonest artifices of a sinister and unprincipled opposition to a plan which ought at least to receive a fair and candid examination from all sincere lovers of their country! How else, he would say, could the authors of them have been tempted to vent such loud censures upon that plan, about a point in which it seems to have conformed itself to the general sense of America as declared in its different forms of government, and in which it has even superadded a new and powerful guard unknown to any of them? If, on the contrary, he happened to be a man of calm and dispassionate feelings, he would indulge a sigh for the frailty of human nature, and would lament that in a matter so interesting to the happiness of millions, the true merits of the question should be perplexed and entangled by expedients so unfriendly to an impartial and right determination. Even such a man could hardly forbear remarking, that a conduct of this kind has too much the appearance of an intention to mislead the people by alarming their passions, rather than to convince them by arguments addressed to their understandings.

But however little this objection may be countenanced, even by precedents among ourselves, it may be satisfactory to take a nearer view of its intrinsic merits. From a close examination it will appear that restraints upon the discretion of the legislature in respect to military establishments in time of peace, would be improper to be imposed, and if imposed, from the necessities of society, would be unlikely to be observed.

Though a wide ocean separates the United States from Europe, yet there are various considerations that warn us against an excess of confidence or security. On one side of us, and stretching far into our rear, are growing settlements subject to the dominion of Britain. On the other side, and extending to meet the British settlements, are colonies and establishments subject to the dominion of Spain. This situation, and the vicinity of the West India Islands, belonging to these two powers, create between them, in respect to their American possessions and in relation to us, a common interest. The savage tribes on our Western frontier ought to be regarded as our natural enemies, their natural allies, because they have most to fear from us, and most to hope from them. The improvements in the art of navigation have, as to the facility of communication, rendered distant nations, in a great measure, neighbors. Britain and Spain are among the principal maritime powers of Europe. A future concert of views between these nations ought not to be regarded as improbable. The increasing remoteness of consanguinity is every day diminishing the force of the family compact between France and Spain. And politicians have ever with great reason considered the ties of blood as feeble and precarious links of political connection. These circumstances combined, admonish us not to be too sanguine in considering ourselves as entirely out of the reach of danger.

Previous to the Revolution, and ever since the peace, there has been a constant necessity for keeping small garrisons on our Western frontier. No person can doubt that these will continue to be indispensable, if it should only be against the ravages and depredations of the Indians. These garrisons must either be furnished by occasional detachments from the militia, or by permanent corps in the pay of the government. The first is impracticable; and if practicable, would be pernicious. The militia would not long, if at all, submit to be dragged from their occupations and families to perform that most disagreeable duty in times of profound peace. And if they could be prevailed upon or compelled to do it, the increased expense of a frequent rotation of service, and the loss of labor and disconcertion of the industrious pursuits of individuals, would form conclusive objections to the scheme. It would be as burdensome and injurious to the public as ruinous to private citizens. The latter resource of permanent corps in the pay of the government amounts to a standing army in time of peace; a small one, indeed, but not the less real for being small. Here is a simple view of the subject that shows us at once the impropriety of a constitutional interdiction of such establishments, and the necessity of leaving the matter to the discretion and prudence of the legislature.

In proportion to our increase in strength, it is probable, nay, it may be said certain, that Britain and Spain would augment their military establishments in our neighborhood. If we should not be willing to be exposed, in a naked and defenceless condition, to their insults and encroachments, we should find it expedient to increase our frontier garrison in some ratio to the force by which our Western settlements might be annoyed. There are, and will be, particular posts, the possession of which will include the command of large districts of territory, and facilitate future invasions of the remainder. It may be added that some of those posts will be keys to the trade with the Indian nations. Can any man think it would be wise to leave such posts in a situation to be at any instant seized by one or the other of two neighboring and formidable powers? To act this part would be to desert all the usual maxims of prudence and policy.

If we mean to be a commercial people, or even to be secure on our Atlantic side, we must endeavor, as soon as possible, to have a navy. To this purpose there must be dockyards and arsenals; and for the defence of these, fortifications, and probably garrisons. When a nation has become so powerful by sea that it can protect its dockyards by its fleets, this supersedes the necessity of garrisons for that purpose; but where naval establishments are in their infancy, moderate garrisons will, in all likelihood, be found an indispensable security against descents for the destruction of the arsenals and dockyards, and sometimes of the fleet itself.   PUBLIUS.

20. THE FEDERALIST (XXXII)

[THE POWER OF TAXATION]

To the People of the State of New York:

Although I am of opinion that there would be no real danger of the consequences which seem to be apprehended to the State governments from a power in the Union to control them in the levies of money, because I am persuaded that the sense of the people, the extreme hazard of provoking the resentments of the State governments, and a conviction of the utility and necessity of local administrations for local purposes, would be a complete barrier against the oppressive use of such a power; yet I am willing here to allow, in its full extent, the justness of the reasoning which requires that the individual States should possess an independent and uncontrollable authority to raise their own revenues for the supply of their own wants. And making this concession, I affirm that (with the sole exception of duties on imports and exports) they would, under the plan of the convention, retain that authority in the most absolute and unqualified sense; and that an attempt on the part of the national government to abridge them in the exercise of it, would be a violent assumption of power, unwarranted by any article or clause of its Constitution.

An entire consolidation of the States into one complete national sovereignty would imply an entire subordination of the parts; and whatever powers might remain in them, would be altogether dependent on the general will. But as the plan of the convention aims only at a partial union or consolidation, the State governments would clearly retain all the rights of sovereignty which they before had, and which were not, by that act, *exclusively* delegated to the United States. This exclusive delegation, or rather this alienation, of State sovereignty, would only exist in three cases: where the Constitution in express terms granted an exclusive authority to the Union; where it granted in one instance an authority to the Union, and in another prohibited the States from exercising the like authority; and where it granted an authority to the Union, to which a similar authority in the States would be absolutely and totally *contradictory* and *repugnant*. I use these terms to distinguish this last case from another which might appear to resemble it, but which would, in fact, be essentially different; I mean where the exercise of a concurrent jurisdiction might be productive of occasional interferences in the *policy* of any branch of administration, but would not imply any direct contradiction of repugnancy in point of constitutional authority. These three cases of exclusive jurisdiction in the federal government may be exemplified by the following instances: The last clause but one in the eighth section of the first article provides expressly that Congress shall exercise *"exclusive legislation"* over the district to be appropriated as the seat of government. This answers to the first case. The first clause of the same section empowers Congress *"to lay and collect taxes, duties, imposts, and excises";* and the second clause of the tenth section of the same article declares that, *"no State shall,* without the consent of Congress, *lay any imposts or duties on imports or exports,* except for the purpose of executing its inspection laws." Hence would result an exclusive power in the Union to lay duties on imports and exports, with the particular exception mentioned; but this power is abridged by another clause, which declares that no tax or duty shall be laid on articles exported from any State; in consequence of which qualification, it now only extends to the *duties on imports.* This answers to the second case. The third will be found in that clause which declares that Congress shall have power "to establish an UNIFORM RULE of naturalization throughout the United States." This must necessarily be exclusive; because if each State had power to prescribe a DISTINCT RULE, there could not be a UNIFORM RULE.

A case which may perhaps be thought to resemble the latter, but which is in fact widely different, affects the question immediately under consideration. I mean the power of imposing taxes on all articles other than exports and imports. This, I contend, is manifestly a concurrent and coequal authority in the United States and in the individual States. There is plainly no expression in the granting clause which makes that power *exclusive* in the Union. There is no independent clause or sentence which prohibits the States from exercising it. So far is this from being the case that a plain and conclusive argument to the contrary is to be deduced from the restraint laid upon the States in relation to duties on imports and exports. This restriction implies an admission that, if it were not inserted, the States would possess the power it excludes; and it implies a further admission, that as to all other taxes, the authority of the

States remains undiminished. In any other view it would be both unnecessary and dangerous; it would be unnecessary, because if the grant to the Union of the power of laying such duties implied the exclusion of the States, or even their subordination in this particular, there could be no need of such a restriction; it would be dangerous, because the introduction of it leads directly to the conclusion which has been mentioned, and which, if the reasoning of the objectors be just, could not have been intended; I mean that the States, in all cases to which the restriction did not apply, would have a concurrent power of taxation with the Union. The restriction in question amounts to what lawyers call a NEGATIVE PREGNANT—this is, a *negation* of one thing, and an *affirmance* of another; a negation of the authority of the States to impose taxes on imports and exports, and an affirmance of their authority to impose them on all other articles. It would be mere sophistry to argue that it was meant to exclude them *absolutely* from the imposition of taxes of the former kind, and to leave them at liberty to lay others *subject to the control* of the national legislature. The restraining or prohibitory clause only says, that they shall not, *without the consent of Congress*, lay such duties; and if we are to understand this in the sense last mentioned, the Constitution would then be made to introduce a formal provision for the sake of a very absurd conclusion; which is, that the States, *with the consent* of the national legislature, might tax imports and exports; and that they might tax every other article, *unless controlled* by the same body. If this was the intention, why not leave it, in the first instance, to what is alleged to be the natural operation of the original clause, conferring a general power of taxation upon the Union? It is evident that this could not have been the intention, and that it will not bear a construction of the kind.

As to a supposition of repugnancy between the power of taxation in the States and in the Union, it cannot be supported in that sense which would be requisite to work an exclusion of the States. It is, indeed, possible that a tax might be laid on a particular article by a State which might render it *inexpedient* that thus a further tax should be laid on the same article by the Union; but it would not imply a constitutional inability to impose a further tax. The quantity of the imposition, the expediency or inexpediency of an increase on either side, would be mutually questions of prudence; but there would be involved no direct contradiction of power. The particular policy of the national and of the State systems of finance might now and then not exactly coincide, and might require reciprocal forbearances. It is not, however, a mere possibility of inconvenience in the exercise of powers, but an immediate constitutional repugnancy that can by implication alienate and extinguish a pre-existing right of sovereignty.

The necessity of a concurrent jurisdiction in certain cases results from the division of the sovereign power; and the rule that all authorities, of which the States are not explicitly divested in favor of the Union, remain with them in full vigor, is not a theoretical consequence of that division, but is clearly admitted by the whole tenor of the instrument which contains the articles of the proposed Constitution. We there find that, notwithstanding the affirmative grants of general authorities, there has been the most pointed care in those cases where it was deemed improper that the like authorities should reside in the States, to insert negative clauses prohibiting the exercise of them by the States. The tenth section of the first article consists altogether of such provisions. This circumstance is a clear indication of the sense of the convention, and furnishes a rule of interpretation out of the body of the act, which justifies the position I have advanced and refutes every hypothesis to the contrary.

PUBLIUS.

21. THE FEDERALIST (LXVII)

[THE EXECUTIVE DEPARTMENT]

To the People of the State of New York:

The constitution of the executive department of the proposed government claims next our attention.

There is hardly any part of the system which could have been attended with greater difficulty in the arrangement of it than this; and there is, perhaps, none which has been inveighed against with less candor or criticized with less judgment.

Here the writers against the Constitution seem to have taken pains to signalize their talent of misrepresentation. Calculating upon the aversion of the people to monarchy, they have endeavored to enlist all their jealousies and apprehensions in opposition to the intended President of the United States; not merely as the embryo, but as the full-grown progeny, of that detested parent. To establish the pretended affinity, they have not scrupled to draw resources even from the regions of fiction. The authorities of a magistrate, in few instances greater, in some instances less, than those of a governor of New York, have been magnified into more than royal prerogatives. He has been decorated with attributes superior in dignity and splendor to those of a king of Great Britain. He has been shown to us with the diadem sparkling on his brow and the imperial purple flowing in his train. He has been seated on a throne surrounded with minions and mistresses, giving audience to the envoys of foreign potentates, in all the supercilious pomp of majesty. The image of Asiatic despotism and voluptuousness have scarcely been wanting to crown the exaggerated scene. We have been taught to tremble at the terrific visages of murdering janizaries, and to blush at the unveiled mysteries of a future seraglio.

Attempts so extravagant as these to disfigure or, it might rather be said, to metamorphose the object, render it necessary to take an accurate view of its real nature and form: in order as well to ascertain its true aspect and genuine appearance, as to unmask the disingenuity and expose the fallacy of the counterfeit resemblances which have been so insidiously, as well as industriously, propagated.

In the execution of this task there is no man who would not find it an arduous effort either to behold with moderation, or to treat with seriousness, the devices, not less weak than wicked, which have been contrived to pervert the public opinion in relation to the subject. They so far exceed the usual though unjustifiable licenses of party artifice, that even in a disposition the most candid and tolerant, they must force the sentiments which favor an indulgent construction of the conduct of political adversaries to give place to a voluntary and unreserved indignation. It is impossible not to bestow the imputation of deliberate imposture and deception upon the gross pretence of a similitude between a king of Great Britain and a magistrate of the character marked out for that of the President of the United States. It is still more impossible to withhold that imputation from the rash and barefaced expedients which have been employed to give success to the attempted imposition.

In one instance, which I cite as a sample of the general spirit, the temerity has proceeded so far as to ascribe to the President of the United States a power which by the instrument reported is *expressly* allotted to the Executives of the individual States. I mean the power of filling casual vacancies in the Senate.

This bold experiment upon the discernment of his countrymen has been hazarded by a writer who (whatever may be his real merit) has had no inconsiderable share in the applauses of his party*;[20] and who, upon this false and unfounded suggestion, has built a series of observations equally false and unfounded. Let him now be confronted with the evidence of the fact, and let him, if he be able, justify or extenuate the shameful outrage he has offered to the dictates of truth and to the rules of fair dealing.

The second clause of the second section of the second article empowers the President of the United States "to nominate, and by and with the advice and consent of the Senate, to appoint ambassadors, other public ministers and consuls, judges of the Supreme Court, and all other *officers* of United States whose appointments are *not* in the Constitution *otherwise provided for*, and *which shall be established by law*." Immediately after this clause follows another in these words: "The President shall have power to fill up all *vacancies* that may happen *during the recess of the Senate*, by granting commissions which shall *expire at the end of their next session*." It is from this last provision that the pretended power of the President to fill vacancies in the

*See Cato, No. V.—PUBLIUS.

Senate has been deduced. A slight attention to the connection of the clauses, and to the obvious meaning of the terms, will satisfy us that the deduction is not even colorable.

The first of these two clauses, it is clear, only provides a mode for appointing such officers, "whose appointments are *not otherwise provided for* in the Constitution, and which *shall be established by law;*" of course it cannot extend to the appointments of senators, whose appointments are *otherwise provided for* in the Constitution,* and who are *established by the Constitution*, and will not require a future establishment by law. This position will hardly be contested.

The last of these two clauses, it is equally clear, cannot be understood to comprehend the power of filling vacancies in the Senate, for the following reasons:—*First*. The relation in which that clause stands to the other, which declares the general mode of appointing officers of the United States, denotes it to be nothing more than a supplement to the other, for the purpose of establishing an auxiliary method of appointment, in cases to which the general method was inadequate. The ordinary power of appointment is confined to the President and Senate *jointly*, and can therefore only be exercised during the session of the Senate; but as it would have been improper to oblige this body to be continually in session for the appointment of officers, and as vacancies might happen *in their recess*, which it might be necessary for the public service to fill without delay, the succeeding clause is evidently intended to authorize the President, *singly*, to make temporary appointments "during the recess of the Senate, by granting commissions which shall expire at the end of their next session." *Secondly*. If this clause is to be considered as supplementary to the one which precedes, the *vacancies* of which it speaks must be construed to relate to the "officers" described in the preceding one; and this, we have seen, excludes from its description the members of the Senate. *Thirdly*. The time within which the power is to operate, "during the recess of the Senate," and the duration of the appointments, "to the end of the next session" of that body, conspire

* Article I, section 3, clause 1.—PUBLIUS.

to elucidate the sense of the provision, which, if it had been intended to comprehend senators, would naturally have referred the temporary power of filling vacancies to the recess of the State legislatures, who are to make the permanent appointments, and not to the recess of the national Senate, who are to have no concern in those appointments; and would have extended the duration in office of the temporary senators to the next session of the legislature of the State, in whose representation the vacancies had happened, instead of making it to expire at the end of the ensuing session of the national Senate. The circumstances of the body authorized to make the permanent appointments would, of course, have governed the modification of a power which related to the temporary appointments; and as the national Senate is the body whose situation is alone contemplated in the clause upon which the suggestion under examination has been founded, the vacancies to which it alludes can only be deemed to respect those officers in whose appointment that body has a concurrent agency with the President. But *lastly*, the first and second clauses of the third section of the first article, not only obviate all possibility of doubt but destroy the pretext of misconception. The former provides that "the Senate of the United States shall be composed of two Senators from each State, chosen *by the legislature thereof* for six years;" and the latter directs that, "if vacancies in that body should happen by resignation or otherwise, *during the recess of the legislature of* ANY STATE, the Executive THEREOF may make temporary appointments until the *next meeting of the legislature,* which shall then fill such vacancies." Here is an express power given, in clear and unambiguous terms, to the State Executives, to fill casual vacancies in the Senate, by temporary appointments; which not only invalidates the supposition, that the clause before considered could have been intended to confer that power upon the President of the United States, but proves that this supposition, destitute as it is even of the merit of plausibility, must have originated in an intention to deceive the people, too palpable to be obscured by sophistry, too atrocious to be palliated by hypocrisy.

I have taken the pains to select this instance of misrepresentation, and to place it in a clear and strong light, as an unequivocal proof of the unwarrantable arts which are practised to prevent a fair and impartial judgment of the real merits of the Constitution submitted to the consideration of the people. Nor have I scrupled, in so flagrant a case, to allow myself a severity of animadversion little congenial with the general spirit of these papers. I hesitate not to submit it to the decision of any candid and honest adversary of the proposed government, whether language can furnish epithets of too much asperity, for so shameless and so prostitute an attempt to impose on the citizens of America.   PUBLIUS.

22. THE FEDERALIST (LXIX)

[THE POWERS OF THE PRESIDENT]

To the People of the State of New York:

I proceed now to trace the real characters of the proposed Executive, as they are marked out in the plan of the convention. This will serve to place in a strong light the unfairness of the representations which have been made in regard to it.

The first thing which strikes our attention is that the executive authority, with few exceptions, is to be vested in a single magistrate. This will scarcely, however, be considered as a point upon which any comparison can be grounded; for if, in this particular, there be a resemblance to the king of Great Britain, there is not less a resemblance to the Grand Seignior, to the khan of Tartary, to the Man of the Seven Mountains, or to the governor of New York.

That magistrate is to be elected for *four* years; and is to be re-eligible as often as the people of the United States shall think him worthy of their confidence. In these circumstances there is a total dissimilitude between *him* and a king of Great Britain, who is an *hereditary* monarch, possessing the crown as a patrimony descendible to his heirs for ever; but there is a close analogy between *him* and a governor of New York, who is elected for *three* years, and is re-eligible without limitation or intermission. If we consider how much less time would be requisite for establishing a dangerous influence in a single State than for establishing a like influence throughout the United States we must conclude that a duration of *four* years for the Chief Magistrate of the Union is a degree of permanency far less to be dreaded in that office than a duration of *three* years for a corresponding office in a single State.

The President of the United States would be liable to be impeached, tried, and, upon conviction of treason, bribery, or other high crimes or misdemeanors, removed from office; and would afterwards be liable to prosecution and punishment in the ordinary course of law. The person of the king of Great Britain is sacred and inviolable; there is no constitutional tribunal to which he is amenable; no punishment to which he can be subjected without involving the crisis of a national revolution. In this delicate and important circumstance of personal responsibility, the President of Confederated America would stand upon no better ground than a governor of New York, and upon worse ground than the governors of Maryland and Delaware.

The President of the United States is to have power to return a bill which shall have passed the two branches of the legislature for reconsideration; and the bill so returned is to become a law if, upon that reconsideration, it be approved by two thirds of both houses. The king of Great Britain, on his part, has an absolute negative upon the acts of the two houses of Parliament. The disuse of that power for a considerable time past does not affect the reality of its existence; and is to be ascribed wholly to the crown's having found the means of substituting influence to authority, or the art of gaining a majority in one or the other of the two houses, to the necessity of exerting a prerogative which could seldom be exerted without hazarding some degree of national agitation. The qualified negative of the President differs widely from this absolute negative of the British sovereign; and tallies exactly with the revisionary authority of the council of revision of this State, of which the governor is a constituent part. In this respect the power of the

President would exceed that of the governor of New York, because the former would possess, singly, what the latter shares with the chancellor and judges; but it would be precisely the same with that of the governor of Massachusetts, whose constitution, as to this article, seems to have been the original from which the convention have copied.

The President is to be the "commander-in-chief of the army and navy of the United States, and of the militia of the several States, when called into the actual service of the United States. He is to have power to grant reprieves and pardons for offences against the United States, *except in cases of impeachment;* to recommend to the consideration of Congress such measures as he shall judge necessary and expedient; to convene, on extraordinary occasions, both houses of the legislature, or either of them, and, in case of disagreement between them *with respect to the time of adjournment,* to adjourn them to such time as he shall think proper; to take care that the laws be faithfully executed; and to commission all officers of the United States." In most of these particulars the power of the President will resemble equally that of the king of Great Britain and of the governor of New York. The most material points of difference are these:—*First.* The President will have only the occasional command of such part of the militia of the nation as by legislative provision may be called into the actual service of the Union. The king of Great Britain and the governor of New York have at all times the entire command of all the militia within their several jurisdictions. In this article, therefore, the power of the President would be inferior to that of either the monarch or the governor. *Secondly.* The President is to be commander-in-chief of the army and navy of the United States. In this respect his authority would be nominally the same with that of the king of Great Britain, but in substance much inferior to it. It would amount to nothing more than the supreme command and direction of the military and naval forces, as first general and admiral of the Confederacy; while that of the British king extends to the *declaring* of war and to the *raising* and *regulating* of fleets and armies—all which, by the Constitution under consideration, would appertain to the legislature.* The governor of New York, on the other hand, is by the constitution of the State vested only with the command of its militia and navy. But the constitutions of several of the States expressly declare their governors to be commanders-in-chief, as well of the army as navy; and it may well be a question whether those of New Hampshire and Massachusetts, in particular, do not, in this instance, confer larger powers upon their respective governors than could be claimed by a President of the United States. *Thirdly.* The power of the President, in respect to pardons, would extend to all cases, *except those of impeachment.* The governor of New York may pardon in all cases, even in those of impeachment, except for treason and murder. Is not the power of the governor, in this article, on a calculation of political consequences, greater than that of the President? All conspiracies and plots against the government which have not been matured into actual treason may be screened from punishment of every kind by the interposition of the prerogative of pardoning. If a governor of New York, therefore, should be at the head of any such conspiracy, until the design had been ripened into actual hostility he could insure his accomplices and adherents an entire impunity. A President of the Union, on the other hand, though he may even pardon treason when prosecuted in the ordinary course of law, could shelter no offender, in any degree, from the effects of impeachment and conviction. Would not the prospect of a total indemnity for all the preliminary steps be a greater temptation

* A writer in a Pennsylvania paper, under the signature of TAMONY, has asserted that the king of Great Britain owes his prerogative as commander-in-chief to an annual mutiny bill. The truth is, on the contrary, that his prerogative, in this respect, is immemorial, and was only disputed, "contrary to all reason and precedent," as Blackstone, vol. I, page 262, expresses it, by the Long Parliament of Charles I; but by the statute the 13th of Charles II, chap. vi, it was declared to be in the king alone, for that the sole supreme government and command of the militia within his Majesty's realms and dominions, and of all forces by sea and land, and of all forts and places of strength, EVER WAS AND IS the undoubted right of his Majesty and his royal predecessors, kings and queens of England, and that both or either house of Parliament cannot nor ought to pretend to the same.— PUBLIUS.

to undertake and persevere in an enterprise against the public liberty than the mere prospect of an exemption from death and confiscation if the final execution of the design, upon an actual appeal to arms, should miscarry? Would this last expectation have any influence at all when the probability was computed that the person who was to afford that exemption might himself be involved in the consequences of the measure, and might be incapacitated by his agency in it from affording the desired impunity? The better to judge of this matter, it will be necessary to recollect that, by the proposed Constitution, the offence of treason is limited "to levying war upon the United States, and adhering to their enemies, giving them aid and comfort;" and that by the laws of New York it is confined within similar bounds. *Fourthly*. The President can only adjourn the national legislature in the single case of disagreement about the time of adjournment. The British monarch may prorogue or even dissolve the Parliament. The governor of New York may also prorogue the legislature of this State for a limited time; a power which, in certain situations, may be employed to very important purposes.

The President is to have power, with the advice and consent of the Senate, to make treaties, provided two thirds of the senators present concur. The king of Great Britain is the sole and absolute representative of the nation in all foreign transactions. He can of his own accord make treaties of peace, commerce, alliance, and of every other description. It has been insinuated that his authority in this respect is not conclusive, and that his conventions with foreign powers are subject to the revision, and stand in need of the ratification, of Parliament. But I believe this doctrine was never heard of until it was broached upon the present occasion. Every jurist* of that kingdom, and every other man acquainted with its Constitution, knows, as an established fact, that the prerogative of making treaties exists in the crown in its utmost plenitude; and that the compacts entered into by the royal authority have the most complete legal validity and perfection, independent of any other

* *Vide* Blackstone's *Commentaries*, Vol. I, p. 257.—PUBLIUS.

sanction. The Parliament, it is true, is sometimes seen employing itself in altering the existing laws to conform them to the stipulations in a new treaty; and this may have possibly given birth to the imagination that its co-operation was necessary to the obligatory efficacy of the treaty. But this parliamentary interposition proceeds from a different cause: from the necessity of adjusting a most artificial and intricate system of revenue and commercial laws to the changes made in them by the operation of the treaty; and of adapting new provisions and precautions to the new state of things to keep the machine from running into disorder. In this respect, therefore, there is no comparison between the intended power of the President and the actual power of the British sovereign. The one can perform alone what the other can do only with the concurrence of a branch of the legislature. It must be admitted that, in this instance, the power of the federal Executive would exceed that of any State Executive. But this arises naturally from the sovereign power which relates to treaties. If the Confederacy were to be dissolved it would become a question whether the Executives of the several States were not solely invested with that delicate and important prerogative.

The President is also to be authorized to receive ambassadors and other public ministers. This, though it has been a rich theme of declamation, is more a matter of dignity than of authority. It is a circumstance which will be without consequence in the administration of the government; and it was far more convenient that it should be arranged in this manner than that there should be a necessity of convening the legislature, or one of its branches, upon every arrival of a foreign minister, though it were merely to take the place of a departed predecessor.

The President is to nominate and, *with the advice and consent of the Senate*, to appoint ambassadors and other public ministers, judges of the Supreme Court, and in general all officers of the United States established by law, and whose appointments are not otherwise provided for by the Constitution. The king of Great Britain is emphatically and truly styled the fountain of honor. He not only appoints to all offices, but can create offices. He can confer titles of nobility at pleasure; and has the disposal of an immense number of church preferments. There is evidently a great inferiority in the power of the President, in this particular, to that of the British king; nor is it equal to that of the governor of New York, if we are to interpret the meaning of the constitution of the State by the practice which has obtained under it. The power of appointment is with us lodged in a council composed of the governor and four members of the Senate chosen by the Assembly. The governor *claims*, and has frequently *exercised*, the right of nomination, and is *entitled* to a casting vote in the appointment. If he really has the right of nominating, his authority is in this respect equal to that of the President and exceeds it in the article of the casting vote. In the national government, if the Senate should be divided, no appointment could be made; in the government of New York, if the council should be divided, the governor can turn the scale and confirm his own nomination.* If we compare the publicity which must necessarily attend the mode of appointment by the President and an entire branch of the national legislature with the privacy in the mode of appointment by the governor of New York, closeted in a secret apartment with at most four, and frequently with only two persons; and if we at the same time consider how much more easy it must be to influence the small number of which a council of appointment consists than the considerable number of which the national Senate would consist, we cannot hesitate to pronounce that the power of the chief magistrate of this State, in the disposition of offices, must, in practice, be greatly superior to that of the Chief Magistrate of the Union.

Hence it appears that, except as to the concurrent authority of the President in the article of treaties, it would be difficult

---

* Candor, however, demands an acknowledgment that I do not think the claim of the governor to a right of nomination well founded. Yet it is always justifiable to reason from the practice of a government, till its propriety has been constitutionally questioned. And independent of this claim, when we take into view the other considerations, and pursue them through all their consequences, we shall be inclined to draw much the same conclusion.—PUBLIUS.

to determine whether that magistrate would, in the aggregate, possess more or less power than the Governor of New York. And it appears yet more unequivocally that there is no pretence for the parallel which has been attempted between him and the king of Great Britain. But to render the contrast in this respect still more striking, it may be of use to throw the principal circumstances of dissimilitude into a closer group.

The President of the United States would be an officer elected by the people for *four* years; the king of Great Britain is a perpetual and *hereditary* prince. The one would be amenable to personal punishment and disgrace; the person of the other is sacred and inviolable. The one would have a *qualified* negative upon the acts of the legislative body; the other has an *absolute* negative. The one would have a right to command the military and naval forces of the nation; the other, in addition to this right, possesses that of *declaring* war, and of *raising* and *regulating* fleets and armies by his own authority. The one would have a concurrent power with a branch of the legislature in the formation of treaties; the other is the *sole possessor* of the power of making treaties. The one would have a like concurrent authority in appointing to offices; the other is the sole author of all appointments. The one can confer no privileges whatever; the other can make denizens of aliens, noblemen of commoners; can erect corporations with all the rights incident to corporate bodies. The one can prescribe no rules concerning the commerce or currency of the nation; the other is in several respects the arbiter of commerce, and in this capacity can establish markets and fairs, can regulate weights and measures, can lay embargoes for a limited time, can coin money, can authorize or prohibit the circulation of foreign coin. The one has no particle of spiritual jurisdiction; the other is the supreme head and governor of the national church! What answer shall we give to those who would persuade us that things so unlike resemble each other? The same that ought to be given to those who tell us that a government, the whole power of which would be in the hands of the elective and periodical servants of the people, is an aristocracy, a monarchy, and a despotism. PUBLIUS.

23. THE FEDERALIST (LXXVIII)

[THE JUDICIARY DEPARTMENT]

To the People of the State of New York:

We proceed now to an examination of the judiciary department of the proposed government.

In unfolding the defects of the existing Confederation, the utility and necessity of a federal judicature have been clearly pointed out. It is the less necessary to recapitulate the considerations there urged, as the propriety of the institution in the abstract is not disputed; the only questions which have been raised being relative to the manner of constituting it, and to its extent. To these points, therefore, our observations shall be confined.

The manner of constituting it seems to embrace these several objects: 1st. The mode of appointing the judges. 2nd. The tenure by which they are to hold their places. 3rd. The partition of the judiciary authority between different courts, and their relations to each other.

First. As to the mode of appointing the judges; this is the same with that of appointing the officers of the Union in general, and has been so fully discussed in the two last numbers that nothing can be said here which would not be useless repetition.

Second. As to the tenure by which the judges are to hold their places: this chiefly concerns their duration in office; the provisions for their support; the precautions for their responsibility.

According to the plan of the convention, all judges who may be appointed by the United States are to hold their offices *during good behavior;* which is conformable to the most approved of the State constitutions, and among the rest, to that of this State. Its propriety having been drawn into question by the adversaries of that plan is no light symptom of the rage for objection which disorders their imaginations and judgments. The standard of good behavior for the continuance in office of the judicial magistracy is certainly one of the most valuable of the modern improvements in the practice of government. In a monarchy it is an excellent barrier to the despotism of the prince; in a republic it is a no less excellent barrier to the encroachments and oppressions of the representative body. And it is the best expedient which can be devised in any government to secure a steady, upright, and impartial administration of the laws.

Whoever attentively considers the different departments of power must perceive that, in a government in which they are separated from each other, the judiciary, from the nature of its functions, will always be the least dangerous to the political rights of the Constitution; because it will be least in a capacity to annoy or injure them. The Executive not only dispenses the honors, but holds the sword of the community. The legislature not only commands the purse, but prescribes the rules by which the duties and rights of every citizen are to be regulated. The judiciary, on the contrary, has no influence over either the sword or the purse; no direction either of the strength or of the wealth of the society; and can take no active resolution whatever. It may truly be said to have neither FORCE nor WILL, but merely judgment; and must ultimately depend upon the aid of the executive arm even for the efficacy of its judgments.

This simple view of the matter suggests several important consequences. It proves incontestably that the judiciary is beyond comparison the weakest of the three departments of power;* that it can never attack with success either of the other two; and that all possible care is requisite to enable it to defend itself against their attacks.[21] It equally proves that though individual oppression may now and then proceed from the courts of justice, the general liberty of the people can never be endangered from that quarter; I mean so long as the judiciary remains truly distinct from both the legislature and the Executive. For I agree that "there is no liberty, if the power of judging be not separated from the legislative and executive powers."† And it proves, in the last place, that as liberty can

*The celebrated Montesquieu, speaking of them, says: "Of the three powers above mentioned, the judiciary is next to nothing."—*Spirit of Laws*, Vol. I, page 186.—PUBLIUS.   †*Idem*, page 181.—PUBLIUS.

have nothing to fear from the judiciary alone, but would have everything to fear from its union with either of the other departments; that as all the effects of such a union must ensue from a dependence of the former on the latter, notwithstanding a nominal and apparent separation; that as, from the natural feebleness of the judiciary, it is in continual jeopardy of being overpowered, awed, or influenced by its co-ordinate branches; and that as nothing can contribute so much to its firmness and independence as permanency in office, this quality may therefore be justly regarded as an indispensable ingredient in its constitution, and, in a great measure, as the citadel of the public justice and the public security.

The complete independence of the courts of justice is peculiarly essential in a limited Constitution. By a limited Constitution I understand one which contains certain specified exceptions to the legislative authority; such, for instance, as that it shall pass no bills of attainder, no *ex post facto* laws, and the like. Limitations of this kind can be preserved in practice no other way than through the medium of courts of justice, whose duty it must be to declare all acts contrary to the manifest tenor of the Constitution void. Without this, all the reservations of particular rights or privileges would amount to nothing.

Some perplexity respecting the rights of the courts to pronounce legislative acts void, because contrary to the Constitution, has arisen from an imagination that the doctrine would imply a superiority of the judiciary to the legislative power. It is urged that the authority which can declare the acts of another void must necessarily be superior to the one whose acts may be declared void. As this doctrine is of great importance in all the American constitutions, a brief discussion of the ground on which it rests cannot be unacceptable.

There is no position which depends on clearer principles than that every act of a delegated authority, contrary to the tenor of the commission under which it is exercised, is void. No legislative act, therefore, contrary to the Constitution can be valid. To deny this would be to affirm that the deputy is greater than his principal; that the servant is above his master; that the representatives of the people are superior to the people themselves; that men acting by virtue of powers may do not only what their powers do not authorize, but what they forbid.

If it be said that the legislative body are themselves the constitutional judges of their own powers, and that the construction they put upon them is conclusive upon the other departments, it may be answered that this cannot be the natural presumption where it is not to be collected from any particular provisions in the Constitution. It is not otherwise to be supposed that the Constitution could intend to enable the representatives of the people to substitute their *will* to that of their constituents. It is far more rational to suppose that the courts were designed to be an intermediate body between the people and the legislature, in order, among other things, to keep the latter within the limits assigned to their authority. The interpretation of the laws is the proper and peculiar province of the courts. A constitution is, in fact, and must be regarded by the judges, as a fundamental law. It therefore belongs to them to ascertain its meaning, as well as the meaning of any particular act proceeding from the legislative body. If there should happen to be an irreconcilable variance between the two, that which has the superior obligation and validity ought, of course, to be preferred; or, in other words, the Constitution ought to be preferred to the statute, the intention of the people to the intention of their agents.

Nor does this conclusion by any means suppose a superiority of the judicial to the legislative power. It only supposes that the power of the people is superior to both; and that where the will of the legislature, declared in its statutes, stands in opposition to that of the people, declared in the Constitution, the judges ought to be governed by the latter rather than the former. They ought to regulate their decisions by the fundamental laws, rather than by those which are not fundamental.

This exercise of judicial discretion, in determining between two contradictory laws, is exemplified in a familiar instance. It not uncommonly happens that there are two statutes existing at one time, clashing in whole or in part with each other, and neither of them containing any repealing clause or expression. In such a case it is the province of the courts to liquidate and fix their meaning and operation. So far as they can, by any fair construction, be reconciled to each other, reason and law conspire to dictate that this should be done; where this is impracticable, it becomes a matter of necessity to give effect to one in exclusion of the other. The rule which has obtained in the courts for determining their relative validity is, that the last in order of time shall be preferred to the first. But this is a mere rule of construction, not derived from any positive law, but from the nature and reason of the thing. It is a rule not enjoined upon the courts by legislative provision, but adopted by themselves, as consonant to truth and propriety, for the direction of their conduct as interpreters of the law. They thought it reasonable that between the interfering acts of an *equal* authority, that which was the last indication of its will should have the preference.

But in regard to the interfering acts of a superior and subordinate authority, of an original and derivative power, the nature and reason of the thing indicate the converse of that rule as proper to be followed. They teach us that the prior act of a superior ought to be preferred to the subsequent act of an inferior and subordinate authority; and that accordingly, whenever a particular statute contravenes the Constitution, it will be the duty of the judicial tribunals to adhere to the latter and disregard the former.

It can be of no weight to say that the courts, on the pretence of a repugnancy, may substitute their own pleasure to the constitutional intentions of the legislature. This might as well happen in the case of two contradictory statutes; or it might as well happen in every adjudication upon any single statute. The courts must declare the sense of the law; and if they should be disposed to exercise WILL instead of JUDGMENT, the consequence would equally be the substitution of their pleasure to that of the legislative body. The observation, if it prove anything, would prove that there ought to be no judges distinct from that body.

If, then, the courts of justice are to be considered as the bulwarks of a limited Constitution against legislative encroachments, this consideration will afford a strong argument for the permanent tenure of judicial offices, since nothing will contribute so much as this to that independent spirit in the judges which must be essential to the faithful performance of so arduous a duty.

This independence of the judges is equally requisite to guard the Constitution and the rights of individuals from the effects of those ill humors, which the arts of designing men, or the influence of particular conjunctures, sometimes disseminate among the people themselves, and which, though they speedily give place to better information, and more deliberate reflection, have a tendency, in the meantime, to occasion dangerous innovations in the government, and serious oppressions of the minor party in the community. Though I trust the friends of the proposed Constitution will never concur with its enemies,* in questioning that fundamental principle of republican government which admits the right of the people to alter or abolish the established Constitution, whenever they find it inconsistent with their happiness, yet it is not to be inferred from this principle that the representatives of the people, whenever a momentary inclination happens to lay hold of a majority of their constituents, incompatible with the provisions in the existing Constitution, would, on that account, be justifiable in a violation of those provisions; or that the courts would be under a greater obligation to connive at infractions in this shape than when they had proceeded wholly from the cabals of the representative body. Until the people have, by some solemn and authoritative act, annulled or changed the established form, it is binding upon themselves collectively, as well as individually; and no presumption, or even knowledge, of their sentiments, can warrant their representatives in a departure from it, prior to such an act. But it is easy to see that it would require an uncommon portion of fortitude in the judges to do their duty as faithful guardians

* *Vide* "Protest of the Minority of the Convention of Pennsylvania," Martin's Speech, etc.—PUBLIUS.

of the Constitution where legislative invasions of it had been instigated by the major voice of the community.

But it is not with a view to infractions of the Constitution only that the independence of the judges may be an essential safeguard against the effects of occasional ill humors in the society. These sometimes extend no farther than to the injury of the private rights of particular classes of citizens by unjust and partial laws. Here also the firmness of the judicial magistracy is of vast importance in mitigating the severity and confining the operation of such laws. It not only serves to moderate the immediate mischiefs of those which may have been passed, but it operates as a check upon the legislative body in passing them; who, perceiving that obstacles to the success of iniquitous intention are to be expected from the scruples of the courts, are in a manner compelled, by the very motives of the injustice they meditate, to qualify their attempts. This is a circumstance calculated to have more influence upon the character of our governments than but few may be aware of. The benefits of the integrity and moderation of the judiciary have already been felt in more States than one; and though they may have displeased those whose sinister expectations they may have disappointed, they must have commanded the esteem and applause of all the virtuous and disinterested. Considerate men, of every description, ought to prize whatever will tend to beget or fortify that temper in the courts; as no man can be sure that he may not be to-morrow the victim of a spirit of injustice, by which he may be a gainer to-day. And every man must now feel that the inevitable tendency of such a spirit is to sap the foundations of public and private confidence, and to introduce in its stead universal distrust and distress.

That inflexible and uniform adherence to the rights of the Constitution, and of individuals, which we perceive to be indispensable in the courts of justice, can certainly not be expected from judges who hold their offices by a temporary commission. Periodical appointments, however regulated, or by whomsoever made, would, in some way or other, be fatal to their necessary independence. If the power of making them was committed either to the Executive or legislature, there would be danger of an improper complaisance to the branch which possessed it; if to both, there would be an unwillingness to hazard the displeasure of either; if to the people, or to persons chosen by them for the special purpose, there would be too great a disposition to consult popularity, to justify a reliance that nothing would be consulted but the Constitution and the laws.

There is yet a further and a weightier reason for the permanency of the judicial offices which is deducible from the nature of the qualifications they require. It has been frequently remarked, with great propriety, that a voluminous code of laws is one of the inconveniences necessarily connected with the advantages of a free government. To avoid an arbitrary discretion in the courts, it is indispensable that they should be bound down by strict rules and precedents, which serve to define and point out their duty in every particular case that comes before them; and it will readily be conceived from the variety of controversies which grow out of the folly and wickedness of mankind that the records of those precedents must unavoidably swell to a very considerable bulk, and must demand long and laborious study to acquire a competent knowledge of them. Hence it is, that there can be but few men in the society who will have sufficient skill in the laws to qualify them for the stations of judges. And making the proper deductions for the ordinary depravity of human nature, the number must be still smaller of those who unite the requisite integrity with the requisite knowledge. These considerations apprise us that the government can have no great option between fit character; and that a temporary duration in office, which would naturally discourage such characters from quitting a lucrative line of practice to accept a seat on the bench, would have a tendency to throw the administration of justice into hands less able, and less well qualified, to conduct it with utility and dignity. In the present circumstances of this country, and in those in which it is likely to be for a long time to come, the disadvantages on this score would be greater than they may at first sight appear; but it must be confessed that they are far inferior to those which present themselves under the other aspects of the subject.

Upon the whole, there can be no room to doubt that the convention acted wisely in copying from the models of those constitutions which have established *good behavior* as the tenure of their judicial offices, in point of duration; and that so far from being blameable on this account, their plan would have been inexcusably defective, if it had wanted this important feature of good government. The experience of Great Britain affords an illustrious comment on the excellence of the institution.   PUBLIUS.

24. TO GEORGE WASHINGTON [22]

[PRESIDENTIAL ETIQUETTE]

NEW YORK, May 5, 1789.

SIR:

In conformity to the intimation you were pleased to honor me with on ——— evening last, I have reflected upon the etiquette proper to be observed by the President, and now submit the ideas which have occurred to me on the subject.

The public good requires as a primary object, that the dignity of the office should be supported.

Whatever is essential to this ought to be pursued, though at the risk of partial or momentary dissatisfaction. But care will be necessary to avoid extensive disgust or discontent. Men's minds are prepared for a pretty high tone in the demeanor of the Executive, but I doubt whether for so high a one as in the abstract might be desirable. The notions of equality are yet, in my opinion, too general and too strong to admit of such a distance being placed between the President and other branches of the government as might even be consistent with a due proportion. The following plan will, I think, steer clear of extremes, and involve no very material inconveniences.

I. The President to have a levee day once a week for receiving visits; an hour to be fixed at which it shall be understood that he will appear, and consequently that the visitors are to be previously assembled.

The President to remain half an hour, in which time he may converse cursorily on indifferent subjects, with such persons as shall invite his attention, and at the end of that half hour disappear. Some regulation will be hereafter necessary to designate those who may visit.

A mode of introduction through particular officers will be indispensable. No visits to be returned.

II. The President to accept no invitations, and to give formal entertainments only twice or four times a year, the anniversaries of important events in the Revolution. If twice, the day of the declaration of independence, and that of the inauguration of the President, which completed the organization of the Constitution, to be preferred; if four times, the day of the treaty of alliance with France, and that of the definitive treaty with Britain to be added. The members of the two Houses of the Legislature, principal officers of the government, foreign ministers and other distinguished strangers only to be invited. The numbers form in my mind an objection; but there may be separate tables in separate rooms. This is practised in some European courts. I see no other method in which foreign ministers can, with propriety, be included in any attentions of the table which the President may think fit to pay.

III. The President, on the levee days, either by himself or some gentleman of his household, to give informal invitations to family dinners on the days of invitation. Not more than six or eight to be invited at a time, and the matter to be confined essentially to members of the Legislature and other official characters. The President never to remain long at table.

I think it probable that the last article will not correspond with the ideas of most of those with whom your Excellency may converse; but on pretty mature reflection, I believe it will be necessary to remove the idea of too immense an inequality, which I fear would excite dissatisfaction and cabal. The thing may be so managed as neither to occasion much waste of time nor to infringe on dignity.

It is an important point to consider what persons may have access to your Excellency on business. The heads of departments will, of course, have this privilege. Foreign ministers of some descriptions will also be entitled to it. In Europe, I am informed, ambassadors only have direct access to the chief magistrate. Something very near what prevails there would, in my opinion, be right. The distinction of rank between diplomatic characters requires attention, and the door of access ought not to be too wide to that class of persons. I have thought that the members of the Senate should also have a right of *individual* access on matters relative to the *public administration*. In England and France, peers of the realm have this right. We have none such in this country, but I believe that it will be satisfactory to the people to know that there is some body of men in the state who have a right of continual communication with the President. It will be considered a safeguard against secret combinations to deceive him.

I have also asked myself, Will not the Representatives expect the same privilege, and be offended if they are not allowed to participate with the Senate? There is sufficient danger of this to merit consideration. But there is reason for the distinction in the Constitution. The Senate are coupled with the President in certain executive functions, treaties, and appointments. This makes them in a degree his constitutional counsellors, and gives them a *peculiar* claim to the right of access. On the whole, I think the discrimination will be proper and may be hazarded.

I have chosen this method of communication because I understood, your Excellency, that it would be most convenient to you. The unstudied and unceremonious manner of it will, I hope, not render it the less acceptable. And if, in the execution of your commands, at any time I consult frankness and simplicity more than ceremony or profession, I flatter myself you will not on that account distrust the sincerity of my cordial wishes for your personal happiness, and the success of your administration.

I have the honor to be, with the highest respect, Your Excellency's most obedient and humble servant.

25. TO LAFAYETTE

[APPREHENSIONS CONCERNING FRANCE]

NEW YORK, October 6, 1789.

MY DEAR MARQUIS:

I have seen, with a mixture of pleasure and apprehension, the progress of the events which have lately taken place in your country. As a friend to mankind and to liberty, I rejoice in the efforts which you are making to establish it, while I fear much for the final success of the attempts, for the fate of those I esteem who are engaged in it, and for the danger, in case of success, of innovations greater than will consist with the real felicity of your nation. If your affairs still go well when this reaches you, you will ask why this foreboding of ill, when all the appearances have been so much in your favor. I will tell you. I dread disagreements among those who are now united (which will be likely to be improved by the adverse party) about the nature of your constitution; I dread the vehement character of your people, whom I fear you may find it more easy to bring on, than to keep within proper bounds after you have put them in motion; I dread the interested refractoriness of your nobles, who cannot be gratified, and who may be unwilling to submit to the requisite sacrifices. And I dread the reveries of your philosophic politicians, who appear in the moment to have great influence, and who, being mere speculatists, may aim at more refinement than suits either with human nature or the composition of your nation.

These, my dear Marquis, are my apprehensions. My wishes for your personal success and that of the cause of liberty are incessant. Be virtuous amidst the seductions of ambition, and you can hardly in any event be unhappy. You are combined with a great and good man; you will anticipate the name of Necker. I trust you and he will never cease to harmonize.

You will, I presume, have heard before this gets to hand, that I have been appointed to the head of the finances of this country. This event, I am sure, will give you pleasure. In undertaking the task I hazard much, but I thought it an occasion that called upon me to hazard. I have no doubt that the reasonable expectation of the public may be satisfied, if I am properly supported by the Legislature, and in this respect I stand at present on the most encouraging footing.

The debt due to France will be among the first objects of my attention. Hitherto it has been from necessity neglected. The session of Congress is now over. It has been exhausted in the organization of the government and in a few laws of immediate urgency respecting navigation and commercial imposts. The subject of the debt, foreign and domestic, has been referred to the next session, which will commence the first Monday in January, with an instruction to me to prepare and report a plan comprehending an adequate provision for the support of the public credit. There were many good reasons for a temporary adjournment.

From this sketch you will perceive that I am not in a situation to address any thing officially to your administration; but I venture to say to you, as my friend, that if the instalments of the principal of the debt could be suspended for a few years, it would be a valuable accommodation to the United States. In this suggestion, I contemplate a speedy payment of the *arrears* of *interest* now due, and effectual provision for the punctual payment of future interest as it arises. Could an arrangement of this sort meet the approbation of your government, it would be best on every account that the offer should come unsolicited as a fresh mark of good will.

I wrote you last by Mr. De Warville. I presume you received my letter. As it touched upon some delicate topics I should be glad to know its fate.

P. S.—The latest accounts from France have abated some of my apprehensions. The abdications of privileges patronized by your nobility in the States-General are truly noble, and bespeak a patriotic and magnanimous policy which promises good both to them and their country.

26. *From* FIRST REPORT ON PUBLIC CREDIT [23]

[SOUND PUBLIC CREDIT]

January 9, 1790.

... To attempt to enumerate the complicated variety of mischiefs, in the whole system of the social economy, which proceed from a neglect of the maxims that uphold public credit, and justify the solicitude manifested by the House on this point, would be an improper intrusion on their time and patience.

In so strong a light, nevertheless, do they appear to the Secretary, that, on their due observance, at the present critical juncture, materially depends, in his judgment, the individual and aggregate prosperity of the citizens of the United States; their relief from the embarrassments they now experience; their character as a people; the cause of good government.

If the maintenance of public credit, then, be truly so important, the next inquiry which suggests itself is: By what means is it to be effected? The ready answer to which question is, by good faith; by a punctual performance of contracts. States, like individuals, who observe their engagements are respected and trusted, while the reverse is the fate of those who pursue an opposite conduct.

Every breach of the public engagements, whether from choice or necessity, is, in different degrees, hurtful to public credit. When such a necessity does truly exist, the evils of it are only to be palliated by a scrupulous attention, on the part of the Government, to carry the violation no further than the necessity absolutely requires, and to manifest, if the nature of the case admit of it, a sincere disposition to make reparation whenever circumstances shall permit. But, with every possible mitigation, credit must suffer, and numerous mischiefs ensue. It is, therefore, highly important, when an appearance of necessity seems to press upon the public councils, that they should examine well its reality, and be perfectly assured that there is no method of escaping from it, before they yield to its suggestions. For, though it cannot safely be affirmed that occasions have never existed, or may not exist, in which violations of the public faith, in this respect, are inevitable; yet there is great reason to believe that they exist far less frequently than precedents indicate, and are oftenest either pretended, through levity or want of firmness; or supposed, through want of knowledge. Expedients often have been devised to effect, consistently with good faith, what has been done in contravention of it. Those who are most commonly creditors of a nation are, generally speaking, enlightened men; and there are signal examples to warrant a conclusion that, when a candid and fair appeal is made to them, they will understand their true interest too well to refuse their concurrence in such modifications of their claims as any real necessity may demand.

While the observance of that good faith, which is the basis of public credit, is recommended by the strongest inducements of political expediency, it is enforced by considerations of still greater authority. There are arguments for it which rest on the immutable principles of moral obligation. And in proportion as the mind is disposed to contemplate, in the order of Providence, an intimate connection between public virtue and public happiness, will be its repugnancy to a violation of those principles.

This reflection derives additional strength from the nature of the debt of the United States. It was the price of liberty. The faith of America has been repeatedly pledged for it, and with solemnities that give peculiar force to the obligation. There is, indeed, reason to regret that it has not hitherto been kept; that the necessities of the war, conspiring with inexperience in the subjects of finance, produced direct infractions; and that the subsequent period has been a continued scene of negative violation or non-compliance. But a diminution of this regret arises from the reflection, that the last seven years have exhibited an earnest and uniform effort, on the part of the Government of the Union, to retrieve the national credit, by doing justice to the creditors of the nation; and that the embarrassments of a defective Constitution, which defeated this laudable effort, have ceased.

From this evidence of a favorable disposition given by the former Government, the institution of a new one, clothed with powers competent to calling forth the resources of the community, has excited correspondent expectations. A general belief accordingly prevails, that the credit of the United States will quickly be established on the firm foundation of an effectual provision for the existing debt. The influence which this has had at home is witnessed by the rapid increase that has taken place in the market value of the public securities. From January to November, they rose thirty-three and a third per cent.; and, from that period to this time, they have risen fifty per cent. more; and the intelligence from abroad announces effects proportionably favorable to our national credit and consequence.

It cannot but merit particular attention, that, among ourselves, the most enlightened friends of good government are those whose expectations are the highest.

To justify and preserve their confidence; to promote the increasing respectability of the American name; to answer the calls of justice; to restore landed property to its due value; to furnish new resources, both to agriculture and commerce; to cement more closely the union of the States; to add to their security against foreign attack; to establish public order on the basis of an upright and liberal policy;—these are the great and invaluable ends to be secured by a proper and adequate provision, at the present period, for the support of public credit. . . .

27. *From* OPINION AS TO THE CONSTITUTIONALITY OF THE BANK OF THE UNITED STATES[24]

[AFFIRMATIVE OPINION]

February 23, 1791.

The Secretary of the Treasury having perused with attention the papers containing the opinions of the Secretary of State and the Attorney-General, concerning the constitutionality of the bill for establishing a national bank, proceeds, according to the order of the President, to submit the reasons which have induced him to entertain a different opinion.

It will naturally have been anticipated, that in performing this task he would feel uncommon solicitude. Personal considerations alone, arising from the reflection that the measure originated with him, would be sufficient to produce it. The sense which he has manifested of the great importance of such an institution to the successful administration of the department under his particular care, and an expectation of serious ill consequences to result from a failure of the measure, do not permit him to be without anxiety on public accounts. But the chief solicitude arises from a firm persuasion, that principles of construction like those espoused by the Secretary of State and the Attorney-General would be fatal to the just and indispensable authority of the United States.

In entering upon the argument, it ought to be premised that the objections of the Secretary of State and the Attorney-General are founded on a general denial of the authority of the United States to erect corporations. The latter, indeed, expressly admits, that if there be anything in the bill which is not warranted by the Constitution, it is the clause of incorporation.

Now it appears to the Secretary of the Treasury that this *general principle* is *inherent* in the very *definition* of government, and *essential* to every step of the progress to be made by that of the United States, namely: That every power vested in a government is in its nature *sovereign*, and includes, by *force* of the *term*, a right to employ all the *means* requisite and fairly applicable to the attainment of the *ends* of such power, and which are not precluded by restrictions and exceptions specified in the Constitution, or not immoral, or not contrary to the *essential ends* of political society.

This principle, in its application to government in general, would be admitted as an axiom; and it will be incumbent upon those who may incline to deny it, to prove a distinction, and to show that a rule which, in the general system of things, is essential to the preservation of the social order, is inapplicable to the United States.

The circumstance that the powers of sovereignty are in this country divided between the National and State governments, does not afford the distinction required. It does not follow from this, that each of the portion of *powers* delegated to the one or to the other, is not sovereign with *regard to its proper objects*. It will only *follow* from it, that each has sovereign power as to *certain things*, and not as to *other things*. To deny that the Government of the United States has sovereign power, as to its declared purposes and trusts, because its power does not extend to all cases, would be equally to deny that the State governments have sovereign power in any case, because their power does not extend to every case. The tenth section of the first article of the Constitution exhibits a long list of very important things which they may not do. And thus the United States would furnish the singular spectacle of a *political society* without *sovereignty*, or of a *people governed*, without *government*.

If it would be necessary to bring proof to a proposition so clear, as that which affirms that the powers of the Federal Government, as to *its objects*, were sovereign, there is a clause of its Constitution which would be decisive. It is that which declares that the Constitution, and the laws of the United States made in pursuance of it, and all treaties made, or which shall be made, under their authority, shall be the *supreme law of the land*. The power which can create the *supreme law of the land* in *any case*, is doubtless *sovereign* as to such case.

This general and indisputable principle puts at once an end to the *abstract* question, whether the United States have power to erect a *corporation;* that is to say, to give a *legal* or *artificial capacity* to one or more persons, distinct from the *natural*. For it is unquestionably incident to *sovereign power* to erect corporations, and consequently to *that* of the United States, in *relation* to the *objects* intrusted to the management of the government. The difference is this: where the authority of the government is general, it can create corporations in *all cases;* where it is confined to certain branches of legislation, it can create corporations *only* in those cases.

Here, then, as far as concerns the reasonings of the Secretary of State and the Attorney-General, the affirmative of the constitutionality of the bill might be permitted to rest. It will occur to the President, that the principle here advanced has been untouched by either of them. . . .

28. *From* REPORT ON MANUFACTURES [25]

[PRODUCTIVENESS OF MANUFACTURES]

December 5, 1791.

. . . II. But, without contending for the superior productiveness of manufacturing industry, it may conduce to a better judgment of the policy which ought to be pursued respecting its encouragement, to contemplate the subject under some additional aspects, tending not only to confirm the idea that this kind of industry has been improperly represented as unproductive in itself, but to evince, in addition, that the establishment and diffusion of manufactures have the effect of rendering the total mass of useful and productive labor, in a community, greater than it would otherwise be. In prosecuting this discussion, it may be necessary briefly to resume and review some of the topics which have been already touched.

To affirm that the labor of the manufacturer is unproductive, because he consumes as much of the produce of land as he adds value to the raw material which he manufactures, is not better founded than it would be to affirm that the labor of the farmer, which furnishes materials to the manufacturer, is unproductive, because he consumes an equal value of manufactured articles. Each furnishes a certain portion of the produce of his labor to the other, and each destroys a corresponding portion of the produce of the labor of the other. In the meantime, the maintenance of two citizens, instead of one, is going on; the State has two members instead of one; and they, together, consume twice the value of what is produced from the land.

If, instead of a farmer and artificer, there were a farmer only, he would be under the necessity of devoting a part of his labor to the fabrication of clothing and other articles, which he would procure of the artificer, in the case of there being such a person; and of course he would be able to devote less labor to the cultivation of his farm, and would draw from it a proportionately less product. The whole quantity of production, in this state of things, in provisions, raw materials, and manufactures, would certainly not exceed in value the amount of what would be produced in provisions and raw materials only, if there were an artificer as well as a farmer.

Again, if there were both an artificer and a farmer, the latter would be left at liberty to pursue exclusively the cultivation of his farm. A greater quantity of provisions and raw materials would, of course, be produced, equal, at least, as has been already observed, to the whole amount of the provisions, raw materials, and manufactures, which would exist on a contrary supposition. The artificer, at the same time, would be going on in the production of manufactured commodities, to an amount sufficient, not only to repay the farmer, in those commodities, for the provisions and materials which were procured from him, but to furnish the artificer himself with a supply of similar commodities for his own use. Thus, then, there would be two quantities or values in existence, instead of one; and the revenue and consumption would be double, in one case, what it would be in the other.

If, in place of both of these suppositions, there were supposed to be two farmers and no artificer, each of whom applied a part of his labor to the culture of land and another part to the fabrication of manufactures; in this case, the portion of the labor of both, bestowed upon land, would produce the same quantity of provisions and raw materials only, as would be produced by the entire sum of the labor of one, applied in the same manner; and the portion of the labor of both, bestowed upon manufactures, would produce the same quantity of manufactures only, as would be produced by the entire sum of the labor of one, applied in the same manner. Hence, the produce of the labor of the two farmers would not be greater than the produce of the labor of the farmer and artificer; and hence it results, that the labor of the artificer is as positively productive as that of the farmer, and as positively augments the revenue of the society.

The labor of the artificer replaces to the farmer that portion of his labor with which he provides the materials of exchange with the artificer, and which he would otherwise have been compelled to apply to manufactures; and while the artificer thus enables the farmer to enlarge his stock of agricultural industry, a portion of which he purchases for his own use, he also supplies himself with the manufactured articles of which he stands in need. He does still more. Besides this equivalent, which he gives for the portion of agricultural labor consumed by him, and this supply of manufactured commodities for his own consumption, he furnishes still a surplus, which compensates for the use of the capital advanced, either by himself or some other person, for carrying on the business. This is the ordinary profit of the stock employed in the manufactory, and is, in every sense, as effective an addition to the income of the society as the rent of land.

The produce of the labor of the artificer, consequently, may be regarded as composed of three parts: one, by which the provisions for his subsistence and the materials for his work are purchased of the farmer; one, by which he supplies himself with manufactured necessaries; and a third, which constitutes the profit on the stock employed. The two last portions seem to have been overlooked in the system which represents manufacturing industry as barren and unproductive.

In the course of the preceding illustrations, the products of equal quantities of the labor of the farmer and artificer have been treated as if equal to each other. But this is not to be understood as intending to assert any such precise equality. It is merely a manner of expression, adopted for the sake of simplicity and perspicuity. Whether the value of the produce of the labor of the farmer be somewhat more or less than that of the artificer, is not material to the main scope of the argument, which, hitherto, has only aimed at showing that the one, as well as the other, occasions a positive augmentation of the total produce and revenue of the society.

It is now proper to proceed a step further, and to enumerate the principal circumstances from which it may be inferred that manufacturing establishments not only occasion a positive augmentation of the produce and revenue of the society, but that they contribute essentially to rendering them greater than they could possibly be without such establishments. These circumstances are:

1. The division of labor.

2. An extension of the use of machinery.

3. Additional employment to classes of the community not ordinarily engaged in the business.

4. The promoting of emigration from foreign countries.

5. The furnishing greater scope for the diversity of talents and dispositions, which discriminate men from each other.

6. The affording a more ample and various field for enterprise.

7. The creating, in some instances, a new, and securing, in all, a more certain and steady demand for the surplus produce of the soil.

Each of these circumstances has a considerable influence upon the total mass of industrious effort in a community; together, they add to it a degree of energy and effect which is not easily conceived. Some comments upon each of them, in the order in which they have been stated, may serve to explain their importance.

1. *As to the division of labor.*[26]

It has justly been observed, that there is scarcely any thing of greater moment in the economy of a nation than the proper division of labor. The separation of occupations causes each to be carried to a much greater perfection than it could possibly acquire if they were blended. This arises principally from three circumstances:

1st. The greater skill and dexterity naturally resulting from a constant and undivided application to a single object. It is evident that these properties must increase in proportion to the separation and simplification of objects, and the steadiness of the attention devoted to each; and must be less in proportion to the complication of objects, and the number among which the attention is distracted.

2d. The economy of time, by avoiding the loss of it, incident to a frequent transition from one operation to another of a different nature. This depends on various circumstances: the transition itself, the orderly disposition of the implements, machines, and materials employed in the operation to be relinquished, the preparatory steps to the commencement of a new one, the interruption of the impulse which the mind of the workman acquires from being engaged in a particular operation, the distractions, hesitations, and reluctances which attend the passage from one kind of business to another.

3d. An extension of the use of machinery. A man occupied on a single object will have it more in his power, and will be more naturally led to exert his imagination, in devising methods to facilitate and abridge labor, than if he were perplexed by a variety of independent and dissimilar operations. Besides this the fabrication of machines, in numerous instances, becoming itself a distinct trade, the artist who follows it has all the advantages which have been enumerated, for improvement in his particular art; and, in both ways, the invention and application of machinery are extended.

And from these causes united, the mere separation of the occupation of the cultivator from that of the artificer, has the effect of augmenting the productive powers of labor, and with them, the total mass of the produce or revenue of a country. In this single view of the subject, therefore, the utility of artificers or manufacturers, towards promoting an increase of productive industry, is apparent.

2. *As to an extension of the use of machinery, a point which, though partly anticipated, requires to be placed in one or two additional lights.*

The employment of machinery forms an item of great importance in the general mass of national industry. It is an artificial force brought in aid of the natural force of man; and, to all the purposes of labor, is an increase of hands, an accession of strength, unencumbered too by the expense of maintaining the laborer. May it not, therefore, be fairly inferred, that those occupations which give greatest scope to the use of this auxiliary, contribute most to the general stock of industrious effort, and, in consequence, to the general product of industry?

It shall be taken for granted, and the truth of the position referred to observation, that manufacturing pursuits are susceptible, in a greater degree, of the application of machinery, than those of agriculture. If so, all the difference is lost to a community which, instead of manufacturing for itself, procures the fabrics requisite to its supply from other countries. The substitution of foreign for domestic manufactures is a transfer to foreign nations of the advantages accruing from the employment of machinery, in the modes in which it is capable of being employed with most utility and to the greatest extent.

The cotton-mill, invented in England, within the last twenty years, is a signal illustration of the general proposition which has been just advanced. In consequence of it, all the different processes for spinning cotton are performed by means of machines, which are put in motion by water, and attended chiefly by women and children—and by a smaller number of persons, in the whole, than are requisite in the ordinary mode of spinning. And it is an advantage of great moment, that the operations of this mill continue with convenience during the night as well as through the day. The prodigious effect of such a machine is easily conceived. To this invention is to be attributed, essentially, the immense progress which has been so suddenly made in Great Britain, in the various fabrics of cotton.

3. *As to the additional employment of classes of the community not originally engaged in the particular business.*

This is not among the least valuable of the means by which manufacturing institutions contribute to augment the general stock of industry and production. In places where those institutions prevail, besides the persons regularly engaged in them, they afford occasional and extra employment to industrious individuals and families, who are willing to devote the leisure resulting from the intermissions of their ordinary pursuits to collateral labors, as a resource for multiplying their acquisitions or their enjoyments. The husbandman himself experiences a new source of profit and support from the increased industry of his wife and daughters, invited and stimulated by the demands of the neighboring manufactories.

Besides this advantage of occasional employment to classes having different occupations, there is another, of a nature allied to it, and of a similar tendency. This is the employment of persons who would otherwise be idle, and in many cases a burden on the community, either from the bias of temper, habit, infirmity of body, or some other cause, indisposing or disqualifying them for the toils of the country. It is worthy of particular remark that, in general, women and children are rendered more useful, and the latter more early useful, by manufacturing establishments, than they would otherwise be. Of the number of persons employed in the cotton manufactories of Great Britain, it is computed that four-sevenths, nearly, are women and children, of whom the greatest proportion are children, and many of them of a tender age.

And thus it appears to be one of the attributes of manufactures, and one of no small consequence, to give occasion to the exertion of a greater quantity of industry, even by the same number of persons, where they happen to prevail, than would exist if there were no such establishments.

4. *As to the promoting of emigration from foreign countries.*

Men reluctantly quit one course of occupation and livelihood for another, unless invited to it by very apparent and proximate advantages. Many who would go from one country to another, if they had a prospect of continuing with more benefit the callings to which they have been educated, will often not be tempted to change their situation by the hope of doing better in some other way. Manufacturers who, listening to the powerful invitations of a better price for their fabrics or their labor, of greater cheapness of provisions and raw materials, of an exemption from the chief part of the taxes, burdens, and restraints which they endure in the Old World, of greater personal independence and consequence, under the operation of a more equal government, and of what is far more precious than mere religious toleration, a perfect equality of religious privileges, would probably flock from Europe to the United States, to pursue their own trades or professions, if they were once made sensible of the advantages they would enjoy, and were inspired with an assurance of encouragement and employment, will, with difficulty, be induced to transplant themselves, with a view to becoming cultivators of land.

If it be true, then, that it is the interest of the United States to open every possible avenue to emigration from abroad, it affords a weighty argument for the encouragement of manufactures; which, for the reasons just assigned, will have the strongest tendency to multiply the inducements to it.

Here is perceived an important resource, not only for extending the population, and with it the useful and productive labor of the country, but likewise for the prosecution of manufactures, without deducting from the number of hands which might otherwise be drawn to tillage, and even for the indemnification of agriculture for such as might happen to be diverted from it. Many, whom manufacturing views would induce to emigrate, would, afterwards, yield to the temptations which the particular situation of this country holds out to agricultural pursuits. And while agriculture would, in other respects, derive many signal and unmingled advantages from the growth of manufactures, it is a problem whether it would gain or lose, as to the article of the number of persons employed in carrying it on.

5. *As to the furnishing greater scope for the diversity of talents and dispositions, which discriminate men from each other.*

This is a much more powerful means of augmenting the fund of national industry, than may at first sight appear. It is a just observation, that minds of the strongest and most active powers for their proper objects, fall below mediocrity, and labor without effect, if confined to uncongenial pursuits. And it is thence to be inferred, that the results of human exertion may be immensely increased by diversifying its objects. When all the different kinds of industry obtain in a community, each individual can find his proper element, and can call into activity the whole vigor of his nature. And the community is benefited by the services of its respective members, in the manner in which each can serve it with most effect.

If there be any thing in a remark often to be met with, namely, that there is, in the genius of the people of this country, a peculiar aptitude for mechanic improvements, it would operate as a forcible reason for giving opportunities to the exercise of that species of talent, by the propagation of manufactures.

6. *As to the affording a more ample and various field for enterprise.*

This also is of greater consequence in the general scale of national exertion than might, perhaps, on a superficial view be supposed, and has effects not altogether dissimilar from those of the circumstance last noticed. To cherish and stimulate the activity of the human mind, by multiplying the objects of enterprise, is not among the least considerable of the expedients by which the wealth of a nation may be promoted. Even things in themselves not positively advantageous sometimes become so, by their tendency to provoke exertion. Every new scene which is opened to the busy nature of man to rouse and exert itself, is the addition of a new energy to the general stock of effort.

The spirit of enterprise, useful and prolific as it is, must necessarily be contracted or expanded, in proportion to the simplicity or variety of the occupations and productions which are to be found in a society. It must be less in a nation of mere cultivators, than in a nation of cultivators and merchants; less in a nation of cultivators and merchants, than in a nation of cultivators, artificers, and merchants.

7. *As to the creating, in some instances, a new, and securing, in all, a more certain and steady demand for the surplus produce of the soil.*

This is among the most important of the circumstances which have been indicated. It is a principal means by which the establishment of manufactures contributes to an augmentation of the produce or revenue of a country, and has an immediate and direct relation to the prosperity of agriculture.

It is evident that the exertions of the husbandman will be steady or fluctuating, vigorous or feeble, in proportion to the steadiness or fluctuation, adequateness or inadequateness of the markets on which he must depend for the vent of the surplus which may be produced by his labor; and that such surplus, in the ordinary course of things, will be greater or less in the same proportion.

For the purpose of this vent, a domestic market is greatly to be preferred to a foreign one; because it is, in the nature of things, far more to be relied upon.

It is a primary object of the policy of nations, to be able to supply themselves with subsistence from their own soils; and manufacturing nations, as far as circumstances permit, endeavor to procure from the same source the raw materials necessary for their own fabrics. This disposition, urged by the spirit of monopoly, is sometimes even carried to an injudicious extreme. It seems not always to be recollected, that nations who have neither mines nor manufactures can only obtain the manufactured articles of which they stand in need, by an exchange of the products of their soils; and that if those who can best furnish them with such articles are unwilling to give a due course to this exchange, they must, of necessity, make every possible effort to manufacture for themselves; the effect of which is, that the manufacturing nations abridge the natural advantages of their situation, through an unwillingness to permit the agricultural countries to enjoy the advantages of theirs, and sacrifice the interests of a mutually beneficial intercourse to the vain project of selling everything and buying nothing.

But it is also a consequence of the policy which has been noted, that the foreign demand for the products of agricultural countries is, in a great degree, rather casual and occasional, than certain or constant. To what extent injurious interruptions of the demand for some of the staple commodities of the United States may have been experienced from that cause, must be referred to the judgment of those who are engaged in carrying on the commerce of the country; but it may be safely affirmed that such interruptions are, at times, very inconveniently felt, and that cases not unfrequently occur, in which markets are so confined and restricted as to render the demand very unequal to the supply.

Independently, likewise, of the artificial impediments which are created by the policy in question, there are natural causes tending to render the external demand for the surplus of agricultural nations a precarious reliance. The differences of seasons in the countries which are the consumers, make immense differences in the produce of their own soils, in different years; and consequently in the degrees of their necessity for foreign supply. Plentiful harvests with them, especially if similar ones occur at the same time in the countries which are the furnishers, occasion, of course, a glut in the markets of the latter.

Considering how fast and how much the progress of new settlements in the United States must increase the surplus produce of the soil, and weighing seriously the tendency of the system which prevails among most of the commercial nations of Europe, whatever dependence may be placed on the force of natural circumstances to counteract the effects of an artificial policy, there appear strong reasons to regard the foreign demand for that surplus as too uncertain a reliance, and to desire a substitute for it in an extensive domestic market.

To secure such a market, there is no other expedient than to promote manufacturing establishments. Manufacturers, who constitute the most numerous class, after the cultivators of land, are for that reason the principal consumers of the surplus of their labor.

This idea of an extensive domestic market for the surplus produce of the soil, is of the first consequence. It is, of all things, that which most effectually conduces to a flourishing state of agriculture. If the effect of manufactories should be to detach a portion of the hands which would otherwise be engaged in tillage, it might possibly cause a smaller quantity of lands to be under cultivation; but, by their tendency to procure a more certain demand for the surplus produce of the soil, they would, at the same time, cause the lands which were in cultivation to be better improved and more productive. And while, by their influence, the condition of each individual farmer would be meliorated, the total mass of agricultural production would probably be increased. For this must evidently depend as much upon the degree of improvement, if not more, than upon the number of acres under culture.

It merits particular observation, that the multiplication of manufactories not only furnishes a market for those articles which have been accustomed to be produced in abundance in a country, but it likewise creates a demand for such as were either unknown or produced in inconsiderable quantities. The bowels as well as the surface of the earth are ransacked for articles which were before neglected. Animals, plants, and minerals acquire a utility and a value which were before unexplored.

The foregoing considerations seem sufficient to establish, as general propositions, that it is the interest of nations to diversify the industrious pursuits of the individuals who compose them; that the establishment of manufactures is calculated not only to increase the general stock of useful and productive labor, but even to improve the state of agriculture in particular,—certainly to advance the interests of those who are engaged in it. There are other views that will be hereafter taken of the subject, which it is conceived will serve to confirm these inferences. . . .

29. TO EDWARD CARRINGTON[27]

[MADISON AND JEFFERSON: POLITICAL CREED]

PHILADELPHIA, May 26, 1792.

MY DEAR SIR:

Believing that I possess a share of your personal friendship and confidence, and yielding to that which I feel towards you; persuaded also, that our political creed is the same on two essential points—first, the necessity of Union to the respectability and happiness of this country, and second, the necessity of an efficient general government to maintain that Union, I have concluded to unbosom myself to you, on the present state of political parties and views. I will ask no reply to what I shall say; I only ask that you will be persuaded the representations I shall make are agreeable to the real and sincere impressions of my mind. You will make the due allowance for the influence of circumstances upon it; you will consult your own observations, and you will draw such a conclusion as shall appear to you proper. When I accepted the office I now hold, it was under full persuasion, that from similarity of thinking, conspiring with personal good will, I should have the firm support of Mr. Madison, in the general course of my administration. Aware of the intrinsic difficulties of the situation, and of the powers of Mr. Madison, I do not believe I should have accepted under a different supposition. I have mentioned the similarity of thinking between that gentleman and myself. This was relative, not merely to the general principles of national policy and government, but to the leading points, which were likely to constitute questions in the administration of the finances. I mean, first, the expediency of funding the debt; second, the inexpediency of discrimination between original and present holders; third, the expediency of assuming the State debts. . . .

In almost all the questions, great and small, which have arisen since the first session of Congress, Mr. Jefferson and Mr. Madison have been found among those who are disposed to narrow the federal authority. The question of a national bank is one example. The question of bounties to the fisheries is another. Mr. Madison resisted it on the ground of constitutionality, till it was evident, by the intermediate questions taken, that the bill would pass; and he then, under the wretched subterfuge of a change of a single word, "bounty" for "allowance," went over to the majority, and voted for the bill. On the militia bill, and in a variety of minor cases, he has leaned to abridging the exercise of federal authority, and leaving as much as possible to the States; and he lost no opportunity of sounding the alarm, with great affected solemnity, at encroachments, meditated on the rights of the States, and of holding up the bugbear of a faction in the government having designs unfriendly to liberty.

This kind of conduct has appeared to me the more extraordinary on the part of Mr. Madison, as I know for a certainty, it was a primary article in his creed, that the real danger in our system was the subversion of the national authority by the preponderancy of the State governments. All his measures have proceeded on an opposite supposition. I recur again to the instance of Freneau's paper. In matters of this kind one cannot have direct proof of men's latent views; they must be inferred from circumstances. As coadjutor of Mr. Jefferson in the establishment of this paper, I include Mr. Madison in the consequences imputable to it. In respect to foreign politics, the views of these gentlemen are, in my judgment, equally unsound and dangerous. They have a womanish attachment to France and a womanish resentment against Great Britain. They would draw us into the closest embrace of the former, and involve us in all the consequences of her politics; and they would risk the peace of the country in their endeavors to keep us at the greatest possible distance from the latter. This disposition goes to a length, particularly in Mr. Jefferson, of which, till lately, I had no adequate idea. Various circumstances prove to me that if these gentlemen were left to pursue their own course, there would be, in less than six months, an open war between the United States and Great Britain. I trust I have a due sense of the conduct of France towards this country in the late revolution; and that I shall always be among the foremost in making her every suitable return; but there is a wide difference between this and implicating ourselves in all her politics; between bearing good will to her and hating and wrangling with all those whom she hates. The neutral and the pacific policy appears to me to mark the true path to the United States.

Having delineated to you what I conceive to be the true complexion of the politics of these gentlemen, I will now attempt a solution of these strange appearances. Mr. Jefferson, it is known, did not in the first instance cordially acquiesce in the new Constitution for the United States; he had many doubts and reserves. He left this country before we had experienced the imbecilities of the former.

In France, he saw government only on the side of its abuses. He drank freely of the French philosophy, in religion, in science, in politics. He came from France in the moment of a fermentation, which he had a share in exciting, and in the passions and feelings of which he shared both from temperament and situation. He came here probably with a too partial idea of his own powers; and with the expectation of a greater share in the direction of our councils than he has in reality enjoyed. I am not sure that he had not peculiarly marked out for himself the department of the finances.

He came, electrified with attachment to France, and with the project of knitting together the two countries in the closest political bands.

Mr. Madison had always entertained an exalted opinion of the talents, knowledge, and virtues of Mr. Jefferson. The sentiment was probably reciprocal. A close correspondence subsisted between them during the time of Mr. Jefferson's absence from the country. A close intimacy arose upon his return.

Whether any peculiar opinions of Mr. Jefferson's concerning the public debt wrought a change in the sentiments of Mr. Madison (for it is certain that the former is more radically wrong than the latter), or whether Mr. Madison, seduced by the expectation of popularity, and possibly by the calculation of advantage to the State of Virginia, was led to change his own opinion, certain it is that a very material change took place, and that the two gentlemen were united in the new ideas. Mr. Jefferson was indiscreetly open in his approbation of Mr. Madison's principles, upon his first coming to the seat of government. I say indiscreetly, because a gentleman in the administration, in one department, ought not to have taken sides against another, in another department. The course of this business and a variety of circumstances which took place left Mr. Madison a very discontented and chagrined man, and begot some degree of ill-humor in Mr. Jefferson. Attempts were made by these gentlemen, in different ways, to produce a commercial warfare with Great Britain. In this, too, they were disappointed. And, as they had the liveliest wishes on the subject, their dissatisfaction has been proportionably great; and, as I had not favored the project, I was comprehended in their displeasure.

These causes, and perhaps some others, created, much sooner than I was aware of it, a systematic opposition to me, on the part of these gentlemen. My subversion, I am now satisfied, has been long an object with them.

Subsequent events have increased the spirit of opposition and the feelings of personal mortification on the part of these gentlemen.

A mighty stand was made on the affair of the bank. There was much commitment in that case. I prevailed. On the mint business I was opposed from the same quarters and with still less success. In the affair of ways and means for the Western expedition, on the supplementary arrangements concerning the debt, except as to the additional assumption, my views have been equally prevalent in opposition to theirs. This current of success on the one side and of defeat on the other has rendered the opposition furious, and has produced a disposition to subvert their competitors, even at the expense of the government.

Another circumstance has contributed to widening the breach. 'T is evident, beyond a question, from every movement, that Mr. Jefferson aims with ardent desire at the Presidential chair. This, too, is an important object of the party-politics. It is supposed, from the nature of my former personal and political connections, that I may favor some other candidate more than Mr. Jefferson, when the question shall occur by the retreat of the present gentleman. My influence, therefore, with the community becomes a thing, on ambitious and personal grounds, to be resisted and destroyed. You know how much it was a point to establish the Secretary of State, as the officer who was to administer the government in defect of the President and Vice-President. Here, I acknowledge, though I took far less part than was supposed, I ran counter to Mr. Jefferson's wishes; but if I had had no other reason for it, I had already experienced opposition from him, which rendered it a measure of self-defence. It is possible, too, (for men easily heat their imaginations when their passions are heated,) that they have by degrees persuaded themselves of what they may have at first only sported to influence others, namely, that there is some dreadful combination against State government and republicanism; which, according to them, are convertible terms. But there is so much absurdity in this supposition, that the admission of it tends to apologize for their hearts at the expense of their heads. Under the influence of all these circumstances the attachment to the government of the United States, originally weak in Mr. Jefferson's mind, has given way to something very like dislike in Mr. Madison's. It is so counteracted by personal feelings as to be more an affair of the head than of the heart; more the result of a conviction of the necessity of Union than of cordiality to the thing itself. I hope it does not stand worse than this with him. In such a state of mind both these gentlemen are prepared to hazard a great deal to effect a change. Most of the important measures of every government are connected with the treasury. To subvert the present head of it, they deem it expedient to risk rendering the government itself odious; perhaps foolishly thinking that they can easily recover the lost affections and confidence of the people, and not appreciating, as they ought to do, the natural resistance to government, which in every community results from the human passions, the degree to which this is strengthened by the organized rivality of State governments, and the infinite danger that the national government, once rendered odious, will be kept so by these powerful and indefatigable enemies. They forget an old, but a very just, though a coarse saying, that it is much easier to raise the devil than to lay him. Poor Knox has come in for a share of their persecutions, as a man who generally thinks with me, and who has a portion of the President's good-will and confidence. In giving you this picture of political parties, my design is, I confess, to awaken your attention, if it has not yet been awakened, to the conduct of the gentlemen in question. If my opinion of them is founded, it is certainly of great moment to the public weal that they should be understood. I rely on the strength of your mind to appreciate men as they merit, when you have a clue to their real views.

A word on another point. I am told that serious apprehensions are disseminated in your State as to the existence of a monarchical party meditating the destruction of State and republican government. If it is possible that so absurd an idea can gain ground, it is necessary that it should be combated. I assure you, on my private faith and honor as a man, that there is not, in my judgment, a shadow of foundation for it. A very small number of men indeed may entertain theories less republican than Mr. Jefferson and Mr. Madison, but I am persuaded there is not a man among them who would not regard as both criminal and visionary any attempt to subvert the republican system of the country. Most of these men rather fear that it may not justify itself by its fruits, than feel a predilection for a different form; and their fears are not diminished by the factious and fanatical politics which they find prevailing among a certain set of gentlemen and threatening to disturb the tranquillity and order of the government.

As to the destruction of State governments, the great and real anxiety is to be able to preserve the national from the too potent and counteracting influence of those governments. As to my own political creed, I give it to you with the utmost sincerity. I am affectionately attached to the republican theory. I desire above all things to see the equality of political rights, exclusive of all hereditary distinction, firmly established by a practical demonstration of its being consistent with the order and happiness of society. As to State governments, the prevailing bias of my judgment is that if they can be circumscribed within bounds, consistent with the preservation of the national government, they will prove useful and salutary. If the States were all of the size of Connecticut, Maryland, or New Jersey, I should decidedly regard the local governments as both safe and useful. As the thing now is, however, I acknowledge the most serious apprehensions, that the government of the United States will not be able to maintain itself against their influence. I see that influence already penetrating into the national councils and preventing their direction. Hence, a disposition on my part towards a liberal construction of the powers of the national government, and to erect every fence, to guard it from depredations, which is, in my opinion, consistent with constitutional propriety. As to any combination to prostrate the State governments, I disavow and deny it. From an apprehension lest the judiciary should not work efficiently or harmoniously, I have been desirous of seeing some national scheme of connection adopted as an amendment to the Constitution, otherwise I am for maintaining things as they are; though I doubt much the possibility of it, from a tendency in the nature of things towards the preponderancy of the State governments.

I said that I was affectionately attached to the republican theory. This is the real language of my heart, which I open to you in the sincerity of friendship; and I add that I have strong hopes of the success of that theory; but, in candor, I ought also to add that I am far from being without doubts. I consider its success as yet a problem. It is yet to be determined by experience whether it be consistent with that stability and order in government which are essential to public strength and private security and happiness.

On the whole, the only enemy which Republicanism has to fear in this country is in the spirit of faction and anarchy. If this will not permit the ends of government to be attained under it, if it engenders disorders in the community, all regular and orderly minds will wish for a change, and the demagogues who have produced the disorder will make it for their own aggrandizement. This is the old story. If I were disposed to promote monarchy and overthrow State governments, I would mount the hobby-horse of popularity; I would cry out "usurpation," "danger to liberty," etc., etc.; I would endeavor to prostrate the national government, raise a ferment, and then "ride in the whirlwind, and direct the storm." That there are men acting with Jefferson and Madison who have this in view, I verily believe; I could lay my finger on some of them. That Madison does not mean it, I also verily believe; and I rather believe the same of Jefferson, but I read him upon the whole thus: "A man of profound ambition and violent passions."

You must be by this time tired of my epistle. Perhaps I have treated certain characters with too much severity. I have, however, not meant to do them injustice, and, from the bottom of my soul, believe I have drawn them truly; and it is of the utmost consequence to the public weal they should be viewed in their true colors. I yield to this impression. I will only add that I make no clandestine attacks on the gentlemen concerned. They are both apprised indirectly from myself of the opinion I entertain of their views.

With the truest regard and esteem.

30. AN AMERICAN (I) [28]

[JEFFERSON AND FRENEAU'S GAZETTE]

August 4, 1792.

MR. FENNO:

It was easy to foresee, when the hint appeared in your *Gazette* of the 25th July, that the editor of the *National Gazette* received a salary from the general government, that advantage would be taken of its want of explicitness and particularity, to make the circumstance matter of merit in Mr. Freneau, and an argument of his independent disinterestedness. Such a turn of the business cannot be permitted to succeed. It is now necessary that the whole truth should be told, and that the real state of the affair should be well understood.

Mr. Freneau, before he came to this city to conduct the *National Gazette*, was employed by Childs & Swaine, printers of the *Daily Advertiser*, in New York, in the capacity of editor or superintendent.

A paper more devoted to the views of a certain party, of which Mr. Jefferson is the head, than any to be found in this city, was wanted. Mr. Freneau was thought a fit instrument; a negotiation was opened with him which ended in the establishment of the *National Gazette*, under his direction.

Mr. Freneau came here, at once editor of the *National Gazette* and clerk for foreign languages in the department of Mr. Jefferson, Secretary of State; an experiment somewhat new in the history of political manœuvres in this country: a newspaper instituted by a public officer, and the editor of it regularly pensioned with the public money in the disposal of that officer; an example savoring not a little of that spirit which, in the enumeration of European abuses, is the continual theme of declamatory censure; an example which could not have been set by the head of any other department, without having long since rung throughout the United States.

Mr. Freneau is not, then, as he would have it supposed, the independent editor of a newspaper, who, though receiving a salary from government, has firmness enough to expose its maladministration: he is the faithful and devoted servant of the head of a party, from whose hands he receives the boon. The whole complexion of his paper exhibits a decisive internal evidence of the influence of that patronage under which he acts.

Whether the services rendered by him are equivalent to the compensation he receives, is best known to his employer and himself; there is, however, some room to doubt. It is well known that his employer is, himself, well acquainted with the French language, the only one of which Mr. Freneau is the translator and it may be a question how often his aid is necessary.

It is somewhat singular, too, that a man acquainted with but one foreign language, engaged in an occupation which, it may be presumed, demands his whole time and attention—the editor of a newspaper,—should be the person selected as the clerk for foreign languages in the department of the United States for foreign affairs. Could no person be found acquainted with more than one foreign language, and who in so confidential a trust could have been regularly attached to, and in the constant employ of, the department, as well as immediately under the eye of the head of it?

But it may be asked—is it possible that Mr. Jefferson, the head of a principal department of the government, can be the patron of a paper, the evident object of which is to decry the government and its measures? If he disapproves of the government itself, and thinks it deserving of his opposition, can he reconcile it to his own personal dignity, and the principles of probity, to hold an office under it, and employ the means of official influence in that opposition? If he disapproves of the leading measures which have been adopted in the course of its administration, can he reconcile it with the principles of delicacy and propriety, to hold a place in that administration, and at the same time to be instrumental in vilifying measures which have been adopted by majorities of both branches of the Legislature, *and sanctioned by the Chief Magistrate of the Union?*

These questions would certainly be natural. An answer might be left to the facts which establish the relation between the Secretary of State and the editor of the *National Gazette* as the text, and to the general tenor of that paper, as the commentary. Let any intelligent man read the paper from the commencement of it, and let him determine for himself whether it be not a paper virulently hostile to the government and its measures. Let him then ask himself whether, considering the connection which has subsisted between the Secretary of State and the editor of that paper, coeval with its first establishment, it be probable that the complexion of the paper is contrary to the views of that officer.

If he wishes for a confirmation of the inference which he cannot fail to draw, as a probable one, let him be informed in addition:

1st. That while the Constitution of the United States was

depending before the people of this country for their consideration and decision, Mr. Jefferson, being in France, was opposed to it in some of its most important features, and wrote his objections to some of his friends in Virginia. That he at first went so far as to discountenance its adoption, though he afterwards recommended it, on the ground of expediency in certain contingencies.[29]

2d. That he is the declared opponent of almost all the important measures which have been devised by the government, more especially the provision which has been made for the public debt, the institution of the Bank of the United States, and such other measures as relate to the public credit, and the finances of the United States.

It is proper that these facts should be known, for if the people of the United States believe that their happiness and their safety are connected with the existence and maintenance of an efficient national or federal government; if they continue to think that which they have created and established worthy of their confidence—if they are willing that the powers they have granted to it should be exercised with sufficient latitude to attain the ends they had in view in granting them, and to do the essential business of the nation; if they feel an honest pride in seeing the credit of their country, so lately prostrate, elevated to an equal station with that of any nation upon earth; if they are conscious that their own importance is increased by the increased respectability of their country, which from an abject and degraded state, owing to the want of government, has, by the establishment of a wise Constitution, and the measures which have been pursued under it, become a theme for the praise and admiration of mankind; if they experience that their own situation is improved and improving—that commerce and navigation have advanced, that manufactures are progressive—that agriculture is thriving—that property is more secure than it was—industry more certain of a real, not nominal reward—personal liberty perfectly protected—that, notwithstanding the unavoidable demands upon them to satisfy the justice, retrieve the reputation, and answer the exigencies of the country, they are either less burthened than they were, or more equal to the burthen they have to sustain;—if these are their opinions and their experience, let them know and understand, that the sentiments of the officer who has been mentioned—both as to the principles and the practice of the Constitution which was framed by them, and has been administered by their representatives, freely chosen—are essentially different from theirs.

If, on the contrary, the people of the United States are of opinion, that they erred in adopting their present Constitution —that it contains pernicious principles and dangerous powers —that it has been administered injudiciously and wickedly; that men whose abilities and patriotism were tried in the worst of times, have entered into a league to deceive, defraud, and oppress them; that they are really oppressed and ruined, or in imminent danger of being so; if they think the preservation of national union a matter of no or small consequence; if they are willing to return to the situation from which they have escaped, and to strip the government of some of the most necessary powers with which they have clothed it; if they are desirous that those which may be permitted to remain should be frittered away by a narrow, timid, and feeble exercise of them; if they are disposed to see the national government transformed into the skeleton of power; if they are persuaded that nations are under no ties of moral obligation—that public credit is useless, or something worse—that public debts may be paid or cancelled at pleasure—that when a provision is not likely to be made for them, the discontents to be expected from the omission may honestly be transferred from a government able to vindicate its rights to the breasts of individuals who may first be encouraged to become the substitutes to the original creditors and may afterwards be defrauded without danger;* if to national union, national respectability, public order, and public credit, they are willing to substitute national disunion, national insignificance, public disorder, and discredit, then let

*Such was the advice given to Congress by Mr. Jefferson, when Minister Plenipotentiary to the court of France, respecting the debt due to the French nation. The precise terms are not recollected, but the substance may be depended upon. The poor Hollanders were to be victims.

them unite their acclamations and plaudits in favor of Mr. Jefferson; let him be the toast of every political club, and the theme of every popular huzza; for to those points, without examining his motives, do the real or pretended political tenets of that gentleman most assuredly tend.

These strictures are made from a conviction that it is important to the people to know the characters intrusted with their public affairs.

As Mr. Jefferson is emulous of being the head of a party whose politics have ever aimed at depressing the national authority, let him enjoy all the glory and all the advantage of it. But let it at the same time be understood by those who are persuaded that the real and permanent welfare of the country is to be promoted by other means, that such are the views by which he is actuated.   AN AMERICAN.

31. *From* OBJECTIONS AND ANSWERS RESPECTING THE ADMINISTRATION OF THE GOVERNMENT [30]

[APPREHENSIONS OF MONARCHY UNFOUNDED]

... OBJECTION 14.—The ultimate object of all this is to prepare the way for a change from the present republican form of government to that of a monarchy, of which the British constitution is to be the model.

ANSWER.—To this there is no other answer than a flat denial, except this: that the project, from its absurdity, refutes itself.

The idea of introducing a monarchy or aristocracy into this country, by employing the influence and force of a government continually changing hands, toward it, is one of those visionary things that none but madmen could meditate, and that no wise man will believe.

If it could be done at all, which is utterly incredible, it would require a long series of time, certainly beyond the life of any individual, to effect it. Who, then, would enter into such a plot? for what purpose of interest or ambition?

To hope that the people may be cajoled into giving their sanctions to such institutions is still more chimerical. A people so enlightened and so diversified as the people of this country can surely never be brought to it, but from convulsions and disorders, in consequence of the arts of popular demagogues.

The truth unquestionably is, that the only path to a subversion of the republican system of the country is by flattering the prejudices of the people, and exciting their jealousies and apprehensions, to throw affairs into confusion, and bring on civil commotion. Tired at length of anarchy or want of government, they may take shelter in the arms of monarchy for repose and security.

Those, then, who resist a confirmation of public order are the true artificers of monarchy. Not that this is the intention of the generality of them. Yet it would not be difficult to lay the finger upon some of their party who may justly be suspected. When a man, unprincipled in private life, desperate in his fortune, bold in his temper, possessed of considerable talents, having the advantage of military habits, despotic in his ordinary demeanor, known to have scoffed in private at the principles of liberty; when such a man is seen to mount the hobby-horse of popularity, to join in the cry of danger to liberty, to take every opportunity of embarrassing the general government and bringing it under suspicion, to flatter and fall in with all the nonsense of the zealots of the day, it may justly be suspected that his object is to throw things into confusion, that he may "ride the storm and direct the whirlwind." [31]

It has aptly been observed, that *Cato* was the *Tory*, *Cæsar* the *Whig* of his day. The former frequently resisted, the latter always flattered, the follies of the people. Yet the former perished with the republic—the latter destroyed it. [32]

No popular government was ever without its Catilines and its Cæsars—these are its true enemies.

As far as I am informed, the anxiety of those who are calumniated is to keep the government in the state in which it is, which they fear will be no easy task, from a natural tendency in the state of things to exalt the local on the ruins of the national government. Some of them appear to wish, in a constitutional way, a change in the judiciary department of the government, from an apprehension that an orderly and effectual administration of justice cannot be obtained without a more intimate connection between the State and National tribunals. But even this is not an object of any set of men as a party. There is a difference of opinion about it, on various grounds, among those who have generally acted together. As to any other change of consequence, I believe nobody dreams of it.

It is curious to observe the anticipations of the different parties. One side appears to believe that there is a serious plot to overturn the State governments, and substitute a monarchy to the present republican system. The other side firmly believes that there is a serious plot to overturn the general government, and elevate the separate power of the States upon its ruins. Both sides may be equally wrong, and their mutual jealousies may be naturally causes of the appearances which mutually disturb them and sharpen them against each other. . . .

32. TO GEORGE WASHINGTON [33]

[DIVISION IN WASHINGTON'S GOVERNMENT]

PHILADELPHIA, September 9, 1792.

SIR:

I have the pleasure of your private letter of the 26th of August. The feelings and views which are manifested in that letter are such as I expected would exist. And I most sincerely regret the causes of the uneasy sensations you experience. It is my most anxious wish, as far as may depend upon me, to smooth the path of your administration, and to render it prosperous and happy. And if any prospect shall open of healing or terminating the differences which exist, I shall most cheerfully embrace it; though I consider myself as the deeply injured party. The recommendation of such a spirit is worthy of the moderation and wisdom which dictated it. And if your endeavors should prove unsuccessful, I do not hesitate to say, that in my opinion the period is not remote, when the public good will require *substitutes* for the *differing members* of your administration. The continuance of a division there must destroy the energy of government, which will be little enough with the strictest union. On my part there will be a most cheerful acquiescence in such a result.

I trust, sir, that the greatest frankness has always marked, and will always mark, every step of my conduct towards you. In this disposition I cannot conceal from you, that I have had some instrumentality of late in the retaliations which have fallen upon certain public characters, and that I find myself placed in a situation not to be able to recede *for the present.*

I considered myself as compelled to this conduct by reasons public as well as personal, of the most cogent nature. I *know* that I have been an object of uniform opposition from Mr. Jefferson, from the moment of his coming to the city of New York to enter upon his present office. I *know* from the most authentic sources, that I have been the frequent subject of the most unkind whispers and insinuations from the same quarter. I have long seen a party formed in the Legislature under his auspices, bent upon my subversion. I cannot doubt from the evidence I possess, that the *National Gazette* was instituted by him for political purposes, and that one leading object of it has been to render me, and all the measures connected with my department, as odious as possible. Nevertheless, I can truly say, that, except explanations to confidential friends, I never directly or indirectly retaliated or countenanced retaliation till very lately. I can even assure you, that I was instrumental in preventing a very severe and systematic attack upon Mr. Jefferson by an association of two or three individuals, in consequence of the persecution which he brought upon the Vice-President, by his indiscreet and light letter to the printer, transmitting *Paine's* pamphlet.[34]

As long as I saw no danger to the government from the machinations which were going on, I resolved to be a silent sufferer of the injuries which were done me. I determined to avoid giving occasion to any thing which could manifest to the world dissensions among the principal characters of the government; a thing which can never happen without weakening its hands, and in some degree throwing a stigma upon it.

But when I no longer doubted that there was a formed party deliberately bent upon the subversion of measures, which in its consequences would subvert the government; when I saw that the undoing of the funding system in particular (which, whatever may be the original merits of that system, would prostrate the credit and the honor of the nation, and bring the government into contempt with that description of men who are in every society the only firm supporters of government) was an avowed object of the party, and that all possible pains were taken to produce that effect, by rendering it odious to the body of the people, I considered it as a duty to endeavor to resist the torrent, and, as an effectual means to this end, to draw aside the veil from the principal actors. To this strong impulse, to this decided conviction, I have yielded. And I think events will prove that I have judged rightly.

Nevertheless, I pledge my honor to you, sir, that if you shall hereafter form a plan to reunite the members of your administration upon some steady principle of coöperation, I will faithfully concur in executing it during my continuance in office; and I will not directly or indirectly say or do a thing that shall endanger a feud.

I have had it very much at heart to make an excursion to Mount Vernon, by way of the federal city, in the course of this month, and have more than once been on the point of asking your permission for it. But I now despair of being able to effect it. I am, nevertheless, equally obliged by your kind invitation.

With the most affectionate and faithful attachment, etc.

33. CATULLUS (III)[35]
[JEFFERSON A PROMOTER OF DISSENSION]

September 29, 1792.

"Aristides" complains that "An American" has charged Mr. Jefferson with being the patron and promoter of *national dis-*

union, national insignificance, public disorder, and *discredit.* "An American," however, has only affirmed, that "the real or pretended political tenets of that gentleman *tend*" to those points.

The facts which have been established clearly demonstrate, that, in the form in which it is made, the charge is well founded.

If Mr. Jefferson's opposition to the funding system, to the bank, and to the other measures which are connected with the administration of the national finances, had ceased, when those measures had received the sanction of law, nothing more could have been said, than, that he had transgressed the rules of official decorum, in entering the lists against the head of another department (between whom and himself there was a reciprocal duty to cultivate harmony); that he had been culpable in pursuing a line of conduct, which was calculated to sow the seeds of discord in the executive branch of the government, in the infancy of its existence.

But when his opposition extended beyond that point, when it was apparent, that he wished to *render odious,* and of course to *subvert* (for in a popular government these are convertible terms), all those deliberate and solemn acts of the Legislature, which had become the pillars of the public credit, his conduct deserved to be regarded with a still severer eye.

Whatever differences of opinion may have preceded those acts, however exceptionable particular features in them may have appeared to certain characters, there is no enlightened nor discreet citizen but must agree that they ought *now* to remain *undisturbed.* To set afloat the funding system, after the faith of the nation has been so deliberately and solemnly pledged to it— after such numerous and extensive alienations of property for full value have been made under its sanction—with adequate revenues little burdensome to the people—in a time of profound peace*—with not even the shadow of any public necessity—on no better ground than that of theoretical and paradoxical dogmas,—would be one of the most wanton and flagitious acts that ever stained the annals of a civilized nation.

---

* The partial Indian hostilities which exist can hardly be deemed an interruption of the general peace.

Yet positions tending to that disgraceful result have been maintained, in public discourses, by individuals known to be devoted to the Secretary of State; and have been privately smiled upon as profound discoveries in political science.

Yet the less discreet, though not least important partisans of that officer, talk familiarly of undoing the funding system as a meritorious work. Yet his gazette (which may fairly be regarded as the mirror of his views), after having labored for months to make it an object of popular detestation, has at length told us, in plain and triumphant terms, that "the funding system has had its day"; and very clearly, if not expressly, that it is the object of the party to overthrow it.

"An American," then, has justly, and from sufficient data, inferred that Mr. Jefferson's politics, whatever may be the motives of them, *tend* to national disunion, insignificance, disorder, and discredit. That the subversion of the funding system would produce national discredit, proves itself. Loss of credit, the reason being the same, must attend nations, as well as individuals, who voluntarily and without necessity violate their formal and positive engagements.

Insignificance and disorder, as applied to communities, equally with individuals, are the natural offspring of a loss of credit, premeditatedly and voluntarily incurred.

Disunion would not long lag behind. Sober-minded and virtuous men in every state would lose all confidence in, and all respect for a government, which has betrayed so much levity and inconstancy, so profligate a disregard to the *rights of property* and to the obligations of good faith. Their support would of course be so far withdrawn or relaxed as to leave it an easy prey to its enemies. These comprise the advocates for separate confederacies; the jealous partisans of unlimited sovereignty, in the State governments—the never to be satiated lovers of innovation and change—the tribe of pretended philosophers, but real fabricators of chimeras and paradoxes, the Catilines and the Cæsars of the community (a description of men to be found in every republic), who, leading the dance to the tune of liberty without law, endeavor to intoxicate the people with delicious but poisonous draughts to render them the easier victims of their rapacious ambition; the vicious and fanatical of every class, who are ever found the willing or deluded followers of those seducing and treacherous leaders.

But this is not all—the invasion of sixty millions of property could not be perpetrated without violent concussions. The States, whose citizens, both as *original* creditors and *purchasers*, own the largest portions of the debt (and several such there are), would not remain long bound in the trammels of a party which had so grossly violated their rights. The consequences in experiment would quickly awaken to a sense of injured right, and interest such of them, whose representatives may have wickedly embarked, or been ignorantly betrayed, into the atrocious and destructive project.

Where would all this end but in disunion and anarchy?—in national disgrace and humiliation?

"Aristides" insinuates that "An American" has distinguished Mr. Jefferson as "the Catiline of the day—the ambitious incendiary." [36] Those epithets are not to be found in either of the papers over that signature. But "An American" has said that Mr. Jefferson "has been the prompter, open or secret, of unwarrantable aspersions on men who, as long as actions, not merely professions, shall be the true tests of patriotism and integrity, need never decline a comparison with him of their titles to the public esteem," and he is supported in the assertion by facts.

Not to cite or trace those foul and pestilent whispers which, clandestinely circulating through the country, have, as far as was practicable, contaminated some of its fairest and worthiest characters, an appeal to known circumstances will justify the charge.

Some time since there appeared in print certain speculations, which have been construed into an advocation of hereditary distinctions in government. [37] These (whether with or without foundation is to this moment matter of conjecture) were ascribed to a particular character, pre-eminent for his early intrepid, faithful, persevering, and comprehensively useful services to his country—a man, pure and unspotted in private life, a citizen having a high and solid title to the esteem, the gratitude, and the confidence of his fellow-citizens.

The first volume of the "Rights of Man" makes its appearance. The opportunity is eagerly seized to answer the double purpose of wounding a competitor, and of laying in an additional stock of popularity, by associating and circulating the name of Thomas Jefferson with a popular production of a favorite writer on a favorite subject.

For this purpose, the Secretary of State sits down and pens an epistle to a printer in the city of Philadelphia, transmitting the work for republication, and expressing his approbation of it in a way which we learn, from the preface of that printer to his edition of the work, was calculated not only to do justice to the rights of Mr. Paine, but to do honor to Mr. Jefferson, by *directing the mind* to a contemplation of that *republican firmness* and *democratic simplicity* which ought to *endear him* to every friend to the "Rights of Man." [38]

The letter, as we learn from the same preface, contained the following passages: "I am extremely pleased to find it will be reprinted here, and that something is at length to be publicly said against the *political heresies* which have sprung up among us." "I have no doubt our citizens will *rally* a second time round the *standard* of common-sense."

There was not a man in the United States acquainted with the insinuations which had been propagated, who did not instantly apply the remark, and the signal was so well understood by the partisans of the writer, that a general attack immediately commenced. The newspapers in different States resounded with invective and scurrility against the patriot, who was marked out as the object of persecution and, if possible, of degradation.

Under certain circumstances, general expressions designate a person or an object as clearly as an indication of it by name. So it happened in the present case. The javelin went directly to its destination.

It was quickly perceived that discerning and respectable men disapproved the step. It was of consequence to endeavor to maintain their good opinion. Protestations and excuses as frivolous as awkward were multiplied to veil the real design.

"The gentleman alluded to never once entered into the mind. It was never imagined that the printer would be so incautious as to publish the letter or any part of it. Nothing more was in view than to turn a handsome period, and avoid the *baldness* of a note that did nothing but present the compliments of the writer."

Thus a solemn invocation to the people of America, on the most serious and important subject, dwindled at once into a brilliant conceit, that tickled the imagination too much to be resisted. The imputation of levity was preferred to that of malice.

But when the people of America presented themselves to the disturbed patriotic fancy, as a routed host, scattered and dispersed by political sorcerers, how was it possible to resist the heroic, the chivalrous desire of erecting for them some magic standard of orthodoxy, and endeavoring to rally them round it for mutual protection and safety?

In so glorious a cause, the considerations that a citizen of the United States had written in a foreign country a book containing strictures on the government of that country which would be regarded by it as libellous and seditious, that he had *dedicated* this book to the Chief Magistrate of the Union, that a republication of it under the auspices of the Secretary of State would wear the appearance of its having been promoted, at least of its being patronized, by the government of this country, were considerations too light and unimportant to occasion a moment's hesitation or pause.

Those who, after an attentive review of circumstances, can be deceived by the artifices which have been employed to varnish over this very exceptional proceeding, must understand little of human nature, must be little read in the history of those arts, which in all countries and at all times have served to disguise the machinations of factious and intriguing men.

The remaining circumstance of public notoriety, which fixes upon Mr. Jefferson the imputation of being the prompter or instigator of detraction, exists in his patronage of the *National Gazette*.

Can any attentive reader of that gazette, doubt for a moment that it has been systematically devoted to the calumniating and blackening of public characters? Can it be a question, that a main object of the paper is to destroy the public confidence in a particular public character, who it seems is to be *hunted down* at all events, for the unpardonable sin of having been the steady, invariable, and decided friend of broad national principles of government? Can it be a question, that the persecution of the officer alluded to is agreeable to the views of the institutor of the paper?

Does all this proceed from motives purely disinterested and patriotic? Can none of a different complexion be imagined, that may at least have operated to give a *stimulus* to *patriotic zeal?*

No. Mr. Jefferson has hitherto been distinguished as the quiet, modest, retiring philosopher; as the plain, simple, unambitious republican. He shall not now, for the first time, be regarded as the intriguing incendiary, the aspiring turbulent competitor.

How long it is since that gentleman's real character may have been *divined*, or whether this is only the *first time* that the *secret* has been disclosed, I am not sufficiently acquainted with the history of his political life to determine; but there is always a *"first time"* when characters studious of artful disguises are unveiled; when the visor of stoicism is plucked from the brow of the epicurean; when the plain garb of Quaker simplicity is stripped from the concealed voluptuary; when Cæsar *coyly refusing* the proffered diadem, is seen to be Cæsar rejecting the trappings, but tenaciously grasping the substance of imperial domination.

It is not unusual to defend one post by attacking another. "Aristides" has shown a disposition to imitate this policy. He by clear implication tells us, and doubtless means it as a justification of the person whom he defends, that attachment to *aristocracy, monarchy, hereditary succession*, a titled order of nobility, and all the *mock pageantry* of kingly government, form the appropriate and prominent features in the character to which he boasts Mr. Jefferson's opposition, and which it seems to be a principal part of the business of his gazette to depreciate. This is no more than what has been long matter for malevolent insinuation. I mistake, however, the man to whom it is applied, if he fears the strictest scrutiny into his political principles and conduct; if he does not wish there "were windows in the breast," and that assembled America might witness the inmost springs of his public actions. I mistake him—however a turn of mind less addicted to *dogmatizing* than *reasoning*, less fond of hypotheses than experience, may have led to speculative doubts concerning the probable success of the republican theory—if he has not uniformly and ardently, since the experiment of it began in the United States, *wished* it success; if he is not sincerely desirous that the sublime idea of a perfect equality of rights among citizens, exclusive of hereditary distinctions, may be practically justified and realized; and if among the sources of the regret which his language and conduct have testified, at the overdriven maxims and doctrines that too long withstood the establishment of firm government in the United States, and now embarrass the execution of the government which has been established, a *principal one* has not been their tendency to counteract a *fair trial* of the theory to which he is represented to be adverse. I mistake him, if his measures proceeding upon the ground of a liberal and efficient exercise of the powers of the national government, have had any other object than to give it stability and duration: *the only solid and rational expedient for preserving republican government in the United States.*

It has been pertinently remarked by a judicious writer, that *Cæsar*, who *overturned* the republic, was the Whig, *Cato*, who *died* for it, the Tory, of Rome; such, at least, was the common cant of political harangues, the insidious tale of hypocritical demagogues. CATULLUS.

34. PACIFICUS (IV) [39]

[A DEFENSE OF NEUTRALITY]

July 10, 1793.

A third objection to the proclamation is, that it is inconsistent with the gratitude due to France for the services rendered to us in our revolution.

Those who make this objection disavow, at the same time, all intention to maintain the position that the United States ought to take part in the war. They profess to be friends to our remaining at peace. What then do they mean by the objection?

If it be no breach of gratitude to refrain from joining France in the war, how can it be a breach of gratitude to declare that such is our disposition and intention?

The two positions are at variance with each other; and the true inference is, either that those who make the objection really wish to engage this country in the war, or that they seek a pretext for censuring the conduct of the Chief Magistrate, for some purpose very different from the public good.

They endeavor in vain to elude this inference by saying that the proclamation places France upon an equal footing with her enemies, while our treaties require distinctions in her favor, and our relative situation would dictate kind offices to her, which ought not be granted to her adversaries.

They are not ignorant that the proclamation is reconcilable with both those objects, as far as they have any foundation in truth or propriety.

It has been shown that the promise of "a friendly and impartial conduct" toward all the belligerent Powers is not incompatible with the performance of any stipulations in our treaties, which would not include our becoming an associate in the war; and it has been observed that the conduct of the executive, in regard to the seventeenth and twenty-second articles of the treaty of commerce, is an unequivocal comment upon the terms. They were, indeed, naturally to be understood, with the exception of those matters of positive compact, which would not amount to taking part in the war; for a nation then observes a friendly and impartial conduct toward two contending Powers, when it only performs to one of them what it is obliged to do by stipulations and antecedent treaties, which do not constitute a participation in the war.

Neither do those expressions imply that the United States will not exercise their discretion in doing kind offices to some of the parties, without extending them to others, so long as they have no relation to war; for kind offices of that description may, consistently with neutrality, be shown to one party and refused to another.

If the objectors mean that the United States ought to favor France, in things relating to war, and where they are not bound to do it by treaty, they must in this case also abandon their pretension of being friends to peace. For such a conduct would be a violation of neutrality, which could not fail to produce war.

It follows then, that the proclamation is reconcilable with all that those who censure it contend for; taking them upon their own ground, that nothing is to be done incompatible with the preservation of peace.

But though this would be a sufficient answer to the objection under consideration, yet it may not be without use to indulge some reflections on this very favorite topic of gratitude to France, since it is at this shrine that we are continually invited to sacrifice the true interests of the country; as if "all for love, and the world well lost," were a fundamental maxim in politics.

Faith and justice between nations are virtues of a nature the most necessary and sacred. They cannot be too strongly inculcated, nor too highly respected. Their obligations are absolute, their utility unquestionable; they relate to objects which, with probity and sincerity, generally admit of being brought within clear and intelligible rules.

But the same cannot be said of gratitude. It is not very often that between nations it can be pronounced with certainty that there exists a solid foundation for the sentiment; and how far it can justifiably be permitted to operate, is always a question of still greater difficulty.

The basis of gratitude is a benefit received or intended, which there was no right to claim, originating in a regard to the interest or advantage of the party on whom the benefit is, or is meant to be, conferred. If a service is rendered from views relative to the immediate interest of the party who performs it, and is productive of reciprocal advantages, there seems scarcely, in such a case, to be an adequate basis for a sentiment like that of gratitude.

The effect at least would be wholly disproportioned to the cause, if such a service ought to beget more than a disposition to render in turn a correspondent good office, founded on mutual interest and reciprocal advantage. But gratitude would require much more than this: it would exact to a certain extent even a sacrifice of the interest of the party obliged to the service or benefit of the one by whom the obligation had been conferred.

Between individuals, occasion is not unfrequently given for the exercise of gratitude. Instances of conferring benefits from kind and benevolent dispositions or feelings toward the person benefited, without any other interest on the part of the person who renders the service, than the pleasure of doing a good action, occur every day among individuals. But among nations they perhaps never occur. It may be affirmed as a general principle, that the predominant motive of good offices from one nation to another, is the interest or advantage of the nation which performs them.

Indeed, the rule of morality in this respect is not precisely the same between nations as between individuals. The duty of making its own welfare the guide of its actions, is much stronger upon the former than upon the latter; in proportion to the greater magnitude and importance of national compared with individual happiness, and to the greater permanency of the effects of national than of individual conduct. Existing millions, and for the most part future generations, are concerned in the present measures of a government; while the consequences of the private actions of an individual ordinarily terminate with himself, or are circumscribed within a narrow compass.

Whence it follows that an individual may, on numerous occasions, meritoriously indulge the emotions of generosity and benevolence, not only without an eye to, but even at the expense of, his own interest. But a government can rarely, if at all, be justifiable in pursuing a similar course; and, if it does so, ought to confine itself within much stricter bounds.* Good offices which are indifferent to the interest of a nation performing them, or which are compensated by the existence or expectation of some reasonable equivalent, or which produce an essential good to the nation to which they are rendered, without real detriment to the affairs of the benefactors, prescribe perhaps the limits of national generosity or benevolence.

It is not here meant to recommend a policy absolutely selfish or interested in nations; but to show, that a policy regulated by their own interest, as far as justice and good faith permit, is, and ought to be, their prevailing one; and that either to ascribe to them a different principle of action, or to deduce, from the supposition of it, arguments for a self-denying and self-sacrificing gratitude on the part of a nation which may have received from another good offices, is to misrepresent or misconceive what usually are, and ought to be, the springs of national conduct.

These general reflections will be auxiliary to a just estimate of our real situation with regard to France, of which a closer view will be taken in a succeeding paper.   PACIFICUS.

35. *From* AMERICANUS (I)[40]

[THE CAUSE OF FRANCE NOT THAT OF LIBERTY]

February 1, 1794.

An examination into the question how far *regard to the cause of Liberty* ought to induce the United States to take part with

* This conclusion derives confirmation from the reflection, that under every form of government rulers are only trustees for the happiness and interest of their nation, and cannot, consistently with their trust, follow the suggestions of kindness or humanity toward others, to the prejudice of their constituents.

France in the present war, is rendered necessary by the efforts which are making to establish an opinion that it ought to have that effect. In order to a right judgment on the point, it is requisite to consider the question under two aspects.

I.—Whether the cause of France be truly the cause of Liberty, pursued with justice and humanity, and in a manner likely to crown it with honorable success.

II.—Whether the degree of service we could render, by participating in the conflict, was likely to compensate, by its utility to the cause, the evils which would probably flow from it to ourselves.

If either of these questions can be answered in the negative, it will result that the consideration which has been stated ought not to embark us in the war.

A discussion of the first point will not be entered upon. It would involve an examination too complicated for the compass of these papers; and, after all, the subject gives so great scope to opinion, to imagination, to feeling, that little could be expected from argument. The great leading facts are before the public; and by this time most men have drawn their conclusions so firmly, that the issue alone can adjust their differences of opinion. There was a time when all men in this country entertained the same favorable view of the French Revolution. At the present time, they all still unite in the wish that the troubles of France may terminate in the establishment of a free and good government; and dispassionate, well-informed men must equally unite in the doubt whether this be likely to take place under the auspices of those who now govern the affairs of that country. But, agreeing in these two points, there is a great and serious diversity of opinion as to the real merits and probable issue of the French Revolution.

None can deny that the cause of France has been stained by excesses and extravagances, for which it is not easy, if possible, to find a parallel in the history of human affairs, and from which reason and humanity recoil. Yet many find apologies and extenuations with which they satisfy themselves; they still see in the cause of France the cause of liberty; they are still sanguine in the hope that it will be crowned with success; that the French nation will establish for themselves not only a free but a republican government, capable of promoting solidly their happiness. Others, on the contrary, discern no adequate apology for the horrid and disgusting scenes which have been, and continue to be, acted. They conceive that the excesses which have been committed, transcend greatly the measure of those which, with every due allowance for circumstances, were reasonably to have been expected. They perceive in them proofs of atrocious depravity in the most influential leaders of the revolution. They observe that among these, a MARAT* and a ROBESPIERRE, assassins still reeking with the blood of their fellow-citizens, monsters who outdo the fabled enormities of a *Busiris* and a *Procrustes*, are predominant in influence as well as iniquity. They find everywhere marks of an unexampled dissolution of all the social and moral ties. They see nowhere any thing but principles and opinions so wild, so extreme, passions so turbulent, so tempestuous, as almost to forbid the hope of agreement in any rational or well-organized system of government. They conclude that a state of things like this is calculated to extend disgust and disaffection throughout the nation, to nourish more and more a spirit of insurrection and mutiny, facilitating the progress of the invading armies, and exciting in the bowels of France commotions, of which it is impossible to compute the mischief, the duration, or the end; that if by the energy of the national character, and the intrinsic difficulty of the enterprise, the enemies of France shall be compelled to leave her to herself, this era may only prove the commencement of greater misfortunes; that after wading through seas of blood, in a furious and sanguinary civil war, France may find herself at length the slave of some victorious Sylla, or Marius, or Cæsar;[41] and they draw this afflicting inference from the whole view of the subject, that there is more reason to fear that the CAUSE OF TRUE LIBERTY has received a deep wound in the mismanagements of

---

*This man has lately met a fate which, though the essential interests of society will not permit us to approve, loses its odium in the contemplation of the character.

it, by those who, unfortunately for the French nation, have for a considerable time past maintained an ascendant in its affairs, than to regard the revolution of France in the form it has lately worn, as entitled to the honors due to that sacred and all-important cause, or as a safe bark in which to freight the fortunes, the liberties, and the reputation of this now respectable and happy land.

Without undertaking to determine which of these opposite opinions rests most firmly on the basis of facts, I shall content myself with observing, that if the latter is conceived to have but a tolerable foundation, it is conclusive against the propriety of our engaging in the war, merely through regard for the cause of Liberty. For when we resolve to put so vast a stake upon the chance of the die, we ought at least to be certain that the object for which we hazard is genuine, is substantial, is real. . . .

36. TULLY (II) [42]

[TRUE AND PRETENDED REPUBLICANS]

August 26, 1794.

It has been observed that the means most likely to be employed to turn the insurrection in the western country to the detriment of the government, would be artfully calculated among other things "to divert your attention from the true question to be decided."

Let us see then what is this question. It is plainly this—Shall the majority govern or be governed? shall the nation rule or be ruled? shall the general will prevail, or the will of a faction? shall there be government or no government? It is impossible to deny that this is the true and the whole question. No art, no sophistry can involve it in the least obscurity.

The Constitution *you* have ordained for yourselves and your posterity contains this express clause: "The Congress *shall have power* to lay and collect taxes, duties, imposts, and *excises*, to pay the debts, and provide for the common defence and general welfare of the United States." You have, then, by a solemn and deliberate act, the most important and sacred that a nation can perform, pronounced and decreed, that your representatives in Congress shall have power to lay *excises*. You have done nothing since to reverse or impair that decree.

Your representatives in Congress, pursuant to the commission derived from you, and with a full knowledge of the public exigencies, have laid an excise. At three succeeding sessions they have revised that act, and have as often, with a degree of unanimity not common, and after the best opportunities of knowing your sense, renewed their sanction to it, you have acquiesced in it, it has gone into general operation, and *you* have actually paid more than a million of dollars on account of it.

But the four western counties of Pennsylvania undertake to rejudge and reverse your decrees. You have said, "The Congress *shall have power* to lay *excises*." They say, "The Congress *shall not have* this power." Or, what is equivalent—they shall not exercise it: for a *power* that may not be exercised is a nullity. Your representatives have said, and four times repeated it, "An excise on distilled spirits *shall* be collected." They say it *shall not* be collected. We will punish, expel, and banish the officers who shall attempt the collection. We will do the same by every other person who shall dare to comply with your decree expressed in the constitutional charter; and with that of your representatives expressed in the laws. The sovereignty shall not reside with you, but with us. If you presume to dispute the point by force, we are ready to measure swords with you, and if unequal ourselves to the contest, we call in the aid of a foreign nation. We will league ourselves with a foreign power.

If there is a man among us who shall affirm that the question is not what it has been stated to be, who shall endeavor to perplex it by ill-timed declamations against excise laws, who shall strive to paralyze the efforts of the community by invectives or insinuations against the government, who shall inculcate, directly or indirectly, that force ought not to be employed to compel the insurgents to a submission to the laws, if the pending experiment to bring them to reason (an experiment which will immortalize the moderation of the government) shall fail,

—such a man is not a good citizen; such a man, however he may prate and babble republicanism, is not a republican; he attempts to set up the *will* of a part against the *will* of the whole, the *will* of a *faction* against the will of the *nation*, the pleasure of a *few* against *your* pleasure, the violence of a lawless combination against the sacred authority of laws pronounced under your indisputable commission.

Mark such a man, if such there be. The occasion may enable you to discriminate the *true* from *pretended republicans; your* friends from the friends of *faction.* 'T is in vain that the latter shall attempt to conceal their pernicious principles under a crowd of odious invectives against the laws. Your answer is this: "*We* have already in the constitutional act decided the point against you, and against those for whom you apologize. *We* have pronounced that *excises* may be laid, and consequently that they are not, as you say, inconsistent with liberty. Let our will be first obeyed, and then we shall be ready to consider the reasons which can be afforded to prove our judgment has been erroneous; and if they convince us, to cause them to be observed. We have not neglected the means of amending in a regular course the constitutional act. And we shall know how to make our sense be respected whenever we shall discover that any part of it needs correction. But as an earnest of this, it is our intention to begin by securing obedience to our authority, from those who have been bold enough to set it at defiance. In a full respect for the laws, we discern the reality of our power and the means of providing for our welfare as occasion may require; in the contempt of the laws we see the annihilation of our power, the possibility and the danger of its being usurped by others, and of the despotism of individuals succeeding to the regular authority of the nation." That a fate like this may never await *you*, let it be deeply imprinted in your minds, and handed down to your latest posterity, that there is no road to *despotism* more sure or more to be dreaded than that which begins at anarchy.

Threats of joining the British are actually thrown out—how far the idea may go is not known.   TULLY.

37. *From* CAMILLUS (VI) [43]

[IMPRESSMENT OF OUR SEAMEN]

1795.

There is one more objection to the treaty for what it does not do, which requires to be noticed. This is an omission to provide against the impressment of our seamen.

It is certain that our trade has suffered embarrassments in this respect, and that there have been abuses which have operated very oppressively upon our seamen; and all will join in the wish that they could have been guarded against in future by the treaty.

But it is easier to desire this, than to see how it could have been done. A general stipulation against the impressment of our seamen would have been nugatory, if not derogatory. Our right to an exemption is perfect by the laws of nations, and a contrary right is not even pretended by Great Britain. The difficulty has been, and is, to fix a rule of evidence, by which to discriminate our seamen from theirs, and by the discrimination to give ours protection, without covering theirs in our service. It happens that the two nations speak the same language, and in every exterior circumstance closely resemble each other; that many of the natives of Great Britain and Ireland are among our citizens, and that others, without being properly our citizens, are employed in our vessels.

Everybody knows that the safety of Great Britain depends upon her marine. This was never more emphatically the case, than in the war in which she is now engaged. Her very existence as an independent power, seems to rest on a maritime superiority.

In this situation, can we be surprised that there are difficulties in bringing her to consent to any arrangement which would enable us, by receiving her seamen into our employment, to detain them from her service? Unfortunately, there can be devised no method of protecting our seamen which does not involve that danger to her. Language and appearance, instead of being a guide, as between other nations, are, between us and Great Britain, sources of mistake and deception. The most familiar experience in the ordinary affairs of society proves that the oaths of parties interested cannot be fully relied upon. Certificates of citizenship, by officers of one party, would be too open to the possibility of collusion and imposition, to expect that the other would admit them to be conclusive. If inconclusive, there must be a discretion to the other party which would destroy their efficacy.

In whatever light they may be viewed, there will be found an intrinsic difficulty in devising a rule of evidence safe for both parties, and consequently, in establishing one by treaty. No nation would readily admit a rule which would make it depend on the good faith of another, and the integrity of its agents, whether her seamen, in time of war, might be drawn from her service, and transferred to that of a neutral power. Such a rule between Great Britain and us would be peculiarly dangerous, on account of circumstances, and would facilitate a transfer of seamen from one party to another. Great Britain has accordingly perseveringly declined any definite arrangement on the subject, notwithstanding earnest and reiterated efforts of our government.

When we consider candidly the peculiar difficulties which various circumstances of similitude between the people of the two countries oppose to a satisfactory arrangement, and that to the belligerent party it is a question of *national safety*, to the neutral party a question of commercial convenience and individual security, we shall be the less disposed to think the want of such a provision as our wishes would dictate a blemish in the treaty.

The truth seems to be, that, from the nature of the thing, it is matter of necessity to leave it to occasional and temporary expedients—to the effects of special interpositions from time to time, to procure the correction of abuses; and if the abuse becomes intolerable, to the *ultima ratio;* the good faith of the parties, and the motives which they have to respect the rights of each other and to avoid causes of offence, and vigilance in noting and remonstrating against the irregularities which are committed, are probably the only peaceable sureties of which the case is susceptible.

Our Minister Plenipotentiary, Mr. Pinckney, it is well known, has long had this matter in charge, and has strenuously exerted himself to have it placed upon some acceptable footing; but his endeavors have been unsuccessful, further than to mitigate the evil by some additional checks, and by drawing the attention of the British Government to the observance of more caution. A more sensible effect of our representations has been lately experienced; and with attention and vigilance that effect may be continued, and perhaps increased. But there is reason to fear that it would constantly be found impracticable to establish an efficacious conventional guard. . . .

38. TO —— HAMILTON [44]

[SKETCHES HIS OWN CAREER]

ALBANY, State of New York, May 2, 1797.

MY DEAR SIR:

Some days since I received with great pleasure your letter of the 10th of March. The mark it affords of your kind attention, and the particular account it gives me of so many relations in Scotland are extremely gratifying to me. You, no doubt, have understood that my father's affairs at a very early day went to wreck, so as to have rendered his situation during the greatest part of his life far from eligible. This state of things occasioned a separation between him and me, when I was very young, and threw me upon the bounty of my mother's relatives, some of whom were then wealthy, though by vicissitudes to which human affairs are so liable, they have been since much reduced and broken up. Myself, at about sixteen, came to this country. Having always had a strong propensity to literary pursuits, by a course of steady and laborious exertion, I was able, by the age of nineteen, to qualify myself for the degree of Bachelor of Arts in the College of New York, and to lay the foundation by preparatory study for the future profession of the law.

The American Revolution supervened. My principles led me to take part in it; at nineteen, I entered into the American army as captain of artillery. Shortly after I became, by his invitation, aide-de-camp to General Washington, in which station I served till the commencement of that campaign which ended with the siege of York in Virginia, and the capture of Cornwallis's army. The campaign I made at the head of a corps of light infantry, with which I was present at the siege of York, and engaged in some interesting operations.

At the period of the peace with Great Britain I found myself a member of Congress, by appointment of the legislature of this State.

After the peace, I settled in the city of New York, in the practice of the law, and was in a very lucrative course of practice, when the derangement of our public affairs, by the feebleness of the general confederation, drew me again reluctantly into public life. I became a member of the Convention which framed the present Constitution of the United States; and having taken part in this measure, I conceived myself to be under an obligation to lend my aid towards putting the machine in some regular motion. Hence, I did not hesitate to accept the offer of President Washington to undertake the office of Secretary of the Treasury.

In that office I met with many intrinsic difficulties, and many artificial ones, proceeding from passions, not very worthy, common to human nature, and which act with peculiar force in republics. The object, however, was effected of establishing public credit and introducing order in the finances.

Public office in this country has few attractions. The pecuniary emolument is so inconsiderable as to amount to a sacrifice to any man who can employ his time with advantage in any liberal profession. The opportunity of doing good, from the jealousy of power and the spirit of faction, is too small in any station to warrant a long continuance of private sacrifices. The enterprises of party had so far succeeded as materially to weaken the necessary influence and energy of the executive authority, and so far diminish the power of doing good in that department, as greatly to take away the motives which a virtuous man might have for making sacrifices. The prospect was even bad for gratifying in future the love of fame, if that passion was to be the spring of action.

The union of these motives, with the reflections of prudence in relation to a growing family, determined me as soon as my plan had attained a certain maturity, to withdraw from office. This I did by a resignation about two years since, when I resumed the profession of the law in the city of New York under every advantage I could desire.

It is a pleasant reflection to me, that since the commencement of my connection with General Washington to the present time, I have possessed a flattering share of his confidence and friendship.

Having given you a brief sketch of my political career, I proceed to some further family details.

In the year 1780, I married the second daughter of General Schuyler, a gentleman of one of the best families of this country, of large fortune, and no less personal and political consequence. It is impossible to be happier than I am in a wife; and I have five children, four sons and a daughter, the eldest a son somewhat past fifteen, who all promise as well as their years permit, and yield me much satisfaction. Though I have been too much in public life to be wealthy, my situation is extremely comfortable, and leaves me nothing to wish for but a continuance of health. With this blessing, the profits of my profession and other prospects authorize an expectation of such addition to my resources, as will render the eve of life easy and agreeable; so far as may depend on this consideration.

It is now several months since I have heard from my father, who continued at the island of St. Vincents. My anxiety at this silence would be greater than it is, were it not for the considerable interruption and precariousness of intercourse which is produced by the war.

I have strongly pressed the old gentleman to come and reside with me, which would afford him every enjoyment of which his advanced age is capable; but he has declined it on the ground that the advice of his physicians leads him to fear that the change of climate would be fatal to him. The next thing for me is, in proportion to my means, to endeavor to increase his comforts where he is.

It will give me the greatest pleasure to receive your son Robert at my house in New York, and still more to be of use to him; to which end, my recommendation and interest will not be wanting, and I hope not unavailing. It is my intention to embrace the opening which your letter affords me to extend my intercourse with my relations in your country, which will be a new source of satisfaction to me.

39. THE STAND (I) [45]

[THE THREAT OF FRANCE]

March 10, 1798.

The enlightened friends of America never saw greater occasion of disquietude than at the present juncture. Our nation, through its official organs, has been treated with studied contempt and systematic insult, essential rights of the country are perseveringly violated, and its independence and liberty eventually threatened by the most flagitious, despotic, and vindictive government that ever disgraced the annals of mankind; by a government marching with hasty and colossal strides to universal empire, and in the execution of this hideous project, wielding with absolute authority the whole physical force of the most enthralled but most powerful nation on earth. In a situation like this, how great is the cause to lament, how afflicting to every heart alive to the honor and interests of its country to observe, that distracted and inefficient councils, that a palsied and unconscious state of the public mind, afford too little assurance of measures adequate either to the urgency of the evils which are felt, or to the magnitude of the dangers which are in prospect.

When Great Britain attempted to wrest from us those rights, without which we must have descended from the rank of freemen, a keen and strong sense of injury and danger ran with electric swiftness through the breasts of our citizens. The mass and weight of talents, property, and character hastened to confederate in the public cause. The great body of our community everywhere burned with a holy zeal to defend it, and were eager to make sacrifices on the altar of their country.

If the nation with which we were called to contend was then the preponderating power of Europe; if by her great wealth and the success of her arms she was in a condition to bias or to awe the cabinets of princes; if her fleets covered and domineered over the ocean, facilitating depredation and invasion; if the penalties of rebellion hung over an unsuccessful contest; if America was yet in the cradle of her political existence; if her population little exceeded two millions; if she was without government, without fleets or armies, arsenals or magazines, without military knowledge; still her citizens had a just and elevated sense of her rights; were thoroughly awake to the violence and injustice of the attack upon them; saw the conduct of her adversary without apology or extenuation; and under the impulse of these impressions and views, determined, with little short of unanimity, to brave every hazard in her defence.

This magnanimous spirit was the sure pledge that all the energies of the country would be exerted to bring all its resources into action; that whatever was possible would be done towards effectual opposition; and this, combined with the immense advantage of distance, warranted the expectation of ultimate success. The event justified the expectation and rewarded the glorious spirit from which it was derived.

Far different is the picture of our present situation! The five tyrants of France, after binding in chains their own countrymen, after prostrating surrounding nations, and vanquishing all external resistance to the revolutionary despotism at home, without the shadow of necessity, with no discernible motive, other than to confirm their usurpation and extend the sphere of their domination abroad,—these implacable tyrants obstinately and remorselessly persist in prolonging the calamities of mankind, and seem resolved, as far as they can, to multiply and perpetuate them. Acting upon the pretension to universal empire, they have at length in fact, though not in name, decreed war against all nations not in league with themselves; and towards this country in particular, they add to a long train of unprovoked aggressions and affronts the insupportable outrage of refusing to receive the extraordinary ambassadors whom we sent to endeavor to appease and conciliate. Thus have they, in regard to us, filled up the measure of national insult and humiliation. 'T is not in their power, unless we are accomplices in the design, to sink us lower. 'T is only in our own power to do this by an abject submission to their will.

But though a knowledge of the true character of the citizens of this country will not permit it to be suspected that a majority either in our public councils or in the community can be so degraded or infatuated; yet to the firm and independent lover of his country, there are appearances at once mortifying and alarming.

Among those who divide our legislative councils, we perceive hitherto, on the one side, unremitting efforts to justify or excuse the despots of France, to vilify and discredit our own government, of course to destroy its necessary vigor, and to distract the opinion and to damp the zeal of our citizens,—what is worse, to divert their affections from their own to a foreign country; on the other side, we have as yet seen neither expanded views of our situation, nor measures at all proportioned to the seriousness and extent of the danger. While our independence is menaced, little more is heard than of guarding our trade, and this too in very feeble and tremulous accents.

In the community, though in a sounder state than its representatives, we discover the vestiges of the same divisions which enervate our councils. A few—happily, a contemptible few,— prostituted to a foreign enemy, seem willing that their country should become a province to France. Some of these dare even to insinuate the treasonable and parricidal sentiment, that in case of invasion they would join the standard of France. Another and a more considerable part are weak enough to appear disposed to sacrifice our commerce, to endure every indignity, and even to become tributary, rather than to encounter war or to increase the chances of it; as if a nation could preserve any rights—could even retain its freedom,—which should conduct itself on the principle of passive obedience to injury and outrage; as if the debasement of the public mind did not include the debasement of the individual mind, and the dereliction of whatever adorns or exalts human nature; as if there could be any security in compounding with tyranny and injustice by degrading compliances; as if submission to the existing violations of our sovereignty would not invite still greater, and whet the appetite to devour us by the allurement of an unresisting prey; as if war was ever to be averted by betraying unequivocally a pusillanimous dread of it as the greatest of all evils.

This country has doubtless powerful motives to cultivate peace. It is its policy, for the sake of this object, to go a great way in yielding secondary interests, and to meet injury with patience, as long as it could be done without the manifest abandonment of essential rights—without absolute dishonor. But to do more than this is suicide in any people who have the least chance of contending with effect. The conduct of our government has corresponded with the cogent inducements to a pacific system. Toward Great Britain it displayed forbearance—toward France it hath shown humility. In the case of Great Britain its moderation was attended with success. But the inexorable arrogance and rapacity of the oppressors of unhappy France bar all the avenues to reconciliation as well as to redress, accumulating upon us injury and insult, till there is no choice left but between resistance and infamy. My countrymen, can ye hesitate which to prefer? Can ye consent to taste the brutalizing cup of disgrace; to wear the livery of foreign masters; to put on the hateful fetters of foreign bondage? Will it make any difference to you, that the badge of your servitude is a *cap* rather than an *epaulet?* Will tyranny be less odious because five instead of one inflict the rod? What is there to deter you from the manful vindication of your rights and your honor?

With an immense ocean rolling between the United States and France; with ample materials for ship-building, and a body of hardy seamen more numerous and more expert than France can boast; with a population exceeding five millions, spread over a wide extent of country, offering no one point, the seizure of which, as of the great capitals of Europe, might decide the issue; with a soil liberal of all the productions that give strength and resource; with the rudiments of the most essential manufactures, capable of being developed in proportion to our want; with a numerous and, in many quarters, well-appointed militia; with respectable revenues and a flourishing credit; with many of the principal sources of taxation yet untouched; with considerable arsenals, and the means of extending them; with experienced officers ready to form an army under the command of the same illustrious chief who before led them to victory and glory, and who, if the occasion should require it, could not hesitate to obey the summons of his country;—what a striking and encouraging contrast does this situation in many respects present, to that in which we defied the thunder of Britain! What is there in it to excuse or palliate the cowardice and baseness of a tame surrender of our rights to France?

The question is unnecessary. The people of America are neither idiots nor dastards. They did not break one yoke to put on another. Though a portion of them have been hitherto misled; yet not even these, still less the great body of the nation, can be long unaware of the true situation, or blind to the treacherous arts by which they are attempted to be hoodwinked. The unfaithful and guilty leaders of a foreign faction, unmasked in all their intrinsic deformity, must quickly shrink from the scene appalled and confounded. The virtuous whom they have led astray will renounce their exotic standard. Honest men of all parties will unite to maintain and defend the honor and the sovereignty of their country.

The crisis demands it. 'T is folly to dissemble. The despots of France are waging war against us. Intoxicated with success and the inordinate love of power, they virtually threaten our independence. All amicable means have in vain been tried towards accommodation. The problem now to be solved is whether we will maintain or surrender our sovereignty. To maintain it with firmness is the most sacred of duties, the most glorious of tasks. The happiness of our country, the honor of the American name, demands it; the genius of independence exhorts to it; the secret mourning voice of oppressed millions in the very country whose despots menace us, admonish to it by their suffering example; the offended dignity of man commands us not to be accessory to its further degradation; reverence to the Supreme Governor of the universe enjoins us not to bow the knee to the modern Titans* who erect their impious crests against him and vainly imagine they can subvert his eternal throne.

But 't is not enough to resist. 'T is requisite to resist with energy. That will be a narrow view of our situation which does not contemplate that we may be called, at our very doors, to defend our independence and liberty, and which does not provide against it by bringing into activity and completely organizing all the resources of our country. A respectable naval force ought to protect our commerce, and a respectable army ought both to diminish the temptation to invasion, by lessening the apparent chance of success, and to guarantee us not only against the signal success of such an attempt, but against the serious though partial calamities which in that case would certainly await us if we have to rely on militia alone against the enterprises of veteran troops, drenched in blood and slaughter, and led by a skilful and daring chief.

Titus Manlius.

40. TO GEORGE WASHINGTON
[A CIRCUIT THROUGH THE SOUTH]

New York. May 19, 1798.

My Dear Sir:

At the present dangerous crisis of public affairs, I make no apology for troubling you with a political letter. Your impressions of our situation, I am persuaded, are not different from

---

* A race of giants fabled of old to have made war on heaven.

mine. There is certainly great probability that we may have to enter into a very serious struggle with France; and it is more and more evident that the powerful faction which has for years opposed the government, is determined to go every length with France. I am sincere in declaring my full conviction, as the result of a long course of observation, that they are ready to *new-model* our Constitution under the *influence* or *coercion* of France, to form with her a perpetual alliance, *offensive* and *defensive*, and to give her a monopoly of our trade by *peculiar* and *exclusive* privileges. This would be in substance, whatever it might be in name, to make this country a province of France. Neither do I doubt that her standard, displayed in this country, would be directly or indirectly seconded by them, in pursuance of the project I have mentioned.

It is painful and alarming to remark, that the opposition faction assumes so much a geographical complexion. As yet, from the south of Maryland nothing has been heard but accounts of disapprobation of our government, and approbation of or apology for France. This is a most portentous symptom, and demands every human effort to change it.

In such a state of public affairs, it is impossible not to look up to you, and to wish that your influence could in some proper mode be brought into direct action. Among the ideas which have passed through my mind for this purpose, I have asked myself whether it might not be expedient for you to make a circuit through Virginia and North Carolina, under some pretence of health, etc. This would call forth addresses, public dinners, etc., which would give you an opportunity of expressing sentiments in answers, toasts, etc., which would throw the weight of your character into the scale of the government, and revive an enthusiasm for your person that may be turned into the right channel.

I am aware that the step is delicate, and ought to be well considered before it is taken. I have even not settled my own opinion as to its propriety, but I have concluded to bring the general idea under your view, confident that your judgment will make a right choice; and that you will take no step which is not well calculated. The conjuncture, however, is extraordinary, and now, or very soon, will demand extraordinary measures.

You ought also to be aware, my dear sir, that in the event of an open rupture with France, the public voice will again call you to command the armies of your country; and, though all who are attached to you will, from attachment, as well as from public considerations, deplore an occasion which should once more tear you from that repose to which you have so good a right, yet it is the opinion of all those with whom I converse, that you will be compelled to make the sacrifice. All your past labor may demand to give it efficacy this further, this very great sacrifice. Adieu, my dear sir.[46]

41. TO GEORGE WASHINGTON

[OFFERING HIS SERVICES]

NEW YORK, June 2, 1798.

MY DEAR SIR:

I have before me your favor of the 27th of May. The suggestion in my last was an indigested thought, begotten by my anxiety. I have no doubt that your view of it is accurate and well founded.

It is a great satisfaction to me to ascertain what I had anticipated in hope, that you are not determined in an *adequate emergency* against affording once more your military services. There is no one but yourself that would unite the public confidence in such an emergency, independent of other considerations, and it is of the last importance that this confidence should be *full and complete*. As to the wish of the country, it is certain that it will be *ardent and universal*. You intimate a desire to be informed what would be my part in such an event as to entering into military service. I have no scruple about opening myself to you on this point. If I am invited to *a station in which the service I may render may be proportionate to the sacrifice I am to make*, I shall be willing to go into the army. If you command, the place in which I should hope to be most useful is that of Inspector-General, with a command in the line. This I would accept. The public must judge for itself as to whom it will employ, but every individual must judge for himself as to the terms on which he will serve, and consequently must estimate his own pretensions.

I have no knowledge of any arrangement contemplated, but I take it for granted the service of all the former officers worth having may be commanded, and that your choice would regulate the Executive. With decision and care in the selection an excellent army may be formed.

The view you give of the prospects in the South is very consoling. The public temper seems everywhere to be travelling to a right point. This promises security to the country in every event.

42. TO LAFAYETTE

[RELATIONS WITH FRANCE]

NEW YORK, January 6, 1799.

DEAR SIR:

I have been made happy, my dear friend, by the receipt of your letter of the 12th of August last. No explanation of your political principles was necessary to satisfy me of the perfect consistency and purity of your conduct. The interpretation may always be left to my attachment for you. Whatever difference of opinion may on any occasion exist between us, it can never lessen my conviction of the goodness both of your head and heart. I expect from you a return of this sentiment so far as concerns the heart. 'T is needless to detail to you my political tenets. I shall only say that I hold with *Montesquieu*, that a government must be fitted to a nation, as much as a coat to the individual; and, consequently, that what may be good at Philadelphia may be bad at Paris, and ridiculous at Petersburgh.

I join with you in regretting the misunderstanding between our two countries. You will have seen by the President's speech that a door is again opened for terminating them amicably. And you may be assured that we are sincere, and that it is in the power of France, by reparation to our merchants for past injury, and the stipulation of justice in future, to put an end to the controversy.

But I do not much like the idea of your being any way implicated in the affair, lest you should be compromitted in the opinion of one or the other of the parties. It is my opinion that it is best for you to stand aloof. Neither have I abandoned the idea that it is most advisable for you to remain in Europe till the difference is adjusted. It would be very difficult for you here to steer a course which would not place you in a party, and not remove you from the broad ground which you now occupy in the hearts of all. It is a favorite point with me that you shall find in the universal regard of this country all the consolations which the loss of your own (for so I consider it) may render requisite.

Mrs. Church and Mrs. Hamilton unite in assurance of their affectionate remembrance.

43. TO TOBIAS LEAR [47]

[ON THE DEATH OF WASHINGTON]

NEW YORK, January 2, 1800.

DEAR SIR:

Your letter of the 15th of December last was delayed in getting to hand by the circumstance of its having gone to New York while I was at Philadelphia, and of its having arrived at Philadelphia after I had set out on my return to New York.

The very painful event which it announces had, previous to the receipt of it, filled my heart with bitterness. Perhaps no man in this community has equal cause with myself to deplore the loss. I have been much indebted to the kindness of the General, and he was an *ægis very essential to me*. But regrets are unavailing. For great misfortunes it is the business of reason to seek consolation. The friends of General Washington have very noble ones. If virtue can secure happiness in another world, he is happy. In this the seal is now put upon *his* glory. It is no longer in jeopardy from the fickleness of fortune.

P. S.—In whose hands are his papers gone? Our very confidential situation will not permit this to be a point of indifference to me.

44. TO JAMES A. BAYARD

[CHARACTER OF AARON BURR]

NEW YORK, January 16, 1801.

I was glad to find, my dear sir, by your letter that you had not yet determined to go with the current of the federal party in the support of Mr. Burr, and that you were resolved to hold yourself disengaged till the moment of final decision.[48] Your resolution to separate yourself in this instance from the federal party, if your conviction shall be strong of the unfitness of Mr. Burr, is certainly laudable. So much does it coincide with my ideas, that if the party shall, by supporting Mr. Burr as President, adopt him for their official chief, I shall be obliged to consider myself as an *isolated* man. It will be impossible for me to reconcile with my notions of *honor* or policy the continuing to be of a party which, according to my apprehension, will have degraded itself and the country.

I am sure, nevertheless, that the motives of many will be good, and I shall never cease to esteem the individuals, though I shall deplore a step which, I fear, experience will show to be a very fatal one. Among the letters which I receive assigning the reasons *pro* and *con* for preferring Burr to J., I observe no small exaggeration to the prejudice of the latter, and some things taken for granted as to the former, which are at least questionable. Perhaps myself the first, at some expense of popularity, to unfold the true character of Jefferson, it is too late for me to become his apologist; nor can I have any disposition to do it.

I admit that his politics are tinctured with fanaticism; that he is too much in earnest in his democracy; that he has been a mischievous enemy to the principal measures of our past administration; that he is crafty and persevering in his objects; that he is not scrupulous about the means of success, nor very mindful of truth, and that he is a contemptible hypocrite. But it is not true, as is alleged, that he is an enemy to the power of the Executive, or that he is for confounding all the powers in the House of Representatives. It is a fact which I have frequently mentioned, that, while we were in the administration together, he was generally for a large construction of the Executive authority and not backward to act upon it in cases which coincided with his views. Let it be added that in his theoretic ideas he has considered as improper the participations of the Senate in the Executive authority. I have more than once made the reflection that, viewing himself as the reversioner, he was solicitous to come into the possession of a good estate. Nor is it true that Jefferson is zealot enough to do any thing in pursuance of his principles which will contravene his popularity or his interest. He is as likely as any man I know to temporize— to calculate what will be likely to promote his own reputation and advantage; and the probable result of such a temper is the preservation of systems, though originally opposed, which, being once established, could not be overturned without danger to the person who did it. To my mind a true estimate of Mr. Jefferson's character warrants the expectation of a temporizing rather than a violent system. That Jefferson has manifested a culpable predilection for France is certainly true; but I think it a question whether it did not proceed quite as much from her *popularity* among us as from sentiment, and, in proportion as that popularity is diminished, his zeal will cool. Add to this that there is no fair reason to suppose him capable of being corrupted, which is a security that he will not go beyond certain limits. It is not at all improbable that under the change of circumstances Jefferson's Gallicism has considerably abated.

As to Burr these things are admitted, and indeed cannot be denied, that he is a man of *extreme* and *irregular* ambition; that he is *selfish* to a degree which excludes all social affections, and that he is decidedly *profligate*. But it is said (1) that he is *artful* and *dexterous* to accomplish his ends; (2) that he holds no pernicious theories, but is a mere *matter-of-fact* man; (3) that his very selfishness* is a guard against mischievous foreign predilections; (4) that his *local situation* has enabled him to appreciate the utility of our commercial and fiscal systems, and the same quality of selfishness will lead him to support and invigorate them; (5) that he is now disliked by the Jacobins; that his elevation will be a mortal stab to them, breed an invincible hatred to him, and compel him to lean on the Federalists; (6) that Burr's ambition will be checked by his good sense, by the manifest impossibility of succeeding in any scheme of usurpation, and that, if attempted, there is nothing to fear from the attempt. These topics are, in my judgment, more plausible than solid. As to the first point, the fact must be admitted, but those qualities are objections rather than recommendations, when they are under the direction of bad principles. As to the second point, too much is taken for granted. If Burr's conversation is to be credited, he is not very far from being a visionary. He has quoted to me *Connecticut* as an example of the success of the democratic theory, and as authority, I have serious doubts whether it was not a good one. It is ascertained in some instances that he has talked perfect *Godwinism*. I have myself heard him speak with applause of the French system, as unshackling the mind and leaving it to its natural energies, and I have been present when he has contended against banking systems† with earnestness and with the same arguments that Jefferson would use.

The truth is, that Burr is a man of very subtle imagination, and a mind of this make is rarely free from ingenious whimsies. Yet I admit that he has no fixed theory, and that his peculiar notions will easily give way to his interest. But is it a recommendation to have *no theory?* Can that man be a systematic or able statesman who has none? I believe not. *No general principles* will hardly work much better than erroneous ones.

---

*It is always very dangerous to look at the *vices* of men for *good.*

† Yet he has lately, by a trick, established a *bank*—a perfect monster in its principles, but a very convenient instrument of *profit* and *influence.*

As to the third point, it is certain that Burr, generally speaking, has been as warm a partisan of France as Jefferson; that he has, in some instances, shown himself to be so with passion. But if it was from calculation, who will say that his calculations will not continue him so? His selfishness,* so far from being an obstacle, may be a prompter. If corrupt as well as selfish, he may be a partisan for gain. If ambitious as well as selfish, he may be a partisan for the sake of aid to his views. No man has trafficked more than he in the floating passions of the multitude. Hatred to Great Britain and attachment to France, in the public mind, will naturally lead a man of his selfishness, attached to place and power, to favor France and oppose Great Britain. The Gallicism of many of our patriots is to be thus resolved, and, in my opinion, it is morally certain that Burr will continue to be influenced by this calculation.

As to the fourth point, the instance I have cited with respect to banks, proves that the argument is not to be relied on. If there was much in it, why does Chancellor Livingston maintain that we ought not to cultivate navigation, but ought to let foreigners be our carriers? France is of the opinion too, and Burr, for some reason or other, will be very apt to be of the opinion of France.

As to the fifth point, nothing can be more fallacious. It is demonstrated by recent facts† that Burr is *solicitous* to *keep* upon *anti-federal* ground, to avoid compromitting himself by any engagements‡ with the Federalists. With or without such engagements, he will easily persuade his former friends that he does stand on that ground, and after their first resentment they will be glad to rally under him. In the meantime he will take care not to disoblige them, and he will always court those among them who are best fitted for tools. He will never choose to lean on good men, because he knows that they will never support his bad projects; but instead of this he will endeavor to disorganize both parties, and to form out of them a third,

---

* Unprincipled selfishness is more apt to seek rapid gain in disorderly practices than slow advantages from orderly systems.
† My letter to Mr. Morris states some of them.
‡ He trusts to their *prejudices* and *hopes* for support.

composed of men fitted by their characters to be conspirators and instruments of such projects.

That this will be his future conduct may be inferred from his past plan, and from the admitted quality of irregular ambition. Let it be remembered that Mr. Burr has ever appeared solicitous for fame, and that great ambition, unchecked by principle or the love of glory, is an unruly tyrant, which never can keep long in a course which good men will approve. As to the last point, the proposition is against the experience of all times. Ambition without principle never was long under the guidance of good sense. Besides that, really, the force of Mr. Burr's understanding is much overrated. He is far more *cunning* than *wise*, far more *dexterous* than *able*.

[*Very, very confidential.*—In my opinion he is inferior in real ability to Jefferson. There are also facts against the supposition. It is past all doubt that he has blamed me for not having improved the situation I once was in to change the government. That when answered that this could not have been done without guilt, he replied, "Les grandes âmes se soucient peu des petits moraux"; that when told the thing was never practicable from the genius and situation of the country, he answered, "That depends on the estimate we form of the human passions, and of the means of influencing them." Does this prove that Mr. Burr would consider a scheme of usurpation as visionary?] [49]

The truth is, with great apparent coldness he is the most sanguine man in the world. He thinks every thing possible to adventure and perseverance, and, though I believe he will fail, I think it almost certain he will attempt usurpation, and the attempt will involve great mischief. But there is one point of view which seems to me decisive. If the Anti-federalists who prevailed in the election are left to take their own man, they remain responsible, and the Federalists remain *free*, *united*, and without *stain*, in a situation to resist, with effect, pernicious measures. If the Federalists substitute Burr, they adopt him and become answerable for him. Whatever may be the theory of the case abroad and at *home* (for so from the beginning will be taught), Mr. Burr will become *in fact* the man of our party;

and if he acts ill, we must share in the blame and disgrace. By adopting him we do all we can to reconcile the minds of the Federalists to him, and we prepare them for the effectual operation of his arts. He will doubtless gain many of them, and the Federalists will become a disorganized and contemptible party. Can there be any serious question between the policy of leaving the Anti-federalists to be answerable for the elevation of an exceptionable man, and that of adopting ourselves and becoming answerable for a man who, on all hands, is acknowledged to be a complete Catiline?[50] 'T is enough to state the question to indicate the answer, if reason, not passion, presides in the decision.

You may communicate this, and my former letter, to discreet and confidential friends.

45. TO BENJAMIN RUSH

[ACKNOWLEDGING CONDOLENCE]

NEW YORK, February 12, 1802.

DEAR SIR:

I felt all the weight of the obligation which I owed to you and your amiable family for the tender concern they manifested in an event beyond comparison the most afflicting of my life, but I was obliged to wait for a moment of greater calm to express my sense of the kindness.

My loss is indeed great.[51] The brightest as well as the eldest hope of my family has been taken from me. You estimated him rightly. He was a fine youth. But why should I repine? It was the will of heaven, and he is now out of the reach of the seductions and calamities of a world full of folly, full of vice, full of danger—of least value in proportion as it is best known. I firmly trust, also, that he has safely reached the haven of eternal repose and felicity.

You will easily imagine that every memorial of the goodness of his heart must be precious to me. You allude to one recorded in a letter to your son. If no special reasons forbid it, I should be very glad to have a copy of that letter.

Mrs. Hamilton, who has drunk deeply of the cup of sorrow, joins me in affectionate thanks to Mrs. Rush and yourself; our wishes for your happiness will be unceasing.

46. TO GOUVERNEUR MORRIS

[AN ODD DESTINY]

NEW YORK, February 27, 1802.

MY DEAR SIR:

Your letter of the 22d is the third favor I am indebted to you since you left New York.

Your frankness in giving me your opinion as to the expediency of an application of our bar to Congress, obliged me.[52] But you know we are not readily persuaded to think we have been wrong. Were the matter to be done over, I should pursue the same course. I did not believe the measure would be useful as a preventive, and for the people an expression of an opinion by letter would be as good as a memorial.

It appeared to be best, because it saved our delicacy, and because in the abstract, I am not over fond of the precedent of the bar addressing Congress. But I did what I thought likely to do more good. I *induced* the Chamber of Commerce to send a memorial. As to the rest, I should be a very unhappy man, if I left my tranquillity at the mercy of the misinterpretations which friends as well as foes are fond of giving to my conduct.

Mine is an odd destiny. Perhaps no man in the United States has sacrificed or done more for the present Constitution than myself; and contrary to all my anticipations of its fate, as you know from the very beginning, I am still laboring to prop the frail and worthless fabric. Yet I have the murmurs of its friends no less than the curses of its foes for my reward. What can I do better than withdraw from the scene? Every day proves to me more and more, that this American world was not made for me.

The suggestions with which you close your letter suppose a much sounder state of the public mind than at present exists. Attempts to make a show of a general *popular* dislike of the pending measures of the government, would only serve to manifest the direct reverse. Impressions are indeed making, but as yet within a very narrow sphere.

The time may erelong arrive when the minds of men will be prepared to make an effort to *recover* the Constitution, but the many cannot now be brought to make a stand for its preservation. We must wait a while.

I have read your speeches with great pleasure. They are truly worthy of you. Your real friends had many sources of satisfaction on account of them. The conspiracy of dulness was at work. It chose to misinterpret your moderation in certain transactions of a personal reference.

A public energetic display of your talents and principles was requisite to silence the cavillers. It is now done. You, friend Morris, are by *birth* a native of this country, but by *genius* an exotic. You mistake, if you fancy that you are more of a favorite than myself, or that you are in any sort upon a theatre suited to you.

47. TO CHARLES COTESWORTH PINCKNEY

[OPPOSITION IN RETIREMENT]

GRANGE (New York), December 29, 1802.

MY DEAR SIR:

A garden, you know, is a very useful refuge of a disappointed politician.[53] Accordingly, I have purchased a few acres about nine miles from town, have built a house, and am cultivating a garden. The *melons* in your country are very fine. Will you have the goodness to send me some seed, both of the water and musk melons? My daughter adds another request, which is for three or four of your paroquets. She is very fond of birds. If there be anything in this quarter the sending of which can give you pleasure, you have only to name them. As *farmers*, a new source of sympathy has arisen between us, and I am pleased with everything in which our likings and tastes can be approximated. Amidst the triumphant reign of democracy, do you retain sufficient interest in public affairs to feel any curiosity about what is going on? In my opinion, the follies and vices of the administration have as yet made no material impression to their disadvantage. On the contrary, I think the malady is rather progressive than upon the decline in our Northern quarter. The last *lullaby* message, instead of inspiring contempt, attracts praise.[54] Mankind are forever destined to be the dupes of bold or cunning imposture. But a difficult knot has been twisted by the incidents of the cession of Louisiana, and the interruption of the deposit of New Orleans. You have seen the soft turn given to this in the message. Yet we are told that the President, in conversation, is very stout. The great embarrassment must be how to carry on the war without taxes. The pretty scheme of substituting economy to taxation will not do here. And a war would be a terrible comment upon the abandonment of the internal revenue. Yet how is popularity to be preserved with the Western partisans if their interests are tamely sacrificed? Will the artifice be for the chief to hold a bold language, and the subalterns to act a feeble part? Time must explain. You know my general theory as to our Western affairs. I have always held that the *unity of our empire* and the best interests of our nation require that we shall annex to the United States all the territory east of the Mississippi, New Orleans included. Of course I infer that, in an emergency like the present, energy is wisdom.

Mrs. Hamilton joins me in affectionate compliments to Mrs. Pinckney.

48. TO TIMOTHY PICKERING

[ATTITUDE IN THE CONSTITUTIONAL CONVENTION]

NEW YORK, September 18, 1803.

MY DEAR SIR:

I will make no apology for my delay in answering your inquiry, some time since made, because I could offer none which would satisfy myself. I pray you only to believe that it proceeded from any thing rather than want of respect or regard. I shall now comply with your request. The highest-toned propositions which I made in the Convention were for a President, Senate, and Judges during good behavior—a House of Representatives for three years. Though I would have enlarged the legislative power of the general government, yet I never contemplated the abolition of the State governments, but on the contrary, they were, in some particulars, constituent parts of my plan. This plan was, in my conception, conformable with the strict theory of a government purely republican, the essential criteria of which are that the principal organs of the executive and legislative departments be elected by the people, and hold their offices by a *responsible* and temporary or *defeasible* tenure. A vote was taken on the proposition respecting the executive. Five States were in favor of it, among these Virginia, and though, from the manner of voting—by delegations,—individuals were not distinguished, it was morally certain, from the known situation of the Virginia members (six in number, two of them *Mason* and *Randolph*, professing popular doctrines), that *Madison* must have concurred in the vote of Virginia; thus, if I sinned against *republicanism*, Mr. Madison was not less guilty. I may truly then say that I never proposed either a President or Senate for life, and that I neither recommended nor meditated the annihilation of the State governments. And I may add that, in the course of the discussions in the convention, neither the propositions thrown out for debate, nor even those voted in the earlier stages of the deliberation, were considered as evidences of a definitive opinion in the proposer or voter. It appeared to me to be in some sort understood that, with a view to free investigation, experimental propositions might be made, which were to be received merely as suggestions for consideration. Accordingly, it is a fact that my final opinion was against an Executive during good behavior, on account of the increased danger to the public tranquillity incident to the election of a magistrate of this degree of permanency. In the plan of a constitution which I drew up while the convention was sitting, and which I communicated to Mr.

Madison about the close of it, perhaps a day or two after, the office of President has no greater duration than for three years. This plan was predicated upon these bases: 1. That the political principles of the people of this country would endure nothing but republican government. 2. That in the actual situation of the country, it was in itself right and proper that the republican theory should have a fair and full trial. 3. That to such a trial it was essential that the government should be so constructed as to give all the energy and stability reconcilable with the principles of that theory.[55]

These were the genuine sentiments of my heart, and upon them I acted. I sincerely hope that it may not hereafter be discovered that, through want of sufficient attention to the last idea, the experiment of republican government, even in this country, has not been as complete, as satisfactory, and as decisive as could be wished.

49. PERICLES

[FAVORING SEIZURE OF LOUISIANA]

1803.

Since the question of independence, none has occurred more deeply interesting to the United States than the cession of Louisiana to France.

This event threatens the early dismemberment of a large portion of the country; more immediately, the safety of all the Southern States; and remotely, the independence of the whole Union. This is the portentous aspect which the affair presents to all men of sound and reflecting minds, of whatever party; and it is not to be concealed, that the only question which now offers itself, is how the evil is to be averted?

The strict right to resort at once to war, if it should be deemed expedient, cannot be doubted. A manifest and great danger to the nation; the nature of the cession to France, extending to ancient limits without respect to our rights by treaty; the direct infraction of an important article of the treaty itself, in withholding the deposit of New Orleans: either of these affords justifiable cause of war, and that they would authorize immediate hostilities is not to be questioned by the most scrupulous mind.

The whole is then a question of expediency. Two courses only present: First, to negotiate and endeavor to purchase; and if this fails, to go to war. Secondly, to seize at once on the Floridas and New Orleans, and then negotiate. A strong objection offers itself to the first. There is not the most distant probability that the ambitious and aggrandizing views of Buonaparte will commute the territory for money. Its acquisition is of immense importance to France, and has long been an object of her extreme solicitude. The attempt, therefore, to purchase, in the first instance, will certainly fail; and in the end, war must be resorted to, under all the accumulation of difficulties caused by a previous and strongly fortified possession of the country by our adversary.

The second plan is, therefore, evidently the best. First, because effectual; the acquisition easy; the preservation afterwards easy. The evils of a war with France at this time are certainly not very formidable: her fleet crippled and powerless; her treasury empty; her resources almost dried up; in short, gasping for breath after a tremendous conflict, which, though it left her victorious, left her nearly exhausted under her extraordinary exertions. On the other hand, we might count with certainty on the aid of Great Britain with her powerful navy.

Secondly, this plan is preferable, because it affords us the only chance of avoiding a long-continued war. When we have once taken possession the business will present itself to France in a new aspect. She will then have to weigh the immense difficulties, if not the utter impracticability, of wresting it from us. In this posture of affairs she will naturally conclude it is her interest to bargain. Now it may become expedient to terminate hostilities by a purchase, and a cheaper one may reasonably be expected. To secure the better prospect of final success, the following auxiliary measures ought to be adopted. The army should be increased to ten thousand men, for the purpose of insuring the preservation of the conquest. Preparations for increasing our naval force should be made. The militia should be classed, and effectual provision made for raising, on an emergency, forty thousand men. Negotiations should be pushed with Great Britain, to induce her to hold herself in readiness to co-operate fully with us, at a moment's warning. This plan should be adopted and proclaimed before the departure of our envoy. Such measures would astonish and disconcert Buonaparte himself; our envoy would be enabled to speak and treat with effect, and all Europe would be taught to respect us. These ideas have been long entertained by the writer, but he has never given himself the trouble to commit them to the public, because he despaired of their being adopted. They are now thrown out with very little hope of their producing any change in the conduct of the Administration, yet with the encouragement that there is a strong current of public feeling in favor of decisive measures. If the President would adopt this course, he might yet retrieve his character, induce the best part of the community to look favorably upon his political career, exalt himself in the eyes of Europe, save the country, and secure a permanent fame. But, for this, alas! Jefferson is not destined.

PERICLES.

50. TO THEODORE SEDGWICK[56]

[AGAINST DIVISION AND DEMOCRACY]

NEW YORK, July 10, 1804.

MY DEAR SIR:

I have received two letters from you since we last saw each other, that of the latest date being the 24th of May. I have had on hand for some time a long letter to you, explaining my view of the course and tendency of our politics, and my intentions as to my own future conduct. But my plan embraced so large a range that, owing to much avocation, some indifferent health, and a growing distaste to politics, the letter is still considerably short of being finished. I write this now to satisfy you that want of regard for you has not been the cause of my silence.

I will here express but one sentiment, which is, that dismemberment of our empire will be a clear sacrifice of great positive advantages without any counterbalancing good, administering no relief to our real disease, which is *democracy*, the poison of which, by a subdivision, will only be the more concentrated in each part, and consequently the more virulent. King is on his way for Boston, where you may chance to see him, and hear from himself his sentiments. God bless you.

*

Selections from
THOMAS   JEFFERSON

*

*Pen drawing by Kerr Eby, after
the bust by Jean Houdon, 1789*

THOMAS JEFFERSON

ÆT. 45

THOMAS JEFFERSON

I. TO ROBERT SKIPWITH

[ADVICE AS TO READING]

MONTICELLO, August 3, 1771.

I sat down with a design of executing your request to form a catalogue of books to the amount of about 50 lib. sterling. But could by no means satisfy myself with any partial choice I could make. Thinking, therefore, it might be as agreeable to you, I have framed such a general collection as I think you would wish and might in time find convenient to procure. Out of this you will choose for yourself to the amount you mentioned for the present year and may hereafter as shall be convenient proceed in completing the whole. A view of the second column in this catalogue would I suppose extort a smile from the face of gravity. Peace to its wisdom! Let me not awaken it. A little attention however to the nature of the human mind evinces that the entertainments of fiction are useful as well as pleasant. That they are pleasant when well written every person feels who reads. But wherein is its utility asks the reverend sage, big with the notion that nothing can be useful but the learned lumber of Greek and Roman reading with which his head is stored?

I answer, everything is useful which contributes to fix in the principles and practices of virtue. When any original act of charity or of gratitude, for instance, is presented either to our sight or imagination, we are deeply impressed with its beauty and feel a strong desire in ourselves of doing charitable and grateful acts also. On the contrary when we see or read of any atrocious deed, we are disgusted with its deformity, and conceive an abhorrence of vice. Now every emotion of this kind is an exercise of our virtuous dispositions, and dispositions of the mind, like limbs of the body acquire strength by exercise.[57]

But exercise produces habit, and in the instance of which we speak the exercise being of the moral feelings produces a habit of thinking and acting virtuously. We never reflect whether the story we read be truth or fiction. If the painting be lively, and a tolerable picture of nature, we are thrown into a reverie, from which if we awaken it is the fault of the writer. I appeal to every reader of feeling and sentiment whether the fictitious murder of Duncan by Macbeth in Shakespeare does not excite in him as great a horror of villany, as the real one of Henry IV by Ravaillac as related by Davila?[58] And whether the fidelity of Nelson and generosity of Blandford in Marmontel do not dilate his breast and elevate his sentiments as much as any similar incident which real history can furnish? Does he not in fact feel himself a better man while reading them, and privately covenant to copy the fair example? We neither know nor care whether Lawrence Sterne really went to France, whether he was there accosted by the Franciscan, at first rebuked him unkindly, and then gave him a peace offering; or whether the whole be not fiction. In either case we equally are sorrowful at the rebuke, and secretly resolve *we* will never do so; we are pleased with the subsequent atonement, and view with emulation a soul candidly acknowledging its fault and making a just reparation. Considering history as a moral exercise, her lessons would be too infrequent if confined to real life. Of those recorded by historians few incidents have been attended with such circumstances as to excite in any high degree this sympathetic emotion of virtue. We are, therefore, wisely framed to be as warmly interested for a fictitious as for a real personage. The field of imagination is thus laid open to our use and lessons may be formed to illustrate and carry home to the heart every moral rule of life. Thus a lively and lasting sense of filial duty is more effectually impressed on the mind of a son or daughter by reading King Lear, than by all the dry volumes of ethics and divinity that ever were written. This is my idea of well written Romance, of Tragedy, Comedy, and Epic poetry.—If you are fond of speculation the books under the head of Criticism will afford you much pleasure. Of Politics and Trade I have given you a few only of the best books, as you would probably choose to be not unacquainted with those commercial principles which bring wealth into our country, and the constitutional security we have for the enjoyment of that wealth. In Law I mention a few systematical books, as a knowledge of the minutiæ of that science is not necessary for a private gentleman. In Religion, History, Natural philosophy, I have followed the same plan in general.—But whence the necessity of this collection? Come to the new Rowanty, from which you may reach your hand to a library formed on a more extensive plan. Separated from each other but a few paces the possessions of each would be open to the other. A spring centrically situated might be the scene of every evening's joy. There we should talk over the lessons of the day, or lose them in music, chess, or the merriments of our family companions. The heart thus lightened, our pillows would be soft, and health and long life would attend the happy scene. Come then and bring our dear Tibby with you, the first in your affections, and second in mine. Offer prayers for me, too, at that shrine to which though absent I pray continual devotions. In every scheme of happiness she is placed in the foreground of the picture, as the principal figure. Take that away, and it is no picture for me. Bear my affections to Wintipock clothed in the warmest expressions of sincerity; and to yourself be every human felicity. Adieu.

2. *From* A SUMMARY VIEW OF THE RIGHTS OF BRITISH AMERICA [59]

[GRIEVANCES OF AMERICA]

Resolved, That it be an instruction to the said deputies, when assembled in General Congress, with the deputies from the other states of British America, to propose to the said Congress, that an humble and dutiful address be presented to his Majesty, begging leave to lay before him, as Chief Magistrate of the British empire, the united complaints of his Majesty's subjects in America; complaints which are excited by many unwarrantable encroachments and usurpations, attempted to be made by the legislature of one part of the empire, upon those rights which God, and the laws, have given equally and independently to all. To represent to his Majesty that these, his States, have often individually made humble application to his imperial Throne, to obtain, through its intervention, some redress of their injured rights; to none of which, was ever even an answer condescended. Humbly to hope that this, their joint address, penned in the language of truth, and divested of those expressions of servility, which would persuade his Majesty that we are asking favors, and not rights, shall obtain from his Majesty a more respectful acceptance; and this his Majesty will think we have reason to expect, when he reflects that he is no more than the chief officer of the people, appointed by the laws, and circumscribed with definite powers, to assist in working the great machine of government, erected for their use, and, consequently, subject to their superintendence; and, in order that these, our rights, as well as the invasions of them, may be laid more fully before his Majesty, to take a view of them, from the origin and first settlement of these countries.

To remind him that our ancestors, before their emigration to America, were the free inhabitants of the British dominions in Europe, and possessed a right, which nature has given to all men, of departing from the country in which chance, not choice, has placed them, of going in quest of new habitations, and of there establishing new societies, under such laws and regulations as, to them, shall seem most likely to promote public happiness.[60] That their Saxon ancestors had, under this universal law, in like manner, left their native wilds and woods in the North of Europe, had possessed themselves of the Island of Britain, then less charged with inhabitants, and had established there that system of laws which has so long been the glory and protection of that country. Nor was ever any claim of superiority or dependence asserted over them, by that mother country from which they had migrated: and were such a claim made, it is believed that his Majesty's subjects in Great Britain have too firm a feeling of the rights derived to them from their ancestors, to bow down the sovereignty of their state before such visionary pretensions. And it is thought that no circumstance has occurred to distinguish, materially, the British from the Saxon emigration. America was conquered, and her settlements made and firmly established, at the expense of individuals, and not of the British public. Their own blood was spilt in acquiring lands for their settlement, their own fortunes expended in making that settlement effectual. For themselves they fought, for themselves they conquered, and for themselves alone they have right to hold. Not a shilling was ever issued from the public treasures of his Majesty, or his ancestors, for their assistance, till of very late times, after the colonies had become established on a firm and permanent footing. That then, indeed, having become valuable to Great Britain for her commercial purposes, his Parliament was pleased to lend them assistance against an enemy who would fain have drawn to herself the benefits of their commerce, to the great aggrandizement of herself, and danger of Great Britain. Such assistance, and in such circumstances, they had often before given to Portugal and other allied states, with whom they carry on a commercial intercourse. Yet these states never supposed, that by calling in her aid, they thereby submitted themselves to her sovereignty. Had such terms been proposed, they would have rejected them with disdain, and trusted for better, to the moderation of their enemies, or to a vigorous exertion of their own force. We do not, however, mean to underrate those aids, which, to us, were doubtless valuable, on whatever principles granted: but we would shew that they cannot give a title to that authority which the British Parliament would arrogate over us; and that may amply be repaid by our giving to the inhabitants of Great Britain such exclusive privileges in trade as may be advantageous to them, and, at the same time, not too restrictive to ourselves. That settlements having been thus effected in the wilds of America, the emigrants thought proper to adopt that system of laws, under which they had hitherto lived in the mother country, and to continue their union with her, by submitting themselves to the same common sovereign, who was thereby made the central link, connecting the several parts of the empire thus newly multiplied. . . .[61]

That, by "an act to discontinue in such manner, and for such time as are therein mentioned, the landing and discharging, lading or shipping of goods, wares and merchandize, at the town and within the harbor of Boston, in the province of Massachusetts Bay, in North America,"* which was passed at the last session of the British Parliament, a large and populous town, whose trade was their sole subsistence, was deprived of that trade, and involved in utter ruin. Let us for a while suppose the question of right suspended, in order to examine this act on principles of justice. An act of Parliament had been passed, imposing duties on teas, to be paid in America, against which act the Americans had protested, as inauthoritative. The East India Company, who till that time, had never sent a pound of tea to America, on their own account, step forth on that occasion the asserters of Parliamentary right, and send hither many ship-loads of that obnoxious commodity. The masters of their several vessels, however, on their arrival in America, wisely attended to admonition, and returned with their cargoes. In the province of New England alone the remonstrances of the people were disregarded, and a compliance, after being many days waited for, was flatly refused. Whether in this, the master of the vessel was governed by his obstinacy, or his instructions, let those who know, say. There are extraordinary situations which require extraordinary interposition. An exasperated people, who feel that they possess power, are not easily restrained within limits strictly regular. A number of them assembled in the town of Boston, threw the tea into the ocean, and dispersed without doing any other act of violence. If in this they did wrong, they were known, and were amenable to the laws of the land; against which, it could not be objected, that they had ever, in any instance, been obstructed or diverted from their regular course, in favor of popular offenders. They should, therefore, not have been distrusted on this occasion. But that ill-fated colony had formerly been bold in their enmi-

*14. G. 3.

ties against the House of Stuart, and were now devoted to ruin, by that unseen hand which governs the momentous affairs of this great empire. On the partial representations of a few worthless ministerial dependants, whose constant office it has been to keep that government embroiled, and who, by their treacheries, hope to obtain the dignity of the British knighthood, without calling for a party accused, without asking a proof, without attempting a distinction between the guilty and the innocent, the whole of that ancient and wealthy town is in a moment reduced from opulence to beggary. Men who had spent their lives in extending the British commerce, who had invested, in that place, the wealth their honest endeavors had merited, found themselves and their families thrown at once on the world, for subsistence by its charities. Not the hundredth part of the inhabitants of that town had been concerned in the act complained of; many of them were in Great Britain, and in other parts beyond sea; yet all were involved in one indiscriminate ruin, by a new executive power, unheard of till then, that of a British Parliament. A property of the value of many millions of money, was sacrificed to revenge, not repay, the loss of a few thousands. This is administering justice with a heavy hand indeed! And when is this tempest to be arrested in its course? Two wharves are to be opened again when his Majesty shall think proper: the residue, which lined the extensive shores of the bay of Boston, are forever interdicted the exercise of commerce. This little exception seems to have been thrown in for no other purpose, than that of setting a precedent for investing his Majesty with legislative powers. If the pulse of his people shall beat calmly under this experiment, another and another will be tried, till the measure of despotism be filled up. It would be an insult on common sense, to pretend that this exception was made in order to restore its commerce to that great town. The trade, which cannot be received at two wharves alone, must of necessity be transferred to some other place; to which it will soon be followed by that of the two wharves. Considered in this light, it would be an insolent and cruel mockery at the annihilation of the town of Boston. By the act for the suppression of riots and tumults in the town of Boston,* passed also in the last session of Parliament, a murder committed there is, if the Governor pleases, to be tried in the court of King's Bench, in the island of Great Britain, by a jury of Middlesex. The witnesses, too, on receipt of such a sum as the Governor shall think it reasonable for them to expend, are to enter into recognizance to appear at the trial. This is, in other words, taxing them to the amount of their recognizance; and that amount may be whatever a Governor pleases. For who does his Majesty think can be prevailed on to cross the Atlantic for the sole purpose of bearing evidence to a fact? His expenses are to be borne, indeed, as they shall be estimated by a Governor; but who are to feed the wife and children whom he leaves behind, and who have had no other subsistence but his daily labor? Those epidemical disorders, too, so terrible in a foreign climate, is the cure of them to be estimated among the articles of expense, and their danger to be warded off by the almighty power of a Parliament? And the wretched criminal, if he happen to have offended on the American side, stripped of his privilege of trial by peers of his vicinage, removed from the place where alone full evidence could be obtained, without money, without counsel, without friends, without exculpatory proof, is tried before Judges predetermined to condemn. The cowards who would suffer a countryman to be torn from the bowels of their society, in order to be thus offered a sacrifice to Parliamentary tyranny, would merit that everlasting infamy now fixed on the authors of the act! . . .

That we shall, at this time also, take notice of an error in the nature of our land holdings, which crept in at a very early period of our settlement. The introduction of the feudal tenures into the kingdom of England, though ancient, is well enough understood to set this matter in a proper light. In the earlier ages of the Saxon settlement, feudal holdings were certainly altogether unknown, and very few, if any, had been introduced at the time of the Norman conquest. Our Saxon ancestors held their lands, as they did their personal property, in absolute dominion, dis-

*14. G. 3.

incumbered with any superior, answering nearly to the nature of those possessions which the feudalists term allodial. William the Norman first introduced that system generally. The lands which had belonged to those who fell in the battle of Hastings, and in the subsequent insurrections of his reign, formed a considerable proportion of the lands of the whole kingdom. These he granted out, subject to feudal duties, as did he also those of a great number of his new subjects, who, by persuasions or threats, were induced to surrender them for that purpose. But still, much was left in the hands of his Saxon subjects, held of no superior, and not subject to feudal conditions. These, therefore, by express laws, enacted to render uniform the system of military defence, were made liable to the same military duties as if they had been feuds; and the Norman lawyers soon found means to saddle them, also, with the other feudal burdens. But still they had not been surrendered to the King, they were not derived from his grant, and therefore they were not holden of him. A general principle, indeed, was introduced, that "all lands in England were held either mediately or immediately of the Crown"; but this was borrowed from those holdings which were truly feudal, and only applied to others for the purposes of illustration. Feudal holdings were, therefore, but exceptions out of the Saxon laws of possession, under which all lands were held in absolute right. These, therefore, still form the basis or groundwork of the common law, to prevail wheresoever the exceptions have not taken place. America was not conquered by William the Norman, nor its lands surrendered to him or any of his successors. Possessions there are, undoubtedly, of the allodial nature. Our ancestors, however, who migrated hither, were laborers, not lawyers. The fictitious principle, that all lands belong originally to the King, they were early persuaded to believe real, and accordingly took grants of their own lands from the Crown. And while the Crown continued to grant for small sums and on reasonable rents, there was no inducement to arrest the error, and lay it open to public view. But his Majesty has lately taken on him to advance the terms of purchase and of holding to the double of what they were; by which means, the acquisition of lands being rendered difficult, the population of our country is likely to be checked. It is time, therefore, for us to lay this matter before his Majesty, and to declare that he has no right to grant lands of himself. From the nature and purpose of civil institutions, all the lands within the limits, which any particular society has circumscribed around itself, are assumed by that society, and subject to their allotment only; this may be done by themselves assembled collectively, or by their legislature, to whom they may have delegated sovereign authority; and, if they are allotted in neither of these ways, each individual of the society may appropriate to himself such lands as he finds vacant, and occupancy will give him title. . . .

That these are our grievances, which we have thus laid before his Majesty, with that freedom of language and sentiment which becomes a free people claiming their rights as derived from the laws of nature, and not as the gift of their Chief Magistrate. Let those flatter, who fear: it is not an American art. To give praise which is not due might be well from the venal, but would ill beseem those who are asserting the rights of human nature. They know, and will, therefore, say, that Kings are the servants, not the proprietors of the people. Open your breast, Sire, to liberal and expanded thought. Let not the name of George the Third be a blot on the page of history. You are surrounded by British counsellors, but remember that they are parties. You have no ministers for American affairs, because you have none taken from among us, nor amenable to the laws on which they are to give you advice. It behooves you, therefore, to think and to act for yourself and your people. The great principles of right and wrong are legible to every reader; to pursue them, requires not the aid of many counsellors. The whole art of government consists in the art of being honest. Only aim to do your duty, and mankind will give you credit where you fail. No longer persevere in sacrificing the rights of one part of the empire to the inordinate desires of another; but deal out to all equal and impartial right. Let no act be passed by any one legislature, which may infringe on the rights and liberties of another.

This is the important post in which fortune has placed you, holding the balance of a great, if a well-poised empire. This, Sire, is the advice of your great American council, on the observance of which may perhaps depend your felicity and future fame, and the preservation of that harmony which alone can continue, both to Great Britain and America, the reciprocal advantages of their connection. It is neither our wish nor our interest to separate from her. We are willing, on our part, to sacrifice everything which reason can ask, to the restoration of that tranquillity for which all must wish. On their part, let them be ready to establish union on a generous plan. Let them name their terms, but let them be just. Accept of every commercial preference it is in our power to give, for such things as we can raise for their use, or they make for ours. But let them not think to exclude us from going to other markets to dispose of those commodities which they cannot use, or to supply those wants which they cannot supply. Still less, let it be proposed that our properties, within our own territories, shall be taxed or regulated by any power on earth, but our own. The God who gave us life, gave us liberty at the same time; the hand of force may destroy, but cannot disjoin them. This, Sire, is our last, our determined resolution. And that you will be pleased to interpose, with that efficacy which your earnest endeavors may insure, to procure redress of these our great grievances, to quiet the minds of your subjects in British America against any apprehensions of future encroachment, to establish fraternal love and harmony through the whole empire, and that these may continue to the latest ages of time, is the fervent prayer of all British America!

3. TO JOHN RANDOLPH, ESQ. [62]

[JUSTICE AND RECONCILIATION]

MONTICELLO, August 25, 1775.

DEAR SIR:

I am sorry the situation of our country should render it not eligible to you to remain longer in it. I hope the returning wisdom of Great Britain will, ere long, put an end to this unnatural contest. There may be people to whose tempers and dispositions contention is pleasing, and who, therefore, wish a continuance of confusion, but to me it is of all states but one, the most horrid. My first wish is a restoration of our just rights; my second, a return of the happy period, when, consistently with duty, I may withdraw myself totally from the public stage, and pass the rest of my days in domestic ease and tranquillity, banishing every desire of ever hearing what passes in the world. Perhaps (for the latter adds considerably to the warmth of the former wish), looking with fondness towards a reconciliation with Great Britain, I cannot help hoping you may be able to contribute towards expediting this good work. I think it must be evident to yourself, that the Ministry have been deceived by their officers on this side of the water, who (for what purpose I cannot tell) have constantly represented the American opposition as that of a small faction, in which the body of the people took little part. This, you can inform them, of your own knowledge is untrue. They have taken it into their heads, too, that we are cowards, and shall surrender at discretion to an armed force. The past and future operations of the war must confirm or undeceive them on that head. I wish they were thoroughly and minutely acquainted with every circumstance relative to America, as it exists in truth. I am persuaded, this would go far towards disposing them to reconciliation. Even those in Parliament who are called friends to America, seem to know nothing of our real determinations. I observe, they pronounced in the last Parliament, that the Congress of 1774 did not mean to insist rigorously on the terms they held out, but kept something in reserve, to give up; and, in fact, that they would give up everything but the article of taxation. Now, the truth is far from this, as I can affirm, and put my honor to the assertion. Their continuance in this error may, perhaps, produce very ill consequences. The Congress stated the lowest terms they thought possible to be accepted, in order to convince the world they were not unreasonable. They gave up the monopoly and regulation of trade, and all acts of Parliament prior to 1764, leaving to British generosity to render these, at some future time, as easy to America as the interest of Britain would admit. But this was before blood was spilt. I cannot affirm, but have reason to think, these terms would not now be accepted. I wish no false sense of honor, no ignorance of our real intentions, no vain hope that partial concessions of right will be accepted, may induce the Ministry to trifle with accommodation, till it shall be out of their power ever to accommodate. If, indeed, Great Britain, disjoined from her colonies, be a match for the most potent nations of Europe, with the colonies thrown into their scale, they may go on securely. But if they are not assured of this, it would be certainly unwise, by trying the event of another campaign, to risk our accepting a foreign aid, which, perhaps, may not be obtainable, but on condition of everlasting avulsion from Great Britain. This would be thought a hard condition, to those who still wish for re-union with their parent country. I am sincerely one of those, and would rather be in dependence on Great Britain, properly limited, than on any other nation on earth, or than on no nation. But I am one of those, too, who, rather than submit to the rights of legislating for us, assumed by the British Parliament, and which late experience has shown they will so cruelly exercise, would lend my hand to sink the whole Island in the ocean.

If undeceiving the Minister, as to matters of fact, may change his disposition, it will, perhaps, be in your power, by assisting to do this, to render service to the whole empire, at the most critical time, certainly, that it has ever seen. Whether Britain shall continue the head of the greatest empire on earth, or shall return to her original station in the political scale of Europe, depends, perhaps, on the resolutions of the succeeding winter. God send they may be wise and salutary for us all. I shall be glad to hear from you as often as you may be disposed to think of things here. You may be at liberty, I expect, to communicate some things, consistently with your honor, and the duties you will owe to a protecting nation. Such a communication among individuals, may be mutually beneficial to the contending parties. On this or any future occasion, if I affirm to you any facts, your knowledge of me will enable you to decide on their credibility; if I hazard opinions on the dispositions of men or other speculative points, you can only know they are my opinions. My best wishes for your felicity, attend you, wherever you go, and believe me to be assuredly,

Your friend and servant.

4. *From* AUTOBIOGRAPHY [63]

[INDEPENDENCE AND REFORM]

. . . It appearing in the course of these debates,[64] that the colonies of New York, New Jersey, Pennsylvania, Delaware, Maryland, and South Carolina were not yet matured for falling from the parent stem, but that they were fast advancing to that state, it was thought most prudent to wait a while for them, and to postpone the final decision to July 1st; but, that this might occasion as little delay as possible, a committee was appointed to prepare a Declaration of Independence. The committee were John Adams, Dr. Franklin, Roger Sherman, Robert R. Livingston, and myself. Committees were also appointed, at the same time, to prepare a plan of confederation for the colonies, and to state the terms proper to be proposed for foreign alliance. The committee for drawing the Declaration of Independence desired me to do it. It was accordingly done, and being approved by them, I reported it to the House on Friday, the 28th of June, when it was read, and ordered to lie on the table. On Monday, the 1st of July, the House resolved itself into a committee of the whole, and resumed the consideration of the original motion made by the delegates of Virginia, which, being again debated through the day, was carried in the affirmative by the votes of New Hampshire, Connecticut, Massachusetts, Rhode Island, New Jersey, Maryland, Virginia, North Carolina, and Georgia. South Carolina and Pennsylvania voted against it. Delaware had but two members present, and they were divided. The delegates from New York declared they were for it themselves, and were assured their constituents were for it; but that their instructions having been drawn near a twelve-month before, when reconciliation was still the general object, they were enjoined by them to do nothing which should impede that object. They, therefore, thought themselves not justifiable in voting on either side, and asked leave to withdraw from the question; which was given them. The committee rose and reported their resolution to the House. Mr. Edward Rutledge, of South Carolina, then requested the determination might be put off to the next day, as he believed his colleagues, though they disapproved of the resolution, would then join in it for the sake of unanimity. The ultimate question, whether the House would agree to the resolution of the committee, was accordingly postponed to the next day, when it was again moved, and South Carolina concurred in voting for it. In the meantime, a third member had come post from the Delaware counties, and turned the vote of that colony in favor of the resolution. Members of a different sentiment attending that morning from Pennsylvania also, her vote was changed, so that the whole twelve colonies, who were authorized to vote at all, gave their voices for it; and, within a few days,* the convention of New York approved of it, and thus supplied the void occasioned by the withdrawing of her delegates from the vote.

Congress proceeded the same day to consider the Declaration of Independence, which had been reported and lain on the table the Friday preceding, and on Monday referred to a committee of the whole. The pusillanimous idea that we had friends in England worth keeping terms with, still haunted the minds of many. For this reason, those passages which conveyed censures on the people of England were struck out, lest they should give them offence. The clause too, reprobating the enslaving the inhabitants of Africa, was struck out in complaisance to South Carolina and Georgia, who had never attempted to restrain the importation of slaves, and who, on the contrary, still wished to continue it. Our northern brethren also, I believe, felt a little tender under those censures; for though their people have very few slaves themselves, yet they had been pretty con-

*July 9.

siderable carriers of them to others. The debates, having taken up the greater parts of the 2d, 3d, and 4th days of July, were, on the evening of the last, closed; the Declaration was reported by the Committee, agreed to by the House, and signed by every member present, except Mr. Dickinson. As the sentiments of men are known not only by what they receive, but what they reject also, I will state the form of the Declaration as originally reported. The parts struck out by Congress shall be distinguished by a black line drawn under them;* and those inserted by them shall be placed in the margin, or in a concurrent column.

A DECLARATION BY THE REPRESENTATIVES OF THE UNITED STATES
OF AMERICA, IN GENERAL CONGRESS ASSEMBLED.[65]

When, in the course of human events, it becomes necessary for one people to dissolve the political bands which have connected them with another, and to assume among the powers of the earth the separate and equal station to which the laws of nature and of nature's God entitle them, a decent respect to the opinions of mankind requires that they should declare the causes which impel them to the separation.

We hold these truths to be self-evident: that all men are created equal; that they are endowed by their creator with [*inherent and*] inalienable rights;   certain that among these are life, liberty, and the pursuit of happiness:[66] that to secure these rights, governments are instituted among men, deriving their just powers from the consent of the governed; that whenever any form of government becomes destructive of these ends, it is the right of the people to alter or to abolish it, and to institute new government, laying its foundation on such principles, and organizing its powers in such form, as to them shall seem most likely to effect their safety and happiness. Prudence, indeed, will dictate that govern-

*The parts struck out are here printed in *Italics* and inclosed in brackets.

ments long established should not be changed for light and transient causes; and accordingly all experience hath shown that mankind are more disposed to suffer while evils are sufferable, than to right themselves by abolishing the forms to which they are accustomed. But when a long train of abuses and usurpations, [*begun at a distinguished period and*] pursuing invariably the same object, evinces a design to reduce them under absolute despotism, it is their right, it is their duty to throw off such government, and to provide new guards for their future security. Such has been the patient sufferance of these colonies; and such is now the necessity which constrains them to [*expunge*] their former   alter systems of government. The history of the present king of Great Britain is a history of [*unremitting*]   repeated injuries and usurpations, [*among which appears no*   all having *solitary fact to contradict the uniform tenor of the rest, but all have*] in direct object the establishment of an absolute tyranny over these states. To prove this, let facts be submitted to a candid world [*for the truth of which we pledge a faith yet unsullied by falsehood*].

He has refused his assent to laws the most wholesome and necessary for the public good.

He has forbidden his governors to pass laws of immediate and pressing importance, unless suspended in their operation till his assent should be obtained; and, when so suspended, he has utterly neglected to attend to them.

He has refused to pass other laws for the accommodation of large districts of people, unless those people would relinquish the right of representation in the legislature, a right inestimable to them, and formidable to tyrants only.

He has called together legislative bodies at places unusual, uncomfortable, and distant from the depository of their public records, for the sole purpose of fatiguing them into compliance with his measures.

He has dissolved representative houses repeatedly [*and continually*] for opposing with manly firmness his invasions on the rights of the people.

He has refused for a long time after such dissolutions to cause others to be elected, whereby the legislative powers, incapable of annihilation, have returned to the people at large for their exercise, the state remaining, in the meantime, exposed to all the dangers of invasion from without and convulsions within.

He has endeavored to prevent the population of these states; for that purpose obstructing the laws for naturalization of foreigners, refusing to pass others to encourage their migrations hither, and raising the conditions of new appropriations of lands.

He has [*suffered*] the administration of justice obstructed [*totally to cease in some of these states*] refusing his by assent to laws for establishing judiciary powers.

He has made [*our*] judges dependent on his will alone for the tenure of their offices, and the amount and payment of their salaries.

He has erected a multitude of new offices, [*by a self-assumed power*] and sent hither swarms of new officers to harass our people and eat out their substance.

He has kept among us in times of peace standing armies [*and ships of war*] without the consent of our legislatures.

He has affected to render the military independent of, and superior to, the civil power.

He has combined with others to subject us to a jurisdiction foreign to our constitutions and unacknowledged by our laws, giving his assent to their acts of pretended legislation for quartering large bodies of armed troops among us; for protecting them by a mock trial from punishment for any murders which they should commit on the inhabitants of these states; for cutting off our trade with all parts of the world; for imposing taxes on us without our consent; for depriving us [ ] of the benefits of trial by jury; for transporting us beyond seas to be tried for pretended offences; for abolishing the free system of English laws in a neighboring province, establishing therein an arbitrary government, and enlarging its boundaries, so as to render it at once an example and fit instrument for introducing the same absolute rule into these [*states*]; for taking away our charters, abolishing our most valuable laws, and altering fundamentally the forms of our governments; for suspending our own legislatures, and declaring themselves invested with power to legislate for us in all cases whatsoever. in many cases colonies

He has abdicated government here [*withdrawing his governors, and declaring us out of his allegiance and protection*]. by declaring us out of his protection, and waging war against us.

He has plundered our seas, ravaged our coasts, burnt our towns, and destroyed the lives of our people.

He is at this time transporting large armies of foreign mercenaries to complete the works of death, desolation, and tyranny already begun with circumstances of cruelty and perfidy [ ] unworthy the head of a civilized nation. scarcely paralleled in the most barbarous ages, and totally

He has constrained our fellow citizens taken captive on the high seas to bear arms against their country, to become the executioners of their friends and brethren, or to fall themselves by their hands.

He has [ ] endeavored to bring on the inhabitants of our frontiers, the merciless Indian savages, whose known rule of warfare is an undistinguished destruction of all ages, sexes, and conditions [*of existence*].

excited domestic insurrection among us, and has

[*He has incited treasonable insurrections of our fellow citizens, with the allurements of forfeiture and confiscation of our property.*

He has waged cruel war against human nature itself, violating its most sacred rights of life and liberty in the persons of a distant people who never offended him, captivating and carrying them into slavery in another hemisphere, or to incur miserable death in their transportation thither. This piratical warfare, the opprobrium of INFIDEL *powers, is the warfare of the* CHRISTIAN *king of Great Britain. Determined to keep open a market where* MEN *should be bought and sold, he has prostituted his negative for suppressing every legislative attempt to prohibit or to restrain this execrable commerce. And that this assemblage of horrors might want no fact of distinguished die, he is now exciting those very people to rise in arms among us, and to purchase that liberty of which he has deprived them, by murdering the people on whom he also obtruded them: thus paying off former crimes committed against the* LIBERTIES *of one people, with crimes which he urges them to commit against the* LIVES *of another.*]

In every stage of these oppressions we have petitioned for redress in the most humble terms: our repeated petitions have been answered only by repeated injuries.

A prince whose character is thus marked by every act which may define a tyrant is unfit to be the ruler of a [ ] people [*who mean to be free.* *Future ages will scarcely believe that the hardiness of one man adventured, within the short compass of*

free

*twelve years only, to lay a foundation so broad and
so undisguised for tyranny over a people fostered and
fixed in principles of freedom*].

Nor have we been wanting in attentions to our
British brethren. We have warned them from time
to time of attempts by their legislature to extend [*a*]
jurisdiction over [*these our states*]. We have re-
minded them of the circumstances of our emigration and settlement here, [*no one of which could
warrant so strange a pretension: that these were
effected at the expense of our own blood and treasure,
unassisted by the wealth or the strength of Great
Britain: that in constituting indeed our several forms
of government, we had adopted one common king,
thereby laying a foundation for perpetual league and
amity with them: but that submission to their parliament was no part of our constitution, nor ever in idea,
if history may be credited: and,*] we [ ] appealed
to their native justice and magnanimity [*as well as
to*] the ties of our common kindred to disavow these
usurpations which [*were likely to*] interrupt our
connection and correspondence. They too have
been deaf to the voice of justice and of consanguinity, [*and when occasions have been given them,
by the regular course of their laws, of removing from
their councils the disturbers of our harmony, they have,
by their free election, re-established them in power. At
this very time too, they are permitting their chief
magistrate to send over not only soldiers of our common blood but Scotch and foreign mercenaries to
invade and destroy us. These facts have given the
last stab to agonizing affection, and manly spirit bids
us to renounce forever these unfeeling brethren. We
must endeavor to forget our former love for them, and
hold them as we hold the rest of mankind, enemies in
war, in peace friends. We might have been a free and
a great people together; but a communication of*

an
unwarrantable
us

have
and we have
conjured
them by
would
inevitably

grandeur and of freedom, it seems, is below their dignity. Be it so, since they will have it. The road to happiness and to glory is open to us, too. We will tread it apart from them, and] acquiesce in the necessity which denounces our [*eternal*] separation [ ]!

We must therefore

and hold them as we hold the rest of mankind, enemies in war, in peace friends.

We, therefore, the representatives of the United States of America in General Congress assembled, do in the name, and by the authority of the good people of these [*states reject and renounce all allegiance and subjection to the kings of Great Britain and all others who may hereafter claim by, through, or under them; we utterly dissolve all political connection which may heretofore have subsisted between us and the people or parliament of Great Britain; and finally we do assert and declare these colonies to be free and independent states,*] and that as free and independent states, they have full power to levy war, conclude peace, contract alliances, establish commerce, and to do all other acts and things which independent states may of right do.

We, therefore, the representatives of the United States of America in General Congress assembled, appealing to the supreme judge of the world for the rectitude of our intentions, do in the name, and by the authority of the good people of these colonies, solemnly publish and declare, that these united colonies are, and of right ought to be free and independent states; that they are absolved from all allegiance to the British crown, and that all political connection between them and the state of Great Britain is, and ought to be, totally dissolved; and that as free and independent states, they have full power to levy war, conclude peace, contract alliances, establish commerce, and to do all other acts and things which independent states may of right do.

And for the support of this declaration, we mutually pledge to each other our lives, our fortunes, and our sacred honor.

And for the support of this declaration, with a firm reliance on the protection of divine providence, we mutually pledge to each other our lives, our fortunes, and our sacred honor.

The Declaration thus signed on the 4th, on paper, was engrossed on parchment, and signed again on the 2d of August. . . . [67]

Our delegation had been renewed for the ensuing year, commencing August 11;[68] but the new government was now organized, a meeting of the legislature was to be held in October, and I had been elected a member by my county. I knew that our legislation, under the regal government, had many very vicious points which urgently required reformation, and I thought I could be of more use in forwarding that work. I therefore retired from my seat in Congress on the 2d of September, resigned it, and took my place in the legislature of my State, on the 7th of October.

On the 11th, I moved for leave to bring in a bill for the establishment of courts of justice, the organization of which was of importance. I drew the bill; it was approved by the committee, reported, and passed, after going through its due course.

On the 12th, I obtained leave to bring in a bill declaring tenants in tail to hold their lands in fee simple. In the earlier times of the colony, when lands were to be obtained for little or nothing, some provident individuals procured large grants; and, desirous of founding great families for themselves, settled them on their descendants in fee tail. The transmission of this property from generation to generation, in the same name, raised up a distinct set of families, who, being privileged by law in the perpetuation of their wealth, were thus formed into a patrician order, distinguished by the splendor and luxury of their establishments. From this order, too, the king habitually

selected his counsellors of state; the hope of which distinction
devoted the whole corps to the interests and will of the crown.
To annul this privilege, and instead of an aristocracy of wealth,
of more harm and danger, than benefit, to society, to make an
opening for the aristocracy of virtue and talent, which nature
has wisely provided for the direction of the interests of society,
and scattered with equal hand through all its conditions, was
deemed essential to a well-ordered republic. To effect it no
violence was necessary, no deprivation of natural right, but
rather an enlargement of it by a repeal of the law. For this
would authorize the present holder to divide the property
among his children equally, as his affections were divided; and
would place them, by natural generation, on the level of their
fellow citizens. But this repeal was strongly opposed by Mr.
Pendleton, who was zealously attached to ancient establishments; and who, taken all in all, was the ablest man in debate I
have ever met with. He had not indeed the poetical fancy of
Mr. Henry, his sublime imagination, his lofty and overwhelm-
ing diction; but he was cool, smooth, and persuasive; his language flowing, chaste, and embellished; his conceptions quick,
acute, and full of resource; never vanquished; for if he lost the
main battle, he returned upon you, and regained so much of it
as to make it a drawn one, by dexterous manœuvres, skirmishes
in detail, and the recovery of small advantages which, little
singly, were important all together. You never knew when you
were clear of him, but were harassed by his perseverance, until
the patience was worn down of all who had less of it than himself. Add to this, that he was one of the most virtuous and
benevolent of men, the kindest friend, the most amiable and
pleasant of companions, which ensured a favorable reception
to whatever came from him. Finding that the general principle
of entails could not be maintained, he took his stand on an
amendment which he proposed, instead of an absolute abolition,
to permit the tenant in tail to convey in fee simple, if he chose
it; and he was within a few votes of saving so much of the old
law. But the bill passed finally for entire abolition.

In that one of the bills for organizing our judiciary system, which proposed a court of Chancery, I had provided for a trial by jury of all matters of fact, in that as well as in the courts of law. He defeated it by the introduction of four words only, "*if either party choose.*" The consequence has been, that as no suitor will say to his judge, "Sir, I distrust you, give me a jury," juries are rarely, I might say, perhaps, never, seen in that court, but when called for by the Chancellor of his own accord.

The first establishment in Virginia which became permanent was made in 1607. I have found no mention of negroes in the colony until about 1650. The first brought here as slaves were by a Dutch ship; after which the English commenced the trade, and continued it until the revolutionary war. That suspended, *ipso facto*, their further importation for the present, and the business of the war pressing constantly on the legislature, this subject was not acted on finally until the year '78, when I brought in a bill to prevent their further importation.[69] This passed without opposition, and stopped the increase of the evil by importation, leaving to future efforts its final eradication.

The first settlers of this colony were Englishmen, loyal subjects to their king and church, and the grant to Sir Walter Raleigh contained an express proviso that their laws "should not be against the true Christian faith, now professed in the church of England." As soon as the state of the colony admitted, it was divided into parishes, in each of which was established a minister of the Anglican church, endowed with a fixed salary, in tobacco, a glebe house and land, with the other necessary appendages. To meet these expenses, all the inhabitants of the parishes were assessed, whether they were or not, members of the established church. Towards Quakers who came here, they were most cruelly intolerant, driving them from the colony by the severest penalties. In process of time, however, other sectarisms were introduced, chiefly of the Presbyterian family; and the established clergy, secure for life in their glebes and salaries, adding to these, generally, the emoluments of a classical school, found employment enough, in their farms and schoolrooms, for the rest of the week, and devoted Sunday only to the edification of their flock, by service, and a sermon at their

parish church. Their other pastoral functions were little attended to. Against this inactivity, the zeal and industry of sectarian preachers had an open and undisputed field; and by the
time of the revolution, a majority of the inhabitants had become dissenters from the established church, but were still
obliged to pay contributions to support the pastors of the
minority. This unrighteous compulsion, to maintain teachers
of what they deemed religious errors, was grievously felt during the regal government, and without a hope of relief. But the
first republican legislature, which met in '76, was crowded with
petitions to abolish this spiritual tyranny. These brought on
the severest contests in which I have ever been engaged. Our
great opponents were Mr. Pendleton and Robert Carter
Nicholas; honest men, but zealous churchmen. The petitions
were referred to the committee of the whole house on the state
of the country; and, after desperate contests in that committee,
almost daily from the 11th of October to the 5th of December,
we prevailed so far only, as to repeal the laws which rendered
criminal the maintenance of any religious opinions, the forbearance of repairing to church, or the exercise of any mode of
worship; and further, to exempt dissenters from contributions
to the support of the established church; and to suspend, only
until the next session, levies on the members of that church for
the salaries of their own incumbents. For although the majority
of our citizens were dissenters, as has been observed, a majority
of the legislature were churchmen. Among these, however, were
some reasonable and liberal men, who enabled us, on some
points, to obtain feeble majorities. But our opponents carried,
in the general resolutions of the committee of November 19,
a declaration that religious assemblies ought to be regulated,
and that provision ought to be made for continuing the succession of the clergy, and superintending their conduct. And, in the
bill now passed, was inserted an express reservation of the question, Whether a general assessment should not be established by
law, on every one, to the support of the pastor of his choice; or
whether all should be left to voluntary contributions; and on this
question, debated at every session, from '76 to '79, (some of our

dissenting allies, having now secured their particular object, going over to the advocates of a general assessment,) we could only obtain a suspension from session to session until '79, when the question against a general assessment was finally carried, and the establishment of the Anglican church entirely put down.[70] In justice to the two honest but zealous opponents who have been named, I must add, that although, from their natural temperaments, they were more disposed generally to acquiesce in things as they are, than to risk innovations, yet whenever the public will had once decided, none were more faithful or exact in their obedience to it.

The seat of our government had been originally fixed in the peninsula of Jamestown, the first settlement of the colonists; and had been afterwards removed a few miles inland to Williamsburg. But this was at a time when our settlements had not extended beyond the tide water. Now they had crossed the Alleghany; and the centre of population was very far removed from what it had been. Yet Williamsburg was still the depository of our archives, the habitual residence of the Governor and many other of the public functionaries, the established place for the sessions of the legislature, and the magazine of our military stores; and its situation was so exposed that it might be taken at any time in war, and, at this time particularly, an enemy might in the night run up either of the rivers between which it lies, land a force above, and take possession of the place, without the possibility of saving either persons or things. I had proposed its removal so early as October, '76; but it did not prevail until the session of May, '79.

Early in the session of May, '79, I prepared, and obtained leave to bring in a bill, declaring who should be deemed citizens, asserting the natural right of expatriation, and prescribing the mode of exercising it. This, when I withdrew from the House, on the 1st of June following, I left in the hands of George Mason, and it was passed on the 26th of that month. . . .

Mr. Madison came into the House in 1776, a new member and young; which circumstances, concurring with his extreme modesty, prevented his venturing himself in debate before his removal to the Council of State, in November, '77. From thence he went to Congress, then consisting of few members. Trained in these successive schools, he acquired a habit of self-possession, which placed at ready command the rich resources of his luminous and discriminating mind, and of his extensive information, and rendered him the first of every assembly afterwards, of which he became a member. Never wandering from his subject into vain declamation, but pursuing it closely, in language pure, classical, and copious, soothing always the feelings of his adversaries by civilities and softness of expression, he rose to the eminent station which he held in the great National Convention of 1787; and in that of Virginia which followed, he sustained the new constitution in all its parts, bearing off the palm against the logic of George Mason, and the fervid declamation of Mr. Henry. With these consummate powers, were united a pure and spotless virtue, which no calumny has ever attempted to sully. Of the powers and polish of his pen, and of the wisdom of his administration in the highest office of the nation, I need say nothing. They have spoken, and will forever speak for themselves. . . .

The acts of Assembly concerning the College of William and Mary, were properly within Mr. Pendleton's portion of our work; but these related chiefly to its revenue, while its constitution, organization, and scope of science were derived from its charter. We thought that on this subject, a systematical plan of general education should be proposed, and I was requested to undertake it.[71] I accordingly prepared three bills for the Revisal, proposing three distinct grades of education, reaching all classes. 1st. Elementary schools, for all children generally, rich and poor. 2d. Colleges, for a middle degree of instruction, calculated for the common purposes of life, and such as would be desirable for all who were in easy circumstances. And, 3d, an ultimate grade for teaching the sciences generally, and in their highest degree. The first bill proposed to lay off every county into Hundreds, or Wards, of a proper size and population for a school, in which reading, writing, and common arithmetic should be taught; and that the whole State should be divided into twenty-four districts, in each of which should be a school for classical learning, grammar, geography, and the higher branches of numerical arithmetic. The second bill proposed to amend the constitution of William and Mary College, to enlarge its sphere of science, and to make it in fact an University. The third was for the establishment of a library. These bills were not acted on until the same year, '96, and then only so much of the first as provided for elementary schools. The College of William and Mary was an establishment purely of the Church of England; the Visitors were required to be all of that Church; the Professors to subscribe its thirty-nine Articles; its Students to learn its Catechism; and one of its fundamental objects was declared to be, to raise up ministers for that church. The religious jealousies, therefore, of all the dissenters took alarm lest this might give an ascendancy to the Anglican sect, and refused acting on that bill. Its local eccentricity, too, and unhealthy autumnal climate lessened the general inclination towards it. And in the Elementary bill, they inserted a provision which completely defeated it; for they left it to the court of each county to determine for itself, when this act should be carried into execution, within their county. One provision of the bill was that the expenses of these schools should be borne by the inhabitants of the county, every one in proportion to his general tax rate. This would throw on wealth the education of the poor; and the justices, being generally of the more wealthy class, were unwilling to incur that burden, and I believe it was not suffered to commence in a single county. I shall recur again to this subject, towards the close of my story, if I should have life and resolution enough to reach that term; for I am already tired of talking about myself.

The bill on the subject of slaves was a mere digest of the existing laws respecting them, without any intimation of a plan for a future and general emancipation. It was thought better that this should be kept back, and attempted only by way of amendment, whenever the bill should be brought on. The principles of the amendment, however, were agreed on, that is to say, the freedom of all born after a certain day, and deportation at a proper age. But it was found that the public mind would not yet bear the proposition, nor will it bear it even at this day. Yet the day is not distant when it must bear and adopt it, or worse will follow. Nothing is more certainly written in the book of fate, than that these people are to be free; nor is it less certain that the two races, equally free, cannot live in the same government. Nature, habit, opinion have drawn indelible lines of distinction between them. It is still in our power to direct the process of emancipation and deportation peaceably, and in such slow degree, as that the evil will wear off insensibly, and their place be, *pari passu*, filled up by free white laborers. If, on the contrary, it is left to force itself on, human nature must shudder at the prospect held up. We should in vain look for an example in the Spanish deportation or deletion of the Moors. This precedent would fall far short of our case.

I considered four of these bills, passed or reported, as forming a system by which every fibre would be eradicated of ancient or future aristocracy; and a foundation laid for a government truly republican. The repeal of the laws of entail would prevent the accumulation and perpetuation of wealth, in select families, and preserve the soil of the country from being daily more and more absorbed in mortmain. The abolition of primogeniture, and equal partition of inheritances, removed the feudal and unnatural distinctions which made one member of every family rich, and all the rest poor, substituting equal partition, the best of all Agrarian laws. The restoration of the rights of conscience relieved the people from taxation for the support of a religion not theirs; for the establishment was truly of the religion of the rich, the dissenting sects being entirely composed of the less wealthy people; and these, by the bill for a general education, would be qualified to understand their rights, to maintain them, and to exercise with intelligence their parts in self-government; and all this would be effected without the violation of a single natural right of any one individual citizen. To these, too, might be added, as a further security, the introduction of the trial by jury, into the Chancery courts, which have already engulfed, and continue to engulf, so great a proportion of the jurisdiction over our property. . . .

Our body was little numerous, but very contentious.[72] Day after day was wasted on the most unimportant questions. My colleague Mercer was one of those afflicted with the morbid rage of debate, of an ardent mind, prompt imagination, and copious flow of words. He heard with impatience any logic which was not his own. Sitting near me on some occasion of a trifling but wordy debate, he asked how I could sit in silence, hearing so much false reasoning, which a word should refute. I observed to him, that to refute indeed was easy, but to silence impossible; that in measures brought forward by myself, I took the laboring oar, as was incumbent on me; but that in general, I was willing to listen. If every sound argument or objection was used by some one or other of the numerous debaters, it was enough; if not, I thought it sufficient to suggest the omission, without going into a repetition of what had been already said by others; that this was a waste and abuse of the time and patience of the House, which could not be justified. And I believe, that if the members of deliberative bodies were to observe this course generally, they would do in a day, what takes them a week; and it is really more questionable, than may at first be thought, whether Bonaparte's dumb legislature, which said nothing, and did much, may not be preferable to one which talks much, and does nothing. I served with General Washington in the legislature of Virginia, before the revolution, and, during it, with Dr. Franklin in Congress. I never heard either of them speak ten minutes at a time, nor to any but the main point, which was to decide the question. They laid their shoulders to the great points, knowing that the little ones would follow of themselves. If the present Congress errs in too much talking, how can it be otherwise in a body to which the people send one hundred and fifty lawyers, whose trade it is to question everything, yield nothing, and talk by the hour? That one hundred and fifty lawyers should do business together ought not to be expected. . . .

5. TO BENJAMIN FRANKLIN

[CONDITIONS IN VIRGINIA]

VIRGINIA, August 13, 1777.

HONORABLE SIR,—

I forbear to write you news, as the time of Mr. Short's departure being uncertain, it might be old before you receive it, and he can, in person, possess you of all we have. With respect to the State of Virginia in particular, the people seem to have laid aside the monarchical, and taken up the republican government, with as much ease as would have attended their throwing off an old, and putting on a new suit of clothes. Not a single throe has attended this important transformation. A half-dozen aristocratical gentlemen, agonizing under the loss of pre-eminence, have sometimes ventured their sarcasms on our political metamorphosis. They have been thought fitter objects of pity, than of punishment. We are, at present, in the complete and quiet exercise of well-organized government, save only that our courts of justice do not open till the fall. I think nothing can bring the security of our continent and its cause into danger, if we can support the credit of our paper. To do that, I apprehend, one of two steps must be taken. Either to procure free trade by alliance with some naval power able to protect it; or, if we find there is no prospect of that, to shut our ports totally, to all the world, and turn our colonies into manufactories. The former would be most eligible, because most conformable to the habits and wishes of our people. Were the British Court to return to their senses in time to seize the little advantage which still remains within their reach, from this quarter, I judge that, on acknowledging our absolute independence and sovereignty, a commercial treaty beneficial to them, and perhaps even a league of mutual offence and defence, might, not seeing the expense or consequences of such a measure, be approved by our people, if nothing, in the mean time, done on your part, should prevent it. But they will continue to grasp at their desperate sovereignty, till every benefit short of that is forever out of their reach. I wish my domestic situation had rendered it possible for me to join you in the very honorable charge confided to you. Residence in a polite Court, society of literati of the first order, a just cause and an approving God, will add length to a life for which all men pray, and none more than

Your most obedient and humble servant.

6. TO DAVID RITTENHOUSE

[THE GREAT ECLIPSE]

MONTICELLO IN ALBEMARLE, VA., July 19, 1778.

DEAR SIR,—

I sincerely congratulate you on the recovery of Philadelphia, and wish it may be found uninjured by the enemy. How far the interests of literature may have suffered by the injury, or removal of the orrery (as it is miscalled), the public libraries, your papers and implements, are doubts which still excite anxiety. We were much disappointed in Virginia generally, on the day of the great eclipse, which proved to be cloudy. In Williamsburg, where it was total, I understand only the beginning was seen. At this place, which is in lat. 38° 8', and longitude west from Williamsburg, about 1° 45', as is conjectured, eleven digits only were supposed to be covered, as it was not seen at all till the moon had advanced nearly one-third over the sun's disc. Afterwards it was seen at intervals through the whole. The egress particularly was visible. It proved, however, of little use to me, for want of a time-piece that could be depended on; which circumstance, together with the subsequent restoration of Philadelphia to you, has induced me to trouble you with this letter, to remind you of your kind promise of making me an accurate clock; which, being intended for astronomical purposes only, I would have divested of all apparatus for striking, or for any other purpose, which, by increasing its complication, might disturb its accuracy. A companion to it for keeping seconds, and which might be moved easily, would greatly add to its value. The theodolite, for which I spoke to you also, I can now dispense with, having since purchased a most excellent one.

7. TO BENEDICT ARNOLD[73]

[THREATENING RETALIATION]

IN COUNCIL, March 24, 1781.

SIR,—

Some of the citizens of this State taken prisoners when not in arms and enlarged on parole have reported the commanding officer as affirming to them that they should be punished with death if found in arms. This has given occasion to the enclosed resolution of the General Assembly of this State. It suffices to observe at present that by the law of nations, a breach of parole (even where the validity of parole is not questioned) can only be punished by strict confinement.

No usage has permitted the putting to death a prisoner for this cause. I would willingly suppose that no British officer had ever expressed a contrary purpose. It has, however, become my duty to declare that should such a threat be carried into execution, it will be deemed as putting prisoners to death in cold blood, and shall be followed by the execution of so many British prisoners in our possession. I trust, however, that this horrid necessity will not be introduced by you and that you will on the contrary concur with us in endeavoring as far as possible to alleviate the inevitable miseries of war by treating captives as humanity and natural honor requires. The event of this contest will hardly be affected by the fate of a few miserable captives in war.

8. *From* NOTES ON VIRGINIA[74]

QUERY IV

A notice of its Mountains?

For the particular geography of our mountains I must refer to Fry and Jefferson's map of Virginia;[75] and to Evans's analysis of his map of America, for a more philosophical view of them than is to be found in any other work. It is worthy of notice, that our mountains are not solitary and scattered confusedly over the face of the country; but that they commence at about one hundred and fifty miles from the sea-coast, are disposed in ridges, one behind another, running nearly parallel with the sea-coast, though rather approaching it as they advance north-eastwardly. To the south-west, as the tract of country between the sea-coast and the Mississippi becomes narrower, the mountains converge into a single ridge, which, as it approaches the Gulf of Mexico, subsides into plain country, and gives rise to some of the waters of that gulf, and particularly to a river called the Apalachicola, probably from the Apalachies, an Indian nation formerly residing on it. Hence the mountains giving rise to that river, and seen from its various parts, were called the Apalachian mountains, being in fact the end or termination only of the great ridges passing through the continent. European geographers, however, extended the name northwardly as far as the mountains extended; some giving it, after their separation into different ridges, to the Blue Ridge, others to the North Mountain, others to the Alleghany, others to the Laurel Ridge, as may be seen by their different maps. But the fact I believe is, that none of these ridges were ever known by that name to the inhabitants, either native or emigrant, but as they saw them so called in European maps. In the same direction, generally, are the veins of limestone, coal, and other minerals hitherto discovered; and so range the falls of our great rivers. But the courses of the great rivers are at right angles with these. James and Potomac penetrate through all the ridges of mountains eastward of the Alleghany; that is broken by no water course. It is in fact the spine of the country between the Atlantic on one side, and the Mississippi and St. Lawrence on the other. The passage of the Potomac through the Blue Ridge is, perhaps, one of the most stupendous scenes in nature. You stand on a very high point of land. On your right comes up the Shenandoah, having ranged along the foot of the mountain an hundred miles to seek a vent. On your left approaches the Potomac, in quest of a passage also. In the moment of their junction, they rush together against the mountain, rend it asunder, and pass off to the sea. The first glance of this scene hurries our senses into the opinion, that this earth has been created in time, that the mountains were formed first, that the rivers began to flow afterwards, that in this place, particularly, they have been dammed up by the Blue Ridge of mountains, and have formed an ocean which filled the whole valley; that continuing to rise they have at length broken over at this spot, and have torn the mountain down from its summit to its base. The piles of rock on each hand, but particularly on the Shenandoah, the evident marks of their disrupture and avulsion from their beds by the most powerful agents of nature, corroborate the impression. But the distant finishing which nature has given to the picture is of a very different character. It is a true contrast to the foreground. It is as placid and delightful as that is wild and tremendous. For the mountain being cloven asunder, she presents to your eye, through the cleft, a small catch of smooth blue horizon, at an infinite distance in the plain country, inviting you, as it were, from the riot and tumult roaring around, to pass through the breach and participate of the calm below. Here the eye ultimately composes itself; and that way, too, the road happens actually to lead. You cross the Potomac above the junction, pass along its side through the base of the mountain for three miles, its terrible precipices hanging in fragments over you, and within about twenty miles reach Frederic town, and the fine country round that. This scene is worth a voyage across the Atlantic. Yet here, as in the neighborhood of the Natural Bridge, are people who have passed their lives within half a dozen miles, and have never been to survey these monuments of a war between rivers and mountains, which must have shaken the earth itself to its centre.

The height of our mountains has not yet been estimated with any degree of exactness. The Alleghany being the great ridge which divides the waters of the Atlantic from those of the Mississippi, its summit is doubtless more elevated above the ocean than that of any other mountain. But its relative height, compared with the base on which it stands, is not so great as that of some others, the country rising behind the successive ridges like the steps of stairs. The mountains of the Blue Ridge, and of these the Peaks of Otter, are thought to be of a greater height, measured from their base, than any others in our country, and perhaps in North America. From data, which may found a tolerable conjecture, we suppose the highest peak to be about four thousand feet perpendicular, which is not a fifth part of the height of the mountains of South America, nor one-third of the height which would be necessary in our latitude to preserve ice in the open air unmelted through the year. The ridge of mountains next beyond the Blue Ridge, called by us the North mountain, is of the greatest extent; for which reason they were named by the Indians the Endless mountains.

A substance supposed to be pumice, found floating on the Mississippi, has induced a conjecture that there is a volcano on some of its waters; and as these are mostly known to their sources, except the Missouri, our expectations of verifying the conjecture would of course be led to the mountains which divide the waters of the Mexican Gulf from those of the South Sea; but no volcano having ever yet been known at such a distance from the sea, we must rather suppose that this floating substance has been erroneously deemed pumice. . . .

QUERY V

Its Cascades and Caverns?

. . . The Natural Bridge, the most sublime of nature's works, though not comprehended under the present head, must not be pretermitted. It is on the ascent of a hill, which seems to have been cloven through its length by some great convulsion. The fissure, just at the bridge, is, by some admeasurements, two hundred and seventy feet deep, by others only two hundred and five. It is about forty-five feet wide at the bottom and ninety feet at the top; this of course determines the length of the bridge, and its height from the water. Its breadth in the middle is about sixty feet, but more at the ends, and the

thickness of the mass, at the summit of the arch, about forty feet.
A part of this thickness is constituted by a coat of earth, which
gives growth to many large trees. The residue, with the hill on
both sides, is one solid rock of limestone. The arch approaches
the semi-elliptical form; but the larger axis of the ellipse, which
would be the cord of the arch, is many times longer than the
transverse. Though the sides of this bridge are provided in
some parts with a parapet of fixed rocks, yet few men have resolution to walk to them, and look over into the abyss. You involuntarily fall on your hands and feet, creep to the parapet,
and peep over it. Looking down from this height about a
minute gave me a violent head-ache. If the view from the top
be painful and intolerable, that from below is delightful in an
equal extreme. It is impossible for the emotions arising from
the sublime to be felt beyond what they are here; so beautiful
an arch, so elevated, so light, and springing as it were up to
heaven! The rapture of the spectator is really indescribable!
The fissure continuing narrow, deep, and straight, for a considerable distance above and below the bridge, opens a short
but very pleasing view of the North mountain on one side, and
the Blue Ridge on the other, at the distance each of them of
about five miles. This bridge is in the county of Rockbridge,
to which it has given name, and affords a public and commodious passage over a valley which cannot be crossed elsewhere
for a considerable distance. The stream passing under it is
called Cedar creek. It is a water of James river, and sufficient in
the driest seasons to turn a grist-mill, though its fountain is not
more than two miles above. . . .[76]

QUERY VI

*A notice of the mines and other subterraneous riches; its trees,
plants, fruits, etc.?*

. . . Of the Indian of South America I know nothing; for I would
not honor with the appellation of knowledge, what I derive
from the fables published of them. These I believe to be just
as true as the fables of Æsop. This belief is founded on what I

have seen of man, white, red, and black, and what has been
written of him by authors, enlightened themselves, and writing
among an enlightened people. The Indian of North America
being more within our reach, I can speak of him somewhat from
my own knowledge, but more from the information of others
better acquainted with him, and on whose truth and judgment
I can rely. From these sources I am able to say, in contradiction to this representation, that he is neither more defective in
ardor, nor more impotent with his female, than the white
reduced to the same diet and exercise; that he is brave, when an
enterprise depends on bravery; education with him making the
point of honor consist in the destruction of an enemy by strata-
gem, and in the preservation of his own person free from injury; or, perhaps, this is nature, while it is education which
teaches us to honor force more than finesse;* that he will
defend himself against a host of enemies, always choosing to be
killed, rather than to surrender, though it be to the whites,
who he knows will treat him well; that in other situations, also,
he meets death with more deliberation, and endures tortures
with a firmness unknown almost to religious enthusiasm with
us; that he is affectionate to his children, careful of them, and
indulgent in the extreme; that his affections comprehend his
other connections, weakening, as with us, from circle to circle,
as they recede from the centre; that his friendships are strong
and faithful to the uttermost extremity; that his sensibility is
keen, even the warriors weeping most bitterly on the loss of
their children, though in general they endeavor to appear superior to human events; that his vivacity and activity of mind is
equal to ours in the same situation; hence his eagerness for
hunting, and for games of chance. The women are submitted
to unjust drudgery. This I believe is the case with every barbarous people. With such, force is law. The stronger sex
therefore imposes on the weaker. It is civilization alone which
replaces women in the enjoyment of their natural equality.
That first teaches us to subdue the selfish passions, and to

---

* Sol Rodomonte sprezza di venire
  Se non, dove la via meno è sicura.—ARIOSTO, 14, 117.

respect those rights in others which we value in ourselves. Were we in equal barbarism, our females would be equal drudges. The man with them is less strong than with us, but their woman stronger than ours; and both for the same obvious reason; because our man and their woman is habituated to labor, and formed by it. With both races the sex which is indulged with ease is the least athletic. An Indian man is small in the hand and wrist, for the same reason for which a sailor is large and strong in the arms and shoulders, and a porter in the legs and thighs. They raise fewer children than we do. The causes of this are to be found, not in a difference of nature, but of circumstance. The women very frequently attending the men in their parties of war and of hunting, child-bearing becomes extremely inconvenient to them. It is said, therefore, that they have learned the practice of procuring abortion by the use of some vegetable; and that it even extends to prevent conception for a considerable time after. During these parties they are exposed to numerous hazards, to excessive exertions, to the greatest extremities of hunger. Even at their homes the nation depends for food, through a certain part of every year, on the gleanings of the forest; that is, they experience a famine once in every year. With all animals, if the female be illy fed, or not fed at all, her young perish; and if both male and female be reduced to like want, generation becomes less active, less productive. To the obstacles, then, of want and hazard, which nature has opposed to the multiplication of wild animals, for the purpose of restraining their numbers within certain bounds, those of labor and of voluntary abortion are added with the Indian. No wonder, then, if they multiply less than we do. Where food is regularly supplied, a single farm will show more of cattle, than a whole country of forests can of buffaloes. The same Indian women, when married to white traders, who feed them and their children plentifully and regularly, who exempt them from excessive drudgery, who keep them stationary and unexposed to accident, produce and raise as many children as the white women. Instances are known, under these circumstances, of their rearing a dozen children. An inhuman practice once prevailed in this country, of making slaves of the Indians. It is a fact well known with us, that the Indian women so enslaved produced and raised as numerous families as either the whites or blacks among whom they lived. It has been said that Indians have less hair than the whites, except on the head. But this is a fact of which fair proof can scarcely be had. With them it is disgraceful to be hairy on the body. They say it likens them to hogs. They therefore pluck the hair as fast as it appears. But the traders who marry their women, and prevail on them to discontinue this practice, say that nature is the same with them as with the whites. Nor, if the fact be true, is the consequence necessary which has been drawn from it. Negroes have notoriously less hair than the whites; yet they are more ardent. But if cold and moisture be the agents of nature for diminishing the races of animals, how comes she all at once to suspend their operation as to the physical man of the new world, whom the Count acknowledges to be "à peu près de même stature que l'homme de notre monde," and to let loose their influence on his moral faculties?[77] How has this "combination of the elements and other physical causes, so contrary to the enlargement of animal nature in this new world, these obstacles to the development and formation of great germs,"* been arrested and suspended, so as to permit the human body to acquire its just dimensions, and by what inconceivable process has their action been directed on his mind alone? To judge of the truth of this, to form a just estimate of their genius and mental powers, more facts are wanting, and great allowance to be made for those circumstances of their situation which call for a display of particular talents only. This done, we shall probably find that they are formed in mind as well as body, on the same module with the "Homo sapiens Europæus."† The principles of their society forbidding all compulsion, they are to be led to duty and to enterprise by personal influence and persuasion. Hence eloquence in council, bravery and address in war, become the foundations of all consequence with them. To these acquirements all their faculties are directed. Of their bravery and

*XVIII, 146.   †Linn. Syst. Definition of a Man.

address in war we have multiplied proofs, because we have been the subjects on which they were exercised. Of their eminence in oratory we have fewer examples, because it is displayed chiefly in their own councils. Some, however, we have, of very superior lustre. I may challenge the whole orations of Demosthenes and Cicero, and of any more eminent orator, if Europe has furnished any more eminent, to produce a single passage, superior to the speech of Logan, a Mingo chief, to Lord Dunmore, when governor of this State. . . .

QUERY VIII

The number of its inhabitants?

. . . But are there no inconveniences to be thrown into the scale against the advantage expected from a multiplication of numbers by the importation of foreigners? It is for the happiness of those united in society to harmonize as much as possible in matters which they must of necessity transact together. Civil government being the sole object of forming societies, its administration must be conducted by common consent. Every species of government has its specific principles. Ours perhaps are more peculiar than those of any other in the universe. It is a composition of the freest principles of the English constitution, with others derived from natural right and natural reason. To these nothing can be more opposed than the maxims of absolute monarchies. Yet from such we are to expect the greatest number of emigrants. They will bring with them the principles of the governments they leave, imbibed in their early youth; or, if able to throw them off, it will be in exchange for an unbounded licentiousness, passing, as is usual, from one extreme to another. It would be a miracle were they to stop precisely at the point of temperate liberty. These principles, with their language, they will transmit to their children. In proportion to their numbers, they will share with us the legislation. They will infuse into it their spirit, warp and bias its directions, and render it a heterogeneous, incoherent, distracted mass. I may appeal to experience, during the present contest, for a verification of these conjectures. But, if they be not certain in event, are they not possible, are they not probable? Is it not safer to wait with patience twenty-seven years and three months longer, for the attainment of any degree of population desired or expected? May not our government be more homogeneous, more peaceable, more durable? Suppose twenty millions of republican Americans thrown all of a sudden into France, what would be the condition of that kingdom? If it would be more turbulent, less happy, less strong, we may believe that the addition of half a million of foreigners to our present numbers would produce a similar effect here. If they come of themselves they are entitled to all the rights of citizenship; but I doubt the expediency of inviting them by extraordinary encouragements. I mean not that these doubts should be extended to the importation of useful artificers. The policy of that measure depends on very different considerations. Spare no expense in obtaining them. They will after a while go to the plough and the hoe; but, in the mean time, they will teach us something we do not know. It is not so in agriculture. The indifferent state of that among us does not proceed from a want of knowledge merely; it is from our having such quantities of land to waste as we please. In Europe the object is to make the most of their land, labor being abundant; here it is to make the most of our labor, land being abundant. . . .

QUERY XI

A description of the Indians established in that State?

. . . I know of no such thing existing as an Indian monument; for I would not honor with that name arrow points, stone hatchets, stone pipes, and half-shapen images. Of labor on the large scale, I think there is no remain as respectable as would be a common ditch for the draining of lands; unless indeed it would be the barrows, of which many are to be found all over this country. These are of different sizes, some of them constructed of earth, and some of loose stones. That they were repositories of the dead has been obvious to all; but on what particular occasion constructed was a matter of doubt. Some have thought they covered the bones of those who have fallen in battles fought on the spot of interment. Some ascribed them to the custom, said to prevail among the Indians, of collecting, at certain periods, the bones of all their dead, wheresoever deposited at the time of death. Others again supposed them the general sepulchres for towns, conjectured to have been on or near these grounds; and this opinion was supported by the quality of the lands in which they are found, (those constructed of earth being generally in the softest and most fertile meadow-grounds on river sides), and by a tradition, said to be handed down from the aboriginal Indians, that, when they settled in a town, the first person who died was placed erect, and earth put about him, so as to cover and support him; that when another died, a narrow passage was dug to the first, the second reclined against him, and the cover of earth replaced, and so on. There being one of these in my neighborhood, I wished to satisfy myself whether any, and which of these opinions were just. For this purpose I determined to open and examine it thoroughly. It was situated on the low grounds of the Rivanna, about two miles above its principal fork, and opposite to some hills, on which had been an Indian town. It was of a spheroidical form, of about forty feet diameter at the base, and had been of about twelve feet altitude, though now reduced by the plough to seven and a half, having been under cultivation about a dozen years. Before this it was covered with trees of twelve inches diameter, and round the base was an excavation of five feet depth and width, from whence the earth had been taken of which the hillock was formed. I first dug superficially in several parts of it, and came to collections of human bones, at different depths, from six inches to three feet below the surface. These were lying in the utmost confusion, some verticle, some oblique, some horizontal, and directed to every point of the compass, entangled and held together in clusters by the earth. Bones of the most distant parts were found together, as, for instance, the small bones of the foot in the hollow of a scull; many sculls would sometimes be in contact, lying on the face, on the side, on the back, top or bottom, so as, on the whole, to give the idea of bones emptied promiscuously from a bag or a basket, and covered over with earth, without any attention to their order. The bones of which the greatest numbers remained, were sculls, jaw-bones, teeth, the bones of the arms, thighs, legs, feet, and hands. A few ribs remained, some vertebræ of the neck and spine, without their processes, and one instance only of the bone* which serves as a base to the vertebral column. The sculls were so tender, that they generally fell to pieces on being touched. The other bones were stronger. There were some teeth which were judged to be smaller than those of an adult; a scull, which on a slight view, appeared to be that of an infant, but it fell to pieces on being taken out, so as to prevent satisfactory examination; a rib, and a fragment of the under-jaw of a person about half grown; another rib of an infant; and a part of the jaw of a child, which had not cut its teeth. This last furnishing the most decisive proof of the burial of children here, I was particular in my attention to it. It was part of the right half of the under-jaw. The processes, by which it was articulated to the temporal bones, were entire, and the bone itself firm to where it had been broken off, which, as nearly as I could judge, was about the place of the eye-tooth. Its upper edge, wherein would have been the sockets of the teeth, was perfectly smooth. Measuring it with that of an adult, by placing their hinder processes together, its broken end extended to the penultimate grinder of the adult. This bone was white, all the others of a sand color. The bones of infants being soft, they probably decay sooner, which might be the cause so few were found here. I proceeded then to make a perpendicular cut through the body of the barrow, that I might examine its internal structure. This passed about three feet from its centre, was opened to the former surface of the earth, and was wide enough for a man to walk through and examine its sides. At the bottom, that is, on the level of the circumjacent plain, I found bones; above these a few stones, brought from a cliff a quarter of a mile off, and from the river one-eighth of a mile off; then a large interval of earth, then a stratum of bones, and so

* The os sacrum.

on. At one end of the section were four strata of bones plainly distinguishable; at the other, three; the strata in one part not ranging with those in another. The bones nearest the surface were least decayed. No holes were discovered in any of them, as if made with bullets, arrows, or other weapons. I conjectured that in this barrow might have been a thousand skeletons. Every one will readily seize the circumstances above related, which militate against the opinion, that it covered the bones only of persons fallen in battle; and against the tradition also, which would make it the common sepulchre of a town, in which the bodies were placed upright, and touching each other. Appearances certainly indicate that it has derived both origin and growth from the accustomary collection of bones, and deposition of them together; that the first collection had been deposited on the common surface of the earth, a few stones put over it, and then a covering of earth, that the second had been laid on this, had covered more or less of it in proportion to the number of bones, and was then also covered with earth; and so on. The following are the particular circumstances which give it this aspect. 1. The number of bones. 2. Their confused position. 3. Their being in different strata. 4. The strata in one part having no correspondence with those in another. 5. The different states of decay in these strata, which seem to indicate a difference in the time of inhumation. 6. The existence of infant bones among them.

But on whatever occasion they may have been made, they are of considerable notoriety among the Indians; for a party passing, about thirty years ago, through the part of the country where this barrow is, went through the woods directly to it, without any instructions or inquiry, and having staid about it for some time, with expressions which were construed to be those of sorrow, they returned to the high road, which they had left about half a dozen miles to pay this visit, and pursued their journey. There is another barrow much resembling this, in the low grounds of the south branch of Shenandoah, where it is crossed by the road leading from the Rockfish gap to Staunton. Both of these have, within these dozen years, been cleared of their trees and put under cultivation, are much reduced in their height, and spread in width, by the plough, and will probably disappear in time. There is another on a hill in the Blue Ridge of mountains, a few miles north of Wood's gap, which is made up of small stones thrown together. This has been opened and found to contain human bones, as the others do. There are also many others in other parts of the country. . . .[78]

QUERY XIII

The Constitution of the State and its several charters?

. . . In enumerating the defects of the Constitution, it would be wrong to count among them what is only the error of particular persons. In December 1776, our circumstances being much distressed, it was proposed in the house of delegates to create a *dictator*, invested with every power legislative, executive, and judiciary, civil and military, of life and of death, over our persons and over our properties; and in June 1781, again under calamity, the same proposition was repeated, and wanted a few votes only of being passed. One who entered into this contest from a pure love of liberty, and a sense of injured rights, who determined to make every sacrifice, and to meet every danger, for the re-establishment of those rights on a firm basis, who did not mean to expend his blood and substance for the wretched purpose of changing this matter for that, but to place the powers of governing him in a plurality of hands of his own choice, so that the corrupt will of no one man might in future oppress him, must stand confounded and dismayed when he is told, that a considerable portion of that plurality had meditated the surrender of them into a single hand, and, in lieu of a limited monarch, to deliver him over to a despotic one![79] How must he find his efforts and sacrifices abused and baffled, if he may still, by a single vote, be laid prostrate at the feet of one man! In God's name, from whence have they derived this power? Is it from our ancient laws? None such can be produced. Is it from any principle in our new Constitution expressed or implied? Every lineament of that expressed or implied is in full opposition to it. Its fundamental principle is, that the State shall be governed as a commonwealth. It provides a republican organization, proscribes under the name of *prerogative* the exercise of all powers undefined by the laws; places on this basis the whole system of our laws; and by consolidating them together, chooses that they shall be left to stand or fall together, never providing for any circumstances, nor admitting that such could arise, wherein either should be suspended; no, not for a moment. Our ancient laws expressly declare, that those who are but delegates themselves shall not delegate to others powers which require judgment and integrity in their exercise. Or was this proposition moved on a supposed right in the movers, of abandoning their posts in a moment of distress? The same laws forbid the abandonment of that post, even on ordinary occasions; and much more a transfer of their powers into other hands and other forms, without consulting the people. They never admit the idea that these, like sheep or cattle, may be given from hand to hand without an appeal to their own will. Was it from the necessity of the case? Necessities which dissolve a government do not convey its authority to an oligarchy or a monarchy. They throw back, into the hands of the people, the powers they had delegated, and leave them as individuals to shift for themselves. A leader may offer, but not impose himself, nor be imposed on them. Much less can their necks be submitted to his sword, their breath be held at his will or caprice. The necessity which should operate these tremendous effects should at least be palpable and irresistible. Yet in both instances, where it was feared, or pretended with us, it was belied by the event. It was belied, too, by the preceding experience of our sister States, several of whom had grappled through greater difficulties without abandoning their forms of government. When the proposition was first made, Massachusetts had found even the government of committees sufficient to carry them through an invasion. But we at the time of that proposition were under no invasion. When the second was made, there had been added to this example those of Rhode Island, New York, New Jersey, and Pennsylvania, in all of which the republican form had been found equal to the task of carrying them through the severest trials. In this State alone did there exist so little virtue, that fear was to be fixed in the hearts of the people, and to become the motive of their exertions, and the principle of their government? The very thought alone was treason against the people; was treason against mankind in general; as riveting forever the chains which bow down their necks, by giving to their oppressors a proof, which they would have trumpeted through the universe, of the imbecility of republican government, in times of pressing danger, to shield them from harm. Those who assume the right of giving away the reins of government in any case, must be sure that the herd, whom they hand on to the rods and hatchet of the dictator, will lay their necks on the block when he shall nod to them. But if our assemblies supposed such a resignation in the people, I hope they mistook their character. I am of opinion, that the government, instead of being braced and invigorated for greater exertions under their difficulties, would have been thrown back upon the bungling machinery of county committees for administration, till a convention could have been called, and its wheels again set into regular motion. What a cruel moment was this for creating such an embarrassment, for putting to the proof the attachment of our countrymen to republican government! Those who meant well, of the advocates for this measure, (and most of them meant well, for I know them personally, had been their fellow-laborer in the common cause, and had often proved the purity of their principles), had been seduced in their judgment by the example of an ancient republic, whose constitution and circumstances were fundamentally different. They had sought this precedent in the history of Rome, where alone it was to be found, and where at length, too, it had proved fatal. They had taken it from a republic rent by the most bitter factions and tumults, where the government was of a heavy-handed unfeeling aristocracy, over a people ferocious, and rendered desperate by poverty and wretchedness; tumults which could not be allayed under the most trying circumstances, but by the omnipotent hand of a single despot. Their constitution, therefore, allowed a temporary tyrant to be erected, under the name of a dictator; and that temporary tyrant, after a few examples, became perpetual. They misapplied this precedent to a people mild in their dispositions, patient under their trial, united for the public liberty, and affectionate to their leaders. But if from the constitution of the Roman government there resulted to their senate a power of submitting all their rights to the will of one man, does it follow that the assembly of Virginia have the same authority? What clause in our constitution has substituted that of Rome, by way of residuary provision, for all cases not otherwise provided for? Or if they may step *ad libitum* into any other form of government for precedents to rule us by, for what oppression may not a precedent be found in this world of the *bellum omnium in omnia?* Searching for the foundations of this proposition, I can find none which may pretend a color of right or reason, but the defect before developed, that there being no barrier between the legislative, executive, and judiciary departments, the legislature may seize the whole; that having seized it, and possessing a right to fix their own quorum, they may reduce that quorum to one, whom they may call a chairman, speaker, dictator, or by any other name they please. Our situation is indeed perilous, and I hope my countrymen will be sensible of it, and will apply, at a proper season, the proper remedy; which is a convention to fix the constitution, to amend its defects, to bind up the several branches of government by certain laws, which, when they transgress, their acts shall become nullities; to render unnecessary an appeal to the people, or in other words a rebellion, on every infraction of their rights, on the peril that their acquiescence shall be construed into an intention to surrender those rights.

QUERY XIV

The administration of justice and the description of the laws?

. . . Another object of the revisal is to diffuse knowledge more generally through the mass of the people.[80] This bill proposes to lay off every county into small districts of five or six miles square, called hundreds, and in each of them to establish a school for teaching reading, writing, and arithmetic. The tutor to be supported by the hundred, and every person in it entitled to send their children three years gratis, and as much longer as they please, paying for it. These schools to be under a visitor who is annually to choose the boy of best genius in the school, of those whose parents are too poor to give them further education, and to send him forward to one of the grammar schools, of which twenty are proposed to be erected in different parts of the country, for teaching Greek, Latin, geography, and the higher branches of numerical arithmetic. Of the boys thus sent in any one year, trial is to be made at the grammar schools one or two years, and the best genius of the whole selected, and continued six years, and the residue dismissed. By this means twenty of the best geniuses will be raked from the rubbish annually, and be instructed, at the public expense, so far as the grammar schools go. At the end of six years' instruction, one-half are to be discontinued (from among whom the grammar schools will probably be supplied with future masters); and the other half, who are to be chosen for the superiority of their parts and disposition, are to be sent and continued three years in the study of such sciences as they shall choose, at William and Mary College, the plan of which is proposed to be enlarged, as will be hereafter explained, and extended to all the useful sciences. The ultimate result of the whole scheme of education would be the teaching all the children of the State reading, writing, and common arithmetic; turning out ten annually, of superior genius, well taught in Greek, Latin, geography, and the higher branches of arithmetic; turning out ten others annually, of still superior parts, who, to those branches of learning, shall have added such of the sciences as their genius shall have led them to; the furnishing to the wealthier part of the people convenient schools at which their children may be educated at their own expense. The general objects of this law are to provide an education adapted to the years, to the capacity, and the condition of every one, and directed to their freedom and happiness. Specific details were not proper for the law.

These must be the business of the visitors entrusted with its execution. The first stage of this education being the schools of the hundreds, wherein the great mass of the people will receive their instruction, the principal foundations of future order will be laid here. Instead, therefore, of putting the Bible and Testament into the hands of the children at an age when their judgments are not sufficiently matured for religious inquiries, their memories may here be stored with the most useful facts from Grecian, Roman, European and American history. The first elements of morality too may be instilled into their minds; such as, when further developed as their judgments advance in strength, may teach them how to work out their own greatest happiness, by showing them that it does not depend on the condition of life in which chance has placed them, but is always the result of a good conscience, good health, occupation, and freedom in all just pursuits. Those whom either the wealth of their parents or the adoption of the State shall destine to higher degrees of learning, will go on to the grammar schools, which constitute the next stage, there to be instructed in the languages. The learning Greek and Latin, I am told, is going into disuse in Europe. I know not what their manners and occupations may call for; but it would be very ill-judged in us to follow their example in this instance. There is a certain period of life, say from eight to fifteen or sixteen years of age, when the mind like the body is not yet firm enough for laborious and close operations. If applied to such, it falls an early victim to premature exertion; exhibiting, indeed, at first, in these young and tender subjects, the flattering appearance of their being men while they are yet children, but ending in reducing them to be children when they should be men. The memory is then most susceptible and tenacious of impressions; and the learning of languages being chiefly a work of memory, it seems precisely fitted to the powers of this period, which is long enough, too, for acquiring the most useful languages, ancient and modern. I do not pretend that language is science. It is only an instrument for the attainment of science. But that time is not lost which is employed in providing tools for future operation; more especially as in this case the books put into the hands of the youth for this purpose may be such as will at the same time impress their minds with useful facts and good principles. If this period be suffered to pass in idleness, the mind becomes lethargic and impotent, as would the body it inhabits if unexercised during the same time. The sympathy between body and mind during their rise, progress and decline, is too strict and obvious to endanger our being misled while we reason from the one to the other. As soon as they are of sufficient age, it is supposed they will be sent on from the grammar schools to the university, which constitutes our third and last stage, there to study those sciences which may be adapted to their views. By that part of our plan which prescribes the selection of the youths of genius from among the classes of the poor, we hope to avail the State of those talents which nature has sown as liberally among the poor as the rich, but which perish without use, if not sought for and cultivated. But of all the views of this law none is more important, none more legitimate, than that of rendering the people the safe, as they are the ultimate, guardians of their own liberty. For this purpose the reading in the first stage, where *they* will receive their whole education, is proposed, as has been said, to be chiefly historical. History, by apprising them of the past, will enable them to judge of the future; it will avail them of the experience of other times and other nations; it will qualify them as judges of the actions and designs of men; it will enable them to know ambition under every disguise it may assume; and knowing it, to defeat its views. In every government on earth is some trace of human weakness, some germ of corruption and degeneracy, which cunning will discover, and wickedness insensibly open, cultivate, and improve. Every government degenerates when trusted to the rulers of the people alone. The people themselves, therefore, are its only safe depositories. And to render even them safe, their minds must be improved to a certain degree. This indeed is not all that is necessary, though it be essentially necessary. An amendment of our constitution must here come in aid of the public education. The influence over government must be shared among all the people. If every individual which composes their mass participates of the ultimate authority, the government will be safe; because the corrupting the whole mass will exceed any private resources of wealth; and public ones cannot be provided but by levies on the people. In this case every man would have to pay his own price. The government of Great Britain has been corrupted, because but one man in ten has a right to vote for members of parliament. The sellers of the government, therefore, get nine-tenths of their price clear. It has been thought that corruption is restrained by confining the right of suffrage to a few of the wealthier of the people; but it would be more effectually restrained by an extension of that right to such members as would bid defiance to the means of corruption.

Lastly, it is proposed, by a bill in this revisal, to begin a public library and gallery, by laying out a certain sum annually in books, paintings, and statues.

QUERY XV

The Colleges and Public Establishments, the Roads, Buildings, etc.?

... The private buildings are very rarely constructed of stone or brick, much the greatest proportion being of scantling and boards, plastered with lime. It is impossible to devise things more ugly, uncomfortable, and happily more perishable. There are two or three plans, on one of which, according to its size, most of the houses in the State are built. The poorest people build huts of logs, laid horizontally in pens, stopping the interstices with mud. These are warmer in winter, and cooler in summer, than the more expensive constructions of scantling and plank. The wealthy are attentive to the raising of vegetables, but very little so to fruits. The poorer people attend to neither, living principally on milk and animal diet. This is the more inexcusable, as the climate requires indispensably a free use of vegetable food, for health as well as comfort, and is very friendly to the raising of fruits. The only public buildings worthy of mention are the capitol, the palace, the college, and the hospital for lunatics, all of them in Williamsburg, heretofore the seat of our government. The capitol is a light and airy structure, with a portico in front of two orders, the lower of which, being Doric, is tolerably just in its proportions and ornaments, save only that the intercolonations are too large. The upper is Ionic, much too small for that on which it is mounted, its ornaments not proper to the order, nor proportioned within themselves. It is crowned with a pediment, which is too high for its span. Yet, on the whole, it is the most pleasing piece of architecture we have. The palace is not handsome without, but it is spacious and commodious within, is prettily situated, and with the grounds annexed to it, is capable of being made an elegant seat. The college and hospital are rude, misshapen piles, which, but that they have roofs, would be taken for brick-kilns. There are no other public buildings but churches and courthouses, in which no attempts are made at elegance. Indeed, it would not be easy to execute such an attempt, as a workman could scarcely be found here capable of drawing an order. The genius of architecture seems to have shed its maledictions over this land. Buildings are often erected, by individuals, of considerable expense. To give these symmetry and taste would not increase their cost. It would only change the arrangement of the materials, the form and combination of the members. This would often cost less than the burden of barbarous ornaments with which these buildings are sometimes charged. But the first principles of the art are unknown, and there exists scarcely a model among us sufficiently chaste to give an idea of them. Architecture being one of the fine arts, and as such within the department of a professor of the college, according to the new arrangement, perhaps a spark may fall on some young subjects of natural taste, kindle up their genius, and produce a reformation in this elegant and useful art. . . .

QUERY XVII

The different religions received into that state?

. . . The present state of our laws on the subject of religion is this. The convention of May, 1776, in their declaration of rights, declared it to be a truth, and a natural right, that the exercise of religion should be free; but when they proceeded to form on that declaration the ordinance of government, instead of taking up every principle declared in the bill of rights, and guarding it by legislative sanction, they passed over that which asserted our religious rights, leaving them as they found them. The same convention, however, when they met as a member of the general assembly in October, 1776, repealed all *acts of Parliament* which had rendered criminal the maintaining any opinions in matters of religion, the forbearing to repair to church, and the exercising any mode of worship; and suspended the laws giving salaries to the clergy, which suspension was made perpetual in October, 1779. Statutory oppressions in religion being thus wiped away, we remain at present under those only imposed by the common law, or by our own acts of assembly. At the common law, *heresy* was a capital offence, punishable by burning. Its definition was left to the ecclesiastical judges, before whom the conviction was, till the statute of the 1 El. c. 1 circumscribed it, by declaring, that nothing should be deemed heresy, but what had been so determined by authority of the canonical scriptures, or by one of the four first general councils, or by some other council, having for the grounds of their declaration the express and plain words of the scriptures. Heresy, thus circumscribed, being an offence at the common law, our act of assembly of October, 1777, c. 17, gives cognizance of it to the general court, by declaring that the jurisdiction of that court shall be general in all matters at the common law. The execution is by the writ *De hæretico comburendo*. By our own act of assembly of 1705, c. 30, if a person brought up in the Christian religion denies the being of a God, or the Trinity, or asserts there are more gods than one, or denies the Christian religion to be true, or the scriptures to be of divine authority, he is punishable on the first offence by incapacity to hold any office or employment ecclesiastical, civil, or military; on the second by disability to sue, to take any gift or legacy, to be guardian, executor, or administrator, and by three years' imprisonment without bail. A father's right to the custody of his own children being founded in law on his right of guardianship, this being taken away, they may of course be severed from him, and put by the authority of a court into more orthodox hands. This is a summary view of that religious slavery under which a people have been willing to remain, who have lavished their lives and fortunes for the establishment of their civil freedom. The error seems not sufficiently eradicated, that the operations of the mind, as well as the acts of the body, are subject to the coercion of the laws.* But our rulers can have authority over such natural rights, only as we have submitted to them. The rights of conscience we never submitted, we could not submit. We are answerable for them to our God. The legitimate powers of government extend to such acts only as are injurious to others. But it does me no injury for my neighbor to say there are twenty gods, or no god. It neither picks my pocket nor breaks my leg. If it be said, his testimony in a court of justice cannot be relied on, reject it then, and be the stigma on him. Constraint may make him worse by making him a hypocrite, but it will never make him a truer man. It may fix him obstinately in his errors, but will not cure them. Reason and free inquiry are the only effectual agents against error. Give a loose to them, they will support the true religion by bringing every false one to their tribunal, to the test of their investigation. They are the natural enemies of error, and of error only. Had not the Roman government permitted free inquiry, Christianity could never have been introduced. Had not free inquiry been indulged, at the era of the Reformation, the corruptions of Christianity could not have been purged away. If it be restrained now, the present corruptions will be protected, and new ones encouraged. Was the government to prescribe to us our medicine and diet, our bodies would be in such keeping as our souls are now. Thus in France the emetic was once forbidden as a medicine, and the potato as an article of food. Government is just as infallible, too, when it fixes systems in physics. Galileo was sent to the Inquisition for affirming that the earth was a sphere; the government had declared it to be as flat as a trencher, and Galileo was

* Furneaux passim.

obliged to abjure his error. This error, however, at length prevailed, the earth became a globe, and Descartes declared it was whirled round its axis by a vortex. The government in which he lived was wise enough to see that this was no question of civil jurisdiction, or we should all have been involved by authority in vortices. In fact, the vortices have been exploded, and the Newtonian principle of gravitation is now more firmly established, on the basis of reason, than it would be were the government to step in, and to make it an article of necessary faith. Reason and experiment have been indulged, and error has fled before them. It is error alone which needs the support of government. Truth can stand by itself. Subject opinion to coercion: whom will you make your inquisitors? Fallible men; men governed by bad passions, by private as well as public reasons. And why subject it to coercion? To produce uniformity. But is uniformity of opinion desirable? No more than of face and stature. Introduce the bed of Procrustes then, and as there is danger that the large men may beat the small, make us all of a size, by lopping the former and stretching the latter. Difference of opinion is advantageous in religion. The several sects perform the office of a *censor morum* over each other. Is uniformity attainable? Millions of innocent men, women, and children, since the introduction of Christianity, have been burnt, tortured, fined, imprisoned; yet we have not advanced one inch towards uniformity. What has been the effect of coercion? To make one-half the world fools, and the other half hypocrites. To support roguery and error all over the earth. Let us reflect that it is inhabited by a thousand millions of people. That these profess probably a thousand different systems of religion. That ours is but one of that thousand. That if there be but one right, and ours that one, we should wish to see the nine hundred and ninety-nine wandering sects gathered into the fold of truth. But against such a majority we cannot effect this by force. Reason and persuasion are the only practicable instruments. To make way for these, free inquiry must be indulged; and how can we wish others to indulge it while we refuse it ourselves. But every state, says an inquisitor, has established some religion. No two, say I, have established the same. Is this a proof of the infallibility of establishments? Our sister States of Pennsylvania and New York, however, have long subsisted without any establishment at all. The experiment was new and doubtful when they made it. It has answered beyond conception. They flourish infinitely. Religion is well supported; of various kinds, indeed, but all good enough; all sufficient to preserve peace and order; or if a sect arises, whose tenets would subvert morals, good sense has fair play, and reasons and laughs it out of doors, without suffering the State to be troubled with it. They do not hang more malefactors than we do. They are not more disturbed with religious dissensions. On the contrary, their harmony is unparalleled, and can be ascribed to nothing but their unbounded tolerance, because there is no other circumstance in which they differ from every nation on earth. They have made the happy discovery, that the way to silence religious disputes, is to take no notice of them. Let us too give this experiment fair play, and get rid, while we may, of those tyrannical laws. It is true, we are as yet secured against them by the spirit of the times. I doubt whether the people of this country would suffer an execution for heresy, or a three years' imprisonment for not comprehending the mysteries of the Trinity. But is the spirit of the people an infallible, a permanent reliance? Is it government? Is this the kind of protection we receive in return for the rights we give up? Besides, the spirit of the times may alter, will alter. Our rulers will become corrupt, our people careless. A single zealot may commence persecutor, and better men be his victims. It can never be too often repeated, that the time for fixing every essential right on a legal basis is while our rulers are honest, and ourselves united. From the conclusion of this war we shall be going down hill. It will not then be necessary to resort every moment to the people for support. They will be forgotten, therefore, and their rights disregarded. They will forget themselves, but in the sole faculty of making money, and will never think of uniting to effect a due respect for their rights. The shackles, therefore, which shall not be knocked off at the conclusion of this war will remain on us long, will be made heavier and heavier, till our rights shall revive or expire in a convulsion.[81]

QUERY XVIII

The particular customs and manners that may happen to be received in that State?

It is difficult to determine on the standard by which the manners of a nation may be tried, whether *catholic* or *particular*. It is more difficult for a native to bring to that standard the manners of his own nation, familiarized to him by habit. There must doubtless be an unhappy influence on the manners of our people produced by the existence of slavery among us.[82] The whole commerce between master and slave is a perpetual exercise of the most boisterous passions, the most unremitting despotism on the one part, and degrading submissions on the other. Our children see this, and learn to imitate it; for man is an imitative animal. This quality is the germ of all education in him. From his cradle to his grave he is learning to do what he sees others do. If a parent could find no motive either in his philanthropy or his self-love, for restraining the intemperance of passion towards his slave, it should always be a sufficient one that his child is present. But generally it is not sufficient. The parent storms, the child looks on, catches the lineaments of wrath, puts on the same airs in the circle of smaller slaves, gives a loose to the worst of passions, and thus nursed, educated, and daily exercised in tyranny, cannot but be stamped by it with odious peculiarities. The man must be a prodigy who can retain his manners and morals undepraved by such circumstances. And with what execration should the statesman be loaded, who, permitting one-half the citizens thus to trample on the rights of the other, transforms those into despots, and these into enemies, destroys the morals of the one part, and the *amor patriæ* of the other. For if a slave can have a country in this world, it must be any other in preference to that in which he is born to live and labor for another; in which he must lock up the faculties of his nature, contribute as far as depends on his individual endeavors to the evanishment of the human race, or entail his own miserable condition on the endless generations proceeding from him. With the morals of the people, their industry also is destroyed. For in a warm climate, no man will labor for himself who can make another labor for him. This is so true, that of the proprietors of slaves a very small proportion indeed are ever seen to labor. And can the liberties of a nation be thought secure when we have removed their only firm basis, a conviction in the minds of the people that these liberties are of the gift of God? That they are not to be violated but with His wrath? Indeed I tremble for my country when I reflect that God is just; that his justice cannot sleep forever; that considering numbers, nature and natural means only, a revolution of the wheel of fortune, an exchange of situation is among possible events; that it may become probable by supernatural interference! The Almighty has no attribute which can take side with us in such a contest. But it is impossible to be temperate and to pursue this subject through the various considerations of policy, of morals, of history natural and civil. We must be contented to hope they will force their way into every one's mind. I think a change already perceptible, since the origin of the present revolution. The spirit of the master is abating, that of the slave rising from the dust, his condition mollifying, the way I hope preparing, under the auspices of heaven, for a total emancipation, and that this is disposed, in the order of events, to be with the consent of the masters, rather than by their extirpation.

QUERY XXII

The Public Income and Expenses?

. . . To this estimate of our abilities, let me add a word as to the application of them, if, when cleared of the present contest, and of the debts with which that will charge us, we come to measure force hereafter with any European power. Such events are devoutly to be deprecated. Young as we are, and with such a country before us to fill with people and with happiness, we should point in that direction the whole generative force of nature, wasting none of it in efforts of mutual destruction. It should be our endeavor to cultivate the peace and friendship of every nation, even of that which has injured us most, when we shall have carried our point against her. Our interest will be to throw open the doors of commerce, and to knock off all its shackles, giving perfect freedom to all persons for the vent of whatever they may choose to bring into our ports, and asking the same in theirs. Never was so much false arithmetic employed on any subject, as that which has been employed to persuade nations that it is their interest to go to war.[83] Were the money which it has cost to gain, at the close of a long war, a little town, or a little territory, the right to cut wood here, or to catch fish there, expended in improving what they already possess, in making roads, opening rivers, building ports, improving the arts, and finding employment for their idle poor, it would render them much stronger, much wealthier and happier. This I hope will be our wisdom. And, perhaps, to remove as much as possible the occasions of making war, it might be better for us to abandon the ocean altogether,[84] that being the element whereon we shall be principally exposed to jostle with other nations; to leave to others to bring what we shall want, and to carry what we can spare. This would make us invulnerable to Europe, by offering none of our property to their prize, and would turn all our citizens to the cultivation of the earth; and, I repeat it again, cultivators of the earth are the most virtuous and independent citizens. It might be time enough to seek employment for them at sea, when the land no longer offers it. But the actual habits of our countrymen attach them to commerce. They will exercise it for themselves. Wars then must sometimes be our lot; and all the wise can do, will be to avoid that half of them which would be produced by our own follies and our own acts of injustice; and to make for the other half the best preparations we can. Of what nature should these be? A land army would be useless for offence, and not the best nor safest instrument of defence. For either of these purposes, the sea is the field on which we should meet an European enemy. On that element it is necessary we should possess some power.[85]

To aim at such a navy as the greater nations of Europe possess, would be a foolish and wicked waste of the energies of our countrymen. It would be to pull on our own heads that load of military expense which makes the European laborer go supperless to bed, and moistens his bread with the sweat of his brows. It will be enough if we enable ourselves to prevent insults from those nations of Europe which are weak on the sea, because circumstances exist, which render even the stronger ones weak as to us. Providence has placed their richest and most defenceless possessions at our door; has obliged their most precious commerce to pass, as it were, in review before us. To protect this, or to assail, a small part only of their naval force will ever be risked across the Atlantic. The dangers to which the elements expose them here are too well known, and the greater dangers to which they would be exposed at home were any general calamity to involve their whole fleet. They can attack us by detachment only; and it will suffice to make ourselves equal to what they may detach. Even a smaller force than they may detach will be rendered equal or superior by the quickness with which any check may be repaired with us, while losses with them will be irreparable till too late. A small naval force then is sufficient for us, and a small one is necessary. What this should be, I will not undertake to say. I will only say, it should by no means be so great as we are able to make it. Suppose the million dollars, or three hundred thousand pounds, which Virginia could annually spare without distress, to be applied to the creating a navy. A single year's contribution would build, equip, man, and send to sea a force which should carry three hundred guns. The rest of the confederacy, exerting themselves in the same proportion, would equip in the same time fifteen hundred guns more. So that one year's contributions would set up a navy of eighteen hundred guns. The British ships of the line average seventy-six guns; their frigates thirty-eight. Eighteen hundred guns then would form a fleet of thirty ships, eighteen of which might be of the line, and twelve frigates. Allowing eight men, the British average, for every gun, their annual expense, including subsistence, clothing, pay, and ordinary repairs, would be about $1,280 for every gun, or $2,304,000 for the whole. I state this only as one year's possible exertion, without deciding whether more or less than a year's exertion should be thus applied. . . .

9. TO GEORGE WASHINGTON

[A TRIBUTE TO WASHINGTON]

PHILADELPHIA, January 22, 1783.

SIR:

Having lately received a call from Congress to pass the Atlantic in the character of one of their ministers for negotiating peace, I cannot leave the continent without separating myself for a moment from the general gratitude of my country, to offer my individual tribute to your Excellency for all you have suffered and all you have effected for us. Were I to indulge myself in those warm effusions which this subject forever prompts, they would wear an appearance of adulation very foreign to my nature; for such is become the prostitution of language that sincerity has no longer distinct terms in which to express her own truths. Should you give me occasion, during the short mission on which I go, to render you any service beyond the water, I shall, for a proof of my gratitude, appeal from language to the zeal with which I shall embrace it. The negotiations to which I am joined may perhaps be protracted beyond our present expectation, in which case, though I know you must receive much better intelligence from the gentlemen whose residence there has brought them into a more intimate acquaintance with the characters and views of the European courts, yet I shall certainly presume to add my mite, should it only serve to convince you of the warmth of those sentiments of respect and esteem with which I have the honor to be, your Excellency's most obedient, and most humble servant.

10. TO MARTHA JEFFERSON

[PATERNAL ADVICE]

ANNAPOLIS, November 28, 1783.

DEAR PATSY:

After four days' journey, I arrived here without any accident, and in as good health as when I left Philadelphia. The conviction that you would be more improved in the situation I have placed you than if still with me, has solaced me on my parting with you, which my love for you has rendered a difficult thing. The acquirements which I hope you will make under the tutors I have provided for you will render you more worthy of my love; and if they cannot increase it, they will prevent its diminution. Consider the good lady who has taken you under her roof, who has undertaken to see that you perform all your exercises, and to admonish you in all those wanderings from what is right or what is clever, to which your inexperience would expose you: consider her, I say, as your mother, as the only person to whom, since the loss with which Heaven has pleased to afflict you, you can now look up; and that her displeasure or disapprobation, on any occasion, will be an immense misfortune, which should you be so unhappy as to incur by any unguarded act, think no concession too much to regain her good-will. With respect to the distribution of your time, the following is what I should approve:

From 8 to 10, practice music.

From 10 to 1, dance one day and draw another.

From 1 to 2, draw on the day you dance, and write a letter next day.

From 3 to 4, read French.

From 4 to 5, exercise yourself in music.

From 5 till bed-time, read English, write, etc.

Communicate this plan to Mrs. Hopkinson, and if she approves of it, pursue it. As long as Mrs. Trist remains in Philadelphia, cultivate her affection. She has been a valuable friend to you, and her good sense and good heart make her valued by all who know her, and by nobody on earth more than me. I expect you will write me by every post. Inform me what books you read, what tunes you learn, and enclose me your best copy of every lesson in drawing. Write also one letter a week either to your Aunt Eppes, your Aunt Skipwith, your Aunt Carr, or the little lady from whom I now enclose a letter, and always put the letter you so write under cover to me. Take care that you never spell a word wrong. Always before you write a word, consider how it is spelt, and if you do not remember it, turn to a dictionary. It produces great praise to a lady to spell well. I have placed my happiness on seeing you good and accomplished; and no distress this world can now bring on me would equal that of your disappointing my hopes. If you love me, then strive to be good under every situation and to all living creatures, and to acquire those accomplishments which I have put in your power, and which will go far towards ensuring you the warmest love of your affectionate father.

P. S. Keep my letters and read them at times, that you may always have present in your mind those things which will endear you to me.

II. TO EZRA STILES [86]

[ON SCIENTIFIC MATTERS]

PARIS, July 17, 1785.

SIR:

I have long deferred doing myself the honor of writing to you, wishing for an opportunity to accompany my letter with a copy of the *Bibliothèque Physico-œconomique;* a book published here lately in four small volumes, and which gives an account of all the improvements in the arts which have been made for some years past. I flatter myself you will find in it many things agreeable and useful. I accompany it with the volumes of the *Connoisance des Tems* for the years 1781, 1784, 1785, 1786, 1787. But why, you will ask, do I send you old almanacs, which are proverbially useless? Because in these publications have appeared, from time to time, some of the most precious things in astronomy. I have searched out those particular volumes which might be valuable to you on this account. That of 1781 contains de la Caille's catalogue of fixed stars reduced to the commencement of that year, and a table of the aberrations and mutations of the principal stars. 1784 contains the same catalogue with the *nébuleuses* of Messier. 1785 contains the famous catalogue of Hamsteed, with the positions of the stars reduced to the beginning of the year 1784, and which supersedes the use of that immense book. 1786 gives you Euler's lunar tables corrected; and 1787, the tables for the planet Herschel. The two last needed not an apology, as not being within the description of old almanacs. It is fixed on grounds which scarcely admit a doubt that the planet Herschel was seen by Mayer in the year 1756, and was considered by him as one of the zodiacal stars, and, as such, arranged in his catalogue, being the 964th which he describes. This 964th of Mayer has been since missing, and the calculations for the planet Herschel show that it should have been, at the time of Mayer's observation, where he places his 964th star. The volume of 1787 gives you Mayer's catalogue of the zodiacal stars. The researches of the natural philosophers of Europe seem mostly in the field of chemistry, and here, principally, on the subjects of air and fire. The analysis of these two subjects presents to us very new ideas. When speaking of the *Bibliothèque Physico-œconomique*, I should have observed that since its publication a man in this city has invented a method of moving a vessel on the water, by a machine worked within the vessel. I went to see it. He did not know himself the principle of his own invention. It is a screw with a very broad thin worm, or rather it is a thin plate with its edge applied spirally round an axis. This being turned operates on the air, as a screw does, and may be literally said to screw the vessel along; the thinness of the medium, and its want of resistance, occasion a loss of much of the force. The screw, I think, would be more effectual if placed below the surface of the water. I very much suspect that a countryman of ours, Mr. Bushnel of Connecticut, is entitled to the merit of a prior discovery of this use of the screw.

I remember to have heard of his submarine navigation during the war, and, from what Colonel Humphreys now tells me, I conjecture that the screw was the power he used. He joined to this a machine for exploding under water at a given moment. If it were not too great a liberty for a stranger to take, I would ask from him a narration of his actual experiments, with or without a communication of his principle, as he should choose. If he thought proper to communicate it, I would engage never to disclose it, unless I could find an opportunity of doing it for his benefit. I thank you for your information as to the great bones found on the Hudson river. I suspect that they must have been of the same animal with those found on the Ohio; and, if so, they could not have belonged to any human figure, because they are accompanied with tusks of the size, form, and substance of those of the elephant. I have seen a part of the ivory, which was very good. The animal itself must have been much larger than an elephant. Mrs. Adams gives me an account of a flower found in Connecticut, which vegetates when suspended in the air. She brought one to Europe. What can be this flower? It would be a curious present to this continent.

The accommodation likely to take place between the Dutch and the Emperor, leaves us without that unfortunate resource for news which wars give us. The Emperor has certainly had in view the Bavarian exchange of which you have heard; but so formidable an opposition presented itself, that he has thought proper to disavow it. The Turks show a disposition to go to war with him, but, if this country can prevail on them to remain in peace, they will do so. It has been thought that the two Imperial courts have a plan of expelling the Turks from Europe. It is really a pity so charming a country should remain in the hands of a people whose religion forbids the admission of science and the arts among them. We should wish success to the object of the two empires, if they meant to leave the country in possession of the Greek inhabitants. We might then expect, once more, to see the language of Homer and Demosthenes a living language. For I am persuaded the modern Greek would easily get back to its classical models. But this is not intended.

They only propose to put the Greeks under other masters: to substitute one set of barbarians for another.

Colonel Humphreys, having satisfied you that all attempts would be fruitless here to obtain money or other advantages for your college, I need add nothing on that head. It is a method of supporting colleges of which they have no idea, though they practice it for the support of their lazy monkish institutions.

I have the honor to be, with the highest respect and esteem, Sir, your most obedient and most humble servant.

12. TO CHARLES BELLINI

[IMPRESSIONS OF FRANCE]

PARIS, September 30, 1785.

DEAR SIR:

Your estimable favor, covering a letter to Mr. Mazzei, came to hand on the 26th instant. The letter to Mr. Mazzei was put into his hands in the same moment, as he happened to be present. I leave to him to convey to you all his complaints, as it will be more agreeable to me to express to you the satisfaction I received, on being informed of your perfect health. Though I could not receive the same pleasing news of Mrs. Bellini, yet the philosophy with which I am told she bears the loss of health is a testimony the more how much she deserved the esteem I bear her.

Behold me at length on the vaunted scene of Europe! It is not necessary for your information, that I should enter into details concerning it. But you are, perhaps, curious to know how this new scene has struck a savage of the mountains of America. Not advantageously, I assure you. I find the general fate of humanity here most deplorable. The truth of Voltaire's observation offers itself perpetually, that every man here must be either the hammer or the anvil. It is a true picture of that country to which they say we shall pass hereafter, and where we are to see God and his angels in splendor, and crowds of the damned trampled under their feet. While the great mass of the people are thus suffering under physical and moral oppression, I have endeavored to examine more nearly the condition of the great, to appreciate the true value of the circumstances in their situation, which dazzle the bulk of spectators, and, especially, to compare it with that degree of happiness which is enjoyed in America, by every class of people. Intrigues of love occupy the younger, and those of ambition, the elder part of the great. Conjugal love having no existence among them, domestic happiness, of which that is the basis, is utterly unknown. In lieu of this, are substituted pursuits which nourish and invigorate all our bad passions, and which offer only moments of ecstasy, amidst days and months of restlessness and torment. Much, very much inferior, this, to the tranquil, permanent felicity with which domestic society in America blesses most of its inhabitants; leaving them to follow steadily those pursuits which health and reason approve, and rendering truly delicious the intervals of those pursuits.

In science, the mass of the people are two centuries behind ours; their literati, half a dozen years before us. Books really good acquire just reputation in that time, and so become known to us, and communicate to us all their advances in knowledge. Is not this delay compensated, by our being placed out of the reach of that swarm of nonsensical publications which issues daily from a thousand presses, and perishes almost in issuing? With respect to what are termed polite manners, without sacrificing too much the sincerity of language, I would wish my countrymen to adopt just so much of European politeness, as to be ready to make all those little sacrifices of self, which really render European manners amiable, and relieve society from the disagreeable scenes to which rudeness often subjects it. Here, it seems that a man might pass a life without encountering a single rudeness. In the pleasures of the table they are far before us, because with good taste they unite temperance. They do not terminate the most sociable meals by transforming themselves into brutes. I have never yet seen a man drunk in France, even among the lowest of the people. Were I to proceed to tell you how much I enjoyed their architecture, sculpture, painting, music, I should want words. It is in these arts they shine. The last of them, particularly, is an enjoyment, the deprivation of which with us, cannot be calculated. I am almost ready to say, it is the only thing which from my heart I envy them, and which, in spite of all the authority of the Decalogue, I do covet. But I am running on in an estimate of things infinitely better known to you than to me, and which will only serve to convince you that I have brought with me all the prejudices of country, habit, and age. But whatever I may allow to be charged to me as prejudice, in every other instance, I have one sentiment at least, founded on reality: it is that of the perfect esteem which your merit and that of Mrs. Bellini have produced, and which will forever enable me to assure you of the sincere regard with which I am, dear Sir, your friend and servant.

13. AN ACT FOR ESTABLISHING RELIGIOUS FREEDOM

Passed in the Assembly of Virginia in the beginning of the year 1786

Well aware that Almighty God hath created the mind free; that all attempts to influence it by temporal punishments or burdens, or by civil incapacitations, tend only to beget habits of hypocrisy and meanness, and are a departure from the plan of the Holy Author of our religion, who being Lord both of body and mind, yet chose not to propagate it by coercions on either, as was in his Almighty power to do; that the impious presumption of legislators and rulers, civil as well as ecclesiastical, who, being themselves but fallible and uninspired men, have assumed dominion over the faith of others, setting up their own opinions and modes of thinking as the only true and infallible, and as such endeavoring to impose them on others, hath established and maintained false religions over the greatest part of the world, and through all time; that to compel a man to furnish contributions of money for the propagation of opinions which he disbelieves, is sinful and tyrannical; that even the forcing him to support this or that teacher of his own religious persuasion, is depriving him of the comfortable liberty of giving his contributions to the particular pastor whose morals he would make his pattern, and whose powers he feels most persuasive to righteousness, and is withdrawing from the ministry those temporal rewards, which, proceeding from an approbation of their personal conduct, are an additional incitement to earnest and unremitting labors for the instruction of mankind; that our civil rights have no dependence on our religious opinions, more than our opinions in physics or geometry; that, therefore, the proscribing any citizen as unworthy the public confidence by laying upon him an incapacity of being called to the offices of trust and emolument, unless he profess or renounce this or that religious opinion, is depriving him injuriously of those privileges and advantages to which in common with his fellow citizens he has a natural right; that it tends also to corrupt the principles of that very religion it is meant to encourage, by bribing, with a monopoly of worldly honors and emoluments, those who will externally profess and conform to it; that though indeed these are criminal who do not withstand such temptation, yet neither are those innocent who lay the bait in their way; that to suffer the civil magistrate to intrude his powers into the field of opinion and to restrain the profession or propagation of principles, on the supposition of their ill tendency, is a dangerous fallacy, which at once destroys all religious liberty, because he being of course judge of that tendency, will make his opinions the rule of judgment, and approve or condemn the sentiments of others only as they shall square with or differ from his own; that it is time enough for the rightful purposes of civil government, for its officers to interfere when principles break out into overt acts against peace and good order; and finally, that truth is great and will prevail if left to herself, that she is the proper and sufficient antagonist to error, and has nothing to fear from the conflict, unless by human interposition disarmed of her natural weapons, free argument and debate, errors ceasing to be dangerous when it is permitted freely to contradict them.

Be it therefore enacted by the General Assembly, That no man shall be compelled to frequent or support any religious worship, place, or ministry whatsoever, nor shall be enforced, restrained, molested, or burdened in his body or goods, nor shall otherwise suffer on account of his religious opinions or belief; but that all men shall be free to profess, and by argument to maintain, their opinions in matters of religion, and that the same shall in nowise diminish, enlarge, or affect their civil capacities.

And though we well know this Assembly, elected by the people for the ordinary purposes of legislation only, have no power to restrain the acts of succeeding assemblies, constituted with the powers equal to our own, and that therefore to declare this act irrevocable would be of no effect in law, yet we are free to declare, and do declare, that the rights hereby asserted are of the natural rights of mankind, and that if any act shall be hereafter passed to repeal the present or to narrow its operation, such act will be an infringement of natural right.[87]

14. TO GEORGE WYTHE

[COMPARING FRANCE AND AMERICA]

Paris, August 13, 1786.

Dear Sir:

Your favors of January 10th and February 10th, came to hand on the 20th and 23d of May. I availed myself of the first opportunity which occurred, by a gentleman going to England, of sending to Mr. Joddrel a copy of the Notes [88] on our country, with a line informing him that it was you who had emboldened me to take that liberty. Madison, no doubt, informed you of the reason why I had sent only a single copy to Virginia. Being assured by him that they will not do the harm I had apprehended, but on the contrary, may do some good, I propose to send thither the copies remaining on hand, which are fewer than I had intended. But, of the numerous corrections they need, there are one or two so essential, that I must have them made, by printing a few new leaves, and substituting them for the old. This will be done while they are engraving a map which I have constructed, of the country from Albemarle sound to Lake Erie, and which will be inserted in the book. A bad French translation which is getting out here, will probably oblige me to publish the original more freely; which it neither deserved nor was ever intended. Your wishes, which are laws to me, will justify my destining a copy for you, otherwise I should as soon have thought of sending you a horn-book; for there is no truth there which is not familiar to you, and its errors I should hardly have proposed to treat you with.

Immediately on the receipt of your letter, I wrote to a correspondent at Florence to inquire after the family of Tagliaferro, as you desired. I received his answer two days ago, a copy of which I now enclose. The original shall be sent by some other occasion. I will have the copper-plate immediately engraved. This may be ready within a few days, but the probability is, that I shall be long getting an opportunity of sending it to you, as these rarely occur. You do not mention the size of the plate, but presuming it is intended for labels for the inside of books, I shall have it made of a proper size for that. I shall omit the word *agisos*, according to the license you allow me, because I think the beauty of a motto is to condense much matter in as few words as possible. The word omitted will be supplied by every reader.

The European papers have announced that the Assembly of Virginia were occupied on the revisal of their code of laws. This, with some other similar intelligence, has contributed much to convince the people of Europe, that what the English papers are constantly publishing of our anarchy, is false; as they are sensible that such a work is that of a people only, who are in perfect tranquillity. Our act for freedom of religion is extremely applauded. The ambassadors and ministers of the several nations of Europe, resident at this Court, have asked of me copies of it, to send to their sovereigns, and it is inserted at full length in several books now in the press; among others, in the new "Encyclopédie." I think it will produce considerable good even in these countries, where ignorance, superstition, poverty, and oppression of body and mind, in every form, are so firmly settled on the mass of the people, that their redemption from them can never be hoped. If the Almighty had begotten a thousand sons, instead of one, they would not have sufficed for this task. If all the sovereigns of Europe were to set themselves to work, to emancipate the minds of their subjects from their present ignorance and prejudices, and that as zealously as they now endeavor the contrary, a thousand years would not place them on that high ground on which our common people are now setting out. Ours could not have been so fairly put into the hands of their own common sense, had they not been separated from their parent stock, and kept from contamination, either from them, or the other people of the old world, by the intervention of so wide an ocean. To know the worth of this, one must see the want of it here. I think by far the most important bill in our whole code is that for the diffusion of knowledge among the people. No other sure foundation can be devised, for the preservation of freedom and happiness. If anybody thinks that kings, nobles, or priests are good conservators of the public happiness, send them here. It is the best school in the universe to cure them of that folly. They will see here, with their own eyes, that these descriptions of men are an abandoned confederacy against the happiness of the mass of the people. The omnipotence of their effect cannot be better proved than in this country particularly, where, notwithstanding the finest soil upon earth, the finest climate under heaven, and a people of the most benevolent, the most gay and amiable character of which the human form is susceptible; where such a people, I say, surrounded by so many blessings from nature, are yet loaded with misery, by kings, nobles, and priests, and by them alone. Preach, my dear Sir, a crusade against ignorance; establish and improve the law for educating the common people. Let our countrymen know that the people alone can protect us against these evils, and that the tax which will be paid for this purpose is not more than the thousandth part of what will be paid to kings, priests, and nobles, who will rise up among us if we leave the people in ignorance. The people of England, I think, are less oppressed than here. But it needs but half an eye to see, when among them, that the foundation is laid in their dispositions for the establishment of a despotism. Nobility, wealth, and pomp are the objects of their adoration. They are by no means the free-minded people we suppose them in America. Their learned men, too, are few in number, and are less learned, and infinitely less emancipated from prejudice, than those of this country. An event, too, seems to be preparing, in the order of things, which will probably decide the fate of that country. It is no longer doubtful, that the harbor of Cherbourg will be complete, that it will be a most excellent one, and capacious enough to hold the whole navy of France. Nothing has ever been wanting to enable this country to invade that, but a naval force conveniently stationed to protect the transports. This change of situation must oblige the English to keep up a great standing army, and there is no king, who, with sufficient force, is not always ready to make himself absolute. My paper warns me it is time to recommend myself to the friendly recollection of Mrs. Wythe, of Colonel Tagliaferro and his family, and particularly of Mr. R. T.; and to assure you of the affectionate esteem with which I am, dear Sir, your friend and servant.

15. TO JAMES MADISON

[ON MATTERS POLITICAL]

Paris, December 16, 1786.

Dear Sir,—

After a very long silence, I am at length able to write to you. An unlucky dislocation of my right wrist has disabled me from using my pen for three months. I now begin to use it a little, but with great pain; so that this letter must be taken up at such intervals as the state of my hand will permit, and will probably be the work of some days. Though the joint seems to be well set, the swelling does not abate, nor the use of it return. I am now, therefore, on the point of setting out to the south of France, to try the use of some mineral waters there, by immersion. This journey will be of two or three months. . . .

I enclose you herein a copy of the letter from the Minister of Finance to me, making several advantageous regulations for our commerce. The obtaining this has occupied us a twelve-month. I say *us*, because I find the Marquis de Lafayette so useful an auxiliary, that acknowledgments for his co-operation are always due. There remains still something to do for the articles of rice, turpentine, and ship duties. What can be done for tobacco, when the late regulation expires, is very uncertain. The commerce between the United States and this country being put on a good footing, we may afterwards proceed to try if anything can be done to favor our intercourse with her colonies. Admission into them for our fish and flour, is very desirable; but, unfortunately, both those articles would raise a competition against their own.

I find by the public papers that your commercial convention failed in point of representation.[89] If it should produce a full meeting in May, and a broader reformation, it will still be well. To make us one nation as to foreign concerns, and keep us distinct in domestic ones, gives the outline of the proper division of power between the general and particular governments. But, to enable the federal head to exercise the power given it to best advantage, it should be organized as the particular ones are, into legislative, executive, and judiciary. The first and last are already separated. The second should also be. When last with Congress, I often proposed to members to do this, by making of the committee of the States, an executive committee during the recess of Congress, and, during its sessions, to appoint a committee to receive and despatch all executive business, so that Congress itself should meddle only with what should be legislative. But I question if any Congress (much less all successively) can have self-denial enough to go through with this distribution. The distribution should be imposed on them then. I find Congress have reversed their division of the western States, and proposed to make them fewer and larger. This is reversing the natural order of things. A tractable people may be governed in large bodies; but, in proportion as they depart from this character, the extent of their government must be less. We see into what small divisions the Indians are obliged to reduce their societies. This measure, with the disposition to shut up the Mississippi, gives me serious apprehensions of the severance of the eastern and western parts of our confederacy. It might have been made the interest of the western States to remain united with us, by managing their interests honestly, and for their own good. But, the moment we sacrifice their interests to our own, they will see it is better to govern themselves. The moment they resolve to do this, the point is settled. A forced connection is neither our interest, nor within our power.

The Virginia act for religious freedom has been received with infinite approbation in Europe, and propagated with enthusiasm. I do not mean by the governments, but by the individuals which compose them. It has been translated into French and Italian, has been sent to most of the courts of Europe, and has been the best evidence of the falsehood of those reports which stated us to be in anarchy. It is inserted in the new "Encyclopédie," and is appearing in most of the publications respecting America. In fact, it is comfortable to see the standard of reason at length erected, after so many ages, during which the human mind has been held in vassalage by kings, priests, and nobles; and it is honorable for us to have produced the first legislature who had the courage to declare, that the reason of man may be trusted with the formation of his own opinions. . . .

I thank you for your communications in Natural History. The several instances of trees, etc., found far below the surface of the earth, as in the case of Mr. Hay's well, seem to set the reason of man at defiance. . . .

I am, dear Sir, with sincere esteem, your friend and servant.

16. TO FRANCIS HOPKINSON

[ON MATTERS SCIENTIFIC]

PARIS, December 23, 1786.

DEAR SIR,—

My last letter to you was dated August 14th. Yours of May 27th and June 28th were not then received, but have been since.

I take the liberty of putting under your cover another letter to Mrs. Champis, as also an inquiry after a Dr. Griffiths. A letter to M. le Vieillard, from the person he had consulted about the essence L'Orient, will convey to you the result of my researches into that article. Your spring-block for assisting a vessel in sailing cannot be tried here, because the Seine, being not more than about forty toises wide, and running swiftly, there is no such thing on it as a vessel with sails. I thank you for the volume of the Philadelphia transactions, which came safely to hand, and is, in my opinion, a very valuable volume, and contains many precious papers. The paccan-nut is, as you conjecture, the Illinois nut. The former is the vulgar name south of the Potomac, as also with the Indians and Spaniards, and enters also into the botanical name which is Juglano Paccan. I have many volumes of the "Encyclopédie" for yourself and Dr. Franklin; but, as a winter passage is bad for books, and before the spring the packets will begin to sail from Havre to New York, I shall detain them till then. You must not presume too strongly that your comb-footed bird is known to M. de Buffon. He did not know our panther. I gave him the stripped skin of one I bought in Philadelphia, and it presents him a new species, which will appear in his next volumes. I have convinced him that our deer is not a *chevreuil*, and would you believe that many letters to different acquaintances in Virginia, where this animal is so common, have never enabled me to present him with a large pair of their horns, a blue and red skin stuffed, to show him their colors, at different seasons. He has never seen the horns of what we call the elk. This would decide whether it be an elk or a deer. I am very much pleased with your project on the harmonica, and the prospect of your succeeding in the application of keys to it. It will be the greatest present which has been made to the musical world this century, not excepting the piano-forte. If its tone approaches that given by the finger as nearly only as the harpsichord does that of the harp, it will be very valuable. I have lately examined a foot-bass newly invented here, by the celebrated Krumfoltz. It is precisely a piano-forte, about ten feet long, eighteen inches broad, and nine inches deep. It is of one octave only, from fa to fa. The part where the keys are projects at the side in order to lengthen the levers of the keys. It is placed on the floor, and the harpsichord or other piano-forte is set over it, the foot acting in concert on that, while the fingers play on this. There are three unison chords to every note, of strong brass wire, and the lowest have wire wrapped on them as the lowest in the piano-forte. The chords give a fine, clear, deep tone, almost like the pipe of an organ. Have they connected you with our mint? My friend Monroe promised me he would take care for you in that, or perhaps the establishment of that at New York may have been incompatible with your residence in Philadelphia. A person here has invented a method of coining the French écu of six livres, so as to strike both faces and the edge at one stroke, and makes a coin as beautiful as a medal. No country has ever yet produced such a coin. They are made cheaper, too. As yet, he has only made a few to show the perfection of his manner. I am endeavoring to procure one to send to Congress as a model for their coinage. They will consider whether, on establishing a new mint, it will be worth while to buy his machines, if he will furnish them. A dislocation of my right wrist, which happened to me about a month after the date of my last letter to you, has disabled me from writing three months. I do it now in pain, and only in cases of necessity, or of strong inclination, having as yet no other use of my hand. I put under your cover a letter from my daughter to her friend. She joins me in respects to your good mother, to Mrs. Hopkinson and yourself, to whom I proffer assurances of the esteem with which I am, dear Sir, your sincere friend and servant.

17. TO JAMES MADISON[90]

[PUBLIC AFFAIRS AND CHARACTERS]

PARIS, January 30, 1787.

DEAR SIR,—

My last to you was of the 16th of December; since which, I have received yours of November 25th, and December 4th, which afforded me, as your letters always do, a treat on matters public, individual, and economical. I am impatient to learn your sentiments on the late troubles in the Eastern States.[91] So far as I have yet seen, they do not appear to threaten serious consequences. Those States have suffered by the stoppage of the channels of their commerce, which have not yet found other issues. This must render money scarce, and make the people uneasy. This uneasiness has produced acts absolutely unjustifiable; but I hope they will provoke no severities from their governments. A consciousness of those in power that their administration of the public affairs has been honest, may, perhaps, produce too great a degree of indignation; and those characters, wherein fear predominates over hope, may apprehend too much from these instances of irregularity. They may conclude too hastily that nature has formed man insusceptible of any other government but that of force, a conclusion not founded in truth nor experience. Societies exist under three forms, sufficiently distinguishable. 1. Without government, as among our Indians. 2. Under governments, wherein the will of every one has a just influence; as is the case in England, in a slight degree, and in our States, in a great one. 3. Under governments of force; as is the case in all other monarchies, and in most of the other republics. To have an idea of the curse of existence under these last, they must be seen. It is a government of wolves over sheep. It is a problem, not clear in my mind, that the first condition is not the best. But I believe it to be inconsistent with any great degree of population. The second state has a great deal of good in it. The mass of mankind under that enjoys a precious degree of liberty and happiness. It has its evils, too; the principal of which is the turbulence to which it is subject. But weigh this against the oppressions of monarchy, and it becomes nothing. *Malo periculosam libertatem quam quietam servitutem.* Even this evil is productive of good. It prevents the degeneracy of government, and nourishes a general attention to the public affairs. I hold it that a little rebellion, now and then, is a good thing, and as necessary in the political world as storms in the physical. Unsuccessful rebellions, indeed, generally establish the encroachments on the rights of the people, which have produced them. An observation of this truth should render honest republican governors so mild in their punishment of rebellions, as not to discourage them too much. It is a medicine necessary for the sound health of government.

If these transactions give me no uneasiness, I feel very differently at another piece of intelligence, to wit, the possibility that the navigation of the Mississippi may be abandoned to Spain. I never had any interest westward of the Alleghany; and I never will have any. But I have had great opportunities of knowing the character of the people who inhabit that country; and I will venture to say that the act which abandons the navigation of the Mississippi is an act of separation between the eastern and western country. It is a relinquishment of five parts out of eight, of the territory of the United States; an abandonment of the fairest subject for the payment of our public debts, and the chaining those debts on our own necks, *in perpetuum*. I have the utmost confidence in the honest intentions of those who concur in this measure; but I lament their want of acquaintance with the character and physical advantages of the people, who, right or wrong, will suppose their interest sacrificed on this occasion, to the contrary interests of that part of the confederacy in possession of present power. If they declare themselves a separate people, we are incapable of a single effort to retain them. Our citizens can never be induced, either as militia or as soldiers, to go there to cut the throats of their own brothers and sons, or rather, to be themselves the subjects, instead of the perpetrators of the parricide. Nor would that country requite the cost of being retained against the will of its inhabitants, could it be done. But it cannot be done. They are able already to rescue the navigation of the Mississippi out of the hands of Spain, and to add New Orleans to their own territory. They will be joined by the inhabitants of Louisiana. This will bring on a war between them and Spain; and that will produce the question with us, whether it will not be worth our while to become parties with them in the war, in order to reunite them with us, and thus correct our error. And were I to permit my forebodings to go one step further, I should predict that the inhabitants of the United States would force their rulers to take the affirmative of that question. I wish I may be mistaken in all these opinions.

We have, for some time, expected that the Chevalier de La Luzerne would obtain a promotion in the diplomatic line, by being appointed to some of the courts where this country keeps an ambassador. But none of the vacancies taking place which had been counted on, I think the present disposition is to require his return to his station in America. He told me himself lately, that he should return in the spring. I have never pressed this matter on the court, though I knew it to be desirable and desired on our part; because, if the compulsion on him to return had been the work of Congress, he would have returned in such ill temper with them, as to disappoint them in the good they expected from it. He would forever have laid at their door his failure of promotion. I did not press it for another reason, which is, that I have great reason to believe that the character of the Count de Moutier, who would go, were the Chevalier to be otherwise provided for, would give the most perfect satisfaction in America.

As you are now returned into Congress, it will become of importance that you should form a just estimate of certain public characters; on which, therefore, I will give you such notes as my knowledge of them has furnished me with. You will compare them with the materials you are otherwise possessed of, and decide on a view of the whole.

You know the opinion I formerly entertained of my friend, Mr. Adams. —— and the Governor were the first who shook that opinion. I afterwards saw proofs which convicted him of a degree of vanity, and of a blindness to it, of which no germ appeared in Congress. A seven months' intimacy with him here, and as many weeks in London, have given me opportunities of studying him closely. He is vain, irritable, and a bad calculator of the force and probable effect of the motives which govern men. This is all the ill which can possibly be said of him. He is as disinterested as the being who made him: he is profound in his views; and accurate in his judgment, except where knowledge of the world is necessary to form a judgment. He is so amiable, that I pronounce you will love him, if ever you become acquainted with him. He would be, as he was, a great man in Congress.[92]

Mr. Carmichael is, I think, very little known in America.[93] I never saw him, and while I was in Congress I formed rather a disadvantageous idea of him. His letters, received then, showed him vain, and more attentive to ceremony and etiquette, than we suppose men of sense should be. I have now a constant correspondence with him, and find him a little hypochondriac and discontented. He possesses very good understanding, though not of the first order. I have had great opportunities of searching into his character, and have availed myself of them. Many persons of different nations, coming from Madrid to Paris, all speak of him as in high esteem, and I think it certain that he has more of the Count de Florida Blanca's friendship, than any diplomatic character at that court. As long as this minister is in office, Carmichael can do more than any other person who could be sent there.

You will see Franks, and doubtless he will be asking some appointment. I wish there may be any one for which he is fit. He is light, indiscreet, active, honest, affectionate. Though Bingham is not in diplomatic office, yet as he wishes to be so, I will mention such circumstances of him, as you might otherwise be deceived in. He will make you believe he was on the most intimate footing with the first characters in Europe, and versed in the secrets of every cabinet. Not a word of this is true. He had a rage for being presented to great men, and had no modesty in the methods by which he could, if he attained acquaintance, effect it. . . .

The Marquis de Lafayette is a most valuable auxiliary to me. His zeal is unbounded, and his weight with those in power great. His education having been merely military, commerce was an unknown field to him. But his good sense enabling him to comprehend perfectly whatever is explained to him, his agency has been very efficacious. He has a great deal of sound genius, is well remarked by the King, and rising in popularity. He has nothing against him, but the suspicion of republican principles. I think he will one day be of the ministry. His foible is a canine appetite for popularity and fame; but he will get above this. The Count de Vergennes is ill.[94] The possibility of his recovery, renders it dangerous for us to express a doubt of it; but he is in danger. He is a great minister in European affairs, but has very imperfect ideas of our institutions, and no confidence in them. His devotion to the principles of pure despotism renders him unaffectionate to our governments. But his fear of England makes him value us as a make-weight. He is cool, reserved in political conversations, but free and familiar on other subjects, and a very attentive, agreeable person to do business with. It is impossible to have a clearer, better organized head; but age has chilled his heart.

Nothing should be spared, on our part, to attach this country to us. It is the only one on which we can rely for support, under every event. Its inhabitants love us more, I think, than they do any other nation on earth. This is very much the effect of the good dispositions with which the French officers returned. In a former letter, I mentioned to you the dislocation of my wrist. I can make not the least use of it, except for the single article of writing, though it is going on five months since the accident happened. I have great anxieties, lest I should never recover any considerable use of it. I shall, by the advice of my surgeons, set out in a fortnight for the waters of Aix, in Provence. I chose these out of several they proposed to me, because if they fail to be effectual, my journey will not be useless altogether. It will give me an opportunity of examining the canal of Languedoc, and of acquiring knowledge of that species of navigation, which may be useful hereafter; but more immediately, it will enable me to make the tour of the ports concerned in commerce with us, to examine, on the spot, the defects of the late regulations respecting our commerce, to learn the further improvements which may be made in it, and on my return, to get this business finished. I shall be absent between two and three months, unless anything happens to recall me here sooner, which may always be effected in ten days, in whatever part of my route I may be.

In speaking of characters, I omitted those of Reyneval and Hennin, the two eyes of Count de Vergennes. The former is the most important character, because possessing the most of the confidence of the Count. He is rather cunning than wise, his views of things being neither great nor liberal. He governs himself by principles which he has learned by rote, and is fit only for the details of execution. His heart is susceptible of little passions, but not of good ones. He is brother-in-law to M. Gerard, from whom he received disadvantageous impressions of us, which cannot be effaced. He has much duplicity. Hennin is a philosopher, sincere, friendly, liberal, learned, beloved by everybody; the other by nobody. I think it a great misfortune that the United States are in the department of the former. As particulars of this kind may be useful to you, in your present situation, I may hereafter continue the chapter. I know it will be safely lodged in your discretion.

Feb. 5. Since writing thus far, Franks is returned from England. I learn that Mr. Adams desires to be recalled, and that Smith should be appointed Chargé des Affaires there. It is not for me to decide whether any diplomatic character should be kept at a court, which keeps none with us. You can judge of Smith's abilities by his letters. They are not of the first order, but they are good. For his honesty, he is like our friend Monroe; turn his soul wrong side outwards, and there is not a speck on it. He has one foible, an excessive inflammability of temper, but he feels it when it comes on, and has resolution enough to suppress it, and to remain silent till it passes over.

I send you, by Colonel Franks, your pocket telescope, walking stick, and chemical box. The two former could not be combined together. The latter could not be had in the form you referred to. Having a great desire to have a portable copying machine, and being satisfied, from some experiments, that the principle of the large machine might be applied in a small one, I planned one when in England, and had it made. It answers perfectly. I have since set a workman to making them here, and they are in such demand that he has his hands full. Being assured that you will be pleased to have one, when you shall have tried its convenience, I send you one by Colonel Franks. The machine costs ninety-six livres, the appendages twenty-four livres, and I send you paper and ink for twelve livres; in all, one hundred and thirty-two livres. There is a printed paper of directions; but you must expect to make many essays before you succeed perfectly. A soft brush, like a shaving brush, is more convenient than the sponge. You can get as much ink and paper as you please from London. The paper costs a guinea a ream.

I am, dear Sir, with sincere esteem and affection, your most obedient humble servant.

18. TO MADAME LA COMTESSE DE TESSE [95]

[SENTIMENTAL JOURNEYS]

NISMES, March 20, 1787.

Here I am, Madam, gazing whole hours at the Maison Quarrée, like a lover at his mistress. The stocking weavers and silk spinners around it consider me a hypochondriac Englishman, about to write with a pistol the last chapter of his history. This is the second time I have been in love since I left Paris. The first was with a Diana at the Château de Laye-Epinaye in Beaujolais, a delicious morsel of sculpture, by M. A. Slodtz. This, you will say, was in rule, to fall in love with a female beauty; but with a house! it is out of all precedent. No, Madam, it is not without a precedent in my own history. While in Paris, I was violently smitten with the Hôtel de Salm, and used to go to the Tuileries almost daily, to look at it. The *loueuse des chaises,* inattentive to my passion, never had the complaisance to place a chair there, so that, sitting on the parapet, and twisting my neck round to see the object of my admiration, I generally left it with a *torti-colli.*

From Lyons to Nismes I have been nourished with the remains of Roman grandeur. They have always brought you to my mind, because I know your affection for whatever is Roman and noble. At Vienna I thought of you. But I am glad you were not there; for you would have seen me more angry than, I hope, you will ever see me. The Prætorian Palace, as it is called, comparable, for its fine proportions, to the Maison Quarrée, defaced by the barbarians who have converted it to its present purpose, its beautiful fluted Corinthian columns cut out, in part, to make space for Gothic windows, and hewed down, in the residue, to the plane of the building, was enough, you must admit, to disturb my composure. At Orange, too, I thought of you. I was sure you had seen with pleasure the sublime triumphal arch of Marius at the entrance of the city. I went then to the Arenæ. Would you believe, Madam, that in this eighteenth century, in France, under the reign of Louis XVI, they are at this moment pulling down the circular wall of this superb remain, to pave a road? And that, too, from a hill which is itself an entire mass of stone, just as fit, and more accessible? A former intendant, a M. de Basville, has rendered his memory dear to the traveller and amateur, by the pains he took to preserve and restore these monuments of antiquity. The present one (I do not know who he is) is demolishing the object, to make a good road to it. I thought of you again, and I was then in great good humor, at the Pont du Gard, a sublime antiquity, and well preserved. But most of all here, where Roman taste, genius, and magnificence excite ideas analogous to yours at every step. I could no longer oppose the inclination to avail myself of your permission to write to you, a permission given with too much complaisance by you, and used by me with too much indiscretion. Madame de Tott did me the same honor. But she, being only the descendant of some of those puny heroes who boiled their own kettles before the walls of Troy, I shall write to her from a Grecian, rather than a Roman canton; when I shall find myself, for example, among her Phocæan relations at Marseilles.

Loving, as you do, Madam, the precious remains of antiquity, loving architecture, gardening, a warm sun and a clear sky, I wonder you have never thought of moving Chaville to Nismes.

This, as you know, has not always been deemed impracticable; and, therefore, the next time a *sur-intendant des bâtiments du roi*, after the example of M. Colbert, sends persons to Nismes to move the Maison Quarrée to Paris, that they may not come empty handed, desire them to bring Chaville with them, to replace it. *A propos* of Paris. I have now been three weeks from there, without knowing anything of what has passed. I suppose I shall meet it all at Aix, where I have directed my letters to be lodged, *poste restante*. My journey has given me leisure to reflect on this Assemblée des Notables.[96] Under a good and a young King, as the present, I think good may be made of it. I would have the deputies then, by all means, so conduct themselves as to encourage him to repeat the calls of this Assembly. Their first step should be, to get themselves divided into two chambers instead of seven; the Noblesse and the Commons separately. The second, to persuade the King, instead of choosing the deputies of the Commons himself, to summon those chosen by the people for the Provincial administrations. The third, as the Noblesse is too numerous to be all of the Assemblée, to obtain permission for that body to choose its own deputies. Two Houses, so elected, would contain a mass of wisdom which would make the people happy, and the King great; would place him in history where no other act can possibly place him. They would thus put themselves in the track of the best guide they can follow; they would soon overtake it, become its guide in turn, and lead to the wholesome modifications wanting in that model, and necessary to constitute a rational government. Should they attempt more than the established habits of the people are ripe for, they may lose all, and retard indefinitely the ultimate object of their aim. These, Madam, are my opinions; but I wish to know yours, which, I am sure, will be better.

From a correspondent at Nismes, you will not expect news. Were I to attempt to give you news, I should tell you stories one thousand years old. I should detail to you the intrigues of the courts of the Cæsars, how they affect us here, the oppressions of their prætors, prefects, etc. I am immersed in antiquities from morning to night. For me, the city of Rome is actually existing in all the splendor of its empire. I am filled with alarms for the event of the irruptions daily making on us, by the Goths, the Visigoths, Ostrogoths, and Vandals, lest they should reconquer us to our original barbarism. If I am sometimes induced to look forward to the eighteenth century, it is only when recalled to it by the recollection of your goodness and friendship, and by those sentiments of sincere esteem and respect with which I have the honor to be, Madam, your most obedient, and most humble servant.

19. TO PETER CARR[97]

[ADVICE AS TO EDUCATION]

Paris, August 10, 1787.

Dear Peter,—

I have received your two letters of December 30th and April 18th, and am very happy to find by them, as well as by letters from Mr. Wythe, that you have been so fortunate as to attract his notice and good will; I am sure you will find this to have been one of the most fortunate events of your life, as I have ever been sensible it was of mine. I enclose you a sketch of the sciences to which I would wish you to apply, in such order as Mr. Wythe shall advise; I mention, also, the books in them worth your reading, which submit to his correction. Many of these are among your father's books, which you should have brought to you. As I do not recollect those of them not in his library, you must write to me for them, making out a catalogue of such as you think you shall have occasion for, in eighteen months from the date of your letter, and consulting Mr. Wythe on the subject. To this sketch, I will add a few particular observations:

1. Italian. I fear the learning this language will confound your French and Spanish. Being all of them degenerated dialects of the Latin, they are apt to mix in conversation. I have never seen a person speaking the three languages who did not mix them. It is a delightful language, but late events having

rendered the Spanish more useful, lay it aside to prosecute that.

2. Spanish. Bestow great attention on this, and endeavor to acquire an accurate knowledge of it. Our future connections with Spain and Spanish America will render that language a valuable acquisition. The ancient history of that part of America, too, is written in that language. I send you a dictionary.

3. Moral Philosophy. I think it lost time to attend lectures in this branch. He who made us would have been a pitiful bungler, if he had made the rules of our moral conduct a matter of science. For one man of science, there are thousands who are not. What would have become of them? Man was destined for society. His morality, therefore, was to be formed to this object. He was endowed with a sense of right and wrong merely relative to this. This sense is as much a part of his nature, as the sense of hearing, seeing, feeling; it is the true foundation of morality, and not the τὸ καλόν, truth, etc., as fanciful writers have imagined. The moral sense, or conscience, is as much a part of man as his leg or arm. It is given to all human beings in a stronger or weaker degree, as force of members is given them in a greater or less degree. It may be strengthened by exercise, as may any particular limb of the body. This sense is submitted, indeed, in some degree, to the guidance of reason; but it is a small stock which is required for this; even a less one than what we call common sense. State a moral case to a ploughman and a professor. The former will decide it as well, and often better than the latter, because he has not been led astray by artificial rules. In this branch, therefore, read good books, because they will encourage, as well as direct your feelings. The writings of Sterne, particularly, form the best course of morality that ever was written. Besides these, read the books mentioned in the enclosed paper; and, above all things, lose no occasion of exercising your dispositions to be grateful, to be generous, to be charitable, to be humane, to be true, just, firm, orderly, courageous, etc. Consider every act of this kind, as an exercise which will strengthen your moral faculties and increase your worth.

4. Religion. Your reason is now mature enough to examine

this object. In the first place, divest yourself of all bias in favor of novelty and singularity of opinion. Indulge them in any other subject rather than that of religion. It is too important, and the consequences of error may be too serious. On the other hand, shake off all the fears and servile prejudices, under which weak minds are servilely crouched. Fix reason firmly in her seat, and call to her tribunal every fact, every opinion. Question with boldness even the existence of a God; because, if there be one, he must more approve of the homage of reason, than that of blindfolded fear. You will naturally examine first the religion of your own country. Read the Bible, then, as you would read Livy or Tacitus. The facts which are within the ordinary course of nature you will believe on the authority of the writer, as you do those of the same kind in Livy and Tacitus. The testimony of the writer weighs in their favor, in one scale, and their not being against the laws of nature does not weigh against them. But those facts in the Bible which contradict the laws of nature, must be examined with more care, and under a variety of faces. Here you must recur to the pretensions of the writer to inspiration from God. Examine upon what evidence his pretensions are founded, and whether that evidence is so strong, as that its falsehood would be more improbable than a change in the laws of nature, in the case he relates. For example, in the book of Joshua, we are told the sun stood still several hours. Were we to read that fact in Livy or Tacitus, we should class it with their showers of blood, speaking of statues, beasts, etc. But it is said that the writer of that book was inspired. Examine, therefore, candidly, what evidence there is of his having been inspired. The pretension is entitled to your inquiry, because millions believe it. On the other hand, you are astronomer enough to know how contrary it is to the law of nature that a body revolving on its axis, as the earth does, should have stopped, should not, by that sudden stoppage, have prostrated animals, trees, buildings, and should after a certain time have resumed its revolution, and that without a second general prostration. Is this arrest of the earth's motion, or the evidence which affirms it, most within the law of probabilities? You will next read the New Testament. It is the history of a personage called Jesus. Keep in your eye the opposite pretensions: 1, of those who say he was begotten by God, born of a virgin, suspended and reversed the laws of nature at will, and ascended bodily into heaven; and 2, of those who say he was a man of illegitimate birth, of a benevolent heart, enthusiastic mind, who set out without pretensions to divinity, ended in believing them, and was punished capitally for sedition, by being gibbeted, according to the Roman law, which punished the first commission of that offence by whipping, and the second by exile, or death *in furca*. See this law in the Digest, Lib. 48, tit. 19, §28.3 and Lipsius Lib. 2, de cruce, cap. 2. These questions are examined in the books I have mentioned, under the head of Religion, and several others. They will assist you in your inquiries; but keep your reason firmly on the watch in reading them all. Do not be frightened from this inquiry by any fear of its consequences. If it ends in a belief that there is no God, you will find incitements to virtue in the comfort and pleasantness you feel in its exercise, and the love of others which it will procure you. If you find reason to believe there is a God, a consciousness that you are acting under his eye, and that he approves you, will be a vast additional incitement; if that there be a future state, the hope of a happy existence in that increases the appetite to deserve it; if that Jesus was also a God, you will be comforted by a belief of his aid and love. In fine, I repeat, you must lay aside all prejudice on both sides, and neither believe nor reject anything, because any other persons, or description of persons, have rejected or believed it. Your own reason is the only oracle given you by heaven, and you are answerable, not for the rightness, but uprightness of the decision. I forgot to observe, when speaking of the New Testament, that you should read all the histories of Christ, as well of those whom a council of ecclesiastics have decided for us, to be Pseudo-evangelists, as those they named Evangelists. Because these Pseudo-evangelists pretended to inspiration, as much as the others, and you are to judge their pretensions by your own reason, and not by the reason of those ecclesiastics. Most of these are lost.

There are some, however, still extant, collected by Fabricius, which I will endeavor to get and send you.

5. Travelling. This makes men wiser, but less happy. When men of sober age travel, they gather knowledge, which they may apply usefully for their country; but they are subject ever after to recollections mixed with regret; their affections are weakened by being extended over more objects; and they learn new habits which cannot be gratified when they return home. Young men, who travel, are exposed to all these inconveniences in a higher degree, to others still more serious, and do not acquire that wisdom for which a previous foundation is requisite, by repeated and just observations at home. The glare of pomp and pleasure is analogous to the motion of their blood; it absorbs all their affection and attention; they are torn from it as from the only good in this world, and return to their home as to a place of exile and condemnation. Their eyes are forever turned back to the object they have lost, and its recollection poisons the residue of their lives. Their first and most delicate passions are hackneyed on unworthy objects here, and they carry home only the dregs, insufficient to make themselves or anybody else happy. Add to this, that a habit of idleness, an inability to apply themselves to business is acquired, and renders them useless to themselves and their country. These observations are founded in experience. There is no place where your pursuit of knowledge will be so little obstructed by foreign objects, as in your own country, nor any wherein the virtues of the heart will be less exposed to be weakened. Be good, be learned, and be industrious, and you will not want the aid of travelling to render you precious to your country, dear to your friends, happy within yourself. I repeat my advice, to take a great deal of exercise, and on foot. Health is the first requisite after morality. Write to me often, and be assured of the interest I take in your success, as well as of the warmth of those sentiments of attachment with which I am, dear Peter, your affectionate friend.

P. S. Let me know your age in your next letter. Your cousins here are well and desire to be remembered to you.

20. TO JAMES MADISON

[OBSERVATIONS ON THE CONSTITUTION]

PARIS, December 20, 1787.

DEAR SIR,—

My last to you was of October 8th, by the Count de Moutier. Yours of July 18th, September 6th and October 24th, have been successively received, yesterday, the day before, and three or four days before that. I have only had time to read the letters; the printed papers communicated with them, however interesting, being obliged to lie over till I finish my despatches for the packet, which despatches must go from hence the day after to-morrow. I have much to thank you for; first and most for the ciphered paragraph respecting myself. These little informations are very material towards forming my own decisions. I would be glad even to know when any individual member thinks I have gone wrong in any instance. If I know myself, it would not excite ill blood in me, while it would assist to guide my conduct, perhaps to justify it, and to keep me to my duty, alert. I must thank you, too, for the information in Thomas Burke's case; though you will have found by a subsequent letter, that I have asked of you a further investigation of that matter. It is to gratify the lady who is at the head of the convent wherein my daughters are, and who, by her attachment and attention to them, lays me under great obligations. I shall hope, therefore, still to receive from you the result of the further inquiries my second letter had asked. The parcel of rice which you informed me had miscarried accompanied my letter to the Delegates of South Carolina. Mr. Bourgoin was to be the bearer of both, and both were delivered together into the hands of his relation here, who introduced him to me, and who, at a subsequent moment, undertook to convey them to Mr. Bourgoin. This person was an engraver, particularly recommended to Dr. Franklin and Mr. Hopkinson. Perhaps he may have mislaid the little parcel of rice among his baggage.[98] I am much pleased that the sale of western lands is so successful. I hope they will absorb all the certificates of our domestic debt speedily, in the first place, and that then, offered for cash, they will do the same by our foreign ones.

The season admitting only of operations in the cabinet, and these being in a great measure secret, I have little to fill a letter. I will, therefore, make up the deficiency, by adding a few words on the Constitution proposed by our Convention.

I like much the general idea of framing a government, which should go on of itself, peaceably, without needing continual recurrence to the State legislatures. I like the organization of the government into legislative, judiciary, and executive. I like the power given the legislature to levy taxes, and for that reason solely, I approve of the greater house being chosen by the people directly. For though I think a house chosen by them will be very illy qualified to legislate for the Union, for foreign nations, etc., yet this evil does not weigh against the good, of preserving inviolate the fundamental principle, that the people are not to be taxed but by representatives chosen immediately by themselves. I am captivated by the compromise of the opposite claims of the great and little States, of the latter to equal, and the former to proportional influence. I am much pleased, too, with the substitution of the method of voting by persons, instead of that of voting by States; and I like the negative given to the Executive, with a third of either house; though I should have liked it better, had the judiciary been associated for that purpose, or invested with a similar and separate power. There are other good things of less moment. I will now add what I do not like. First, the omission of a bill of rights, providing clearly, and without the aid of sophisms, for freedom of religion, freedom of the press, protection against standing armies, restriction against monopolies, the eternal and unremitting force of the habeas corpus laws, and trials by jury in all matters of fact triable by the laws of the land, and not by the laws of nations. To say, as Mr. Wilson does, that a bill of rights was not necessary, because all is reserved in the case of the general government which is not given, while in the particular ones, all is given which is not reserved, might do for the audience to whom it was addressed; but it is surely a *gratis dictum*, opposed by strong inferences from the body of the instrument, as well as from the omission of the clause of our present Confederation, which had declared that in express terms. It was a hard conclusion to say, because there has been no uniformity among the States as to the cases triable by jury, because some have been so incautious as to abandon this mode of trial in certain cases, therefore, the more prudent States shall be reduced to the same level of calamity. It would have been much more just and wise to have concluded the other way, that as most of the States had judiciously preserved this palladium, those who had wandered, should be brought back to it; and to have established general right instead of general wrong. Let me add, that a bill of rights is what the people are entitled to against every government on earth, general or particular; and what no just government should refuse, or rest on inferences.

The second feature I dislike, and greatly dislike, is the abandonment, in every instance, of the necessity of rotation in office, and most particularly in the case of the President. Experience concurs with reason in concluding, that the first magistrate will always be re-elected if the Constitution permits it. He is then an officer for life. This once observed, it becomes of so much consequence to certain nations, to have a friend or a foe at the head of our affairs, that they will interfere with money and with arms. A Galloman, or an Angloman, will be supported by the nation he befriends. If once elected, and at a second or third election outvoted by one or two votes, he will pretend false votes, foul play, hold possession of the reins of government, be supported by the States voting for him, especially if they are the central ones, lying in a compact body themselves, and separating their opponents; and they will be aided by one nation of Europe, while the majority are aided by another. The election of a President of America, some years hence, will be much more interesting to certain nations of Europe, than ever the election of a king of Poland was. Reflect on all the instances in history, ancient and modern, of elective monarchies, and say if they do not give foundation for my fears; the Roman emperors, the popes while they were of any importance, the German emperors till they became hereditary in practice, the kings of Poland, the deys of the Ottoman dependencies. It may be said that if elections are to be attended with these disorders, the seldomer they are renewed the better. But experience shows, that the only way to prevent disorder is to render them uninteresting by frequent changes. An incapacity to be elected a second time would have been effectual preventative. The power of removing him every fourth year by the vote of the people is a power which will not be exercised. The King of Poland is removable every day by the diet, yet he is never removed. Smaller objections are, the appeal in fact as well as law; and the binding all persons, legislative, executive, and judiciary by oath, to maintain that constitution. I do not pretend to decide, what would be the best method of procuring the establishment of the manifold good things in this constitution, and of getting rid of the bad. Whether by adopting it, in hopes of future amendment; or after it shall have been duly weighed and canvassed by the people, after seeing the parts they generally dislike, and those they generally approve, to say to them, "We see now what you wish. Send together your deputies again. Let them frame a Constitution for you, omitting what you have condemned, and establishing the powers you approve. Even these will be a great addition to the energy of your government."

At all events, I hope you will not be discouraged from other trials, if the present one should fail of its full effect. I have thus told you freely what I like, and dislike, merely as a matter of curiosity; for I know your own judgment has been formed on all these points after having heard everything which could be urged on them. I own, I am not a friend to a very energetic government. It is always oppressive. The late rebellion in Massachusetts has given more alarm than I think it should have done.[99] Calculate that one rebellion in thirteen States in the course of eleven years is but one for each State in a century and a half. No country should be so long without one. Nor will any degree of power in the hands of government prevent insurrections. France, with all its despotism, and two or three hundred thou-

sand men always in arms, has had three insurrections in the
three years I have been here, in every one of which greater numbers were engaged than in Massachusetts and a great deal more
blood was spilt. In Turkey, which Montesquieu supposes more
despotic, insurrections are the events of every day. In England,
where the hand of power is lighter than here, but heavier than
with us, they happen every half dozen years. Compare again
the ferocious depredations of their insurgents, with the order,
the moderation and the almost self-extinguishment of ours.
(And say, finally, whether peace is best preserved by giving
energy to the government, or information to the people. This
last is the most certain, and the most legitimate engine of government. Educate and inform the whole mass of the people.
Enable them to see that it is their interest to preserve peace and
order, and they will preserve them. And it requires no very
high degree of education to convince them of this. They are
the only sure reliance for the preservation of our liberty.) After
all, it is my principle that the will of the majority should always
prevail. If they approve the proposed convention in all its
parts, I shall concur in it cheerfully, in hopes that they will
amend it, whenever they shall find it work wrong.[100] I think
our governments will remain virtuous for many centuries; as
long as they are chiefly agricultural; and this will be as long as
there shall be vacant lands in any part of America. When they
get piled upon one another in large cities, as in Europe, they
shall become corrupt as in Europe. Above all things, I hope the
education of the common people will be attended to; convinced
that on their good sense we may rely with the most sincerity for
the preservation of a due degree of liberty. I have tired you by
this time with my disquisitions and will therefore only add
assurances of the sincerity of those sentiments of esteem and
attachment with which I am, dear Sir, your affectionate friend
and servant.

P. S. The instability of our laws is really an immense evil. I
think it would be well to provide in our constitutions, that there
shall always be a twelvemonth between the engrossing a bill and
passing it; that it should then be offered to its passage without

changing a word; and that if circumstances should be thought to require a speedier passage, it should take two-thirds of both houses, instead of a bare majority.

21. *From* AUTOBIOGRAPHY

[THE CONSTITUTION: THE FALL OF THE BASTILE]

Our first essay, in America, to establish a federative government had fallen, on trial, very short of its object. During the war of Independence, while the pressure of an external enemy hooped us together, and their enterprises kept us necessarily on the alert, the spirit of the people, excited by danger, was a supplement to the Confederation, and urged them to zealous exertions, whether claimed by that instrument or not; but, when peace and safety were restored, and every man became engaged in useful and profitable occupation, less attention was paid to the calls of Congress. The fundamental defect of the Confederation was, that Congress was not authorized to act immediately on the people, and by its own officers. Their power was only requisitory, and these requisitions were addressed to the several Legislatures, to be by them carried into execution, without other coercion than the moral principle of duty. This allowed, in fact, a negative to every Legislature, on every measure proposed by Congress; a negative so frequently exercised in practice, as to benumb the action of the Federal government, and to render it inefficient in its general objects, and more especially in pecuniary and foreign concerns. The want, too, of a separation of the legislative, executive, and judiciary functions, worked disadvantageously in practice. Yet this state of things afforded a happy augury of the future march of our Confederacy, when it was seen that the good sense and good dispositions of the people, as soon as they perceived the incompetence of their first compact, instead of leaving its correction to insurrection and civil war, agreed, with one voice, to elect deputies to a general Convention, who should peaceably meet and agree on such a Constitution as "would ensure peace, justice, liberty, the common defence and general welfare."

This Convention met at Philadelphia on the 25th of May, '87. It sat with closed doors, and kept all its proceedings secret, until its dissolution on the 17th of September, when the results of its labors were published all together. I received a copy, early in November, and read and contemplated its provisions with great satisfaction. As not a member of the Convention, however, nor probably a single citizen of the Union, had approved it in all its parts, so I, too, found articles which I thought objectionable.[101] The absence of express declarations ensuring freedom of religion, freedom of the press, freedom of the person under the uninterrupted protection of the habeas corpus, and trial by jury in civil as well as in criminal cases, excited my jealousy; and the re-eligibility of the President for life, I quite disapproved. I expressed freely, in letters to my friends, and most particularly to Mr. Madison and General Washington, my approbations and objections. How the good should be secured and the ill brought to rights was the difficulty. To refer it back to a new Convention might endanger the loss of the whole. My first idea was, that the nine States first acting, should accept it unconditionally, and thus secure what in it was good, and that the four last should accept on the previous condition, that certain amendments should be agreed to; but a better course was devised, of accepting the whole, and trusting that the good sense and honest intentions of our citizens would make the alterations which should be deemed necessary. Accordingly, all accepted, six without objection, and seven with recommendations of specified amendments. Those respecting the press, religion, and juries, with several others, of great value, were accordingly made; but the habeas corpus was left to the discretion of Congress, and the amendment against the re-eligibility of the President was not proposed by that body. My fears of that feature were founded on the importance of the office, on the fierce contentions it might excite among ourselves, if continuable for life, and the dangers of interference, either with money or arms, by foreign nations, to whom the choice of an American President might become interesting. Examples of this abounded in history; in the case of the Roman Emperors, for instance; of the

Popes, while of any significance; of the German Emperors; the Kings of Poland, and the Deys of Barbary. I had observed, too, in the feudal history, and in the recent instance, particularly, of the Stadtholder of Holland, how easily offices, or tenures for life, slide into inheritances. My wish, therefore, was, that the President should be elected for seven years, and be ineligible afterwards. This term I thought sufficient to enable him, with the concurrence of the Legislature, to carry through and establish any system of improvement he should propose for the general good. But the practice adopted, I think, is better, allowing his continuance for eight years, with a liability to be dropped at half way of the term, making that a period of probation. That his continuance should be restrained to seven years, was the opinion of the Convention at an earlier stage of its session, when it voted that term, by a majority of eight against two, and by a simple majority that he should be ineligible a second time. This opinion was confirmed by the House so late as July 26, referred to the Committee of detail, reported favorably by them, and changed to the present form by final vote, on the last day but one only of their session. Of this change, three States expressed their disapprobation; New York, by recommending an amendment, that the President should not be eligible a third time, and Virginia and North Carolina that he should not be capable of serving more than eight, in any term of sixteen years; and although this amendment has not been made in form, yet practice seems to have established it. The example of four Presidents voluntarily retiring at the end of their eighth year, and the progress of public opinion, that the principle is salutary, have given it in practice the force of precedent and usage; insomuch that, should a President consent to be a candidate for a third election, I trust he would be rejected, on this demonstration of ambitious views.

But there was another amendment,[102] of which none of us thought at the time, and in the omission of which lurks the germ that is to destroy this happy combination of National powers in the General government, for matters of National concern, and independent powers in the States, for what concerns the

States severally. In England, it was a great point gained at the Revolution, that the commissions of the judges, which had hitherto been during pleasure, should thenceforth be made during good behavior. A judiciary, dependent on the will of the King, had proved itself the most oppressive of all tools, in the hands of that magistrate. Nothing, then, could be more salutary than a change there, to the tenure of good behavior; and the question of good behavior left to the vote of a simple majority in the two Houses of Parliament. Before the Revolution, we were all good English Whigs, cordial in their free principles, and in their jealousies of their executive magistrate. These jealousies are very apparent in all our state Constitutions; and, in the general government in this instance, we have gone even beyond the English caution, by requiring a vote of two-thirds, in one of the Houses, for removing a judge; a vote so impossible, where any defence is made,* before men of ordinary prejudices and passions, that our judges are effectually independent of the nation. But this ought not to be. I would not, indeed, make them dependent on the executive authority, as they formerly were in England; but I deem it indispensable to the continuance of this government, that they should be submitted to some practical and impartial control; and that this, to be imparted, must be compounded of a mixture of State and Federal authorities. It is not enough that honest men are appointed judges. All know the influence of interest on the mind of man, and how unconsciously his judgment is warped by that influence. To this bias add that of the *esprit de corps*, of their peculiar maxim and creed, that "it is the office of a good judge to enlarge his jurisdiction," and the absence of responsibility; and how can we expect impartial decision between the general government, of which they are themselves so eminent a part, and an individual state, from which they have nothing to hope or fear? We have seen, too, that contrary to all correct example, they are in the habit of going out of the question before them, to throw an

*In the impeachment of Judge Pickering, of New Hampshire, a habitual and maniac drunkard, no defence was made. Had there been, the party vote of more than one-third of the Senate would have acquitted him.

anchor ahead, and grapple further hold for future advances of power. They are then, in fact, the corps of sappers and miners, steadily working to undermine the independent rights of the states, and to consolidate all power in the hands of that government in which they have so important a freehold estate. But it is not by the consolidation, or concentration of powers, but by their distribution, that good government is effected. Were not this great country already divided into states, that division must be made, that each might do for itself what concerns itself directly, and what it can so much better do than a distant authority. Every state again is divided into counties, each to take care of what lies within its local bounds; each county again into townships or wards, to manage minuter details; and every ward into farms, to be governed each by its individual proprietor. Were we directed from Washington when to sow, and when to reap, we should soon want bread. It is by this partition of cares, descending in gradation from general to particular, that the mass of human affairs may be best managed, for the good and prosperity of all. I repeat, that I do not charge the judges with wilful and ill-intentioned error; but honest error must be arrested, where its toleration leads to public ruin. As, for the safety of society, we commit honest maniacs to Bedlam, so judges should be withdrawn from their bench, whose erroneous biases are leading us to dissolution. It may, indeed, injure them in fame or in fortune; but it saves the Republic, which is the first and supreme law. . . .

The King was now completely in the hands of men, the principal among whom had been noted, through their lives, for the Turkish despotism of their characters, and who were associated around the King, as proper instruments for what was to be executed.[103] The news of this change began to be known at Paris, about one or two o'clock. In the afternoon, a body of about one hundred German cavalry were advanced, and drawn up in the Place Louis XV, and about two hundred Swiss posted at a little distance in their rear. This drew people to the spot, who thus accidentally found themselves in front of the troops, merely at first as spectators; but, as their numbers increased, their indignation rose. They retired a few steps, and posted themselves on and behind large piles of stones, large and small, collected in that Place for a bridge, which was to be built adjacent to it. In this position, happening to be in my carriage on a visit, I passed through the lane they had formed, without interruption. But the moment after I had passed, the people attacked the cavalry with stones. They charged, but the advantageous position of the people, and the showers of stones, obliged the horse to retire, and quit the field altogether, leaving one of their number on the ground, and the Swiss in their rear not moving to their aid. This was the signal for universal insurrection, and this body of cavalry, to avoid being massacred, retired towards Versailles. The people now armed themselves with such weapons as they could find in armorer's shops, and private houses, and with bludgeons; and were roaming all night, through all parts of the city, without any decided object. The next day (the 13th), the Assembly pressed on the King to send away the troops, to permit the Bourgeoisie of Paris to arm for the preservation of order in the city, and offered to send a deputation from their body to tranquillize them; but their propositions were refused. A committee of magistrates and electors of the city are appointed by those bodies, to take upon them its government. The people, now openly joined by the French guards, force the prison of St. Lazare, release all the prisoners, and take a great store of corn, which they carried to the corn-market. Here they get some arms, and the French guards begin to form and train them. The city committee determined to raise forty-eight thousand Bourgeoise, or rather to restrain their numbers to forty-eight thousand. On the 14th, they send one of their members (Monsieur de Corny) to the Hôtel des Invalides, to ask arms for their Garde Bourgeoise. He was followed by, and he found there, a great collection of people. The Governor of the Invalids came out, and represented the impossibility of his delivering arms, without the orders of those from whom he received them. De Corny advised the people then to retire, and retired himself; but the people took possession of the arms. It was remarkable, that not only the Invalids themselves made no opposition, but that a body of five thousand foreign troops, within four hundred yards, never stirred. M. de Corny, and five others, were then sent to ask arms of M. de Launay, Governor of the Bastile. They found a great collection of people already before the place, and they immediately planted a flag of truce, which was answered by a like flag hoisted on the parapet. The deputation prevailed on the people to fall back a little, advanced themselves to make their demand of the Governor, and in that instant, a discharge from the Bastile killed four persons of those nearest to the deputies. The deputies retired. I happened to be at the house of M. de Corny, when he returned to it, and received from him a narrative of these transactions. On the retirement of the deputies, the people rushed forward, and almost in an instant, were in possession of a fortification of infinite strength, defended by one hundred men, which in other times had stood several regular sieges, and had never been taken. How they forced their entrance has never been explained. They took all the arms, discharged the prisoners, and such of the garrison as were not killed in the first moment of fury; carried the Governor and Lieutenant Governor, to the Place de Grève (the place of public execution), cut off their heads, and sent them through the city, in triumph, to the Palais royal. About the same instant, a treacherous correspondence having been discovered in M. de Fless6lles, Prévôt des Marchands, they seized him in the Hôtel de Ville, where he was in the execution of his office, and cut off his head. These events, carried imperfectly to Versailles, were the subject of two successive deputations from the Assembly to the King, to both of which he gave dry and hard answers; for nobody had as yet been permitted to inform him, truly and fully, of what had passed at Paris. But at night, the Duke de Liancourt forced his way into the King's bed-chamber, and obliged him to hear a full and animated detail of the disasters of the day in Paris. He went to bed fearfully impressed. The decapitation of de Launay worked powerfully through the night on the whole aristocratic party; insomuch, that in the morning, those of the greatest influence on the Count d'Artois represented to him the absolute necessity that the King should give up everything to the Assembly. This according with the dispositions of the King, he went about eleven o'clock, accompanied only by his brothers, to the Assembly, and there read to them a speech, in which he asked their interposition to reestablish order. Although couched in terms of some caution, yet the manner in which it was delivered made it evident that it was meant as a surrender at discretion. He returned to the Château afoot, accompanied by the Assembly. They sent off a deputation to quiet Paris, at the head of which was the Marquis de Lafayette, who had, the same morning, been named Commandant en chef of the Milice Bourgeoise; and Monsieur Bailly, former President of the States General, was called for as Prévôt des Marchands. The demolition of the Bastile was now ordered and begun. A body of the Swiss guards, of the regiment of Ventimille, and the city horse guards joined the people. The alarm at Versailles increased. The foreign troops were ordered off instantly. Every Minister resigned. The King confirmed Bailly as Prévôt des Marchands, wrote to M. Necker, to recall him, sent his letter open to the Assembly, to be forwarded by them, and invited them to go with him to Paris the next day, to satisfy the city of his dispositions; and that night, and the next morning, the Count d'Artois, and M. de Montesson, a deputy connected with him, Madame de Polignac, Madame de Guiche, and the Count de Vaudreuil, favorites of the Queen, the Abbé de Vermont, her confessor, the Prince of Condé, and Duke of Bourbon fled. The King came to Paris, leaving the Queen in consternation for his return. Omitting the less important figures of the procession, the King's carriage was in the centre; on each side of it, the Assembly, in two ranks afoot; at their head the Marquis de Lafayette, as Commander-in-chief, on horseback, and Bourgeois guards before and behind. About sixty thousand citizens, of all forms and conditions, armed with the muskets of the Bastile and Invalids, as far as they would go, the rest with pistols, swords, pikes, pruning-hooks, scythes, etc., lined all the streets through which the procession passed, and with the crowds of people in the streets, doors, and windows, saluted them everywhere with the cries of "vive la nation," but not a single "vive le Roi" was heard. The King stopped at the Hôtel de Ville. There M. Bailly presented, and put into his hat, the popular cockade, and addressed him. The King being unprepared, and unable to answer, Bailly went to him, gathered from him some scraps of sentences, and made out an answer, which he delivered to the audience, as from the King. On their return, the popular cries were "vive le Roi et la nation." He was conducted by a garde Bourgeoise to his palace at Versailles, and thus concluded an "amende honorable," as no sovereign ever made, and no people ever received.

And here, again, was lost another precious occasion of sparing to France the crimes and cruelties through which she has since passed, and to Europe, and finally America, the evils which flowed on them also from this mortal source. The King was now become a passive machine in the hands of the National Assembly, and had he been left to himself, he would have willingly acquiesced in whatever they should devise as best for the nation. A wise constitution would have been formed, hereditary in his line, himself placed at its head, with powers so large as to enable him to do all the good of his station, and so limited, as to restrain him from its abuse. This he would have faithfully administered, and more than this I do not believe he ever wished. But he had a Queen of absolute sway over his weak mind and timid virtue, and of a character the reverse of his in all points. This angel, as gaudily painted in the rhapsodies of the rhetor Burke, with some smartness of fancy, but no sound sense, was proud, disdainful of restraint, indignant at all obstacles to her will, eager in the pursuit of pleasure, and firm enough to hold to her desires, or perish in their wreck. Her inordinate gambling and dissipations, with those of the Count d'Artois, and others of her *clique*, had been a sensible item in the exhaustion of the treasury, which called into action the reforming hand of the nation; and her opposition to it, her inflexible perverseness, and dauntless spirit, led herself to the guillotine, drew the King on with her, and plunged the world into crimes and calamities which will forever stain the pages of modern history. I have ever believed, that had there been no Queen, there would have been no revolution. No force would have been provoked, nor exercised. The King would have gone hand in hand with the wisdom of his sounder counsellors, who, guided by the increased lights of the age, wished only, with the same pace, to advance the principles of their social institution. The deed which closed the mortal course of these sovereigns, I shall neither approve nor condemn. I am not prepared to say, that the first magistrate of a nation cannot commit treason against his country, or is unamenable to its punishment; nor yet, that where there is no written law, no regulated tribunal, there is not a law in our hearts, and a power in our hands, given for righteous employment in maintaining right, and redressing wrong. Of those who judged the King, many thought him wilfully criminal; many, that his existence would keep the nation in perpetual conflict with the horde of kings who would war against a regeneration which might come home to themselves, and that it were better that one should die than all. I should not have voted with this portion of the legislature. I should have shut up the Queen in a convent, putting harm out of her power, and placed the King in his station, investing him with limited powers, which, I verily believe, he would have honestly exercised, according to the measure of his understanding. In this way, no void would have been created, courting the usurpation of a military adventurer, nor occasion given for those enormities which demoralized the nations of the world, and destroyed, and is yet to destroy, millions and millions of its inhabitants. There are three epochs in history signalized by the total extinction of national morality. The first was of the successors of Alexander, not omitting himself; the next, the successors of the first Cæsar; the third, our own age. This was begun by the partition of Poland, followed by that of the treaty of Pilnitz; next the conflagration of Copenhagen; then the enormities of Bonaparte, partitioning the earth at his will, and devastating it with fire and sword; now the conspiracy of kings, the successors of Bonaparte, blasphemously calling themselves the Holy Alliance, and treading in the footsteps of their incarcerated leader; not yet, indeed, usurping the government of other nations, avowedly and in detail, but controlling by their armies the forms in which they will permit them to be governed; and reserving, *in petto*, the order and extent of the usurpations further meditated. But I will return from a digression, anticipated, too, in time, into which I have been led by reflection on the criminal passions which refused to the world a favorable occasion of saving it from the afflictions it has since suffered. . . .

22. TO FRANCIS HOPKINSON

[FURTHER OBSERVATIONS ON THE CONSTITUTION]

Paris, March 13, 1789.

Dear Sir,—

Since my last, which was of December 21st, yours of December 9th and 21st are received. Accept my thanks for the papers and pamphlets which accompanied them, and mine and my daughter's, for the book of songs. I will not tell you how much they have pleased us, nor how well the last of them merits praise for its pathos, but relate a fact only, which is, that while my elder daughter was playing it on the harpsichord, I happened to look towards the fire, and saw the younger one all in tears. I asked her if she was sick? She said "no; but the tune was so mournful."

The Editor of the *Encyclopédie* has published something as to an advanced price on his future volumes, which, I understand, alarms the subscribers. It was in a paper which I do not take, and therefore I have not yet seen it, nor can I say what it is. I hope that by this time you have ceased to make wry faces about your vinegar, and that you have received it safe and good.

You say that I have been dished up to you as an antifederalist, and ask me if it be just. My opinion was never worthy enough of notice to merit citing; but since you ask it, I will tell it you. I am not a federalist, because I never submitted the whole system of my opinions to the creed of any party of men whatever, in religion, in philosophy, in politics, or in anything else, where I was capable of thinking for myself. Such an addiction is the last degradation of a free and moral agent. If I could not go to heaven but with a party, I would not go there at all. Therefore, I protest to you, I am not of the party of federalists. But I am much farther from that of the anti-federalists. I approved, from the first moment, of the great mass of what is in the new Constitution; the consolidation of the government; the organization into executive, legislative, and judiciary; the subdivision of the legislative; the happy compromise of interests between the great and little States, by the different manner of voting in the different Houses; the voting by persons instead of States; the qualified negative on laws given to the executive, which, however, I should have liked better if associated with the judiciary also, as in New York; and the power of taxation. I thought at first that the latter might have been limited. A little reflection soon convinced me it ought not to be. What I disapproved from the first moment also was the want of a bill of rights, to guard liberty against the legislative as well as executive branches of the government; that is to say, to secure freedom in religion, freedom of the press, freedom from monopolies, freedom from unlawful imprisonment, freedom from a permanent military, and a trial by jury, in all cases determinable by the laws of the land. I disapproved, also, the perpetual reeligibility of the President. To these points of disapprobation I adhere. My first wish was that the nine first conventions might accept the Constitution, as the means of securing to us the great mass of good it contained, and that the four last might reject it, as the means of obtaining amendments. But I was corrected in this wish the moment I saw the much better plan of Massachusetts, and which had never occurred to me. With respect to the declaration of rights, I suppose the majority of the United States are of my opinion; for I apprehend all the anti-federalists, and a very respectable proportion of the federalists, think that such a declaration should now be annexed. The enlightened part of Europe have given us the greatest credit for inventing this instrument of security for the rights of the people, and have been not a little surprised to see us so soon give it up. With respect to the re-eligibility of the President, I find myself differing from the majority of my countrymen; for I think there are but three States out of the eleven which have desired an alteration of this. And indeed, since the thing is established, I would wish it not to be altered during the life of our great leader, whose executive talents are superior to those, I believe, of any man in the world, and who, alone, by the authority of his name and the confidence reposed in his perfect integrity, is fully qualified to put the new government so under way, as to secure it against the efforts of opposition. But, having derived from our error all the good there was in it, I hope we shall correct it the moment we can no longer have the same name at the helm.

These, my dear friend, are my sentiments, by which you will see I was right in saying I am neither federalist nor anti-federalist;[104] that I am of neither party, nor yet a trimmer between parties. These, my opinions, I wrote within a few hours after I had read the Constitution, to one or two friends in America. I had not then read one single word printed on the subject. I never had an opinion in politics or religion, which I was afraid to own. A costive reserve on these subjects might have procured me more esteem from some people, but less from myself. My great wish is to go on in a strict but silent performance of my duty; to avoid attracting notice, and to keep my name out of newspapers, because I find the pain of a little censure, even when it is unfounded, is more acute than the pleasure of much praise. The attaching circumstance of my present office, is that I can do its duties unseen by those for whom they are done. You did not think, by so short a phrase in your letter, to have drawn on yourself such an egotistical dissertation. I beg your pardon for it, and will endeavor to merit that pardon by the constant sentiments of esteem and attachment with which I am, dear Sir, your sincere friend and servant.

23. *From* THE ANAS [105]

[RELATIONS WITH THE NEW GOVERNMENT]

. . . The alliance between the States under the old Articles of Confederation, for the purpose of joint defence against the aggression of Great Britain, was found insufficient, as treaties of alliance generally are, to enforce compliance with their mutual stipulations; and these, once fulfilled, that bond was to expire of itself, and each State to become sovereign and independent in all things. Yet it could not but occur to every one that these separate independencies, like the petty states of Greece, would be eternally at war with each other, and would become at length the mere partisans and satellites of the leading powers of Europe. All then must have looked forward to some further bond of union, which would insure eternal peace, and a political system of our own, independent of that of Europe. Whether all should be consolidated into a single government, or each remain independent as to internal matters, and the whole form a single nation as to what was foreign only, and whether that national government should be a monarchy or republic, would of course divide opinions, according to the constitutions, the habits, and the circumstances of each individual. Some officers of the army, as it has always been said and believed (and Steuben and Knox have even been named as the leading agents), trained to monarchy by military habits, are understood to have proposed to General Washington to decide this great question by the army before its disbandment, and to assume himself the crown on the assurance of their support. The indignation with which he is said to have scouted this parricide proposition was equally worthy of his virtue and wisdom.

The next effort was (on suggestion of the same individuals, in the moment of their separation) the establishment of an hereditary order, under the name of the Cincinnati, ready prepared by that distinction to be ingrafted into the future frame of government, and placing General Washington still at their

head. The General wrote to me on this subject,* while I was in
Congress at Annapolis, and an extract from my letter is inserted
in 5th Marshall's history, page 28. He afterwards called on me
at that place, on his way to a meeting of the society, and after a
whole evening of consultation, he left that place fully determined
to use all his endeavors for its total suppression. But he found
it so firmly riveted in the affections of the members that,
strengthened as they happened to be by an adventitious occurrence of the moment, he could effect no more than the abolition
of its hereditary principle. He called again on his return, and
explained to me fully the opposition which had been made, the
effect of the occurrence from France, and the difficulty with
which its duration had been limited to the lives of the present
members. Further details will be found among my papers, in
his and my letters, and some in the *Encyclopédie Méthodique et
Dictionnaire d'Economie Politique*, communicated by myself to
M. Meunier,[106] its author, who had made the establishment of
this society the ground, in that work, of a libel on our country.

The want of some authority which should procure justice to
the public creditors, and an observance of treaties with foreign
nations, produced, some time after, the call of a convention of
the States at Annapolis. Although, at this meeting, a difference
of opinion was evident on the question of a republican or kingly
government, yet, so general through the States was the sentiment in favor of the former, that the friends of the latter confined themselves to a course of obstruction only, and delay, to
everything proposed; they hoped that nothing being done, and
all things going from bad to worse, a kingly government might
be usurped, and submitted to by the people, as better than
anarchy and wars internal and external, the certain consequences
of the present want of a general government. The effect of their
manœuvres, with the defective attendance of deputies from the
States, resulted in the measure of calling a more general convention, to be held at Philadelphia. At this, the same party exhibited
the same practices, and with the same views of preventing a government of concord, which they foresaw would be republican,

*See his letter, April 8, 1784.

and of forcing through anarchy their way to monarchy. But the mass of that convention was too honest, too wise, and too steady, to be baffled and misled by their manœuvres.

One of these was a form of government proposed by Colonel Hamilton, which would have been in fact a compromise between the two parties of royalism and republicanism. According to this, the executive and one branch of the legislature were to be during good behavior, *i.e.* for life, and the governors of the States were to be named by these two permanent organs. This, however, was rejected; on which Hamilton left the Convention, as desperate, and never returned again until near its final conclusion. These opinions and efforts, secret or avowed, of the advocates for monarchy, had begotten great jealousy through the States generally; and this jealousy it was which excited the strong opposition to the conventional constitution; a jealousy which yielded at last only to a general determination to establish certain amendments as barriers against a government either monarchical or consolidated. In what passed through the whole period of these conventions, I have gone on the information of those who were members of them, being absent myself on my mission to France.

I returned from that mission in the first year of the new government, having landed in Virginia in December, 1789, and proceeded to New York in March, 1790, to enter on the office of Secretary of State. Here, certainly, I found a state of things which, of all I had ever contemplated, I the least expected. I had left France in the first year of its revolution, in the fervor of natural rights, and zeal for reformation. My conscientious devotion to these rights could not be heightened, but it had been aroused and excited by daily exercise. The President received me cordially, and my colleagues and the circle of principal citizens apparently with welcome. The courtesies of dinner parties given me, as a stranger newly arrived among them, placed me at once in their familiar society. But I cannot describe the wonder and mortification with which the table conversations filled me. Politics were the chief topic, and a preference of kingly over republican government was evidently the favorite sentiment. An apostate I could not be, nor yet a hypocrite; and I found myself, for the most part, the only advocate on the republican side of the question, unless among the guests there chanced to be some member of that party from the legislative Houses. Hamilton's financial system had then passed. It had two objects: 1st, as a puzzle, to exclude popular understanding and inquiry; 2d, as a machine for the corruption of the legislature; for he avowed the opinion that man could be governed by one of two motives only, force or interest; force, he observed, in this country was out of the question; and the interests, therefore, of the members must be laid hold of, to keep the legislative in unison with the executive. And with grief and shame it must be acknowledged that his machine was not without effect; that even in this, the birth of our government, some members were found sordid enough to bend their duty to their interests, and to look after personal rather than public good.

It is well known that during the war the greatest difficulty we encountered was the want of money or means to pay our soldiers who fought, or our farmers, manufacturers, and merchants, who furnished the necessary supplies of food and clothing for them. After the expedient of paper money had exhausted itself, certificates of debt were given to the individual creditors, with assurance of payment so soon as the United States should be able. But the distresses of these people often obliged them to part with these for the half, the fifth, and even a tenth of their value; and speculators had made a trade of cozening them from the holders by the most fraudulent practices, and persuasions that they would never be paid. In the bill for funding and paying these, Hamilton made no difference between the original holders and the fraudulent purchasers of this paper. Great and just repugnance arose at putting these two classes of creditors on the same footing, and great exertions were used to pay to the former the full value, and to the latter, the price only which he had paid, with interest. But this would have prevented the game which was to be played, and for which the minds of greedy members were already tutored and prepared. When the trial of strength on these several efforts had indicated the form in which the bill would finally pass, this being known within doors sooner than without, and especially than to those who were in distant parts of the Union, the base scramble began. Couriers and relay horses by land, and swift sailing pilot-boats by sea, were flying in all directions. Active partners and agents were associated and employed in every state, town, and country neighborhood, and this paper was bought up at five shillings, and even as low as two shillings in the pound, before the holder knew that Congress had already provided for its redemption at par. Immense sums were thus filched from the poor and ignorant, and fortunes accumulated by those who had themselves been poor enough before. Men thus enriched by the dexterity of a leader, would follow of course the chief who was leading them to fortune, and become the zealous instruments of all his enterprises.

This game was over, and another was on the carpet at the moment of my arrival; [107] and to this I was most ignorantly and innocently made to hold the candle.[108] This fiscal manœuvre is well known by the name of the Assumption. Independently of the debts of Congress, the States had during the war contracted separate and heavy debts; and Massachusetts particularly, in an absurd attempt, absurdly conducted, on the British post of Penobscot; and the more debt Hamilton could rake up, the more plunder for his mercenaries. This money, whether wisely or foolishly spent, was pretended to have been spent for general purposes, and ought, therefore, to be paid from the general purse. But it was objected that nobody knew what these debts were, what their amount, or what their proofs. No matter; we will guess them to be twenty millions. But of these twenty millions, we do not know how much should be reimbursed to one State, nor how much to another. No matter; we will guess. And so another scramble was set on foot among the several States, and some got much, some little, some nothing. But the main object was obtained, the phalanx of the Treasury was re-enforced by additional recruits. This measure produced the most bitter and angry contest ever known in Congress, before or since the Union of the States. I arrived in the midst of it.

But a stranger to the ground, a stranger to the actors on it, so long absent as to have lost all familiarity with the subject, and as yet unaware of its object, I took no concern in it.

The great and trying question, however, was lost in the House of Representatives. So high were the feuds excited by this subject that on its rejection business was suspended. Congress met and adjourned from day to day without doing anything, the parties being too much out of temper to do business together. The eastern members particularly, who, with Smith from South Carolina, were the principal gamblers in these scenes, threatened a secession and dissolution. Hamilton was in despair. As I was going to the President's one day, I met him in the street. He walked me backwards and forwards before the President's door for half an hour. He painted pathetically the temper into which the legislature had been wrought; the disgust of those who were called the creditor States; the danger of the secession of their members, and the separation of the States. He observed that the members of the administration ought to act in concert; that though this question was not of my department, yet a common duty should make it a common concern; that the President was the centre on which all administrative questions ultimately rested, and that all of us should rally around him, and support, with joint efforts, measures approved by him; and that the question having been lost by a small majority only, it was probable that an appeal from me to the judgment and discretion of some of my friends might effect a change in the vote, and the machine of government, now suspended, might be again set into motion. I told him that I was really a stranger to the whole subject; not having yet informed myself of the system of finances adopted, I knew not how far this was a necessary sequence; that undoubtedly, if its rejection endangered a dissolution of our Union at this incipient stage, I should deem that the most unfortunate of all consequences, to avert which all partial and temporary evils should be yielded. I proposed to him, however, to dine with me the next day, and I would invite another friend or two, bring them into conference together, and I thought it impossible that reasonable men, consulting together coolly, could fail, by some mutual sacrifices of opinion, to form a compromise which was to save the Union.

The discussion took place. I could take no part in it but an exhortatory one, because I was a stranger to the circumstances which should govern it. But it was finally agreed that, whatever importance had been attached to the rejection of this proposition, the preservation of the Union and of concord among the States was more important, and that therefore it would be better that the vote of rejection should be rescinded, to effect which some members should change their votes. But it was observed that this pill would be peculiarly bitter to the southern States, and that some concomitant measure should be adopted, to sweeten it a little to them. There had before been propositions to fix the seat of government either at Philadelphia, or at Georgetown on the Potomac; and it was thought that by giving it to Philadelphia for ten years, and to Georgetown permanently afterwards, this might, as an anodyne, calm in some degree the ferment which might be excited by the other measure alone. So two of the Potomac members (White and Lee, but White with a revulsion of stomach almost convulsive) agreed to change their votes, and Hamilton undertook to carry the other point. In doing this, the influence he had established over the eastern members, with the agency of Robert Morris with those of the middle States, effected his side of the engagement; and so the Assumption was passed, and twenty millions of stock divided among favored States, and thrown in as pabulum to the stock-jobbing herd. This added to the number of votaries to the Treasury, and made its chief the master of every vote in the legislature, which might give to the government the direction suited to his political views.

I know well, and so must be understood, that nothing like a majority in Congress had yielded to this corruption. Far from it. But a division, not very unequal, had already taken place in the honest part of that body, between the parties styled republican and federal. The latter being monarchists in principle, adhered to Hamilton of course, as their leader in that principle, and this mercenary phalanx added to them, insured him always a majority in both Houses; so that the whole action of legislature was now under the direction of the Treasury. Still the machine was not complete. The effect of the funding system, and of the Assumption, would be temporary; it would be lost with the loss of the individual members whom it had enriched, and some engine of influence more permanent must be contrived, while these myrmidons were yet in place to carry it through all opposition. This engine was the Bank of the United States. All that history is known, so I shall say nothing about it. While the government remained at Philadelphia, a selection of members of both Houses were constantly kept as directors, who, on every question interesting to that institution, or to the views of the federal head, voted at the will of that head; and, together with the stock-holding members, could always make the federal vote that of the majority. By this combination, legislative expositions were given to the constitution, and all the administrative laws were shaped on the model of England, and so passed. And from this influence we were not relieved until the removal from the precincts of the bank, to Washington.

Here then was the real ground of the opposition which was made to the course of administration. Its object was to preserve the legislature pure and independent of the executive, to restrain the administration to republican forms and principles, and not permit the constitution to be construed into a monarchy, and to be warped, in practice, into all the principles and pollutions of their favorite English model. Nor was this an opposition to General Washington. He was true to the republican charge confided to him; and has solemnly and repeatedly protested to me, in our private conversations, that he would lose the last drop of his blood in support of it; and he did this the oftener and with the more earnestness, because he knew my suspicions of Hamilton's designs against it, and wished to quiet them. For he was not aware of the drift, or of the effect of Hamilton's schemes. Unversed in financial projects and calculations and budgets, his approbation of them was bottomed on his confidence in the man.

But Hamilton was not only a monarchist, but for a monarchy bottomed on corruption.[109] In proof of this, I will relate an anecdote, for the truth of which I attest the God who made me. Before the President set out on his southern tour in April, 1791, he addressed a letter of the fourth of that month, from Mount Vernon, to the Secretaries of State, Treasury, and War, desiring that if any serious and important cases should arise during his absence, they would consult and act on them. And he requested that the Vice President should also be consulted. This was the only occasion on which that officer was ever requested to take part in a cabinet question. Some occasion for consultation arising, I invited those gentlemen (and the Attorney General, as well as I remember) to dine with me, in order to confer on the subject. After the cloth was removed, and our question agreed and dismissed, conversation began on other matters, and by some circumstance, was led to the British constitution, on which Mr. Adams observed, "Purge that constitution of its corruption, and give to its popular branch equality of representation, and it would be the most perfect constitution ever devised by the wit of man." Hamilton paused and said, "Purge it of its corruption, and give to its popular branch equality of representation, and it would become an *impracticable* government; as it stands at present, with all its supposed defects, it is the most perfect government which ever existed." And this was assuredly the exact line which separated the political creeds of these two gentlemen. The one was for two hereditary branches and an honest elective one; the other, for a hereditary King, with a House of Lords and Commons corrupted to his will, and standing between him and the people.

Hamilton was, indeed, a singular character. Of acute understanding, disinterested, honest, and honorable in all private transactions, amiable in society, and duly valuing virtue in private life, yet so bewitched and perverted by the British example, as to be under thorough conviction that corruption was essential to the government of a nation. Mr. Adams had originally been a republican. The glare of royalty and nobility, during his mission to England, had made him believe their fascination a necessary ingredient in government; and Shays's rebellion, not sufficiently understood where he then was, seemed to prove that the absence of want and oppression was not a sufficient guarantee of order. His book on the American constitutions having made known his political bias, he was taken up by the monarchical federalists in his absence, and on his return to the United States, he was by them made to believe that the general disposition of our citizens was favorable to monarchy. He here wrote his "Davila," as a supplement to the former work,[110] and his election to the Presidency confirmed his errors. Innumerable addresses, too, artfully and industriously poured in upon him, deceived him into a confidence that he was on the pinnacle of popularity, when the gulf was yawning at his feet, which was to swallow up him and his deceivers. For when General Washington was withdrawn, these energumeni of royalism, kept in check hitherto by the dread of his honesty, his firmness, his patriotism, and the authority of his name, now mounted on the car of State and free from control, like Phaeton on that of the sun, drove headlong and wild, looking neither to right nor left, nor regarding anything but the objects they were driving at; until, displaying these fully, the eyes of the nation were opened, and a general disbandment of them from the public councils took place. . . .   February 4, 1818.

CONVERSATION WITH ALEXANDER HAMILTON

August the 13th, 1791. Notes of a conversation between Alexander Hamilton and Thomas Jefferson. Thomas Jefferson mentioned to him a letter received from John Adams, disavowing "Publicola," [111] and denying that he ever entertained a wish to bring this country under a hereditary executive, or introduce an hereditary branch of legislature, etc. See his letter. Alexander Hamilton condemning Mr. Adams' writings, and most particularly "Davila," as having a tendency to weaken the present government, declared in substance as follows: "I own it is my own opinion, though I do not publish it in Dan and Beersheba, that the present government is not that which will answer the ends of society, by giving stability and protection to its rights, and that it will probably be found expedient to go into the British form. However, since we have undertaken the experiment, I am for giving it a fair course, whatever my expectations. The success, indeed, so far, is greater than I had expected, and therefore, at present, success seems more possible than it had done heretofore, and there are still other and other stages of improvement which, if the present does not succeed, may be tried, and ought to be tried, before we give up the republican form altogether; for that mind must be really depraved which would not prefer the equality of political rights, which is the foundation of pure republicanism, if it can be obtained consistently with order. Therefore, whoever by his writings disturbs the present order of things, is really blameable, however pure his intentions may be, and he was sure Mr. Adams' were pure." This is the substance of a declaration made in much more lengthy terms, and which seemed to be more formal than usual for a private conversation between two, and as if intended to qualify some less guarded expressions which had been dropped on former occasions. Thomas Jefferson has committed it to writing in the moment of Alexander Hamilton's leaving the room. . . .

24. OPINION AGAINST THE CONSTITUTIONALITY OF A NATIONAL BANK [112]

[THE NEGATIVE ARGUMENT]

February 15, 1791.

The bill for establishing a National Bank undertakes among other things:

1. To form the subscribers into a corporation.

2. To enable them in their corporate capacities to receive grants of land; and so far is against the laws of *Mortmain.**

*Though the Constitution controls the laws of Mortmain so far as to permit Congress itself to hold land for certain purposes, yet not so far as to permit them to communicate a similar right to other corporate bodies.

3. To make alien subscribers capable of holding lands; and so far is against the laws of *Alienage*.

4. To transmit these lands, on the death of a proprietor, to a certain line of successors; and so far changes the course of *Descents*.

5. To put the lands out of the reach of forfeiture or escheat; and so far is against the laws of *Forfeiture and Escheat*.

6. To transmit personal chattels to successors in a certain line; and so far is against the laws of *Distribution*.

7. To give them the sole and exclusive right of banking under the national authority; and so far is against the laws of *Monopoly*.

8. To communicate to them a power to make laws paramount to the laws of the States; for so they must be construed, to protect the institution from the control of the State legislatures; and so, probably, they will be construed.

I consider the foundation of the Constitution as laid on this ground: That "all powers not delegated to the United States, by the Constitution, nor prohibited by it to the States, are reserved to the States or to the people." [XIIth amendment.] To take a single step beyond the boundaries thus specially drawn around the powers of Congress is to take possession of a boundless field of power, no longer susceptible of any definition.

The incorporation of a bank, and the powers assumed by this bill, have not, in my opinion, been delegated to the United States, by the Constitution.

I. They are not among the powers specially enumerated; for these are: 1st. A power to lay taxes for the purpose of paying the debts of the United States; but no debt is paid by this bill, nor any tax laid. Were it a bill to raise money, its origination in the Senate would condemn it by the Constitution.

2d. "To borrow money." But this bill neither borrows money nor ensures the borrowing it. The proprietors of the bank will be just as free as any other money-holders, to lend or not to lend their money to the public. The operation proposed in the bill, first, to lend them two millions, and then to borrow them back again, cannot change the nature of the latter act, which will still be a payment, and not a loan, call it by what name you please.

3d. To "regulate commerce with foreign nations, and among the States, and with the Indian tribes." To erect a bank, and to regulate commerce, are very different acts. He who erects a bank creates a subject of commerce in its bills; so does he who makes a bushel of wheat, or digs a dollar out of the mines; yet neither of these persons regulates commerce thereby. To make a thing which may be bought and sold is not to prescribe regulations for buying and selling. Besides, if this was an exercise of the power of regulating commerce, it would be void, as extending as much to the internal commerce of every State, as to its external. For the power given to Congress by the Constitution does not extend to the internal regulation of the commerce of a State (that is to say of the commerce between citizen and citizen), which remains exclusively with its own legislature; but to its external commerce only, that is to say, its commerce with another State, or with foreign nations, or with the Indian tribes. Accordingly the bill does not propose the measure as a regulation of trade, but as "productive of considerable advantages to trade." Still less are these powers covered by any other of the special enumerations.

II. Nor are they within either of the general phrases, which are the two following:

1. To lay taxes to provide for the general welfare of the United States, that is to say, "to lay taxes for *the purpose* of providing for the general welfare." For the laying of taxes is the *power*, and the general welfare the *purpose* for which the power is to be exercised. They are not to lay taxes *ad libitum for any purpose they please;* but only *to pay the debts or provide for the welfare of the Union.* In like manner, they are not *to do anything they please* to provide for the general welfare, but only to *lay taxes* for that purpose. To consider the latter phrase, not as describing the purpose of the first, but as giving a distinct and independent power to do any act they please, which might be for the good of the Union, would render all the preceding and subsequent enumerations of power completely useless.

It would reduce the whole instrument to a single phrase, that of instituting a Congress with power to do whatever would be for the good of the United States; and, as they would be the sole judges of the good or evil, it would be also a power to do whatever evil they please.

It is an established rule of construction where a phrase will bear either of two meanings, to give it that which will allow some meaning to the other parts of the instrument, and not that which would render all the others useless. Certainly no such universal power was meant to be given them. It was intended to lace them up straitly within the enumerated powers, and those without which, as means, these powers could not be carried into effect. It is known that the very power now proposed *as a means* was rejected as *an end* by the Convention which formed the Constitution. A proposition was made to them to authorize Congress to open canals, and an amendatory one to empower them to incorporate. But the whole was rejected, and one of the reasons for rejection urged in debate was that then they would have a power to erect a bank, which would render the great cities, where there were prejudices and jealousies on the subject, adverse to the reception of the Constitution.

2. The second general phrase is, "to make all laws *necessary* and proper for carrying into execution the enumerated powers." But they can all be carried into execution without a bank. A bank therefore is not *necessary*, and consequently not authorized by this phrase.

It has been urged that a bank will give great facility or convenience in the collection of taxes. Suppose this were true; yet the Constitution allows only the means which are "*necessary*," not those which are merely "*convenient*" for effecting the enumerated powers. If such a latitude of construction be allowed to this phrase as to give any non-enumerated power, it will go to every one, for there is not one which ingenuity may not torture into a *convenience* in some instance *or other*, to *some one* of so long a list of enumerated powers. It would swallow up all the delegated powers, and reduce the whole to one power, as before observed. Therefore it was that the Constitution restrained them to the *necessary* means, that is to say, to those means without which the grant of power would be nugatory.

But let us examine this convenience and see what it is. The report on this subject, page 3, states the only *general* convenience to be, the preventing the transportation and re-transportation of money between the States and the Treasury (for I pass over the increase of circulating medium, ascribed to it as a want, and which, according to my ideas of paper money, is clearly a demerit). Every State will have to pay a sum of tax money into the Treasury; and the Treasury will have to pay, in every State, a part of the interest on the public debt, and salaries to the officers of government resident in that State. In most of the States there will still be a surplus of tax money to come up to the seat of government for the officers residing there. The payments of interest and salary in each State may be made by Treasury orders on the State collector. This will take up the greater part of the money he has collected in his State, and consequently prevent the great mass of it from being drawn out of the State. If there be a balance of commerce in favor of that State against the one in which the government resides, the surplus of taxes will be remitted by the bills of exchange drawn for that commercial balance. And so it must be if there was a bank. But if there be no balance of commerce, either direct or circuitous, all the banks in the world could not bring up the surplus of taxes, but in the form of money. Treasury orders then, and bills of exchange may prevent the displacement of the main mass of the money collected, without the aid of any bank; and where these fail, it cannot be prevented even with that aid.

Perhaps, indeed, bank bills may be a more *convenient* vehicle than treasury orders. But a little *difference* in the degree of *convenience* cannot constitute the necessity which the constitution makes the ground for assuming any non-enumerated power.

Besides; the existing banks will, without a doubt, enter into arrangements for lending their agency, and the more favorable, as there will be a competition among them for it; whereas the bill delivers us up bound to the national bank, who are free to refuse all arrangement, but on their own terms, and the public not free, on such refusal, to employ any other bank. That of Philadelphia, I believe, now does this business, by their post-notes, which, by an arrangement with the Treasury, are paid by any State collector to whom they are presented. This expedient alone suffices to prevent the existence of that *necessity* which may justify the assumption of a non-enumerated power as a means for carrying into effect an enumerated one. The thing may be done, and has been done, and well done, without this assumption; therefore, it does not stand on that degree of *necessity* which can honestly justify it.

It may be said that a bank whose bills would have a currency all over the States, would be more convenient than one whose currency is limited to a single State. So it would be still more convenient that there should be a bank whose bills should have a currency all over the world. But it does not follow from this superior conveniency, that there exists anywhere a power to establish such a bank; or that the world may not go on very well without it.

Can it be thought that the Constitution intended that for a shade or two of *convenience*, more or less, Congress should be authorized to break down the most ancient and fundamental laws of the several States; such as those against mortmain, the laws of alienage, the rules of descent, the acts of distribution, the laws of escheat and forfeiture, the laws of monopoly? Nothing but a necessity invincible by any other means can justify such a prostitution of laws, which constitute the pillars of our whole system of jurisprudence. Will Congress be too strait-laced to carry the Constitution into honest effect, unless they may pass over the foundation-laws of the State government for the slightest convenience of theirs?

The negative of the President is the shield provided by the Constitution to protect against the invasions of the legislature: 1. The right of the Executive. 2. Of the Judiciary. 3. Of the States and State legislatures. The present is the case of a right remaining exclusively with the States, and consequently one of those intended by the Constitution to be placed under its protection.

It must be added, however, that unless the President's mind, on a view of everything which is urged for and against this bill, is tolerably clear that it is unauthorized by the Constitution; if the pro and the con hang so even as to balance his judgment, a just respect for the wisdom of the legislature would naturally decide the balance in favor of their opinion. It is chiefly for cases where they are clearly misled by error, ambition, or interest, that the Constitution has placed a check in the negative of the President.

25. TO LAFAYETTE [113]

[STOCK-JOBBERS AND KING-JOBBERS]

PHILADELPHIA, June 16, 1792.

Behold you, then, my dear friend, at the head of a great army establishing the liberties of your country against a foreign enemy. May heaven favor your cause, and make you the channel through which it may pour its favors. While you are exterminating the monster Aristocracy, and pulling out the teeth and fangs of its associate, Monarchy, a contrary tendency is discovered in some here. A sect has shown itself among us, who declare they espoused our new Constitution not as a good and sufficient thing itself, but only as a step to an English constitution, the only thing good and sufficient in itself, in their eye. It is happy for us that these are preachers without followers, and that our people are firm and constant in their republican purity. You will wonder to be told that it is from the eastward chiefly that these champions for a king, lords, and commons, come. They get some important associates from New York, and are puffed up by a tribe of Agioteurs which have been hatched in a bed of corruption made up after the model of their beloved England. Too many of these stock-jobbers and king-jobbers have come into our Legislature, or rather too many of our Legislature have become stock-jobbers and king-jobbers. However, the voice of the people is beginning to make itself heard, and will probably cleanse their seats at the ensuing election. The machinations of our old enemies are such as to keep us still at bay with our Indian neighbors. What are you doing for your colonies? They will be lost, if not more effectually succored. Indeed, no future efforts you can make will ever be able to reduce the blacks. All that can be done, in my opinion, will be to compound with them, as has been done formerly in Jamaica. We have been less zealous in aiding them, lest your government should feel any jealousy on our account. But, in truth, we as sincerely wish their restoration and their connection with you, as you do yourselves. We are satisfied that neither your justice nor their distresses will ever again permit their being forced to seek at dear and distant markets those first necessaries of life which they may have at cheaper markets, placed by nature at their door, and formed by her for their support. What is become of Madame de Tessy and Madame de Tott? I have not heard of them since they went to Switzerland. I think they would have done better to have come and reposed under the poplars of Virginia. Pour into their bosoms the warmest effusions of my friendship, and tell them they will be warm and constant unto death. Accept of them also for Madame de Lafayette, and your dear children; but I am forgetting that you are in the field of war, and they I hope in those of peace. Adieu, my dear friend! God bless you all. Yours affectionately.

26. TO THE PRESIDENT OF THE UNITED STATES [114]

[DISSENSIONS IN THE GOVERNMENT]

MONTICELLO, September 9, 1792.

DEAR SIR,—

I received on the 2d instant the letter of August 23d, which you did me the honor to write me; but the immediate return of our post, contrary to his custom, prevented my answer by that occasion. The proceedings of Spain, mentioned in your letter, are really of a complexion to excite uneasiness, and a suspicion that their friendly overtures about the Mississippi, have been merely to lull us while they should be strengthening their holds on that river. Mr. Carmichael's silence has been long my astonishment; and however it might have justified something very different from a new appointment, yet the public interest certainly called for his junction with Mr. Short, as it is impossible but that his knowledge of the ground of negotiation, of persons and characters, must be useful and even necessary to the success of the mission. That Spain and Great Britain may understand one another on our frontiers is very possible; for however opposite their interests or disposition may be in the affairs of Europe, yet while these do not call them into opposite action, they may concur as against us. I consider their keeping an agent in the Indian country as a circumstance which requires serious interference on our part; and I submit to your decision whether it does not furnish a proper occasion to us to send an additional instruction to Messrs. Carmichael and Short to insist on a mutual and formal stipulation to forbear employing agents or pensioning any persons within each other's limits; and if this be refused, to propose the contrary stipulation, to wit, that each party may freely keep agents within the Indian territories of the other, in which case we might soon sicken them of the license.

I now take the liberty of proceeding to that part of your letter wherein you notice the internal dissensions which have taken place within our government, and their disagreeable effect on its movements. That such dissensions have taken place is certain, and even among those who are nearest to you in the administration. To no one have they given deeper concern than myself; to no one equal mortification at being myself a part of them. Though I take to myself no more than my share of the general observations of your letter, yet I am so desirous ever that you should know the whole truth, and believe no more than the truth, that I am glad to seize every occasion of developing to you whatever I do or think relative to the government; and shall, therefore, ask permission to be more lengthy now than the occasion particularly calls for, or could otherwise perhaps justify.

When I embarked in the government, it was with a determination to intermeddle not at all with the Legislature, and as little as possible with my co-departments. The first and only instance of variance from the former part of my resolution, I was duped into by the Secretary of the Treasury, and made a tool for forwarding his schemes, not then sufficiently understood by me; and of all the errors of my political life, this has occasioned me the deepest regret.[115] It has ever been my purpose to explain this to you, when, from being actors on the scene, we shall have become uninterested spectators only. The second part of my resolution has been religiously observed with the War Department; and as to that of the Treasury, has never been farther swerved from than by the mere enunciation of my sentiments in conversation, and chiefly among those who, expressing the same sentiments, drew mine from me. If it has been supposed that I have ever intrigued among the members of the Legislatures to defeat the plans of the Secretary of the Treasury, it is contrary to all truth. As I never had the desire to influence the members, so neither had I any other means than my friendships, which I valued too highly to risk by usurpations on their freedom of judgment, and the conscientious pursuit of their own sense of duty. That I have utterly, in my private conversations, disapproved of the system of the Secretary of the Treasury, I acknowledge and avow; and this was not merely a speculative difference. His system flowed from principles adverse to liberty, and was calculated to undermine and demolish the Republic, by creating an influence of his department over the members of the Legislature. I saw this influence actually produced, and its first fruits to be the establishment of the great outlines of his project by the votes of the very persons who, having swallowed his bait, were laying themselves out to profit by his plans; and that had these persons withdrawn, as those interested in a question ever should, the vote of the disinterested majority was clearly the reverse of what they made it. These were no longer the votes then of the representatives of the people, but of deserters from the rights and interests of the people; and it was impossible to consider their decisions, which had nothing in view but to enrich themselves, as the measures of the fair majority, which ought always to be respected. If what was actually doing begat uneasiness in those who wished for virtuous government, what was further proposed was not less threatening to the friends of the Constitution. For, in a report on the subject of manufactures (still to be acted on), it was expressly assumed that the General Government has a right to exercise all powers which may be for the *general welfare*, that is to say, all the legitimate powers of government; since no government has a legitimate right to do what is not for the welfare of the governed. There was, indeed, a sham limitation of the universality of this power *to cases where money is to be employed*. But about what is it that money cannot be employed? Thus the object of these plans, taken together, is to draw all the powers of government into the hands of the general Legislature, to establish means for corrupting a sufficient corps in that Legislature to divide the honest votes, and preponderate, by their own, the scale which suited, and to have that corps under the command of the Secretary of the Treasury, for the purpose of subverting, step by step, the principles of the Constitution, which he has so often declared to be a thing of nothing, which must be changed. Such views might have justified something more than mere expressions of dissent, beyond which, nevertheless, I never went. Has abstinence from the department, committed to me, been equally observed by him? To say nothing of other interferences equally known, in the case of the two nations, with which we have the most intimate connections, France and England, my system was to give some satisfactory distinctions to the former, of little cost to us, in return for the solid advantages yielded us by them; and to have met the English with some restrictions which might induce them to abate their severities against our commerce. I have always supposed this coincided with your sentiments. Yet the Secretary of the Treasury, by his cabals with members of the Legislature, and by high-toned declamations on other occasions, has forced down his own system, which was exactly the reverse. He undertook, of his own authority, the conferences with the ministers of those two nations, and was, on every consultation, provided with some report of a conversation with the one or the other of them, adapted to his views. These views, thus made to prevail, their execution fell, of course, to me; and I can safely appeal to you, who have seen all my letters and proceedings, whether I have not carried them into execution as sincerely as if they had been my own, though I ever considered them as inconsistent with the honor and interest of our country. That they have been inconsistent with our interest is but too fatally proved by the stab to our navigation given by the French. So that if the question be by whose fault is it that Colonel Hamilton and myself have not drawn together? the answer will depend on that to two other questions: whose principles of administration best justify, by their purity, conscientious adherence? and which of us has, notwithstanding, stepped farthest into the control of the department of the other?

To this justification of opinions, expressed in the way of conversation, against the views of Colonel Hamilton, I beg leave to add some notice of his late charges against me in Fenno's Gazette; for neither the style, matter, nor venom of the pieces alluded to, can leave a doubt of their author. Spelling my name and character at full length to the public, while he conceals his own under the signature of "An American," [116] he charges me, 1st. With having written letters from Europe to my friends to oppose the present Constitution, while depending. 2d. With a desire of not paying the public debt. 3d. With setting up a paper to decry and slander the government. 1st. The first charge is most false. No man in the United States, I suppose, approved of every tittle in the Constitution; no one, I believe, approved more of it than I did, and more of it was certainly disapproved by my accuser than by me, and of its parts most vitally republican. Of this the few letters I wrote on the subject (not half a dozen I believe) will be a proof; [117] and for my own satisfaction and justification, I must tax you with the reading of them when I return to where they are. You will there see that my objection to the Constitution was that it wanted a bill of rights securing freedom of religion, freedom of the press, freedom from standing armies, trial by jury, and a constant habeas corpus act. Colonel Hamilton's was that it wanted a king and house of lords. The sense of America has approved my objection and added the bill of rights, not the king and lords. I also thought a longer term of service, insusceptible of renewal, would have made a President more independent. My country has thought otherwise, I have acquiesced implicitly. He wishes the General Government should have power to make laws binding the States in all cases whatsoever. Our country has thought otherwise: has he acquiesced? Notwithstanding my wish for a bill of rights, my letters strongly urged the adoption of the Constitution, by nine States at least, to secure the good it contained. I at first thought that the best method of securing the bill of rights would be for four States to hold off till such a bill should be agreed to. But the moment I saw Mr. Hancock's proposition to pass the Constitution as it stood, and give perpetual instructions to the representatives of every State to insist on a bill of rights, I acknowledged the superiority of his plan, and advocated universal adoption. 2d. The second charge is equally untrue. My whole correspondence while in France, and every word, letter, and act on the subject, since my return, prove that no man is more ardently intent to see the public debt soon and sacredly paid off than I am. This exactly marks the difference between Colonel Hamilton's views and mine, that I would wish the debt paid tomorrow; he wishes it never to be paid, but always to be a thing wherewith to corrupt and manage the Legislature.[118] 3d. I have never enquired what number of sons, relatives, and friends of Senators, Representatives, printers or other useful partisans Colonel Hamilton has provided for among the hundred clerks of his department, the thousand excisemen, custom-house officers, loan-officers, etc., etc., etc., appointed by him, or at his nod, and spread over the Union; nor could ever have imagined that the man who has the shuffling of millions backwards and forwards from paper into money and money into paper, from Europe to America, and America to Europe, the dealing out of treasury secrets among his friends in what time and measure he pleases, and who never slips an occasion of making friends with his means, that such an one, I say, would have brought forward a charge against me for having appointed the poet Freneau,[119] translating clerk to my office, with a salary of 250 dollars a year. That fact stands thus. While the government was at New York I was applied to on behalf of Freneau to know if there was any place within my department to which he could be appointed. I answered there were but four clerkships, all of which I found full, and continued without any change. When we removed to Philadelphia, Mr. Pintard, the translating clerk, did not choose to remove with us. His office then became vacant. I was again applied to there for Freneau, and had no hesitation to promise the clerkship for him. I cannot recollect whether it was at the same time, or afterwards, that I was told he had a thought of setting up a newspaper there. But whether then, or afterwards, I considered it as a circumstance of some value, as it might enable me to do, what I had long wished to have done, that is, to have the material parts of the Leyden Gazette brought under your eye, and that of the public, in order to possess yourself and them of a juster view of the affairs of Europe than could be obtained from any other public source. This I had ineffectually attempted through the press of Mr. Fenno, while in New York, selecting and translating passages myself at first, then having it done by Mr. Pintard, the translating clerk, but they found their way too slowly into Mr. Fenno's papers. Mr. Bache essayed it for me in Philadelphia, but his being a daily paper, did not circulate sufficiently in the other States. He even tried, at my request, the plan of a weekly paper of recapitulation from his daily paper, in hopes that that might go into the other States, but in this too we failed. Freneau, as translating clerk, and the printer of a periodical paper likely to circulate through the States (uniting in one person the parts of Pintard and Fenno), revived my hopes that the thing could at length be effected. On the establishment of his paper, therefore, I furnished him with the Leyden Gazettes, with an expression of my wish that he could always translate and publish the material intelligence they contained, and have continued to furnish them from time to time, as regularly as I received them. But as to any other direction or indication of my wish how his press should be conducted, what sort of intelligence he should give, what essays encourage, I can protest, in the presence of heaven, that I never did by myself, or any other, directly or indirectly, say a syllable, nor attempt any kind of influence.[120] I can further protest, in the same awful presence, that I never did by myself, or any other, directly or indirectly, write, dictate, or procure any one sentence or sentiment to be inserted *in his, or any other gazette*, to which my name was not affixed or that of my office. I surely need not except here a thing so foreign to the present subject as a little paragraph about our Algerine captives, which I put once into Fenno's paper. Freneau's proposition to publish a paper, having been about the time that the writings of Publicola, and the discourses on Davila,[121] had a good deal excited the public attention, I took for granted from Freneau's character, which had been marked as that of a good whig, that he would give free place to pieces written against the aristocratical and monarchical principles these papers had inculcated. This having been in my mind, it is likely enough I may have expressed it in conversation with others, though I do not recollect that I did. To Freneau I think I could not, because I had still seen him but once, and that was at a public table, at breakfast, at Mrs. Elsworth's, as I passed through New York the last year. And I can safely declare that my expectations looked only to the chastisement of the aristocratical and monarchical writers, and not to any criticisms on the proceedings of government. Colonel Hamilton can see no motive for any appointment, but that of making a convenient partisan. But you, Sir, who have received from me recommendations of a Rittenhouse, Barlow, Paine, will believe that talents and science are sufficient motives with me in appointments to which they are fitted; and that Freneau, as a man of genius, might find a preference in my eye to be a translating clerk, and make good title to the little aids I could give him as the editor of a gazette, by procuring subscriptions to his paper, as I did some before it appeared, and as I have with pleasure done for the labors of other men of genius. I hold it to be one of the distinguishing excellences of elective over hereditary successions, that the talents, which nature has provided in sufficient proportion, should be selected by the society for the government of their affairs, rather than that this should be transmitted through the loins of knaves and fools, passing from the debauches of the table to those of the bed. Colonel Hamilton, alias "Plain Facts,"[122] says that Freneau's salary began before he resided in Philadelphia. I do not know what quibble he may have in reserve on the word "residence." He may mean to include under that idea the removal of his family; for I believe he removed himself, before his family did, to Philadelphia. But no act of mine gave commencement to his salary before he so far took up his abode in Philadelphia as to be sufficiently in readiness for the duties of the office. As to the merits or demerits of his paper, they certainly concern me not. He and Fenno are rivals for the public favor. The one courts them by flattery, the other by censure, and I believe it will be admitted that the one has been as servile, as the other severe. But is not the dignity, and even decency of government committed, when one of its principal ministers enlists himself as an anonymous writer or paragraphist for either the one or the other of them? No government ought to be without censors; and where the press is free, no one ever will. If virtuous, it need not fear the fair operation of attack and defence. Nature has given to man no other means of sifting out the truth, either in religion, law, or politics. I think it as honorable to the government neither to know, nor notice, its sycophants or censors, as it would be undignified and criminal to pamper the former and persecute the latter. So much for the past, a word now of the future.

When I came into this office, it was with a resolution to retire from it as soon as I could with decency. It pretty early appeared to me that the proper moment would be the first of those epochs at which the Constitution seems to have contemplated a periodical change or renewal of the public servants. In this I was confirmed by your resolution respecting the same period; from which, however, I am happy in hoping you have departed. I look to that period with the longing of a wave-worn mariner, who has at length the land in view, and shall count the days and hours which still lie between me and it. In the meanwhile, my main object will be to wind up the business of my office, avoiding as much as possible all new enterprise. With the affairs of the Legislature, as I never did intermeddle, so I certainly shall not now begin. I am more desirous to predispose everything for the repose to which I am withdrawing, than expose it to be disturbed by newspaper contests. If these, however, cannot be avoided altogether, yet a regard for your quiet will be a sufficient motive for my deferring it till I become merely a private citizen, when the propriety or impropriety of what I may say or do, may fall on myself alone. I may then, too, avoid the charge of misapplying that time which now, belonging to those who employ me, should be wholly devoted to their service. If my own justification, or the interests of the republic shall require it, I reserve to myself the right of then appealing to my country, subscribing my name to whatever I write, and using with freedom and truth the facts and names necessary to place the cause in its just form before that tribunal.[123] To a thorough disregard of the honors and emoluments of office, I join as great a value for the esteem of my countrymen, and conscious of having merited it by an integrity which cannot be reproached, and by an enthusiastic devotion to their rights and liberty, I will not suffer my retirement to be clouded by the slanders of a man whose history, from the moment at which history can stoop to notice him, is a tissue of machinations against the liberty of the country which has not only received and given him bread, but heaped its honors on his head. Still, however, I repeat the hope that it will not be necessary to make such an appeal. Though little known to the people of America, I believe, that as far as I am known, it is not as an enemy to the Republic, nor an intriguer against it, nor a waster of its revenue, nor prostitutor of it to the purposes of corruption, as the "American" represents me; and I confide that yourself are satisfied that as to dissensions in the newspapers, not a syllable of them has ever proceeded from me, and that no cabals or intrigues of mine have produced those in the Legislature, and I hope I may promise both to you and myself, that none will receive aliment from me during the short space I have to remain in office, which will find ample employment in closing the present business of the department.

Observing that letters written at Mount Vernon on the Monday, and arriving at Richmond on the Wednesday, reach me on Saturday, I have now the honor to mention that the 22d instant will be the last of our post-days that I shall be here, and consequently that no letter from you after the 17th, will find me here. Soon after that I shall have the honor of receiving at Mount Vernon your orders for Philadelphia, and of there also delivering you the little matter which occurs to me as proper for the opening of Congress, exclusive of what has been recommended in former speeches, and not yet acted on. In the meantime and ever I am, with great and sincere affection and respect, dear Sir, your most obedient, and most humble servant.

27. TO PHILLIP MAZZEI [124]

[AN ANGLICAN PARTY]

Monticello, April 24, 1796.

My Dear Friend,—

...The aspect of our politics has wonderfully changed since you left us. In place of that noble love of liberty and republican government which carried us triumphantly through the war, an Anglican monarchical and aristocratical party has sprung up, whose avowed object is to draw over us the substance, as they have already done the forms, of the British government. The main body of our citizens, however, remain true to their republican principles; the whole landed interest is republican, and so is a great mass of talents. Against us are the Executive, the Judiciary, two out of three branches of the Legislature, all the officers of the government, all who want to be officers, all timid men who prefer the calm of despotism to the boisterous sea of liberty, British merchants and Americans trading on British capitals, speculators and holders in the banks and public funds, a contrivance invented for the purposes of corruption, and for assimilating us in all things to the rotten as well as the sound parts of the British model. It would give you a fever were I to name to you the apostates who have gone over to these heresies, men who were Samsons in the field and Solomons in the council, but who have had their heads shorn by the harlot England. In short, we are likely to preserve the liberty we have obtained only by unremitting labors and perils. But we shall preserve it; and our mass of weight and wealth on the good side is so great, as to leave no danger that force will ever be attempted against us. We have only to awake and snap the Lilliputian cords with which they have been entangling us during the first sleep which succeeded our labors.

I will forward the testimonial of the death of Mrs. Mazzei, which I can do the more incontrovertibly as she is buried in my graveyard, and I pass her grave daily. The formalities of the proof you require, will occasion delay. . . . I begin to feel the effects of age. My health has suddenly broken down, with symptoms which give me to believe I shall not have much to encounter of the *tedium vitæ*. While it remains, however, my heart will be warm in its friendships, and among these, will always foster the affection with which I am, dear Sir, your friend and servant.

28. TO HERBERT CROFT, ESQ., LL.B., LONDON

[LINGUISTIC STUDIES]

MONTICELLO, October 30, 1798.

SIR,—

The copy of your printed letter on the English and German languages, which you have been so kind as to send me, has come to hand; and I pray you to accept of my thanks for this mark of your attention. I have perused it with singular pleasure, and, having long been sensible of the importance of a knowledge of the Northern languages to the understanding of English, I see it, in this letter, proved and specifically exemplified by your collations of the English and German. I shall look with impatience for the publication of your "English and German

Dictionary." Johnson, besides the want of precision in his definitions, and of accurate distinction in passing from one shade of meaning to another of the same word, is most objectionable in his derivations. From a want probably of intimacy with our own language while in the Anglo-Saxon form and type, and of its kindred languages of the North, he has a constant leaning towards Greek and Latin for English etymon. Even Skinner has a little of this, who, when he has given the true Northern parentage of a word, often tells you from what Greek and Latin source it might be derived by those who have that kind of partiality. He is, however, on the whole, our best etymologist, unless we ascend a step higher to the Anglo-Saxon vocabulary; and he has set the good example of collating the English word with its kindred word in the several Northern dialects, which often assist in ascertaining its true meaning.

Your idea is an excellent one, in producing authorities for the meaning of words, "to select the prominent passages in our best writers, to make your dictionary a general index to English literature, and thus intersperse with verdure and flowers the barren deserts of philology." And I believe with you that "wisdom, morality, religion, thus thrown down, as if without intention, before the reader, in quotations, may often produce more effect than the very passages in the books themselves."— "that the cowardly suicide, in search of a strong word for his dying letter, might light on a passage which would excite him to blush at his want of fortitude, and to forego his purpose;"— "and that a dictionary with examples at the words may, in regard to every branch of knowledge, produce more real effect than the whole collection of books which it quotes." I have sometimes myself used Johnson as a repertory, to find favorite passages which I wished to recollect, but too rarely with success.

I was led to set a due value on the study of the Northern languages, and especially of our Anglo-Saxon, while I was a student of the law, by being obliged to recur to that source for explanation of a multitude of law terms. A preface to Fortescue on Monarchies, written by Fortescue Aland, and afterwards premised to his volume of Reports, develops the advantages to be derived to the English student generally, and particularly the student of law, from an acquaintance with the Anglo-Saxon; and mentions the books to which the learner may have recourse for acquiring the language. I accordingly devoted some time to its study, but my busy life has not permitted me to indulge in a pursuit to which I felt great attraction. While engaged in it, however, some ideas occurred for facilitating the study by simplifying its grammar, by reducing the infinite diversities of its unfixed orthography to single and settled forms, indicating at the same time the pronunciation of the word by its correspondence with the characters and powers of the English alphabet. Some of these ideas I noted at the time on the blank leaves of my Elstob's Anglo-Saxon Grammar: but there I have left them, and must leave them, unpursued, although I still think them sound and useful. Among the works which I proposed for the Anglo-Saxon student, you will find such literal and verbal translations of the Anglo-Saxon writers recommended, as you have given us of the German in your printed letter. Thinking that I cannot submit those ideas to a better judge than yourself, and that if you find them of any value you may put them to some use, either as hints in your dictionary, or in some other way, I will copy them as a sequel to this letter, and commit them without reserve to your better knowledge of the subject.[125] Adding my sincere wishes for the speedy publication of your valuable dictionary, I tender you the assurance of my high respect and consideration.

29. TO ELBRIDGE GERRY[126]

[PROFESSION OF POLITICAL FAITH]

PHILADELPHIA, January 26, 1799.

MY DEAR SIR,—

Your favor of November 12th was safely delivered to me by Mr. Binney; but not till December 28th, as I arrived here only three days before that date. It was received with great satisfaction. Our very long intimacy as fellow-laborers in the same cause, the recent expressions of mutual confidence which had preceded your mission, the interesting course which that had taken, and particularly and personally as it regarded yourself, made me anxious to hear from you on your return. I was the more so too, as I had myself, during the whole of your absence, as well as since your return, been a constant butt for every shaft of calumny which malice and falsehood could form, and the presses, public speakers, or private letters disseminate. One of these, too, was of a nature to touch yourself; as if, wanting confidence in your efforts, I had been capable of usurping powers committed to you, and authorizing negotiations private and collateral to yours. The real truth is, that though Doctor Logan, the pretended missionary, about four or five days before he sailed for Hamburg, told me he was going there, and thence to Paris, and asked and received from me a certificate of his citizenship, character, and circumstances of life, merely as a protection, should he be molested on his journey, in the present turbulent and suspicious state of Europe, yet I had been led to consider his object as relative to his private affairs; and though, from an intimacy of some standing, he knew well my wishes for peace and my political sentiments in general, he nevertheless received then no particular declaration of them, no authority to communicate them to any mortal, nor to speak to any one in my name, or in anybody's name, on that, or on any other subject whatever; nor did I write by him a scrip of a pen to any person whatever. This he has himself honestly and publicly declared since his return; and from his well-known character and every other circumstance, every candid man must perceive that his enterprise was dictated by his own enthusiasm, without consultation or communication with any one; that he acted in Paris on his own ground, and made his own way. Yet to give some color to his proceedings, which might implicate the republicans in general, and myself particularly, they have not been ashamed to bring forward a supposititious paper, drawn by one of their own party in the name of Logan, and falsely pretended to have been presented by him to the government of France; counting that the bare mention of my name therein, would connect that in the eye of the public with this transaction. In confutation of these and all future calumnies, by way of anticipation, I shall make to you a profession of my political faith;[127] in confidence that you will consider every future imputation on me of a contrary complexion, as bearing on its front the mark of falsehood and calumny.

I do then, with sincere zeal, wish an inviolable preservation of our present federal Constitution, according to the true sense in which it was adopted by the States, that in which it was advocated by its friends, and not that which its enemies apprehended, who therefore became its enemies; and I am opposed to the monarchising its features by the forms of its administration, with a view to conciliate a first transition to a President and Senate for life, and from that to a hereditary tenure of these offices, and thus to worm out the elective principle. I am for preserving to the States the powers not yielded by them to the Union, and to the legislature of the Union its constitutional share in the division of powers; and I am not for transferring all the powers of the States to the General Government, and all those of that government to the executive branch. I am for a government rigorously frugal and simple, applying all the possible savings of the public revenue to the discharge of the national debt; and not for a multiplication of officers and salaries merely to make partisans, and for increasing, by every device, the public debt, on the principle of its being a public blessing.[128] I am for relying, for internal defence, on our militia solely, till actual invasion, and for such a naval force only as may protect our coasts and harbors from such depredations as we have experienced; and not for a standing army in time of peace, which may overawe the public sentiment; nor for a navy, which, by its own expenses and the eternal wars in which it will implicate us, will grind us with public burdens, and sink us under them. I am for free commerce with all nations; political connection with none; and little or no diplomatic establishment. And I am not for linking ourselves by new treaties with the quarrels of Europe; entering that field of slaughter to preserve their balance, or joining in the confederacy of kings to war against the principles of liberty. I am for freedom of religion, and against all manœuvres to bring about a legal ascendancy of one sect over another; for freedom of the press, and against all violations of the Constitution to silence by force and not by reason the complaints or criticisms, just or unjust, of our citizens against the conduct of their agents. And I am for encouraging the progress of science in all its branches; and not for raising a hue and cry against the sacred name of philosophy;[129] for awing the human mind by stories of raw head and bloody bones to a distrust of its own vision, and to repose implicitly on that of others; to go backwards instead of forwards to look for improvement; to believe that government, religion, morality, and every other science were in the highest perfection in ages of the darkest ignorance, and that nothing can ever be devised more perfect than what was established by our forefathers. To these I will add, that I was a sincere well-wisher to the success of the French revolution, and still wish it may end in the establishment of a free and well-ordered republic; but I have not been insensible under the atrocious depredations they have committed on our commerce. The first object of my heart is my own country. In that is embarked my family, my fortune, and my own existence. I have not one farthing of interest, nor one fibre of attachment out of it, nor a single motive of preference of any one nation to another, but in proportion as they are more or less friendly to us. But though deeply feeling the injuries of France, I did not think war the surest means of redressing them. I did believe, that a mission sincerely disposed to preserve peace, would obtain for us a peaceable and honorable settlement and retribution; and I appeal to you to say, whether this might not have been obtained, if either of your colleagues had been of the same sentiment with yourself.

These, my friend, are my principles; they are unquestionably the principles of the great body of our fellow citizens, and I know there is not one of them which is not yours also. In truth, we never differed but on one ground, the funding system; and as, from the moment of its being adopted by the constituted authorities, I became religiously principled in the sacred discharge of it to the uttermost farthing, we are united now even on that single ground of difference. . . .

When I sat down to answer your letter, but two courses presented themselves, either to say nothing or everything; for half-confidences are not in my character. I could not hesitate which was due to you. I have unbosomed myself fully; and it will certainly be highly gratifying if I receive like confidence from you. For even if we differ in principle more than I believe we do, you and I know too well the texture of the human mind, and the slipperiness of human reason, to consider differences of opinion otherwise than differences of form or feature. Integrity of views more than their soundness is the basis of esteem. I shall follow your direction in conveying this by a private hand; though I know not as yet when one worthy of confidence will occur. And my trust in you leaves me without a fear that this letter, meant as a confidential communication of my impressions, will ever go out of your own hand, or be suffered in anywise to commit my name. Indeed, besides the accidents which might happen to it even under your care, considering the accident of death to which you are liable, I think it safest to pray you, after reading it as often as you please, to destroy at least the second and third leaves. The first contains principles only, which I fear not to avow; but the second and third contain facts stated for your information, and which, though sacredly conformable to my firm belief, yet would be galling to some, and expose me to illiberal attacks. I therefore repeat my prayer to burn the second and third leaves. And did we ever expect to see the day, when, breathing nothing but sentiments of love to our country and its freedom and happiness, our correspondence must be as secret as if we were hatching its destruction! Adieu, my friend, and accept my sincere and affectionate salutations. I need not add my signature.

30. TO GIDEON GRANGER [130]

[DANGERS OF FEDERALISM]

MONTICELLO, August 13, 1800.

DEAR SIR,—

I received with great pleasure your favor of June 4th, and am much comforted by the appearance of a change of opinion in your State; for though we may obtain, and I believe shall obtain, a majority in the Legislature of the United States, attached to the preservation of the federal Constitution according to its obvious principles, and those on which it was known to be received; attached equally to the preservation to the States of those rights unquestionably remaining with them; friends to the freedom of religion, freedom of the press, trial by jury and to economical government; opposed to standing armies, paper systems, war, and all connection, other than commerce, with any foreign nation; in short, a majority firm in all those principles which we have espoused and the federalists have opposed uniformly; still, should the whole body of New England continue in opposition to these principles of government, either knowingly or through delusion, our government will be a very uneasy one. It can never be harmonious and solid, while so respectable a portion of its citizens support principles which go directly to a change of the federal Constitution, to sink the State governments, consolidate them into one, and to monarchize that. Our country is too large to have all its affairs directed by a single government. Public servants at such a distance, and from under the eye of their constituents, must, from the circumstance of distance, be unable to administer and overlook all the details necessary for the good government of the citizens, and the same circumstance, by rendering detection impossible to their constituents, will invite the public agents to corruption, plunder, and waste. And I do verily believe that if the principle were to prevail of a common law being in force in the United States, (which principle possesses the General Government at once of all the powers of the State governments, and reduces us to a single consolidated government), it would become the most corrupt government on the earth. You have seen the practises by which the public servants have been able to cover their conduct, or, where that could not be done, delusions by which they have varnished it for the eye of their constituents. What an augmentation of the field for jobbing, speculating, plundering, office-building and office-hunting would be produced by an assumption of all the State powers into the hands of the General Government! The true theory of our Constitution is surely the wisest and best, that the States are independent as to everything within themselves, and united as to everything respecting foreign nations. Let the General Government be reduced to foreign concerns only, and let our affairs be disentangled from those of all other nations, except as to commerce, which the merchants will manage the better, the more they are left free to manage for themselves, and our General Government may be reduced to a very simple organization, and a very unexpensive one; a few plain duties to be performed by a few servants. But I repeat, that this simple and economical mode of government can never be secured, if the New England States continue to support the contrary system. I rejoice, therefore, in every appearance of their returning to those principles which I had always imagined to be almost innate in them. In this State, a few persons were deluded by the X. Y. Z. duperies. You saw the effect of it in our last Congressional representatives, chosen under their influence. This experiment on their credulity is now seen into, and our next representation will be as republican as it has heretofore been. On the whole, we hope, that by a part of the Union having held on to the principles of the Constitution, time has been given to the States to recover from the temporary frenzy into which they had been decoyed, to rally round the Constitution, and to rescue it from the destruction with which it had been threatened even at their own hands. I see copied from the "American Magazine" two numbers of a paper signed Don Quixote, most excellently adapted to introduce the real truth to the minds even of the most prejudiced.

I would, with great pleasure, have written the letter you

desired in behalf of your friend, but there are existing circumstances which render a letter from me to that magistrate as improper as it would be unavailing. I shall be happy, on some more fortunate occasion, to prove to you my desire of serving your wishes.

I sometime ago received a letter from a Mr. M'Gregory of Derby, in your State; it is written with such a degree of good sense and appearance of candor, as entitles it to an answer. Yet the writer being entirely unknown to me, and the stratagems of the times very multifarious, I have thought it best to avail myself of your friendship, and enclose the answer to you. You will see its nature. If you find from the character of the person to whom it is addressed, that no improper use would probably be made of it, be so good as to seal and send it. Otherwise suppress it.

How will the vote of your State and Rhode Island be as to A. and P.? [131]

I am, with great and sincere esteem, dear Sir, your friend and servant.

31. INAUGURATION ADDRESS

MARCH 4, 1801

Friends and Fellow Citizens:

Called upon to undertake the duties of the first executive office of our country, I avail myself of the presence of that portion of my fellow citizens which is here assembled, to express my grateful thanks for the favor with which they have been pleased to look towards me, to declare a sincere consciousness that the task is above my talents, and that I approach it with those anxious and awful presentiments which the greatness of the charge and the weakness of my powers so justly inspire. A rising nation, spread over a wide and fruitful land, traversing all the seas with the rich productions of their industry, engaged in commerce with nations who feel power and forget right, advancing rapidly to destinies beyond the reach of mortal eye—when I contemplate these transcendent objects, and see the honor, the happiness, and the hopes of this beloved country committed to the issue and the auspices of this day, I shrink from the contemplation, and humble myself before the magnitude of the undertaking. Utterly indeed should I despair, did not the presence of many whom I here see remind me, that in the other high authorities provided by our Constitution, I shall find resources of wisdom, of virtue, and of zeal, on which to rely under all difficulties. To you, then, gentlemen, who are charged with the sovereign functions of legislation, and to those associated with you, I look with encouragement for that guidance and support which may enable us to steer with safety the vessel in which we are all embarked amidst the conflicting elements of a troubled world.

During the contest of opinion through which we have passed, the animation of discussions and of exertions has sometimes worn an aspect which might impose on strangers unused to think freely and to speak and to write what they think; but this being now decided by the voice of the nation, enounced according to the rules of the Constitution, all will, of course, arrange themselves under the will of the law, and unite in common efforts for the common good. All, too, will bear in mind this sacred principle, that though the will of the majority is in all cases to prevail, that will, to be rightful, must be reasonable; that the minority possess their equal rights, which equal laws must protect, and to violate would be oppression. Let us, then, fellow citizens, unite with one heart and one mind. Let us restore to social intercourse that harmony and affection without which liberty and even life itself are but dreary things. And let us reflect that having banished from our land that religious intolerance under which mankind so long bled and suffered, we have yet gained little if we countenance a political intolerance as despotic, as wicked, and capable of as bitter and bloody persecutions. During the throes and convulsions of the ancient world, during the agonizing spasms of infuriated man, seeking through blood and slaughter his long-lost liberty, it was not wonderful that the agitation of the billows should reach even this distant and peaceful shore; [132] that this should be more felt and feared by some and less by others; that this should divide opinions as to measures of safety. But every difference of opinion is not a difference of principle. We have called by different names brethren of the same principle. We are all republicans; we are all federalists.[133] If there be any among us who would wish to dissolve this Union or to change its republican form, let them stand undisturbed as monuments of the safety with which error of opinion may be tolerated where reason is left free to combat it. I know, indeed, that some honest men fear that a republican government cannot be strong; that this government is not strong enough. But would the honest patriot, in the full tide of successful experiment, abandon a government which has so far kept us free and firm, on the theoretic and visionary fear that this government, the world's best hope, may by possibility want energy to preserve itself? I trust not. I believe this, on the contrary, the strongest government on earth. I believe it the only one where every man, at the call of the law, would fly to the standard of the law, and would meet invasions of the public order as his own personal concern. Sometimes it is said that man cannot be trusted with the government of himself. Can he, then, be trusted with the government of others? Or have we found angels in the form of kings to govern him? Let history answer this question.

Let us, then, with courage and confidence pursue our own federal and republican principles, our attachment to our union and representative government. Kindly separated by nature and a wide ocean from the exterminating havoc of one quarter of the globe; too high-minded to endure the degradations of the others; possessing a chosen country, with room enough for our descendants to the hundredth and thousandth generation; entertaining a due sense of our equal right to the use of our own faculties, to the acquisitions of our own industry, to honor and confidence from our fellow citizens, resulting not from birth but from our actions and their sense of them; enlightened by a benign religion, professed, indeed, and practiced in various forms, yet all of them inculcating honesty, truth, temperance, gratitude, and the love of man; acknowledging and adoring an overruling Providence, which by all its dispensations proves that it delights in the happiness of man here and his greater happiness hereafter; with all these blessings, what more is necessary to make us a happy and a prosperous people? Still one thing more, fellow citizens—a wise and frugal government, which shall restrain men from injuring one another, shall leave them otherwise free to regulate their own pursuits of industry and improvement, and shall not take from the mouth of labor the bread it has earned. This is the sum of good government, and this is necessary to close the circle of our felicities.

About to enter, fellow citizens, on the exercise of duties which comprehend everything dear and valuable to you, it is proper you should understand what I deem the essential principles of our government, and consequently those which ought to shape its administration. I will compress them within the narrowest compass they will bear, stating the general principle, but not all its limitations. Equal and exact justice to all men, of whatever state or persuasion, religious or political; peace, commerce, and honest friendship, with all nations; entangling alliances with none; the support of the state governments in all their rights, as the most competent administrations for our domestic concerns and the surest bulwarks against anti-republican tendencies; the preservation of the General Government in its whole constitutional vigor, as the sheet anchor of our peace at home and safety abroad; a jealous care of the right of election by the people—a mild and safe corrective of abuses which are lopped by the sword of revolution where peaceable remedies are unprovided; absolute acquiescence in the decisions of the majority—the vital principle of republics, from which is no appeal but to force, the vital principle and immediate parent of despotism; a well-disciplined militia—our best reliance in peace and for the first moments of war, till regulars may relieve them; the supremacy of the civil over the military authority; economy in the public expense, that labor may be lightly burdened; the honest payment of our debts and sacred preservation of the public faith; encouragement of agriculture, and of commerce as its handmaid; the diffusion of information and arraignment of all abuses at the bar of public reason; freedom of religion; freedom of the press; and freedom of person under the protection of the *habeas corpus;* and trial by juries impartially selected—these principles form the bright constellation which has gone before us, and guided our steps through an age of revolution and reformation. The wisdom of our sages and blood of our heroes have been devoted to their attainment. They should be the creed of our political faith, the text of civil instruction, the touchstone by which to try the services of those we trust; and should we wander from them in moments of error or alarm, let us hasten to retrace our steps and to regain the road which alone leads to peace, liberty, and safety.

I repair, then, fellow citizens, to the post you have assigned me. With experience enough in subordinate offices to have seen the difficulties of this, the greatest of all, I have learned to expect that it will rarely fall to the lot of imperfect man to retire from this station with the reputation and the favor which bring him into it. Without pretensions to that high confidence you reposed in our first and great revolutionary character, whose preëminent services had entitled him to the first place in his country's love, and destined for him the fairest page in the volume of faithful history, I ask so much confidence only as may give firmness and effect to the legal administration of your affairs. I shall often go wrong through defect of judgment. When right, I shall often be thought wrong by those whose positions will not command a view of the whole ground. I ask your indulgence for my own errors, which will never be intentional; and your support against the errors of others who may condemn what they would not if seen in all its parts. The approbation implied by your suffrage is a great consolation to me for the past; and my future solicitude will be to retain the good opinion of those who have bestowed it in advance, to conciliate that of others by doing them all the good in my power, and to be instrumental to the happiness and freedom of all.

Relying, then, on the patronage of your good will, I advance with obedience to the work, ready to retire from it whenever you become sensible how much better choice it is in your power to make. And may that Infinite Power which rules the destinies of the universe lead our councils to what is best, and give them a favorable issue for your peace and prosperity.

32. TO HENRY KNOX [134]
[PRESIDENTIAL POLICY]

WASHINGTON, March 27, 1801.

DEAR SIR,—

I received with great pleasure your favor of the 16th, and it is with the greatest satisfaction I learn from all quarters that my inaugural address is considered as holding out a ground for conciliation and union. I am the more pleased with this, because the opinion therein stated as to the real ground of difference among us (to wit: the measures rendered most expedient by French enormities), is that which I have long entertained. I was always satisfied that the great body of those called federalists were real republicans as well as federalists. I know, indeed, that there are monarchists among us. One character of these is in theory only, and perfectly acquiescent in our form of government as it is, and not entertaining a thought of destroying it merely on their theoretic opinions. A second class, at the head of which is our quondam colleague, are ardent for the introduction of monarchy, eager for armies, making more noise for a great naval establishment than better patriots who wish it on a rational scale only, commensurate to our wants and our means. This last class ought to be tolerated, but not trusted. Believing that (excepting the ardent monarchists) all our citizens agreed in ancient whig principles, I thought it advisable to define and declare them, and let them see the ground on which we could rally. And the fact proving to be so, that they agree in these principles, I shall pursue them with more encouragement. I am aware that the necessity of a few removals for legal oppressions, delinquencies, and other official malversations, may be misconstrued as done for political opinions, and produce hesitation in the coalition so much to be desired; but the extent of these will be too limited to make permanent impressions. [135] In the class of removals, however, I do not rank the new appointments which Mr. A. crowded in with whip and spur from the 12th of December, when the event of the election was known, (and, consequently, that he was making appointments, not for himself, but his successor), until 9 o'clock of the night, at 12 o'clock of which he was to go out of office. This outrage on decency should not have its effect, except in the life appointments which are irremovable. But as to the others I consider the nominations as nullities, and will not view the persons appointed as even candidates for their office, much less as possessing it by any title meriting respect. I mention these things that the grounds and extent of the removals may be understood, and may not disturb the tendency to union. Indeed that union is already effected, from New York southwardly, almost completely. In the New England States it will be slower than elsewhere, from peculiar circumstances better known to yourself than me. But we will go on attending with the utmost solicitude to their interests, and doing them impartial justice, and I have no doubt they will in time do justice to us. I have opened myself frankly, because I wish to be understood by those who mean well, and are disposed to be just towards me, as you are, and because I know you will use it for good purposes only, and for none unfriendly to me. I leave this place in a few days to make a short excursion home, but some domestic arrangements are necessary previous to my final removal here, which will be about the latter end of April. Be so good as to present my respects to Mrs. Knox, and accept yourself assurances of my high consideration and esteem.

33. TO THE REV. ISAAC STORY
[THE COUNTRY OF SPIRITS]

WASHINGTON, December 5, 1801.

SIR,—

Your favor of October 27 was received some time since, and read with pleasure. It is not for me to pronounce on the hypothesis you present of a transmigration of souls from one body to another in certain cases. The laws of nature have withheld from us the means of physical knowledge of the country of spirits, and revelation has, for reasons unknown to us, chosen to leave us in the dark as we were. When I was young I was fond of the speculations which seemed to promise some insight into that hidden country, but observing at length that they left me in the same ignorance in which they had found me, I have for very many years ceased to read or to think concerning them, and have reposed my head on that pillow of ignorance which a benevolent Creator has made so soft for us, knowing how much we should be forced to use it. I have thought it better, by nourishing the good passions and controlling the bad, to merit an inheritance in a state of being of which I can know so little, and to trust for the future to Him who has been so good for the past. I perceive too that these speculations have with you been only the amusement of leisure hours; while your labors have been devoted to the education of your children, making them good members of society, to the instructing men in their duties, and performing the other offices of a large parish. I am happy in your approbation of the principles I avowed on entering on the government. Ingenious minds, availing themselves of the imperfection of language, have tortured the expressions out of their plain meaning in order to infer departures from them in practice. If revealed language has not been able to guard itself against misinterpretations, I could not expect it. But if an administration "quadrating with the obvious import of my language can conciliate the affections of my opposers," I will merit that conciliation. I pray you to accept assurances of my respect and best wishes.

34. TO BENJAMIN RUSH [136]

[DOCTRINES OF JESUS]

WASHINGTON, April 21, 1803.

DEAR SIR,—

In some of the delightful conversations with you, in the evenings of 1798–99, and which served as an anodyne to the afflictions of the crisis through which our country was then laboring, the Christian religion was sometimes our topic; and I then promised you, that one day or other, I would give you my views of it. They are the result of a life of inquiry and reflection, and very different from that anti-Christian system imputed to me by those who know nothing of my opinions. To the corruptions of Christianity I am, indeed, opposed; but not to the genuine precepts of Jesus himself. I am a Christian, in the only sense he wished any one to be; sincerely attached to his doctrines, in preference to all others; ascribing to himself every *human* excellence; and believing he never claimed any other. At the short interval since these conversations, when I could justifiably abstract my mind from public affairs, the subject has been under my contemplation. But the more I considered it, the more it expanded beyond the measure of either my time or information. In the moment of my late departure from Monticello, I received from Dr. Priestley, his little treatise of "Socrates and Jesus Compared." This being a section of the general view I had taken of the field, it became a subject of reflection while on the road, and unoccupied otherwise. The result was, to arrange in my mind a syllabus, or outline of such an estimate of the comparative merits of Christianity, as I wished to see executed by some one of more leisure and information for the task, than myself. This I now send you, as the only discharge of my promise I can probably ever execute. And in confiding it to you, I know it will not be exposed to the malignant perversions of those who make every word from me a text for new misrepresentations and calumnies. I am moreover averse to the communication of my religious tenets to the public; because it would countenance the presumption of those who have endeavored to draw them before that tribunal, and to seduce public opinion to erect itself into that inquisition over the rights of conscience, which the laws have so justly proscribed. It behooves every man who values liberty of conscience for himself, to resist invasions of it in the case of others; or their case may, by change of circumstances, become his own. It behooves him, too, in his own case, to give no example of concession, betraying the common right of independent opinion, by answering questions of faith, which the laws have left between God and himself. Accept my affectionate salutations.

Syllabus of an Estimate of the Merit of the Doctrines of Jesus, compared with those of others.

In a comparative view of the Ethics of the enlightened nations of antiquity, of the Jews and of Jesus, no notice should be taken of the corruptions of reason among the ancients, to wit, the idolatry and superstition of the vulgar, nor of the corruptions of Christianity by the learned among its professors.

Let a just view be taken of the moral principles inculcated by the most esteemed of the sects of ancient philosophy, or of their individuals; particularly Pythagoras, Socrates, Epicurus, Cicero, Epictetus, Seneca, Antoninus.

I. Philosophers. 1. Their precepts related chiefly to ourselves, and the government of those passions which, unrestrained, would disturb our tranquillity of mind.* In this branch of philosophy they were really great.

2. In developing our duties to others, they were short and defective. They embraced, indeed, the circles of kindred and friends, and inculcated patriotism, or the love of our country in the aggregate, as a primary obligation; toward our neighbors and countrymen they taught justice, but scarcely viewed them as within the circle of benevolence. Still less have they inculcated peace, charity, and love to our fellow men, or embraced with benevolence the whole family of mankind.

II. Jews. 1. Their system was Deism; that is, the belief of

---

*To explain, I will exhibit the heads of Seneca's and Cicero's philosophical works, the most extensive of any we have received from the ancients. Of ten heads in Seneca, seven relate to ourselves, to wit, *de ira, consolatio, de tranquillitate, de constantia sapientis, de otio sapientis, de vita beata, de brevitate vitæ;* two relate to others, *de clementia, de beneficiis;* and one relates to the government of the world, *de providentia.* Of eleven tenets of Cicero, five respect ourselves, viz. *de finibus, Tusculana, academica, paradoxa, de senectute;* one, *de officiis,* relates partly to ourselves, partly to others; one, *de amicitia,* relates to others; and four are on different subjects, to wit, *de natura deorum, de divinatione, de fato,* and *somnium Scipionis.*

one only God. But their ideas of him and of his attributes were degrading and injurious.

2. Their Ethics were not only imperfect, but often irreconcilable with the sound dictates of reason and morality, as they respect intercourse with those around us; and repulsive and anti-social, as respecting other nations. They needed reformation, therefore, in an eminent degree.

III. Jesus. In this state of things among the Jews, Jesus appeared. His parentage was obscure; his condition poor; his education null; his natural endowments great; his life correct and innocent; he was meek, benevolent, patient, firm, disinterested, and of the sublimest eloquence.

The disadvantages under which his doctrines appear are remarkable.

1. Like Socrates and Epictetus, he wrote nothing himself.

2. But he had not, like them, a Xenophon or an Arrian to write for him. I name not Plato, who only used the name of Socrates to cover the whimsies of his own brain. On the contrary, all the learned of his country, entrenched in its power and riches, were opposed to him, lest his labors should undermine their advantages; and the committing to writing his life and doctrines fell on unlettered and ignorant men; who wrote, too, from memory, and not till long after the transactions had passed.

3. According to the ordinary fate of those who attempt to enlighten and reform mankind, he fell an early victim to the jealousy and combination of the altar and the throne, at about thirty-three years of age, his reason having not yet attained the *maximum* of its energy, nor the course of his preaching, which was but of three years at most, presented occasions for developing a complete system of morals.

4. Hence the doctrines which he really delivered were defective as a whole, and fragments only of what he did deliver have come to us mutilated, misstated, and often unintelligible.

5. They have been still more disfigured by the corruptions of schismatizing followers, who have found an interest in sophisticating and perverting the simple doctrines he taught,

by engrafting on them the mysticisms of a Grecian sophist, frittering them into subtleties, and obscuring them with jargon, until they have caused good men to reject the whole in disgust, and to view Jesus himself as an impostor.

Notwithstanding these disadvantages, a system of morals is presented to us, which, if filled up in the true style and spirit of the rich fragments he left us, would be the most perfect and sublime that has ever been taught by man.

The question of his being a member of the Godhead, or in direct communication with it, claimed for him by some of his followers, and denied by others, is foreign to the present view, which is merely an estimate of the intrinsic merit of his doctrines.

1. He corrected the Deism of the Jews, confirming them in their belief of one only God, and giving them juster notions of his attributes and government.

2. His moral doctrines, relating to kindred and friends, were more pure and perfect than those of the most correct of the philosophers, and greatly more so than those of the Jews; and they went far beyond both in inculcating universal philanthropy, not only to kindred and friends, to neighbors and countrymen, but to all mankind, gathering all into one family, under the bonds of love, charity, peace, common wants and common aids. A development of this head will evince the peculiar superiority of the system of Jesus over all others.

3. The precepts of philosophy, and of the Hebrew code, laid hold of actions only. He pushed his scrutinies into the heart of man; erected his tribunal in the region of his thoughts, and purified the waters at the fountain head.

4. He taught, emphatically, the doctrines of a future state, which was either doubted, or disbelieved by the Jews; and wielded it with efficacy, as an important incentive, supplementary to the other motives to moral conduct.

35. *From* THIRD ANNUAL MESSAGE [137]

OCTOBER 17, 1803

[EUROPEAN WAR]

...We have seen with sincere concern the flames of war lighted up again in Europe, and nations with which we have the most friendly and useful relations engaged in mutual destruction. While we regret the miseries in which we see others involved, let us bow with gratitude to that kind Providence which, inspiring with wisdom and moderation our late legislative councils while placed under the urgency of the greatest wrongs, guarded us from hastily entering into the sanguinary contest, and left us only to look on and to pity its ravages. These will be heaviest on those immediately engaged. Yet the nations pursuing peace will not be exempt from all evil. In the course of this conflict, let it be our endeavor, as it is our interest and desire, to cultivate the friendship of the belligerent nations by every act of justice and of incessant kindness; to receive their armed vessels with hospitality from the distresses of the sea, but to administer the means of annoyance to none; to establish in our harbors such a police as may maintain law and order; to restrain our citizens from embarking individually in a war in which their country takes no part; to punish severely those persons, citizen or alien, who shall usurp the cover of our flag for vessels not entitled to it, infecting thereby with suspicion those of real Americans, and committing us into controversies for the redress of wrongs not our own; to exact from every nation the observance, toward our vessels and citizens, of those principles and practices which all civilized people acknowledge; to merit the character of a just nation, and maintain that of an independent one, preferring every consequence to insult and habitual wrong. Congress will consider whether the existing laws enable us efficaciously to maintain this course with our citizens in all places, and with others while within the limits of our jurisdiction, and will give them the new modifications necessary for these objects. Some contraventions of right have already taken place, both within our jurisdictional limits and on the high seas. The friendly disposition of the governments from whose agents they have proceeded, as well as their wisdom and regard for justice, leave us in reasonable expectation that they will be rectified and prevented in future; and that no act will be countenanced by them which threatens to disturb our friendly intercourse. Separated by a wide ocean from the nations of Europe, and from the political interests which entangle them together, with productions and wants which render our commerce and friendship useful to them and theirs to us, it cannot be the interest of any to assail us, nor ours to disturb them. We should be most unwise, indeed, were we to cast away the singular blessings of the position in which nature has placed us, the opportunity she has endowed us with of pursuing, at a distance from foreign contentions, the paths of industry, peace, and happiness; of cultivating general friendship, and of bringing collisions of interest to the umpirage of reason rather than of force. How desirable then must it be, in a government like ours, to see its citizens adopt individually the views, the interests, and the conduct which their country should pursue, divesting themselves of those passions and partialities which tend to lessen useful friendships, and to embarrass and embroil us in the calamitous scenes of Europe. Confident, fellow citizens, that you will duly estimate the importance of neutral dispositions toward the observance of neutral conduct, that you will be sensible how much it is our duty to look on the bloody arena spread before us with commiseration indeed, but with no other wish than to see it closed, I am persuaded you will cordially cherish these dispositions in all discussions among yourselves, and in all communications with your constituents; and I anticipate with satisfaction the measures of wisdom which the great interests now committed to *you* will give you an opportunity of providing, and *myself* that of approving and carrying into execution with the fidelity I owe to my country. . . .

36. TO MRS. JOHN ADAMS [138]

[AN ATTEMPT AT RECONCILIATION]

WASHINGTON, June 13, 1804.

DEAR MADAM,—

The affectionate sentiments which you have had the goodness to express in your letter of May 20th, towards my dear departed daughter, have awakened in me sensibilities natural to the occasion, and recalled your kindnesses to her, which I shall ever remember with gratitude and friendship. I can assure you with truth, they had made an indelible impression on her mind, and that to the last, on our meetings after long separations, whether I had heard lately of you, and how you did, were among the earliest of her inquiries. In giving you this assurance I perform a sacred duty for her, and, at the same time, am thankful for the occasion furnished me, of expressing my regret that circumstances should have arisen, which have seemed to draw a line of separation between us. The friendship with which you honored me has ever been valued, and fully reciprocated; and although events have been passing which might be trying to some minds, I never believed yours to be of that kind, nor felt that my own was. Neither my estimate of your character, nor the esteem founded in that, have ever been lessened for a single moment, although doubts whether it would be acceptable may have forbidden manifestations of it.

Mr. Adams's friendship and mine began at an earlier date. It accompanied us through long and important scenes. The different conclusions we had drawn from our political reading and reflections were not permitted to lessen personal esteem; each party being conscious they were the result of an honest conviction in the other. Like differences of opinion existing among our fellow citizens attached them to one or the other of us, and produced a rivalship in their minds which did not exist in ours. We never stood in one another's way; for if either had been withdrawn at any time, his favorers would not have gone over to the other, but would have sought for some one of homogeneous opinions. This consideration was sufficient to keep down all jealousy between us, and to guard our friendship from any disturbance by sentiments of rivalship; and I can say with truth, that one act of Mr. Adams's life, and one only, ever gave me a moment's personal displeasure. I did consider his last appointments to office as personally unkind. They were from among my most ardent political enemies, from whom no faithful co-operation could ever be expected; and laid me under the embarrassment of acting through men whose views were to defeat mine, or to encounter the odium of putting others in their places. It seemed but common justice to leave a successor free to act by instruments of his own choice. If my respect for him did not permit me to ascribe the whole blame to the influence of others, it left something for friendship to forgive, and after brooding over it for some little time, and not always resisting the expression of it, I forgave it cordially, and returned to the same state of esteem and respect for him which had so long subsisted. Having come into life a little later than Mr. Adams, his career has preceded mine, as mine is followed by some other; and it will probably be closed at the same distance after him which time originally placed between us. I maintain for him, and shall carry into private life, an uniform and high measure of respect and good will, and for yourself a sincere attachment.

I have thus, my dear Madam, opened myself to you without reserve, which I have long wished an opportunity of doing; and without knowing how it will be received, I feel relief from being unbosomed. And I have now only to entreat your forgiveness for this transition from a subject of domestic affliction, to one which seems of a different aspect. But though connected with political events, it has been viewed by me most strongly in its unfortunate bearings on my private friendships. The injury these have sustained has been a heavy price for what has never given me equal pleasure. That you may both be favored with health, tranquillity, and long life, is the prayer of one who tenders you the assurance of his highest consideration and esteem.

37. SECOND INAUGURAL ADDRESS

MARCH 4, 1805

Proceeding, fellow citizens, to that qualification which the Constitution requires, before my entrance on the charge again conferred upon me, it is my duty to express the deep sense I entertain of this new proof of confidence from my fellow citizens at large, and the zeal with which it inspires me, so to conduct myself as may best satisfy their just expectations.

On taking this station on a former occasion, I declared the principles on which I believed it my duty to administer the affairs of our commonwealth. My conscience tells me that I have, on every occasion, acted up to that declaration, according to its obvious import, and to the understanding of every candid mind.

In the transaction of your foreign affairs, we have endeavored to cultivate the friendship of all nations, and especially of those with which we have the most important relations. We have done them justice on all occasions, favored where favor was lawful, and cherished mutual interests and intercourse on fair and equal terms. We are firmly convinced, and we act on that conviction, that with nations, as with individuals, our interests soundly calculated, will ever be found inseparable from our moral duties;[139] and history bears witness to the fact, that a just nation is taken on its word, when recourse is had to armaments and wars to bridle others.

At home, fellow citizens, you best know whether we have done well or ill. The suppression of unnecessary offices, of useless establishments and expenses, enabled us to discontinue our internal taxes. These covering our land with officers, and opening our doors to their intrusions, had already begun that process of domiciliary vexation which, once entered, is scarcely to be restrained from reaching successively every article of produce and property. If among these taxes some minor ones fell which had not been inconvenient, it was because their amount would not have paid the officers who collected them, and because, if they had any merit, the state authorities might adopt them, instead of others less approved.

The remaining revenue on the consumption of foreign articles is paid cheerfully by those who can afford to add foreign luxuries to domestic comforts; being collected on our seaboards and frontiers only, and incorporated with the transactions of our mercantile citizens, it may be the pleasure and pride of an American to ask, what farmer, what mechanic, what laborer, ever sees a tax-gatherer of the United States? These contributions enable us to support the current expenses of the government, to fulfil contracts with foreign nations, to extinguish the native right of soil within our limits, to extend those limits, and to apply such a surplus to our public debts, as places at a short day their final redemption, and that redemption once effected, the revenue thereby liberated may, by a just repartition among the states, and a corresponding amendment of the Constitution, be applied, *in time of peace*, to rivers, canals, roads, arts, manufactures, education, and other great objects within each state. *In time of war*, if injustice, by ourselves or others, must sometimes produce war, increased as the same revenue will be increased by population and consumption, and aided by other resources reserved for that crisis, it may meet within the year all the expenses of the year, without encroaching on the rights of future generations, by burdening them with the debts of the past. War will then be but a suspension of useful works, and a return to a state of peace, a return to the progress of improvement.

I have said, fellow citizens, that the income reserved had enabled us to extend our limits; but that extension may possibly pay for itself before we are called on, and in the meantime, may keep down the accruing interest; in all events, it will repay the advances we have made. I know that the acquisition of Louisiana has been disapproved by some, from a candid apprehension that the enlargement of our territory would endanger its union. But who can limit the extent to which the federative principle may operate effectively? The larger our association, the less will it be shaken by local passions; and in any view, is it not

better that the opposite bank of the Mississippi should be settled by our own brethren and children, than by strangers of
another family? With which shall we be most likely to live in
harmony and friendly intercourse?

In matters of religion, I have considered that its free exercise
is placed by the Constitution independent of the powers of the
general government. I have therefore undertaken, on no occasion, to prescribe the religious exercises suited to it; but have
left them, as the Constitution found them, under the direction
and discipline of state or church authorities acknowledged by
the several religious societies.

The aboriginal inhabitants of these countries I have regarded
with the commiseration their history inspires. Endowed with
the faculties and the rights of men, breathing an ardent love of
liberty and independence, and occupying a country which left
them no desire but to be undisturbed, the stream of overflow-
ing population from other regions directed itself on these
shores; without power to divert, or habits to contend against,
they have been overwhelmed by the current, or driven before
it; now reduced within limits too narrow for the hunter's state,
humanity enjoins us to teach them agriculture and the domestic
arts; to encourage them to that industry which alone can enable
them to maintain their place in existence, and to prepare them
in time for that state of society, which to bodily comforts adds
the improvement of the mind and morals. We have therefore
liberally furnished them with the implements of husbandry
and household use; we have placed among them instructors in
the arts of first necessity; and they are covered with the ægis of
the law against aggressors from among ourselves.

But the endeavors to enlighten them on the fate which awaits
their present course of life, to induce them to exercise their
reason, follow its dictates, and change their pursuits with the
change of circumstances, have powerful obstacles to encounter;
they are combated by the habits of their bodies, prejudice of
their minds, ignorance, pride, and the influence of interested
and crafty individuals among them, who feel themselves something in the present order of things, and fear to become nothing

in any other. These persons inculcate a sanctimonious reverence for the customs of their ancestors; that whatsoever they did, must be done through all time; that reason is a false guide, and to advance under its counsel, in their physical, moral, or political condition, is perilous innovation; that their duty is to remain as their Creator made them, ignorance being safety, and knowledge full of danger; in short, my friends, among them is seen the action and counteraction of good sense and bigotry; they, too, have their anti-philosophers,[140] who find an interest in keeping things in their present state, who dread reformation, and exert all their faculties to maintain the ascendency of habit over the duty of improving our reason, and obeying its mandates.

In giving these outlines, I do not mean, fellow citizens, to arrogate to myself the merit of the measures; that is due, in the first place, to the reflecting character of our citizens at large, who, by the weight of public opinion, influence and strengthen the public measures; it is due to the sound discretion with which they select from among themselves those to whom they confide the legislative duties; it is due to the zeal and wisdom of the characters thus selected, who lay the foundations of public happiness in wholesome laws, the execution of which alone remains for others; and it is due to the able and faithful auxiliaries, whose patriotism has associated with me in the executive functions.

During this course of administration, and in order to disturb it, the artillery of the press has been levelled against us, charged with whatsoever its licentiousness could devise or dare. These abuses of an institution so important to freedom and science, are deeply to be regretted, inasmuch as they tend to lessen its usefulness, and to sap its safety; they might, indeed, have been corrected by the wholesome punishments reserved and provided by the laws of the several States against falsehood and defamation; but public duties more urgent press on the time of public servants, and the offenders have therefore been left to find their punishment in the public indignation.

Nor was it uninteresting to the world, that an experiment should be fairly and fully made, whether freedom of discussion, unaided by power, is not sufficient for the propagation and protection of truth—whether a government, conducting itself in the true spirit of its constitution, with zeal and purity, and doing no act which it would be unwilling the whole world should witness, can be written down by falsehood and defamation. The experiment has been tried; you have witnessed the scene; our fellow citizens have looked on, cool and collected; they saw the latent source from which these outrages proceeded; they gathered around their public functionaries and when the constitution called them to the decision by suffrage, they pronounced their verdict, honorable to those who had served them, and consolatory to the friend of man, who believes he may be intrusted with his own affairs.

No inference is here intended, that the laws, provided by the State against false and defamatory publications, should not be enforced; he who has time, renders a service to public morals and public tranquillity, in reforming these abuses by the salutary coercions of the law; but the experiment is noted, to prove that, since truth and reason have maintained their ground against false opinions in league with false facts, the press, confined to truth, needs no other legal restraint; the public judgment will correct false reasonings and opinions, on a full hearing of all parties; and no other definite line can be drawn between the inestimable liberty of the press and its demoralizing licentiousness. If there be still improprieties which this rule would not restrain, its supplement must be sought in the censorship of public opinion.

Contemplating the union of sentiment now manifested so generally, as auguring harmony and happiness to our future course, I offer to our country sincere congratulations. With those, too, not yet rallied to the same point, the disposition to do so is gaining strength; facts are piercing through the veil drawn over them; and our doubting brethren will at length see, that the mass of their fellow citizens, with whom they cannot yet resolve to act, as to principles and measures, think as they think, and desire what they desire; that our wish, as well as theirs, is, that the public efforts may be directed honestly to the public good, that peace be cultivated, civil and religious liberty unassailed, law and order preserved, equality of rights maintained, and that state of property, equal or unequal, which results to every man from his own industry, or that of his fathers. When satisfied of these views, it is not in human nature that they should not approve and support them; in the meantime, let us cherish them with patient affection; let us do them justice, and more than justice, in all competitions of interest; and we need not doubt that truth, reason, and their own interests, will at length prevail, will gather them into the fold of their country, and will complete their entire union of opinion, which gives to a nation the blessing of harmony, and the benefit of all its strength.

I shall now enter on the duties to which my fellow citizens have again called me, and shall proceed in the spirit of those principles which they have approved. I fear not that any motives of interest may lead me astray; I am sensible of no passion which could seduce me knowingly from the path of justice; but the weakness of human nature, and the limits of my own understanding, will produce errors of judgment sometimes injurious to your interests. I shall need, therefore, all the indulgence I have heretofore experienced; the want of it will certainly not lessen with increasing years. I shall need, too, the favor of that Being in whose hands we are, who led our forefathers, as Israel of old,[141] from their native land, and planted them in a country flowing with all the necessaries and comforts of life; who has covered our infancy with his providence, and our riper years with his wisdom and power; and to whose goodness I ask you to join with me in supplications, that he will so enlighten the minds of your servants, guide their councils, and prosper their measures, that whatsoever they do, shall result in your good, and shall secure to you the peace, friendship, and approbation of all nations.

38. TO THOMAS JEFFERSON RANDOLPH [142]

[A GRANDFATHER'S ADVICE]

WASHINGTON, November 24, 1808.

MY DEAR JEFFERSON,—

...Your situation, thrown at such a distance from us, and alone, cannot but give us all great anxieties for you. As much has been secured for you, by your particular position and the acquaintance to which you have been recommended, as could be done towards shielding you from the dangers which surround you. But thrown on a wide world, among entire strangers, without a friend or guardian to advise, so young too, and with so little experience of mankind, your dangers are great, and still your safety must rest on yourself. A determination never to do what is wrong, prudence and good humor, will go far towards securing to you the estimation of the world. When I recollect that at fourteen years of age, the whole care and direction of myself was thrown on myself entirely, without a relation or friend qualified to advise or guide me, and recollect the various sorts of bad company with which I associated from time to time, I am astonished I did not turn off with some of them, and become as worthless to society as they were. I had the good fortune to become acquainted very early with some characters of very high standing, and to feel the incessant wish that I could ever become what they were. Under temptations and difficulties, I would ask myself, what would Dr. Small, Mr. Wythe, Peyton Randolph do in this situation? What course in it will insure me their approbation? I am certain that this mode of deciding on my conduct tended more to its correctness than any reasoning powers I possessed. Knowing the even and dignified line they pursued, I could never doubt for a moment which of two courses would be in character for them. Whereas, seeking the same object through a process of moral reasoning, and with the jaundiced eye of youth, I should often have erred. From the circumstances of my position, I was often thrown into the society of horse-racers, card-players, fox-hunters, scientific and professional men, and of dignified men; and many a time have I asked myself, in the enthusiastic moment of the death of a fox, the victory of a favorite horse, the issue of a question eloquently argued at the bar, or in the great council of the nation,—well, which of these kinds of reputation should I prefer? That of a horse-jockey? a fox-hunter? an orator? or the honest advocate of my country's rights? Be assured, my dear Jefferson, that these little returns into ourselves, this self-catechising habit, is not trifling nor useless, but leads to the prudent selection and steady pursuit of what is right.

I have mentioned good humor as one of the preservatives of our peace and tranquillity. It is among the most effectual, and its effect is so well imitated and aided, artificially, by politeness, that this also becomes an acquisition of first rate value. In truth, politeness is artificial good humor, it covers the natural want of it, and ends by rendering habitual a substitute nearly equivalent to the real virtue. It is the practice of sacrificing to those whom we meet in society, all the little conveniences and preferences which will gratify them, and deprive us of nothing worth a moment's consideration; it is the giving a pleasing and flattering turn to our expressions, which will conciliate others, and make them pleased with us as well as themselves. How cheap a price for the good will of another! When this is in return for a rude thing said by another, it brings him to his senses, it mortifies and corrects him in the most salutary way, and places him at the feet of your good nature, in the eyes of the company. But in stating prudential rules for our government in society, I must not omit the important one of never entering into dispute or argument with another. I never saw an instance of one of two disputants convincing the other by argument. I have seen many, on their getting warm, becoming rude, and shooting one another. Conviction is the effect of our own dispassionate reasoning, either in solitude, or weighing within ourselves, dispassionately, what we hear from others, standing uncommitted in argument ourselves. It was one of the rules which, above all others, made Doctor Franklin the most amiable of men in society, "never to contradict anybody." If he was urged to announce an opinion, he did it rather by asking questions, as if for information, or by suggesting doubts. When I hear another express an opinion which is not mine, I say to myself, he has a right to his opinion, as I to mine; why should I question it? His error does me no injury, and shall I become a Don Quixote, to bring all men by force of argument to one opinion? If a fact be misstated, it is probable he is gratified by a belief of it, and I have no right to deprive him of the gratification. If he wants information, he will ask it, and then I will give it in measured terms; but if he still believes his own story, and shows a desire to dispute the fact with me, I hear him and say nothing. It is his affair, not mine, if he prefers error. There are two classes of disputants most frequently to be met with among us. The first is of young students, just entered the threshold of science, with a first view of its outlines, not yet filled up with the details and modifications which a further progress would bring to their knowledge. The other consists of the ill-tempered and rude men in society, who have taken up a passion for politics. (Good humor and politeness never introduce into mixed society a question on which they foresee there will be a difference of opinion.) From both of those classes of disputants, my dear Jefferson, keep aloof, as you would from the infected subjects of yellow fever or pestilence. Consider yourself, when with them, as among the patients of Bedlam, needing medical more than moral counsel. Be a listener only, keep within yourself, and endeavor to establish with yourself the habit of silence, especially on politics. In the fevered state of our country, no good can ever result from any attempt to set one of these fiery zealots to rights, either in fact or principle. They are determined as to the facts they will believe, and the opinions on which they will act. Get by them, therefore, as you would by an angry bull; it is not for a man of sense to dispute the road with such an animal. You will be more exposed than others to have these animals shaking their horns at you, because of the relation in which you stand with me. Full of political venom, and willing to see me and to hate me as a chief in the antagonist party, your presence will be to them what the vomit grass is to the sick dog, a nostrum for producing ejaculation. Look upon them exactly with that eye, and pity them as objects to whom you can administer only occasional ease. My character is not within their power. It is in the hands of my fellow citizens at large, and will be consigned to honor or infamy by the verdict of the republican mass of our country, according to what themselves will have seen, not what their enemies and mine shall have said. Never, therefore, consider these puppies in politics as requiring any notice from you, and always show that you are not afraid to leave my character to the umpirage of public opinion. Look steadily to the pursuits which have carried you to Philadelphia, be very select in the society you attach yourself to, avoid taverns, drinkers, smokers, idlers, and dissipated persons generally; for it is with such that broils and contentions arise; and you will find your path more easy and tranquil. The limits of my paper warn me that it is time for me to close with my affectionate adieu.

P. S. Present me affectionately to Mr. Ogilvie, and, in doing the same to Mr. Peale, tell him I am writing with his polygraph, and shall send him mine the first moment I have leisure enough to pack it.

39. TO BENJAMIN RUSH

[RELATIONS WITH JOHN ADAMS]

MONTICELLO, January 16, 1811.

DEAR SIR,—

I had been considering for some days, whether it was not time by a letter, to bring myself to your recollection, when I received your welcome favor of the 2d instant. I had before heard of the heart-rending calamity you mention, and had sincerely sympathized with your afflictions. But I had not made it the subject of a letter, because I knew that condolences were but renewals of grief. Yet I thought, and still think, this is one of the cases wherein we should "not sorrow, even as others who have no hope." . . .

You ask if I have read Hartley? I have not. My present

course of life admits less reading than I wish. From breakfast, or noon at latest, to dinner, I am mostly on horseback, attending to my farm or other concerns, which I find healthful to my body, mind, and affairs; and the few hours I can pass in my cabinet, are devoured by correspondences; not those with my intimate friends, with whom I delight to interchange sentiments, but with others, who, writing to me on concerns of their own in which I have had an agency, or from motives of mere respect and approbation, are entitled to be answered with respect and a return of good will. My hope is that this obstacle to the delights of retirement will wear away with the oblivion which follows that, and that I may at length be indulged in those studious pursuits, from which nothing but revolutionary duties would ever have called me.

I shall receive your proposed publication and read it with the pleasure which everything gives me from your pen. Although much of a sceptic in the practice of medicine, I read with pleasure its ingenious theories.

I receive with sensibility your observations on the discontinuance of friendly correspondence between Mr. Adams and myself, and the concern you take in its restoration. This discontinuance has not proceeded from me, nor from the want of sincere desire and of effort on my part, to renew our intercourse. You know the perfect coincidence of principle and of action, in the early part of the Revolution, which produced a high degree of mutual respect and esteem between Mr. Adams and myself. Certainly no man was ever truer than he was, in that day, to those principles of rational republicanism which, after the necessity of throwing off our monarchy, dictated all our efforts in the establishment of a new government. And although he swerved, afterwards, towards the principles of the English constitution, our friendship did not abate on that account. While he was Vice-President, and I Secretary of State, I received a letter from President Washington, then at Mount Vernon, desiring me to call together the heads of departments, and to invite Mr. Adams to join us (which, by-the-bye, was the only instance of that being done), in order to determine on some measure which required despatch; and he desired me to act on it, as decided, without again recurring to him. I invited them to dine with me, and after dinner, sitting at our wine, having settled our question, other conversation came on, in which a collision of opinion arose between Mr. Adams and Colonel Hamilton, on the merits of the British constitution, Mr. Adams giving it as his opinion, that, if some of its defects and abuses were corrected, it would be the most perfect constitution of government ever devised by man. Hamilton, on the contrary, asserted, that with its existing vices, it was the most perfect model of government that could be formed; and that the correction of its vices would render it an impracticable government. And this you may be assured was the real line of difference between the political principles of these two gentlemen. Another incident took place on the same occasion, which will further delineate Mr. Hamilton's political principles. The room being hung around with a collection of the portraits of remarkable men, among them were those of Bacon, Newton, and Locke, Hamilton asked me who they were. I told him they were my trinity of the three greatest men the world had ever produced, naming them. He paused for some time: "The greatest man," said he, "that ever lived, was Julius Cæsar." Mr. Adams was honest as a politician, as well as a man; Hamilton honest as a man, but, as a politician, believing in the necessity of either force or corruption to govern men.

You remember the machinery which the federalists played off, about that time, to beat down the friends to the real principles of our Constitution, to silence by terror every expression in their favor, to bring us into war with France and alliance with England, and finally to homologize our Constitution with that of England. Mr. Adams, you know, was overwhelmed with feverish addresses, dictated by the fear, and often by the pen, of the *bloody buoy*, and was seduced by them into some open indications of his new principles of government, and in fact, was so elated as to mix with his kindness a little superciliousness towards me. Even Mrs. Adams, with all her good sense and prudence, was sensibly flushed. And you recollect the short suspension of our intercourse, and the circumstance which gave rise to it, which you were so good as to bring to an early explanation, and have set to rights, to the cordial satisfaction of us all. The nation at length passed condemnation on the political principles of the federalists, by refusing to continue Mr. Adams in the Presidency. On the day on which we learned in Philadelphia the vote of the city of New York, which it was well known would decide the vote of the State, and that, again, the vote of the Union, I called on Mr. Adams on some official business. He was very sensibly affected, and accosted me with these words: "Well, I understand that you are to beat me in this contest, and I will only say that I will be as faithful a subject as any you will have." "Mr. Adams," said I, "this is no personal contest between you and me. Two systems of principles on the subject of government divide our fellow citizens into two parties. With one of these you concur, and I with the other. As we have been longer on the public stage than most of those now living, our names happen to be more generally known. One of these parties, therefore, has put your name at its head, the other mine. Were we both to die to-day, to-morrow two other names would be in the place of ours, without any change in the motion of the machinery. Its motion is from its principle, not from you or myself." "I believe you are right," said he, "that we are but passive instruments, and should not suffer this matter to affect our personal dispositions." But he did not long retain this just view of the subject. I have always believed that the thousand calumnies which the federalists, in bitterness of heart, and mortification at their ejection, daily invented against me, were carried to him by their busy intriguers, and made some impression. When the election between Burr and myself was kept in suspense by the federalists, and they were mediating to place the President of the Senate at the head of the government, I called on Mr. Adams with a view to have this desperate measure prevented by his negative. He grew warm in an instant, and said with a vehemence he had not used towards me before, "Sir, the event of the election is within your own power. You have only to say you will do justice to the public creditors, maintain the navy, and not disturb those holding offices, and the government will instantly be put into your hands. We know it is the wish of the people it should be so." "Mr. Adams," said I, "I know not what part of my conduct, in either public or private life, can have authorized a doubt of my fidelity to the public engagements. I say, however, I will not come into the government by capitulation. I will not enter on it, but in perfect freedom to follow the dictates of my own judgment." I had before given the same answer to the same intimation from Gouverneur Morris. "Then," said he, "things must take their course." I turned the conversation to something else, and soon took my leave. It was the first time in our lives we had ever parted with anything like dissatisfaction. And then followed those scenes of midnight appointment, which have been condemned by all men. The last day of his political power, the last hours, and even beyond the midnight, were employed in filling all offices, and especially permanent ones, with the bitterest federalists, and providing for me the alternative, either to execute the government by my enemies, whose study it would be to thwart and defeat all my measures, or to incur the odium of such numerous removals from office, as might bear me down. A little time and reflection effaced in my mind this temporary dissatisfaction with Mr. Adams, and restored me to that just estimate of his virtues and passions, which a long acquaintance had enabled me to fix. And my first wish became that of making his retirement easy by any means in my power; for it was understood he was not rich. I suggested to some republican members of the delegation from his State, the giving him, either directly or indirectly, an office, the most lucrative in that State, and then offered to be resigned, if they thought he would not deem it affrontive. They were of opinion he would take great offence at the offer; and moreover, that the body of republicans would consider such a step in the outset as auguring very ill of the course I meant to pursue. I dropped the idea, therefore, but did not cease to wish for some opportunity of renewing our friendly understanding.

Two or three years after, having had the misfortune to lose a daughter, between whom and Mrs. Adams there had been a considerable attachment, she made it the occasion of writing me a letter, in which, with the tenderest expressions of concern at this event, she carefully avoided a single one of friendship towards myself, and even concluded it with the wishes "of her who *once* took pleasure in subscribing herself your friend, Abigail Adams." Unpromising as was the complexion of this letter, I determined to make an effort towards removing the cloud from between us. This brought on a correspondence which I now enclose for your perusal, after which be so good as to return it to me, as I have never communicated it to any mortal breathing, before. I send it to you, to convince you I have not been wanting either in the desire, or the endeavor to remove this misunderstanding. Indeed, I thought it highly disgraceful to us both, as indicating minds not sufficiently elevated to prevent a public competition from affecting our personal friendship. I soon found from the correspondence that conciliation was desperate, and yielding to an intimation in her last letter, I ceased from further explanation. I have the same good opinion of Mr. Adams which I ever had. I know him to be an honest man, an able one with his pen, and he was a powerful advocate on the floor of Congress. He has been alienated from me, by belief in the lying suggestions contrived for electioneering purposes, that I perhaps mixed in the activity and intrigues of the occasion. My most intimate friends can testify that I was perfectly passive. They would sometimes, indeed, tell me what was going on; but no man ever heard me take part in such conversations; and none ever misrepresented Mr. Adams in my presence, without my asserting his just character. With very confidential persons I have doubtless disapproved of the principles and practices of his administration. This was unavoidable. But never with those with whom it could do him any injury. Decency would have required this conduct from me, if disposition had not; and I am satisfied Mr. Adams's conduct was equally honorable towards me. But I think it part of his character to suspect foul play in those of whom he is jealous, and not easily to relinquish his suspicions.

I have gone, my dear friend, into these details, that you

might know everything which had passed between us, might be fully possessed of the state of facts and dispositions, and judge for yourself whether they admit a revival of that friendly intercourse for which you are so kindly solicitous. I shall certainly not be wanting in anything on my part which may second your efforts, which will be the easier with me, inasmuch as I do not entertain a sentiment of Mr. Adams, the expression of which could give him reasonable offence. And I submit the whole to yourself, with the assurance, that whatever be the issue, my friendship and respect for yourself will remain unaltered and unalterable.

40. TO JOHN ADAMS[143]

[AN OLD FRIENDSHIP RENEWED]

MONTICELLO, January 21, 1812.

DEAR SIR,—

I thank you beforehand (for they are not yet arrived) for the specimens of homespun you have been so kind as to forward me by post. I doubt not their excellence, knowing how far you are advanced in these things in your quarter. Here we do little in the fine way, but in coarse and middling goods a great deal. Every family in the country is a manufactory within itself, and is very generally able to make within itself all the stouter and middling stuffs for its own clothing and household use. We consider a sheep for every person in the family as sufficient to clothe it, in addition to the cotton, hemp, and flax which we raise ourselves. For fine stuff we shall depend on your northern manufactories. Of these, that is to say, of company establishments, we have none. We use little machinery. The spinning-jenny, and loom with the flying shuttle, can be managed in a family; but nothing more complicated. The economy and thriftiness resulting from our household manufactures are such that they will never again be laid aside; and nothing more salutary for us has ever happened than the British obstructions to our demands for their manufactures. Restore free intercourse when they will, their commerce with us will have totally changed its form, and the articles we shall in future want from them will not exceed their own consumption of our produce.

A letter from you calls up recollections very dear to my mind. It carries me back to the times when, beset with difficulties and dangers, we were fellow laborers in the same cause, struggling for what is most valuable to man, his right of self-government. Laboring always at the same oar, with some wave ever ahead, threatening to overwhelm us, and yet passing harmless under our bark, we knew not how we rode through the storm with heart and hand, and made a happy port. Still we did not expect to be without rubs and difficulties; and we have had them. First, the detention of the western posts, then the coalition of Pilnitz, outlawing our commerce with France, and the British enforcement of the outlawry. In your day, French depredations; in mine, English, and the Berlin and Milan decrees; now, the English orders of council, and the piracies they authorize. When these shall be over, it will be the impressment of our seamen or something else; and so we have gone on, and so we shall go on, puzzled and prospering beyond example in the history of man. And I do believe we shall continue to grow, to multiply and prosper, until we exhibit an association, powerful, wise, and happy, beyond what has yet been seen by men. As for France and England, with all their preëminence in science, the one is a den of robbers, and the other of pirates. And if science produces no better fruits than tyranny, murder, rapine, and destitution of national morality, I would rather wish our country to be ignorant, honest, and estimable, as our neighboring savages are. But whither is senile garrulity leading me? Into politics, of which I have taken final leave. I think little of them and say less. I have given up newspapers in exchange for Tacitus and Thucydides, for Newton and Euclid, and I find myself much the happier. Sometimes, indeed, I look back to former occurrences, in remembrance of our old friends and fellow laborers, who have fallen before us. Of the signers of the Declaration of Independence, I see now living not more than half a dozen on your side of the Potomac, and on this side, myself alone. You and I have been wonderfully spared, and myself with remarkable health, and a considerable activity of body and mind. I am on horseback three or four hours of every day; visit three or four times a year a possession I have ninety miles distant, performing the winter journey on horseback. I walk little, however, a single mile being too much for me, and I live in the midst of my grandchildren, one of whom has lately promoted me to be a great-grandfather. I have heard with pleasure that you also retain good health, and a greater power of exercise in walking than I do. But I would rather have heard this from yourself, and that, writing a letter like mine, full of egotisms, and of details of your health, your habits, occupations and enjoyments, I should have the pleasure of knowing that in the race of life, you do not keep, in its physical decline, the same distance ahead of me which you have done in political honors and achievements. No circumstances have lessened the interest I feel in these particulars respecting yourself; none have suspended for one moment my sincere esteem for you, and I now salute you with unchanged affection and respect.

41. TO JOHN MELISH [144]

[GROUNDS FOR PARTY DIVISION]

MONTICELLO, January 13, 1813.

DEAR SIR,—

I received duly your favor of December the 15th, and with it the copies of your map and travels, for which be pleased to accept my thanks. The book I have read with extreme satisfaction and information. As to the Western States, particularly, it has greatly edified me; for of the actual condition of that interesting portion of our country I had not an adequate idea. I feel myself now as familiar with it as with the condition of the maritime States. I had no conception that manufactures had made such progress there, and particularly of the number of carding and spinning machines dispersed through the whole country. We are but beginning here to have them in our private families. Small spinning-jennies of from half a dozen to twenty spindles, will soon, however, make their way into the humblest cottages, as well as the richest houses; and nothing is more certain, than that the coarse and middling clothing for our families, will forever hereafter continue to be made within ourselves. I have hitherto myself depended entirely on foreign manufactures; but I have now thirty-five spindles a-going, a hand carding machine, and looms with the flying shuttle, for the supply of my own farms, which will never be relinquished in my time. The continuance of the war will fix the habit generally, and out of the evils of impressment and of the orders of council a great blessing for us will grow. I have not formerly been an advocate for great manufactories. I doubted whether our labor, employed in agriculture, and aided by the spontaneous energies of the earth, would not procure us more than we could make ourselves of other necessaries. But other considerations entering into the question have settled my doubts.

The candor with which you have viewed the manners and condition of our citizens is so unlike the narrow prejudices of the French and English travellers preceding you, who, considering each the manners and habits of their own people as the only orthodox, have viewed everything differing from that test as boorish and barbarous, that your work will be read here extensively, and operate great good.

Amidst this mass of approbation which is given to every other part of the work, there is a single sentiment which I cannot help wishing to bring to what I think the correct one; and, on a point so interesting, I value your opinion too highly not to ambition its concurrence with my own. Stating in volume one, page sixty-three, the principle of difference between the two great political parties here, you conclude it to be, "whether the controlling power shall be vested in this or that set of men." That each party endeavors to get into the administration of the government, and exclude the other from power, is true, and may be stated as a motive of action; but this is only secondary; the primary motive being a real and radical difference of political principle. I sincerely wish our differences were but personally who should govern, and that the principles of our constitution were those of both parties. Unfortunately, it is otherwise; and the question of preference between monarchy and republicanism, which has so long divided mankind elsewhere, threatens a permanent division here.

Among that section of our citizens called federalists, there are three shades of opinion. Distinguishing between the *leaders* and *people* who compose it, the *leaders* consider the English constitution as a model of perfection, some, with a correction of its vices, others, with all its corruptions and abuses. This last was Alexander Hamilton's opinion, which others, as well as myself, have often heard him declare, and that a correction of what are called its vices, would render the English an impracticable government. This government they wished to have established here, and only accepted and held fast, *at first*, to the present constitution, as a stepping-stone to the final establishment of their favorite model. This party has therefore always clung to England as their prototype, and great auxiliary in promoting and effecting this change. A weighty MINORITY, however, of these *leaders*, considering the voluntary conversion of our government into a monarchy as too distant, if not desperate, wish to break off from our Union its eastern fragment, as being, in truth, the hot-bed of American monarchism, with a view to a commencement of their favorite government, from whence the other States may gangrene by degrees, and the whole be thus brought finally to the desired point. For Massachusetts, the prime mover in this enterprise, is the last State in the Union to mean a *final* separation, as being of all the most dependent on the others. Not raising bread for the sustenance of her own inhabitants, not having a stick of timber for the construction of vessels, her principal occupation, nor an article to export in them, where would she be, excluded from the ports of the other States, and thrown into dependence on England, her direct and natural, but now insidious rival? At the head of this MINORITY is what is called the Essex Junto of Massachusetts. But the MAJORITY of these *leaders* do not aim at separation. In this, they adhere to the known principle of General Hamilton, never, under any views, to break the Union. Anglomany, monarchy, and separation, then, are the principles of the Essex federalists, Anglomany and monarchy, those of the Hamiltonians, and Anglomany alone, that of the portion among the *people* who call themselves federalists. These last are as good republicans as the brethren whom they oppose, and differ from them only in their devotion to England and hatred of France which they have imbibed from their leaders. The moment that these leaders should avowedly propose a separation of the Union, or the establishment of regal government, their popular adherents would quit them to a man, and join the republican standard; and the partisans of this change, even in Massachusetts, would thus find themselves an army of officers without a soldier.

The party called republican is steadily for the support of the present Constitution. They obtained at its commencement all the amendments to it they desired. These reconciled them to it perfectly, and if they have any ulterior view, it is only, perhaps, to popularize it further, by shortening the senatorial term, and devising a process for the responsibility of judges, more practical than that of impeachment. They esteem the people of England and France equally, and equally detest the governing powers of both.

This I verily believe, after an intimacy of forty years with the public councils and characters, is a true statement of the grounds on which they are at present divided, and that it is not merely an ambition for power. An honest man can feel no pleasure in the exercise of power over his fellow citizens. And considering as the only offices of power those conferred by the people directly, that is to say, the executive and legislative functions of the General and State governments, the common refusal of these, and multiplied resignations, are proofs sufficient that power is not alluring to pure minds, and is not, with them, the primary principle of contest. This is my belief of it; it is that on which I have acted; and had it been a mere contest who should be permitted to administer the government according to its genuine republican principles, there has never been a moment of my life in which I should have relinquished for it the enjoyments of my family, my farm, my friends and books.

You expected to discover the difference of our party principles in General Washington's valedictory, and my inaugural address. Not at all. General Washington did not harbor one principle of federalism. He was neither an Angloman, a monarchist, nor a separatist. He sincerely wished the people to have as much self-government as they were competent to exercise themselves. The only point on which he and I ever differed in opinion, was, that I had more confidence than he had in the natural integrity and discretion of the people, and in the safety and extent to which they might trust themselves with a control over their government. He has asseverated to me a thousand times his determination that the existing government should have a fair trial, and that in support of it he would spend the last drop of his blood. He did this the more repeatedly, because he knew General Hamilton's political bias, and my apprehensions from it. It is a mere calumny, therefore, in the monarchists, to associate General Washington with their principles. But that may have happened in this case which has been often seen in ordinary cases, that, by oft repeating an untruth, men come to believe it themselves. It is a mere artifice in this party to bolster themselves up on the revered name of that first of our worthies. If I have dwelt longer on this subject than was necessary, it proves the estimation in which I hold your ultimate opinions, and my desire of placing the subject truly before them. In so doing, I am certain I risk no use of the communication which may draw me into contention before the public. Tranquillity is the *summum bonum* of a septagenaire.

To return to the merits of your work: I consider it as so lively a picture of the real state of our country, that if I can possibly obtain opportunities of conveyance, I propose to send a copy to a friend in France, and another to one in Italy, who, I know, will translate and circulate it as an antidote to the misrepresentations of former travellers. But whatever effect my profession of political faith may have on your general opinion, a part of my object will be obtained, if it satisfies you as to the principles of my own action, and of the high respect and consideration with which I tender you my salutations.

42. TO JOHN ADAMS

[PERSONAL RELATIONS]

MONTICELLO, June 27, 1813.

Ἴδαν ἐς πολύδενδρον ἀνὴρ ὑλατόμος ἐλθὼν
παπταίνει, παρεόντος ἄδην, πόθεν ἄρξεται ἔργου·
τί πρῶτον καταλέξω; ἐπεὶ πάρα μυρία εἰπεῖν.[145]

And I too, my dear Sir, like the wood-cutter of Ida, should doubt where to begin, were I to enter the forest of opinions, discussions, and contentions which have occurred in our day. I should say with Theocritus, Τί πρῶτον καταλέξω; ἐπεὶ πάρα μυρία εἰπεῖν. But I shall not do it. The *summum bonum* with me is now truly epicurean, ease of body and tranquillity of mind; and to these I wish to consign my remaining days. Men have differed in opinion, and been divided into parties by these opinions, from the first origin of societies, and in all governments where they have been permitted freely to think and to speak. The same political parties which now agitate the United States, have existed through all time. Whether the power of the people or that of the ἄριστοι should prevail, were questions which kept the States of Greece and Rome in eternal convulsions, as they now schismatize every people whose minds and mouths are not shut up by the gag of a despot. And in fact, the terms of whig and tory belong to natural as well as to civil history. They denote the temper and constitution of mind of different individuals. To come to our own country, and to the times when you and I became first acquainted, we well remember the violent parties which agitated the old Congress, and their bitter contests. There you and I were together, and the Jays, and the Dickinsons, and other anti-independents, were arrayed against us. They cherished the monarchy of England, and we the rights of our countrymen. When our present government was in the mew, passing from Confederation to Union, how bitter was the schism between the Feds and Antis! Here you and I were together again. For although, for a moment, separated by the Atlantic from the scene of action, I favored the opinion that nine States should confirm the Constitution, in order to secure it, and the others hold off until certain amendments, deemed favorable to freedom, should be made, I rallied in the first instant to the wiser proposition of Massachusetts, that all should confirm, and then all instruct their delegates to urge those amendments. The amendments were made, and all were reconciled to the government. But as soon as it was put into motion, the line of division was again drawn. We broke into two parties, each wishing to give the government a different direction; the one to strengthen the most popular branch, the other the more permanent branches, and to extend their permanence. Here you and I separated for the first time, and as we had been longer than most others on the public theatre, and our names therefore were more familiar to our countrymen, the party which considered you as thinking with them, placed your name at their head; the other, for the same reason, selected mine. But neither decency nor inclination permitted us to become the advocates of ourselves, or to take part personally in the violent contests which followed. We suffered ourselves, as you so well expressed it, to be passive subjects of public discussion. And these discussions, whether relating to men, measures, or opinions, were conducted by the parties with an animosity, a bitterness, and an indecency which had never been exceeded. All the resources of reason and of wrath were exhausted by each party in support of its own, and to prostrate the adversary opinions; one was upbraided with receiving the anti-federalists, the other the old tories and refugees, into their bosom. Of this acrimony, the public papers of the day exhibit ample testimony, in the debates of Congress, of state legislatures, of stump orators, in addresses, answers, and newspaper essays; and to these, without question, may be added the private correspondences of individuals; and the less guarded in these, because not meant for the public eye, not restrained by the respect due to that, but poured forth from the overflowings of the heart into the bosom of a friend, as a momentary easement of our feelings. In this way, and in answers to addresses, you and I could indulge ourselves. We have probably done it, sometimes with warmth, often with prejudice, but always, as we believed, adhering to truth. I have not examined my letters of that day. I have no stomach to revive the memory of its feelings. But one of these letters, it seems, has got before the public, by accident and infidelity, by the death of one friend to whom it was written, and of his friend to whom it had been communicated, and by the malice and treachery of a third person, of whom I had never before heard, merely to make mischief, and in the same satanic spirit in which the same enemy had intercepted and published, in 1776, your letter animadverting on Dickinson's character. How it happened that I quoted you in my letter to Doctor Priestley,[146] and for whom, and not for yourself, the strictures were meant, has been explained to you in my letter of the 15th, which had been committed to the post eight days before I received yours of the 10th, 11th, and 14th. That gave you the reference which these asked to the particular answer alluded to in the one to Priestley. The renewal of these old discussions, my friend, would be equally useless and irksome. To the volumes then written on these subjects, human ingenuity can add nothing new, and the rather, as lapse of time has obliterated many of the facts. And shall you and I, my dear Sir, at our age, like Priam of old, gird on the "*arma, diu desueta, trementibus ævo humeris?*" Shall we, at our age, become the Athletæ of party, and exhibit ourselves as gladiators in the arena of the newspapers? Nothing in the universe could induce me to it. My mind has been long fixed to bow to the judgment of the world, who will judge by my acts, and will never take counsel from me as to what that judgment shall be. If your objects and opinions have been misunderstood, if the measures and principles of others have been wrongfully imputed to you, as I believe they have been, that you should leave an explanation of them would be an act of justice to yourself. I will add that it has been hoped that you would leave such explanations as would place every saddle on its right horse, and replace on the shoulders of others the burdens they shifted on yours.

But all this, my friend, is offered, merely for your consideration and judgment, without presuming to anticipate what you alone are qualified to decide for yourself. I mean to express my own purpose only, and the reflections which have led to it. To me, then, it appears that there have been differences of opinion and party differences, from the first establishment of governments to the present day, and on the same question which now divides our own country; that these will continue through all future time; that every one takes his side in favor of the many, or of the few, according to his constitution, and the circumstances in which he is placed; that opinions, which are equally honest on both sides, should not affect personal esteem or social intercourse; that as we judge between the Claudii and the Gracchi, the Wentworths and the Hampdens of past ages, so of those among us whose names may happen to be remembered for awhile, the next generations will judge, favorably or unfavorably, according to the complexion of individual minds, and the side they shall themselves have taken; that nothing new can be added by you or me to what has been said by others, and will be said in every age in support of the conflicting opinions on government; and that wisdom and duty dictate an humble resignation to the verdict of our future peers. In doing this myself, I shall certainly not suffer moot questions to affect the sentiments of sincere friendship and respect, consecrated to you by so long a course of time, and of which I now repeat sincere assurances.

43. TO JOHN ADAMS

[ARISTOCRACY, NATURAL AND ARTIFICIAL]

MONTICELLO, October 28, 1813.

DEAR SIR,—

According to the reservation between us, of taking up one of the subjects of our correspondence at a time, I turn to your letters of August the 16th and September the 2d.[147]

The passage you quote from Theognis, I think has an ethical rather than a political object. The whole piece is a moral *exhortation*, παραίνεσις, and this passage particularly seems to be a reproof to man, who, while with his domestic animals he is curious to improve the race, by employing always the finest male, pays no attention to the improvement of his own race, but intermarries with the vicious, the ugly, or the old, for considerations of wealth or ambition. It is in conformity with the principle adopted afterwards by the Pythagoreans, and expressed by Ocellus in another form; περὶ δὲ τῆς ἐξ τῶν ἀλλήλων ἀνθρώπων γενέσεως etc.,—οὐχ ἡδονῆς ἕνεκα ἡ μῖξις· which, as literally as intelligibility will admit, may be thus translated: "Concerning the interprocreation of men, how, and of whom it shall be, in a perfect manner, and according to the laws of modesty and sanctity, conjointly, this is what I think right. First to lay it down that we do not commix for the sake of pleasure, but of the procreation of children. For the powers, the organs and desires for coition have not been given by God to man for the sake of pleasure, but for the procreation of the race. For as it were incongruous for a mortal born to partake of divine life, the immortality of the race being taken away, God fulfilled the purpose by making the generations uninterrupted and continuous. This, therefore, we are especially to lay down as a principle, that coition is not for the sake of pleasure." But nature, not trusting to this moral and abstract motive, seems to have provided more securely for the perpetuation of the species, by making it the effect of the *œstrum* implanted in the constitution of both sexes. And not only has the commerce of love been indulged on this unhallowed impulse, but made subservient also to wealth and ambition by marriage, without regard to the beauty, the healthiness, the understanding, or virtue of the subject from which we are to breed. The selecting the best male for a harem of well-chosen females also, which Theognis seems to recommend from the example of our sheep and asses, would doubtless improve the human, as it does the brute animal, and produce a race of veritable ἄριστοι. For experience proves that the moral and physical qualities of man, whether good or evil, are transmissible in a certain degree from father to son. But I suspect that the equal rights of men will rise up against this privileged Solomon and his harem, and oblige us to continue acquiescence under the "ἀμαύρωσις γένεος ἀστῶν" which Theognis complains of, and to content ourselves with the accidental *aristoi* produced by the fortuitous concourse of breeders. For I agree with you that there is a natural aristocracy among men. The grounds of this are virtue and talents. Formerly, bodily powers gave place among the *aristoi*. But since the invention of gunpowder has armed the weak as well as the strong with missile death, bodily strength, like beauty, good humor, politeness, and other accomplishments, has become but an auxiliary ground of distinction. There is also an artificial aristocracy, founded on wealth and birth, without either virtue or talents; for with these it would belong to the first class. The natural aristocracy I consider as the most precious gift of nature, for the instruction, the trusts, and government of society. And indeed, it would have been inconsistent in creation to have formed man for the social state, and not to have provided virtue and wisdom enough to manage the concerns of the society. May we not even say, that that form of government is the best, which provides the most effectually for a pure selection of these natural *aristoi* into the offices of government? The artificial aristocracy is a mischievous ingredient in government, and provision should be made to prevent its ascendency. On the question, what is the best provision, you and I differ; but we differ as rational friends, using the free exercise of our own reason, and mutually indulging its errors. You think it best to put the *pseudo-aristoi* into a separate chamber of legislation, where they may be hindered from doing mischief by their co-ordinate branches, and where, also, they may be a protection to wealth against the agrarian and plundering enterprises of the majority of the people. I think that to give them power in order to prevent them from doing mischief, is arming them for it, and increasing instead of remedying the evil. For if the co-ordinate branches can arrest their action, so may they that of the co-ordinates. Mischief may be done negatively as well as positively. Of this, a cabal in the Senate of the United States has furnished many proofs. Nor do I believe them necessary to protect the wealthy; because enough of these will find their way into every branch of the legislation, to protect themselves. From fifteen to twenty legislatures of our own, in action for thirty years past, have proved that no fears of an equalization of property are to be apprehended from them. I think the best remedy is exactly that provided by all our constitutions, to leave to the citizens the free election and separation of the *aristoi* from the *pseudo-aristoi*, of the wheat from the chaff. In general they will elect the really good and wise. In some instances, wealth may corrupt, and birth blind them; but not in sufficient degree to endanger the society.

It is probable that our difference of opinion may, in some measure, be produced by a difference of character in those among whom we live. From what I have seen of Massachusetts and Connecticut myself, and still more from what I have heard, and the character given of the former by yourself, who know them so much better, there seems to be in those two States a traditionary reverence for certain families; which has rendered the offices of the government nearly hereditary in those families. I presume that from an early period of your history, members of those families happening to possess virtue and talents, have honestly exercised them for the good of the people, and by their services have endeared their names to them. In coupling Connecticut with you, I mean it politically only, not morally. For having made the Bible the common law of their land, they seem to have modeled their morality on the story of Jacob and Laban. But although this hereditary succession to office with you, may, in some degree, be founded in real family merit, yet in a much higher degree, it has proceeded from your strict alliance of Church and State. These families are canonized in the eyes of the people on common principles, "you tickle me, and I will tickle you." In Virginia we have nothing of this. Our clergy, before the Revolution, having been secured against rivalship by fixed salaries, did not give themselves the trouble of acquiring influence over the people. Of wealth, there were great accumulations in particular families, handed down from generation to generation, under the English law of entails. But the only object of ambition for the wealthy was a seat in the King's Council. All their court then was paid to the crown and its creatures; and they Philipized in all collisions between the King and the people. Hence they were unpopular; and that unpopularity continues attached to their names. A Randolph, a Carter, or a Burwell must have great personal superiority over a common competitor to be elected by the people even at this day. At the first session of our legislature after the Declaration of Independence, we passed a law abolishing entails. And this was followed by one abolishing the privilege of primogeniture, and dividing the lands of intestates equally among all their children, or other representatives. These laws, drawn by myself, laid the axe to the foot of pseudo-aristocracy. And had another which I prepared been adopted by the legislature, our work would have been complete. It was a bill for the more general diffusion of learning. This proposed to divide every county into wards of five or six miles square, like your townships; to establish in each ward a free school for reading, writing, and common arithmetic; to provide for the annual selection of the best subjects from these schools, who might receive, at the public expense, a higher degree of education at a district school; and from these district schools to select a certain number of the most promising subjects, to be completed at an university, where all the useful sciences should be taught. Worth and genius would thus have been sought out from every condition of life, and completely prepared by education for defeating the competition of wealth and birth for public trusts. My proposition had, for a further object, to impart to these wards those portions of self-government for which they are best qualified, by confiding to them the care of their poor, their roads, police, elections, the nomination of jurors, administration of justice in small cases, elementary exercises of militia; in short, to have made them little republics, with a warden at the head of each, for all those concerns which, being under their eye, they would better manage than the larger republics of the county or State. A general call of ward meetings by their wardens on the same day through the State would at any time produce the genuine sense of the people on any required point, and would enable the State to act in mass, as your people have so often done, and with so much effect by their town meetings. The law for religious freedom, which made a part of this system, having put down the aristocracy of the clergy, and restored to the citizen the freedom of the mind, and those of entails and descents nurturing an equality of condition among them, this on education would have raised the mass of the people to the high ground of moral respectability necessary to their own safety, and to orderly government; and would have completed the great object of qualifying them to select the veritable *aristoi*, for the trusts of government, to the exclusion of the pseudalists; and the same Theognis who has furnished the epigraphs of your two letters, assures us that "Οὐδεμίαν πω, Κύρν', ἀγαθοὶ πόλιν ὤλεσαν ἄνδρες." Although this law has not yet been acted on but in a small and inefficient degree, it is still considered as before the legislature, with other bills of the revised code, not yet taken up, and I have great hope that some patriotic spirit will, at a favorable moment, call it up, and make it the keystone of the arch of our government.

With respect to aristocracy, we should further consider, that before the establishment of the American States, nothing was known to history but the man of the old world, crowded within limits either small or overcharged, and steeped in the vices which that situation generates. A government adapted to such men would be one thing; but a very different one, that for the man of these States. Here every one may have land to labor for himself, if he chooses; or, preferring the exercise of any other industry, may exact for it such compensation as not only to afford a comfortable subsistence, but wherewith to provide for a cessation from labor in old age. Every one, by his property, or by his satisfactory situation, is interested in the support of law and order. And such men may safely and advantageously reserve to themselves a wholesome control over their public affairs, and a degree of freedom, which, in the hands of the *canaille* of the cities of Europe, would be instantly perverted to the demolition and destruction of everything public and private.

The history of the last twenty-five years of France, and of the last forty years in America, nay of its last two hundred years, proves the truth of both parts of this observation.

But even in Europe a change has sensibly taken place in the mind of man. Science had liberated the ideas of those who read and reflect, and the American example had kindled feelings of right in the people. An insurrection has consequently begun, of science, talents, and courage, against rank and birth, which have fallen into contempt. It has failed in its first effort, because the mobs of the cities, the instrument used for its accomplishment, debased by ignorance, poverty, and vice, could not be restrained to rational action. But the world will recover from the panic of this first catastrophe. Science is progressive, and talents and enterprise on the alert. Resort may be had to the people of the country, a more governable power from their principles and subordination; and rank, and birth, and tinsel-aristocracy will finally shrink into insignificance, even there. This, however, we have no right to meddle with. It suffices for us, if the moral and physical condition of our own citizens qualifies them to select the able and good for the direction of their government, with a recurrence of elections at such short periods as will enable them to displace an unfaithful servant, before the mischief he meditates may be irremediable.

I have thus stated my opinion on a point on which we differ, not with a view to controversy, for we are both too old to change opinions which are the result of a long life of inquiry and reflection; but on the suggestions of a former letter of yours, that we ought not to die before we have explained ourselves to each other. We acted in perfect harmony, through a long and perilous contest for our liberty and independence. A Constitution has been acquired, which, though neither of us thinks perfect, yet both consider as competent to render our fellow citizens the happiest and the securest on whom the sun has ever shone. If we do not think exactly alike as to its imperfections, it matters little to our country, which, after devoting to it long lives of disinterested labor, we have delivered over to our successors in life, who will be able to take care of it and of themselves.

Of the pamphlet on aristocracy which has been sent to you, or who may be its author, I have heard nothing but through your letter. If the person you suspect, it may be known from the quaint, mystical, and hyperbolical ideas, involved in affected, new-fangled, and pedantic terms which stamp his writings. Whatever it be, I hope your quiet is not to be affected at this day by the rudeness or intemperance of scribblers; but that you may continue in tranquillity to live and to rejoice in the prosperity of our country, until it shall be your own wish to take your seat among the *aristoi* who have gone before you. Ever and affectionately yours.

44. TO WALTER JONES

[CHARACTER OF WASHINGTON]

MONTICELLO, January 2, 1814.

DEAR SIR,—

Your favor of November the 25th reached this place December the 21st, having been near a month on the way. How this could happen I know not, as we have two mails a week both from Fredericksburg and Richmond. It found me just returned from a long journey and absence, during which so much business had accumulated, commanding the first attentions, that another week has been added to the delay.

I deplore, with you, the putrid state into which our newspapers have passed, and the malignity, the vulgarity, and mendacious spirit of those who write for them; and I enclose you a recent sample, the production of a New England judge, as a proof of the abyss of degradation into which we are fallen. These ordures are rapidly depraving the public taste, and lessening its relish for sound food. As vehicles of information, and a curb on our functionaries, they have rendered themselves useless, by forfeiting all title to belief. That this has, in a great degree, been produced by the violence and malignity of party spirit, I agree with you; and I have read with great pleasure the paper you enclosed me on that subject, which I now return.

It is at the same time a perfect model of the style of discussion which candor and decency should observe, of the tone which renders difference of opinion even amiable, and a succinct, correct, and dispassionate history of the origin and progress of party among us. It might be incorporated as it stands, and without changing a word, into the history of the present epoch, and would give to posterity a fairer view of the times than they will probably derive from other sources. In reading it with great satisfaction, there was but a single passage where I wished a little more development of a very sound and catholic idea; a single intercalation to rest it solidly on true bottom. It is near the end of the first page, where you make a statement of genuine republican maxims; saying, "that the people ought to possess as much political power as can possibly exist with the order and security of society." Instead of this, I would say, "that the people, being the only safe depository of power, should exercise in person every function which their qualifications enable them to exercise, consistently with the order and security of society; that we now find them equal to the election of those who shall be invested with their executive and legislative powers, and to act themselves in the judiciary, as judges in questions of fact; that the range of their powers ought to be enlarged," etc. This gives both the reason and exemplification of the maxim you express, "that they ought to possess as much political power," etc. I see nothing to correct either in your facts or principles.

You say that in taking General Washington on your shoulders, to bear him harmless through the federal coalition, you encounter a perilous topic. I do not think so. You have given the genuine history of the course of his mind through the trying scenes in which it was engaged, and of the seductions by which it was deceived, but not depraved. I think I knew General Washington intimately and thoroughly; and were I called on to delineate his character, it should be in terms like these.

His mind was great and powerful, without being of the very first order; his penetration strong, though not so acute as that of a Newton, Bacon, or Locke; and as far as he saw, no judgment was ever sounder. It was slow in operation, being little aided by invention or imagination, but sure in conclusion. Hence the common remark of his officers, of the advantage he derived from councils of war, where hearing all suggestions, he selected whatever was best; and certainly no general ever planned his battles more judiciously. But if deranged during the course of the action, if any member of his plan was dislocated by sudden circumstances, he was slow in re-adjustment. The consequence was, that he often failed in the field, and rarely against an enemy in station, as at Boston and York. He was incapable of fear, meeting personal dangers with the calmest unconcern. Perhaps the strongest feature in his character was prudence, never acting until every circumstance, every consideration, was maturely weighed; refraining if he saw a doubt, but, when once decided, going through with his purpose, whatever obstacles opposed. His integrity was most pure, his justice the most inflexible I have ever known, no motives of interest or consanguinity, of friendship or hatred, being able to bias his decision. He was, indeed, in every sense of the words, a wise, a good, and a great man. His temper was naturally high toned; but reflection and resolution had obtained a firm and habitual ascendency over it. If ever, however, it broke its bonds, he was most tremendous in his wrath. In his expenses he was honorable, but exact; liberal in contributions to whatever promised utility; but frowning and unyielding on all visionary projects, and all unworthy calls on his charity. His heart was not warm in its affections; but he exactly calculated every man's value, and gave him a solid esteem proportioned to it. His person, you know, was fine, his stature exactly what one would wish, his deportment easy, erect, and noble; the best horseman of his age, and the most graceful figure that could be seen on horseback. Although in the circle of his friends, where he might be unreserved with safety, he took a free share in conversation, his colloquial talents were not above mediocrity, possessing neither copiousness of ideas, nor fluency of words. In public, when called on for a sudden opinion, he was unready, short, and embarrassed. Yet he wrote readily, rather diffusely, in an easy and correct style. This he had acquired by conversation with the world, for his education was merely reading, writing, and common arithmetic, to which he added surveying at a later day. His time was employed in action chiefly, reading little, and that only in agriculture and English history. His correspondence became necessarily extensive, and, with journalizing his agricultural proceedings, occupied most of his leisure hours within doors. On the whole, his character was, in its mass, perfect, in nothing bad, in few points indifferent; and it may truly be said, that never did nature and fortune combine more perfectly to make a man great, and to place him in the same constellation with whatever worthies have merited from man an everlasting remembrance. For his was the singular destiny and merit, of leading the armies of his country successfully through an arduous war, for the establishment of its independence; of conducting its councils through the birth of a government, new in its forms and principles, until it had settled down into a quiet and orderly train; and of scrupulously obeying the laws through the whole of his career, civil and military, of which the history of the world furnishes no other example.

How, then, can it be perilous for you to take such a man on your shoulders? I am satisfied the great body of republicans think of him as I do. We were, indeed, dissatisfied with him on his ratification of the British treaty. But this was short-lived. We knew his honesty, the wiles with which he was encompassed, and that age had already begun to relax the firmness of his purposes; and I am convinced he is more deeply seated in the love and gratitude of the republicans, than in the pharisaical homage of the federal monarchists. For he was no monarchist from preference of his judgment. The soundness of that gave him correct views of the rights of man, and his severe justice devoted him to them. He has often declared to me that he considered our new Constitution as an experiment on the practicability of republican government, and with what dose of liberty man could be trusted for his own good; that he was determined the experiment should have a fair trial, and would lose the last drop of his blood in support of it. And these declarations he repeated to me the oftener and more pointedly, because he knew my suspicions of Colonel Hamilton's views, and probably had heard from him the same declarations which I had, to wit, "that the British constitution, with its unequal representation, corruption, and other existing abuses, was the most perfect government which had ever been established on earth, and that a reformation of those abuses would make it an impracticable government." I do believe that General Washington had not a firm confidence in the durability of our government. He was naturally distrustful of men, and inclined to gloomy apprehensions; and I was ever persuaded that a belief that we must at length end in something like a British constitution had some weight in his adoption of the ceremonies of levees, birthdays, pompous meetings with Congress, and other forms of the same character, calculated to prepare us gradually for a change which he believed possible, and to let it come on with as little shock as might be to the public mind.

These are my opinions of General Washington, which I would vouch at the judgment seat of God, having been formed on an acquaintance of thirty years. I served with him in the Virginia legislature from 1769 to the Revolutionary war, and again a short time in Congress, until he left us to take command of the army. During the war and after it we corresponded occasionally, and in the four years of my continuance in the office of Secretary of State, our intercourse was daily, confidential, and cordial. After I retired from that office, great and malignant pains were taken by our federal monarchists, and not entirely without effect, to make him view me as a theorist, holding French principles of government, which would lead infallibly to licentiousness and anarchy. And to this he listened the more easily, from my known disapprobation of the British treaty. I never saw him afterwards, or these malignant insinuations should have been dissipated before his just judgment, as mists before the sun. I felt on his death, with my countrymen, that "verily a great man hath fallen this day in Israel."

More time and recollection would enable me to add many other traits of his character; but why add them to you who

knew him well? And I cannot justify to myself a longer detention of your paper.

Vale, proprieque tuum, me esse tibi persuadeas.

45. TO P. S. DUPONT DE NEMOURS

[CONSTITUTIONS COMPARED]

POPLAR FOREST, April 24, 1816.

I received, my dear friend, your letter covering the constitution for your Equinoctial republics, just as I was setting out for
this place. I brought it with me, and have read it with great
satisfaction. I suppose it well formed for those for whom it was
intended, and the excellence of every government is its adaptation to the state of those to be governed by it. For us it would
not do. Distinguishing between the structure of the government and the moral principles on which you prescribe its administration, with the latter we concur cordially, with the
former we should not. We of the United States, you know, are
constitutionally and conscientiously democrats. We consider
society as one of the natural wants with which man has been
created; that he has been endowed with faculties and qualities
to effect its satisfaction by concurrence of others having the
same want; that when, by the exercise of these faculties, he has
procured a state of society, it is one of his acquisitions which he
has a right to regulate and control, jointly indeed with all those
who have concurred in the procurement, whom he cannot exclude from its use or direction more than they him. We think
experience has proved it safer, for the mass of individuals composing the society, to reserve to themselves personally the
exercise of all rightful powers to which they are competent,
and to delegate those to which they are not competent to
deputies named, and removable for unfaithful conduct, by
themselves immediately. Hence, with us, the people (by which
is meant the mass of individuals composing the society) being
competent to judge of the facts occurring in ordinary life, they
have retained the functions of judges of facts, under the name

of jurors; but being unqualified for the management of affairs requiring intelligence above the common level, yet competent judges of human character, they choose, for their management, representatives, some by themselves immediately, others by electors chosen by themselves. Thus our President is chosen by ourselves, directly in *practice*, for we vote for A as elector only on the condition he will vote for B, our representatives by ourselves immediately, our Senate and judges of law through electors chosen by ourselves. And we believe that this proximate choice and power of removal is the best security which experience has sanctioned for ensuring an honest conduct in the functionaries of society. Your three or four alembications have indeed a seducing appearance. We should conceive, *prima facie*, that the last extract would be the pure alcohol of the substance, three or four times rectified. But in proportion as they are more and more sublimated, they are also farther and farther removed from the control of the society; and the human character, we believe, requires in general constant and immediate control, to prevent its being biased from right by the seductions of self-love. Your process produces, therefore, a structure of government from which the fundamental principle of ours is excluded. You first set down as zeros all individuals not having lands, which are the greater number in every society of long standing. Those holding lands are permitted to manage in person the small affairs of their commune or corporation, and to elect a deputy for the canton; in which election, too, every one's vote is to be an unit, a plurality, or a fraction, in proportion to his landed possessions. The assemblies of cantons, then, elect for the districts; those of districts for circles; and those of circles for the national assemblies. Some of these highest councils, too, are in a considerable degree self-elected, the regency partially, the judiciary entirely, and some are for life. Whenever, therefore, an *esprit de corps*, or of party, gets possession of them, which experience shows to be inevitable, there are no means of breaking it up, for they will never elect but those of their own spirit. Juries are allowed in criminal cases only. I acknowledge myself strong in affection to our own form, yet both of us act and think from the same motive, we both consider the people as our children, and love them with parental affection. But you love them as infants whom you are afraid to trust without nurses; and I as adults whom I freely leave to self-government. And you are right in the case referred to you; my criticism being built on a state of society not under your contemplation. It is, in fact, like a critic on Homer by the laws of the Drama.

But when we come to the moral principles on which the government is to be administered, we come to what is proper for all conditions of society. I meet you there in all the benevolence and rectitude of your native character; and I love myself always most where I concur most with you. Liberty, truth, probity, honor, are declared to be the four cardinal principles of your society. I believe with you that morality, compassion, generosity, are innate elements of the human constitution; that there exists a right independent of force; that a right to property is founded in our natural wants, in the means with which we are endowed to satisfy these wants, and the right to what we acquire by those means without violating the similar rights of other sensible beings; that no one has a right to obstruct another, exercising his faculties innocently for the relief of sensibilities made a part of his nature; that justice is the fundamental law of society; that the majority, oppressing an individual, is guilty of a crime, abuses its strength, and by acting on the law of the strongest breaks up the foundations of society; that action by the citizens in person, in affairs within their reach and competence, and in all others by representatives, chosen immediately, and removable by themselves, constitutes the essence of a republic; that all governments are more or less republican in proportion as this principle enters more or less into their composition; and that a government by representation is capable of extension over a greater surface of country than one of any other form. These, my friend, are the essentials in which you and I agree; however, in our zeal for their maintenance, we may be perplexed and divaricate, as to the structure of society most likely to secure them.

In the Constitution of Spain, as proposed by the late Cortes, there was a principle entirely new to me, and not noticed in yours, that no person, born after that day, should ever acquire the rights of citizenship until he could read and write. It is impossible sufficiently to estimate the wisdom of this provision. Of all those which have been thought of for securing fidelity in the administration of the government, constant ralliance to the principles of the Constitution, and progressive amendments with the progressive advances of the human mind, or changes in human affairs, it is the most effectual. Enlighten the people generally, and tyranny and oppressions of body and mind will vanish like evil spirits at the dawn of day. Although I do not, with some enthusiasts, believe that the human condition will ever advance to such a state of perfection as that there shall no longer be pain or vice in the world, yet I believe it susceptible of much improvement, and most of all, in matters of government and religion; and that the diffusion of knowledge among the people is to be the instrument by which it is to be effected. The Constitution of the Cortes had defects enough; but when I saw in it this amendatory provision, I was satisfied all would come right in time, under its salutary operation. No people have more need of a similar provision than those for whom you have felt so much interest. No mortal wishes them more success than I do. But if what I have heard of the ignorance and bigotry of the mass be true, I doubt their capacity to understand and to support a free government; and fear that their emancipation from the foreign tyranny of Spain, will result in a military despotism at home. Palacios may be great; others may be great; but it is the multitude which possess force; and wisdom must yield to that. For such a condition of society, the Constitution you have devised is probably the best imaginable. It is certainly calculated to elicit the best talents; although perhaps not well guarded against the egoism of its functionaries. But that egoism will be light in comparison with the pressure of a military despot, and his army of janissaries. Like Solon to the Athenians, you have given to your Columbians, not the best possible government, but the best they can bear. By-the-bye,

I wish you had called them the Columbian republics, to distinguish them from our American republics. Theirs would be the most honorable name, and they best entitled to it; for Columbus discovered their continent, but never saw ours.

To them liberty and happiness; to you the meed of wisdom and goodness in teaching them how to attain them, with the affectionate respect and friendship of Th. J.

46. TO FRANCIS W. GILMER

[NATURAL RIGHTS AND DUTIES]

MONTICELLO, June 7, 1816.

DEAR SIR,—

I received a few days ago from Mr. Dupont the enclosed manuscript, with permission to read it, and a request, when read, to forward it to you, in expectation that you would translate it. It is well worthy of publication for the instruction of our citizens, being profound, sound, and short. Our legislators are not sufficiently apprised of the rightful limits of their power; that their true office is to declare and enforce only our natural rights and duties, and to take none of them from us. No man has a natural right to commit aggression on the equal rights of another; and this is all from which the laws ought to restrain him; every man is under the natural duty of contributing to the necessities of the society; and this is all the laws should enforce on him; and, no man having a natural right to be the judge between himself and another, it is his natural duty to submit to the umpirage of an impartial third. When the laws have declared and enforced all this, they have fulfilled their functions; and the idea is quite unfounded, that on entering into society we give up any natural right. The trial of every law by one of these texts, would lessen much the labors of our legislators, and lighten equally our municipal codes. There is a work of the first order of merit now in the press at Washington, by Destutt Tracy, on the subject of political economy, which he brings into the compass of three hundred pages, octavo. In a

preliminary discourse on the origin of the right of property, he
coincides much with the principles of the present manuscript;
but is more developed, more demonstrative. He promises a
future work on morals, in which I lament to see that he will
adopt the principles of Hobbes, or humiliation to human nature; that the sense of justice and injustice is not derived from
our natural organization, but founded on convention only. I
lament this the more, as he is unquestionably the ablest writer
living, on abstract subjects. Assuming the fact, that the earth
has been created in time, and consequently the dogma of final
causes, we yield, of course, to this short syllogism. Man was
created for social intercourse; but social intercourse cannot be
maintained without a sense of justice; then man must have been
created with a sense of justice. There is an error into which
most of the speculators on government have fallen, and which
the well-known state of society of our Indians ought, before
now, to have corrected. In their hypothesis of the origin of
government, they suppose it to have commenced in the patriarchal or monarchical form. Our Indians are evidently in
that state of nature which has passed the association of a single
family; and not yet submitted to the authority of positive laws,
or of any acknowledged magistrate. Every man, with them,
is perfectly free to follow his own inclinations. But if, in doing
this, he violates the rights of another, if the case be slight, he is
punished by the disesteem of his society, or, as we say, by public
opinion; if serious, he is tomahawked as a dangerous enemy.
Their leaders conduct them by the influence of their character
only; and they follow, or not, as they please, him of whose character for wisdom or war they have the highest opinion. Hence
the origin of the parties among them adhering to different
leaders, and governed by their advice, not by their command.
The Cherokees, the only tribe I know to be contemplating the
establishment of regular laws, magistrates, and government,
propose a government of representatives, elected from every
town. But of all things, they least think of subjecting themselves to the will of one man. This, the only instance of actual
fact within our knowledge, will be then a beginning by repub-

lican, and not by patriarchal or monarchical government, as speculative writers have generally conjectured.

We have to join in mutual congratulations on the appointment of our friend Correa, to be minister or envoy of Portugal, here. This, I hope, will give him to us for life. Nor will it at all interfere with his botanical rambles or journeys. The government of Portugal is so peaceable and inoffensive, that it has never any altercations with its friends. If their minister abroad writes them once a quarter that all is well, they desire no more. I learn (though not from Correa himself) that he thinks of paying us a visit as soon as he is through his course of lectures. Not to lose this happiness again by my absence, I have informed him I shall set out for Poplar Forest the 20th instant, and be back the first week of July. I wish you and he could concert your movements so as to meet here, and that you would make this your headquarters. It is a good central point from which to visit your connections; and you know our practice of placing our guests at their ease, by showing them we are so ourselves and that we follow our necessary vocations, instead of fatiguing them by hanging unremittingly on their shoulders. I salute you with affectionate esteem and respect.

47. TO VINE UTLEY
[PHYSICAL HABITS]
MONTICELLO, March 21, 1819.

SIR,—

Your letter of February the 18th came to hand on the 1st instant; and the request of the history of my physical habits would have puzzled me not a little, had it not been for the model with which you accompanied it, of Doctor Rush's answer to a similar inquiry. I live so much like other people, that I might refer to ordinary life as the history of my own. Like my friend the Doctor, I have lived temperately, eating little animal food, and that not as an aliment, so much as a condiment for the vegetables, which constitute my principal diet. I double, however, the Doctor's glass and a half of wine, and even treble it with a friend; but halve its effects by drinking the weak wines only. The ardent wines I cannot drink, nor do I use ardent spirits in any form. Malt liquors and cider are my table drinks, and my breakfast, like that also of my friend, is of tea and coffee. I have been blest with organs of digestion which accept and concoct, without ever murmuring, whatever the palate chooses to consign to them, and I have not yet lost a tooth by age. I was a hard student until I entered on the business of life, the duties of which leave no idle time to those disposed to fulfil them; and now, retired, and at the age of seventy-six, I am again a hard student. Indeed, my fondness for reading and study revolts me from the drudgery of letter-writing. And a stiff wrist, the consequence of an early dislocation, makes writing both slow and painful. I am not so regular in my sleep as the Doctor says he was, devoting to it from five to eight hours, according as my company or the book I am reading interests me; and I never go to bed without an hour, or half hour's previous reading of something moral, whereon to ruminate in the intervals of sleep. But whether I retire to bed early or late, I rise with the sun. I use spectacles at night, but not necessarily in the day, unless in reading small print. My hearing is distinct in particular conversation, but confused when several voices cross each other, which unfits me for the society of the table. I have been more fortunate than my friend in the article of health. So free from catarrhs that I have not had one (in the breast, I mean) on an average of eight or ten years through life. I ascribe this exemption partly to the habit of bathing my feet in cold water every morning, for sixty years past. A fever of more than twenty-four hours I have not had above two or three times in my life. A periodical headache has afflicted me occasionally, once, perhaps, in six or eight years, for two or three weeks at a time, which seems now to have left me; and except on a late occasion of indisposition, I enjoy good health; too feeble, indeed, to walk much, but riding without fatigue six or eight miles a day, and sometimes thirty or forty. I may end these egotisms, therefore, as I began, by saying that my life has been so much like that of other people, that I might say with Horace, to every one "*nomine mutato, narratur fabula de te.*" I must not end, however, without due thanks for the kind sentiments of regard you are so good as to express towards myself; and with my acknowledgments for these, be pleased to accept the assurances of my respect and esteem.

48. TO EZRA STILES

[SECTARIAN DIFFERENCES]

MONTICELLO, June 25, 1819.

Your favor, Sir, of the 14th, has been duly received, and with it the book you were so kind as to forward to me. For this mark of attention, be pleased to accept my thanks. The science of the human mind is curious, but is one on which I have not indulged myself in much speculation. The times in which I have lived, and the scenes in which I have been engaged, have required me to keep the mind too much in action to have leisure to study minutely its laws of action. I am therefore little qualified to give an opinion on the comparative worth of books on that subject, and little disposed to do it on any book. Yours has brought the science within a small compass, and that is a merit of the first order; and especially with one to whom the drudgery of letter-writing often denies the leisure of reading a single page in a week. On looking over the summary of the contents of your book, it does not seem likely to bring into collision any of those sectarian differences which you suppose may exist between us. In that branch of religion which regards the moralities of life, and the duties of a social being, which teaches us to love our neighbors as ourselves, and to do good to all men, I am sure that you and I do not differ. We probably differ on the dogmas of theology, the foundation of all sectarianism, and on which no two sects dream alike; for if they did they would then be of the same. You say you are a Calvinist. I am not. I am of a sect by myself, as far as I know. I am not a Jew, and therefore do not adopt their theology, which supposes the God of infinite justice to punish the sins of the

fathers upon their children, unto the third and fourth generation; and the benevolent and sublime Reformer of that religion
has told us only that God is good and perfect, but has not
defined Him. I am, therefore, of His theology, believing that
we have neither words nor ideas adequate to that definition.
And if we could all, after this example, leave the subject as
undefinable, we should all be of one sect, doers of good, and
eschewers of evil. No doctrines of His lead to schism. It is the
speculations of crazy theologists which have made a Babel of
a religion the most moral and sublime ever preached to man,
and calculated to heal, and not to create differences. These
religious animosities I impute to those who call themselves His
ministers, and who engraft their casuistries on the stock of His
simple precepts. I am sometimes more angry with them than
is authorized by the blessed charities which He preaches. To
yourself I pray the acceptance of my great respect.

49. TO TIMOTHY PICKERING [148]

[UNITY OF THE CREATOR]

MONTICELLO, February 27, 1821.

I have received, Sir, your favor of the 12th, and I assure you
I received it with pleasure. It is true, as you say, that we have
differed in political opinions; but I can say with equal truth, that
I never suffered a political to become a personal difference. I
have been left on this ground by some friends whom I dearly
loved, but I was never the first to separate. With some others,
of politics different from mine, I have continued in the warmest
friendship to this day, and to all, and to yourself particularly,
I have ever done moral justice.

I thank you for Mr. Channing's discourse, which you have
been so kind as to forward me. It is not yet at hand, but is
doubtless on its way. I had received it through another channel,
and read it with high satisfaction. No one sees with greater
pleasure than myself the progress of reason in its advances towards rational Christianity. When we shall have done away

the incomprehensible jargon of the Trinitarian arithmetic, that three are one, and one is three; when we shall have knocked down the artificial scaffolding, reared to mask from view the simple structure of Jesus; when, in short, we shall have un-learned everything which has been taught since His day, and got back to the pure and simple doctrines He inculcated, we shall then be truly and worthily His disciples; and my opinion is that if nothing had ever been added to what flowed purely from His lips, the whole world would at this day have been Christian. I know that the case you cite, of Dr. Drake, has been a common one. The religion-builders have so distorted and deformed the doctrines of Jesus, so muffled them in mysticisms, fancies, and falsehoods, have caricatured them into forms so monstrous and inconceivable, as to shock reasonable thinkers, to revolt them against the whole, and drive them rashly to pro-nounce its Founder an impostor. Had there never been a com-mentator, there never would have been an infidel. In the present advance of truth, which we both approve, I do not know that you and I may think alike on all points. As the Creator has made no two faces alike, so no two minds, and probably no two creeds. We well know that among Unitarians themselves there are strong shades of difference, as between Doctors Price and Priestley, for example. So there may be peculiarities in your creed and in mine. They are honestly formed without doubt. I do not wish to trouble the world with mine, nor to be troubled for them. These accounts are to be settled only with Him who made us; and to Him we leave it, with charity for all others, of whom, also, He is the only rightful and competent Judge. I have little doubt that the whole of our country will soon be rallied to the unity of the Creator, and, I hope, to the pure doctrines of Jesus also.

In saying to you so much, and without reserve, on a subject on which I never permit myself to go before the public, I know that I am safe against the infidelities which have so often be-trayed my letters to the strictures of those for whom they were not written, and to whom I never meant to commit my peace. To yourself I wish every happiness, and will conclude, as you have done, in the same simple style of antiquity, *da operam ut valeas; hoc mihi gratius facere nihil potes.*

50. TO BENJAMIN WATERHOUSE

[THE TRUE AND CHARITABLE CHRISTIAN]

MONTICELLO, June 26, 1822.

DEAR SIR,—

I have received and read with thankfulness and pleasure your denunciation of the abuses of tobacco and wine. Yet, however sound in its principles, I expect it will be but a sermon to the wind. You will find it is as difficult to inculcate these sanative precepts on the sensualities of the present day, as to convince an Athanasian that there is but one God. I wish success to both attempts, and am happy to learn from you that the latter, at least, is making progress, and the more rapidly in proportion as our Platonizing Christians make more stir and noise about it. The doctrines of Jesus are simple, and tend all to the happiness of man.

1. That there is one only God, and He all perfect.

2. That there is a future state of rewards and punishments.

3. That to love God with all thy heart and thy neighbor as thyself is the sum of religion. These are the great points on which He endeavored to reform the religion of the Jews. But compare with these the demoralizing dogmas of Calvin.

1. That there are three Gods.

2. That good works, or the love of our neighbor, are nothing.

3. That faith is everything, and the more incomprehensible the proposition, the more merit in its faith.

4. That reason in religion is of unlawful use.

5. That God, from the beginning, elected certain individuals to be saved, and certain others to be damned; and that no crimes of the former can damn them; no virtues of the latter save.

Now, which of these is the true and charitable Christian? He who believes and acts on the simple doctrines of Jesus? Or the impious dogmatists, as Athanasius and Calvin? Verily I say these are the false shepherds foretold as to enter not by the door into the sheepfold, but to climb up some other way. They are mere usurpers of the Christian name, teaching a counter-religion made up of the *deliria* of crazy imaginations, as foreign from Christianity as is that of Mahomet. Their blasphemies have driven thinking men into infidelity, who have too hastily rejected the supposed Author himself, with the horrors so falsely imputed to Him. Had the doctrines of Jesus been preached always as pure as they came from his lips, the whole civilized world would now have been Christian. I rejoice that in this blessed country of free inquiry and belief, which has surrendered its creed and conscience to neither kings nor priests, the genuine doctrine of one only God is reviving, and I trust that there is not a *young man* now living in the United States who will not die an Unitarian.

But much I fear, that when this great truth shall be re-established, its votaries will fall into the fatal error of fabricating formulas of creed and confessions of faith, the engines which so soon destroyed the religion of Jesus, and made of Christendom a mere Aceldama; that they will give up morals for mysteries, and Jesus for Plato. How much wiser are the Quakers, who, agreeing in the fundamental doctrines of the gospel, schismatize about no mysteries, and, keeping within the pale of common sense, suffer no speculative differences of opinion, any more than of feature, to impair the love of their brethren. Be this the wisdom of Unitarians, this the holy mantle which shall cover within its charitable circumference all who believe in one God, and who love their neighbor! I conclude my sermon with sincere assurances of my friendly esteem and respect.

51. TO JOHN ADAMS
[POISONING OF FRIENDSHIP]

MONTICELLO, October 12, 1823.

DEAR SIR,—

I do not write with the ease which your letter of September the 18th supposes. Crippled wrists and fingers make writing

slow and laborious. But while writing to you, I lose the sense of
these things in the recollection of ancient times, when youth and
health made happiness out of everything. I forget for a while
the hoary winter of age, when we can think of nothing but how
to keep ourselves warm, and how to get rid of our heavy hours
until the friendly hand of death shall rid us of all at once.
Against this *tedium vitæ*, however, I am fortunately mounted
on a hobby, which, indeed, I should have better managed some
thirty or forty years ago; but whose easy amble is still sufficient
to give exercise and amusement to an octogenary rider. This is
the establishment of a University, on a scale more comprehensive, and in a country more healthy and central than our old
William and Mary, which these obstacles have long kept in a
state of languor and inefficiency. But the tardiness with which
such works proceed may render it doubtful whether I shall live
to see it go into action.

Putting aside these things, however, for the present, I write
this letter as due to a friendship coeval with our government,
and now attempted to be poisoned, when too late in life to be
replaced by new affections. I had for some time observed in the
public papers, dark hints and mysterious innuendoes of a correspondence of yours with a friend, to whom you had opened
your bosom without reserve, and which was to be made public
by that friend or his representative. And now it is said to be
actually published. It has not yet reached us, but extracts have
been given, and such as seemed most likely to draw a curtain
of separation between you and myself. Were there no other
motive than that of indignation against the author of this outrage on private confidence, whose shaft seems to have been
aimed at yourself more particularly, this would make it the
duty of every honorable mind to disappoint that aim, by opposing to its impression a sevenfold shield of apathy and insensi-
bility. With me, however, no such armor is needed. The circumstances of the times in which we have happened to live, and
the partiality of our friends at a particular period, placed us in a
state of apparent opposition, which some might suppose to be
personal also; and there might not be wanting those who wished

to make it so, by filling our ears with malignant falsehoods, by dressing up hideous phantoms of their own creation, presenting them to you under my name, to me under yours, and endeavoring to instil into our minds things concerning each other the most destitute of truth. And if there had been, at any time, a moment when we were off our guard, and in a temper to let the whispers of these people make us forget what we had known of each other for so many years, and years of so much trial, yet all men who have attended to the workings of the human mind, who have seen the false colors under which passion sometimes dresses the actions and motives of others, have seen also those passions subsiding with time and reflection, dissipating like mists before the rising sun, and restoring to us the sight of all things in their true shape and colors. It would be strange indeed, if, at our years, we were to go back an age to hunt up imaginary or forgotten facts, to disturb the repose of affections so sweetening to the evening of our lives. Be assured, my dear Sir, that I am incapable of receiving the slightest impression from the effort now made to plant thorns on the pillow of age, worth, and wisdom, and to sow tares between friends who have been such for near half a century. Beseeching you then, not to suffer your mind to be disquieted by this wicked attempt to poison its peace, and praying you to throw it by among the things which have never happened, I add sincere assurances of my unabated and constant attachment, friendship, and respect.

52. TO THE PRESIDENT OF THE UNITED STATES (JAMES MONROE)

[MONROE DOCTRINE]

MONTICELLO, October 24, 1823.

DEAR SIR,—

The question presented by the letters you have sent me, is the most momentous which has ever been offered to my contemplation since that of Independence.[149] That made us a nation, this sets our compass and points the course which we are to steer through the ocean of time opening on us. And never could we embark on it under circumstances more auspicious. Our first and fundamental maxim should be, never to entangle ourselves in the broils of Europe. Our second, never to suffer Europe to intermeddle with cis-Atlantic affairs. America, North and South, has a set of interests distinct from those of Europe, and peculiarly her own. She should therefore have a system of her own, separate and apart from that of Europe. While the last is laboring to become the domicile of despotism, our endeavor should surely be, to make our hemisphere that of freedom. One nation, most of all, could disturb us in this pursuit; she now offers to lead, aid, and accompany us in it. By acceding to her proposition, we detach her from the bands, bring her mighty weight into the scale of free government, and emancipate a continent at one stroke, which might otherwise linger long in doubt and difficulty. Great Britain is the nation which can do us the most harm of any one, or all on earth; and with her on our side we need not fear the whole world. With her, then, we should most sedulously cherish a cordial friendship; and nothing would tend more to knit our affections than to be fighting once more, side by side, in the same cause. Not that I would purchase even her amity at the price of taking part in her wars. But the war in which the present proposition might engage us, should that be its consequence, is not her war, but ours. Its object is to introduce and establish the American system, of keeping out of our land all foreign powers, of never permitting those of Europe to intermeddle with the affairs of our nations. It is to maintain our own principle, not to depart from it. And if, to facilitate this, we can effect a division in the body of the European powers, and draw over to our side its most powerful member, surely we should do it. But I am clearly of Mr. Canning's opinion, that it will prevent instead of provoking war. With Great Britain withdrawn from their scale and shifted into that of our two continents, all Europe combined would not undertake such a war. For how would they propose to get at either enemy without superior fleets? Nor is the occasion to be slighted which this proposition offers, of declaring our protest against the atrocious violations of the rights of nations, by the interference of any one in the internal affairs of another, so flagitiously begun by Bonaparte, and now continued by the equally lawless Alliance, calling itself Holy.

But we have first to ask ourselves a question. Do we wish to acquire to our own confederacy any one or more of the Spanish provinces? I candidly confess, that I have ever looked on Cuba as the most interesting addition which could ever be made to our system of States. The control which, with Florida Point, this island would give us over the Gulf of Mexico, and the countries and isthmus bordering on it, as well as all those whose waters flow into it, would fill up the measure of our political well-being. Yet, as I am sensible that this can never be obtained, even with her own consent, but by war; and its independence, which is our second interest, (and especially its independence of England), can be secured without it, I have no hesitation in abandoning my first wish to future chances, and accepting its independence, with peace and the friendship of England, rather than its association, at the expense of war and her enmity.

I could honestly, therefore, join in the declaration proposed, that we aim not at the acquisition of any of those possessions, that we will not stand in the way of any amicable arrangement between them and the mother country; but that we will oppose, with all our means, the forcible interposition of any other power, as auxiliary, stipendiary, or under any other form or pretext, and most especially, their transfer to any power by conquest, cession, or acquisition in any other way. I should think it, therefore, advisable, that the Executive should encourage the British government to a continuance in the dispositions expressed in these letters, by an assurance of his concurrence with them as far as his authority goes; and that as it may lead to war, the declaration of which requires an act of Congress, the case shall be laid before them for consideration at their first meeting, and under the reasonable aspect in which it is seen by himself.

I have been so long weaned from political subjects, and have so long ceased to take any interest in them, that I am sensible I am not qualified to offer opinions on them worthy of any attention. But the question now proposed involves consequences so lasting, and effects so decisive of our future destinies, as to rekindle all the interest I have heretofore felt on such occasions, and to induce me to the hazard of opinions, which will prove only my wish to contribute still my mite towards anything which may be useful to our country. And praying you to accept it at only what it is worth, I add the assurance of my constant and affectionate friendship and respect.

53. TO ROGER C. WEIGHTMAN [150]

[THE RIGHTS OF MAN]

MONTICELLO, June 24, 1826.

RESPECTED SIR,—

The kind invitation I receive from you, on the part of the citizens of the city of Washington, to be present with them at their celebration on the fiftieth anniversary of American Independence, as one of the surviving signers of an instrument pregnant with our own, and the fate of the world, is most flattering to myself, and heightened by the honorable accompaniment proposed for the comfort of such a journey. It adds sensibly to the sufferings of sickness, to be deprived by it of a personal participation in the rejoicings of that day. But acquiescence is a duty, under circumstances not placed among those we are permitted to control. I should, indeed, with peculiar delight, have met and exchanged there congratulations personally with the small band, the remnant of that host of worthies, who joined with us on that day, in the bold and doubtful election we were to make for our country, between submission or the sword; and to have enjoyed with them the consolatory fact, that our fellow citizens, after half a century of experience and prosperity, continue to approve the choice we made. May it be to the world, what I believe it will be, (to some parts sooner, to others later, but finally to all), the signal of arousing men to burst the chains under which monkish ignorance and superstition had persuaded them to bind themselves, and to assume the blessings and security of self-government. That form which we have substituted, restores the free right to the unbounded exercise of reason and freedom of opinion. All eyes are opened, or opening, to the rights of man. The general spread of the light of science has already laid open to every view the palpable truth, that the mass of mankind has not been born with saddles on their backs, nor a favored few booted and spurred, ready to ride them legitimately, by the grace of God. These are grounds of hope for others. For ourselves, let the annual return of this day forever refresh our recollections of these rights, and an undiminished devotion to them.

I will ask permission here to express the pleasure with which I should have met my ancient neighbors of the city of Washington and its vicinities, with whom I passed so many years of a pleasing social intercourse; an intercourse which so much relieved the anxieties of the public cares, and left impressions so deeply engraved in my affections, as never to be forgotten. With my regret that ill health forbids me the gratification of an acceptance, be pleased to receive for yourself, and those for whom you write, the assurance of my highest respect and friendly attachments.

NOTES

ALEXANDER HAMILTON

(References are to Hamilton's *Works*, edited by H. C. Lodge, 9 vols., 1885–6.)

1. Stevens was an intimate boyhood friend, son of a St. Croix merchant.

2. For *The Farmer Refuted* see Introduction, p. xv; and with the references to Hobbes compare Introduction, pp. xiii, xvi.

3. Quoted from Blackstone, *Commentaries on the Laws of England*, Introduction, Sec. I, "Of the Nature of Laws in General"; the second quotation (p. 6) is from Chap. I, "Of the Absolute Rights of Individuals."

4. For the quotation see Hume, *Essays* (London, 1767), I, 37 ("Of the Independency of Parliament").

5. Hamilton's plea for a "representative democracy" in this letter is noteworthy.

6. Conway led an intrigue against Washington known as the "Conway Cabal."

7. For friends coming from New York Miss Livingston, daughter of William Livingston, had asked for safe-conduct through the American lines.

8. This letter is of capital importance, showing how early Hamilton realized not only the defects of the Confederation but the necessary remedies. In a portion here omitted he proposes recruitment for longer terms, measures of taxation, and a national bank. The bank indeed had been proposed earlier; see Introduction, p. xix.

9. A hint of the doctrine of implied powers, further developed in *Federalist*, No. 23 (Selections preceding, p. 62), and especially in "Opinion as to the Constitutionality of the Bank"; see Selections preceding, pp. 103, 305.

10. Though a highly unified government is here considered dangerous as giving the sovereign will too much power, it became Hamilton's unattainable ideal. He later made various proposals for reducing the states to a merely provincial status. In the Convention of 1787 he proposed that the state governors should be appointed "under the authority of the United States," and should have veto powers (Article VIII of his proposed Constitution, *Works*, I, 349). In 1799, evidently spurred by the Virginia and Kentucky Resolutions, he urged that "the subdivision of [the great] states ought to be a cardinal point in federal policy." (To Dayton, *Works*, VIII, 524; and compare *ibid.*, 517.)

11. Hamilton not only advocates the Constitutional Convention, but conceives the idea of the *Federalist*.

12. Refers to the defeat of Gates at Camden, S. C., August 16, 1780.

13. This letter, here included only in part, gives the best first-hand account of the affair of André.

14. "The Continentalist" was a series of six papers, showing that "it is necessary to augment the powers of the Confederation," and "the points which ought to compose that augmentation."—(No. IV.) The most important are the powers of taxing and regulating trade. These essays, advocating a more powerful government, looked toward the Annapolis and Philadelphia conventions and the adoption of the Constitution; and they contain the germs of the *Federalist*. "The great defect of the Confederation is, that it gives the United States no property: or, in other words, no revenue, nor the means of acquiring it, inherent in themselves and independent on the temporary pleasure of the different members. And power without revenue, in a political society, is a name. While Congress continues altogether dependent on the occasional grants of the several States, for the means of defraying the expenses of the Federal Government, it can neither have dignity, vigor, nor credit."—(No. IV.)

15. In 1784 Hamilton wrote two letters, signed "Phocion," on measures proposed in New York for the disfranchisement of those who had been loyalists in the Revolution, arguing that these measures were contrary to the Treaty of 1783 and to public policy. They show his courage and readiness to support justice in the face of popular prejudice. The text includes the conclusion of the second letter.

16. Written in September, 1787, as the Constitutional Convention adjourned, and in the month before the appearance of *Federalist*, No. 1.

17. The Constitution was completed by the federal convention September 17, 1787, and was then submitted by Congress to the people of the several states. Nowhere was opposition to it stronger than in the state of New York. Governor Clinton and two of the three delegates to the convention, Yates and Lansing, were openly opposed to it; the third delegate, Hamilton, became its warmest supporter. On the day of its publication in New York, September 27, Clinton opened fire in the first of a series of essays signed "Cato"; and Yates followed with a series by "Brutus." In reply appeared a series of caustic articles, over the signature of "Cæsar," whose style the public had no difficulty in identifying as that of Hamilton. "Cæsar" was truculent, threatening to follow "Cato" "in all his marches," and contemptuous, professing no attachment "to the majesty of the multitude." (For all these letters see Ford, *Essays on the Constitution*.) Feeling that in adopting this tone he had started on the wrong track, Hamilton soon decided to give up this series for one more impersonal and serious, in which he might "take up the principles of the whole subject."

"Federalist, No. 1," appearing October 27, announced the purpose and outlined the scope of this new work. The task was completed in eighty-five letters—chiefly by Hamilton, but partly by John Jay and James Madison—which appeared during the next seven months. On the much discussed question of the authorship of certain papers, see P. L. Ford, in his edition of the *Federalist*, p. xxix, and also *American Historical Review*, II, p. 443 (E. G. Bourne) and p. 675 (P. L. Ford). First published in the New York *Independent* and *Packet*, the essays were widely reprinted; and even before ratification was complete, they were collected, revised by Hamilton, and published in book form (New York, 1788, 2 vols.). Hamilton's preface says: "The particular circumstances under which these papers have been written, have rendered it impracticable to avoid violations of method and repetitions of ideas, which cannot but displease the critical reader." The essays were written hurriedly to convert the voters of New York—sometimes with arguments local in character—rather than as an abstract treatment of government.

18. This outline covers fairly the contents of Nos. 1 to 51. At some time during the composition the plan was evidently enlarged to include a detailed analysis of the Constitution in the three branches of government (Nos. 52 to 83), a refutation of objections (No. 84), and a conclusion (No. 85).

19. Compare Selections preceding, p. 56, "The great and radical vice," etc.

20. Governor Clinton of New York. The purpose here is immediately controversial—to discredit the strongest opponent of the Constitution in the state of New York.

21. "In the *Federalist* . . . comparatively little is said about the Supreme Court. This is very remarkable, in view of its subsequent history; for if there is any 'sleeping giant' in the Constitution, it has proved to be in the power of the Supreme Court to pass upon the constitutionality of laws." (Sumner, *Hamilton*, p. 139.) If Hamilton overlooked an important means of extending the federal powers, it is perhaps explained by the entire novelty of this function of the Court, with no precedent in experience.

22. After taking the oath of office, Washington, realizing the importance of precedent, gave early attention to the troublesome matter of etiquette, sending a set of nine queries on this point to Hamilton, Jay, Madison, and Adams. Only the replies of Hamilton (here given) and Adams have been preserved. If Hamilton's savors of the "monarchy" which Jefferson deprecated, it should be noted that the reply of Adams went considerably further in recommending "splendor and majesty"; and that at Washington's second inauguration Hamilton concurred with Jefferson in recommending simplicity. Jefferson bears witness to Washington's impatience of form. In 1789 Washington "resisted for three weeks the efforts to introduce levees," and after the first said to his "grand chamberlain," Humphreys: "Well, you have taken me in once, but by God you

shall never take me in a second time."—(The *Anas, Writings of Jefferson*, I, 334.)

23. A long and careful report to Congress furthering the purpose of its resolution: "That adequate provision for the support of the public credit is a matter of high importance to the honor and prosperity of the United States." After insisting on its importance, Hamilton proposes his celebrated measures: 1) the consolidation of the entire public debt; 2) provision for its payment by appropriate taxes and sinking fund. Urging these measures on high grounds of justice and expedience, he does not conceal his main purpose of buttressing the government by enlisting the moneyed classes in its support; see *Works*, II, 65. This expedient had occurred to him as early as 1779; see Introduction, p. xix. C. F. Dunbar (*Quarterly Journal of Economics*, III, 32) shows that in his fiscal measures Hamilton adapted "to his purpose methods and agencies which had been tested by experience," utilizing for the most part English precedents.

24. On December 14, 1790, Hamilton took the second important step in the development of his fiscal policy. To make "further provision for establishing the public credit" he proposed the chartering by the federal government of a National Bank. (Compare note 8.) This measure was assailed by his opponents as inexpedient and particularly as unconstitutional. On Washington's requesting opinions on the latter point from members of his cabinet, adverse opinions were given by Jefferson (see Selections preceding, p. 305) and Randolph; and to these Hamilton here replies. Here he first fully develops the doctrine of "implied" and "resulting powers." "It is not denied that there are *implied*, as well as *express powers*, and that the *former* are as effectually delegated as the *latter*. And for the sake of accuracy it shall be mentioned, that there is another class of powers, which may be properly denominated *resulting powers*. It will not be doubted, that if the United States should make a conquest of any of the territories of its neighbors, they would possess sovereign jurisdiction over the conquered territory. This would be rather a result, from the whole mass of the powers of the government, and from the source of political society, than a consequence of either of the powers specially enumerated." (*Works*, III, 184.) On the passage of the Bank Bill it was signed by the President.

25. On December 5, 1791, in presenting this report, Hamilton took a third important step in the development of his federal policy, by proposing means for "encouraging manufactures in the United States." He bases his argument on two fundamental grounds—national security and balanced economic development. "Not only the wealth but the independence and security of a country appear to be materially connected with the prosperity of manufactures. Every nation, with a view to these great objects, ought to possess within itself all the essentials of national supply."

The report, long and very carefully developed, best of his writings supports his pretensions as a political economist. He begins by examining the principles of Quesnay and the physiocrats, that "agriculture is the most beneficial and productive object of human industry." In Section II, here reprinted, he argues for the productiveness of manufactures. Then, after a long examination of the principal objections, he proposes "the particular measures which it may be advisable to adopt,"—these including protecting duties, bounties and premiums, and the encouragement of inventions. Finally he takes up in turn the different materials of manufacture—iron, wood, skins, etc.—and proposes a board of commissioners "for promoting arts, agriculture, manufactures, and commerce." The report thus contains the germs of our protective system, our Department of Commerce, and our economic commissions.

26. The three reasons for the division of labor are those of Adam Smith, *Wealth of Nations*, Book I, chap. I. E. G. Bourne (*Quarterly Journal of Economics*, VIII, 328) shows, in parallel columns, Hamilton's large use of Smith in this Report. Though he makes only one direct quotation, and does not mention Smith by name, he adopts, among other ideas, Smith's criticism of the physiocratic doctrine, that agriculture is superior to manufacture in productiveness. But with Smith's general conception of the economic world as a system of natural liberty, which is corrupted by government regulation, Hamilton is not in sympathy. He cannot adopt the doctrine of *laissez faire*. It should be noted, however, that even Smith makes concessions to the mercantilist policy of regulation of foreign trade, where such regulation is clearly advantageous. (See J. Viner, *Journal of Political Economy*, XXXV, 229-231.) Hamilton undoubtedly noted these. See also Culbertson, *Hamilton*, p. 127.

27. This letter, to an old friend in Virginia, exhibits the separation, not yet quite public, between Hamilton and his future opponents. Hamilton is now "unequivocally convinced . . . that Mr. Madison, coöperating with Mr. Jefferson, is at the head of a faction decidedly hostile to me and my administration; and actuated by views, in my judgment, subversive of the principles of good government." Too long to be given here entire, the letter may be found in *Works*, VIII, 248-265.

28. The first of three articles published anonymously in Fenno's Federalist *Gazette of the United States*. Freneau's "Whig vehicle of intelligence," the *National Gazette*, first appearing in 1791, had become a thorn in Hamilton's side. Feeling it "now necessary that the whole truth should be told," he sought, perhaps inadvisedly, to discomfit his opponents in these anonymous papers. Ten days earlier he had published, over the initials "T. L.," the following: "The editor of the 'National Gazette' receives a salary from the government. *Quere:* Whether this salary is paid him for *translations*, or for *publications*, the design of which is, to vilify those to whom the voice of the people has committed the administration of our public affairs—to oppose the measures of government, and, by false insinuations, to disturb the public peace? In common life it is thought ungrateful for a man to bite the hand that puts bread into

his mouth; but if the man is hired to do it the case is altered." Hamilton soon published other similar papers, under various pseudonyms, including "Catullus"; see Selections preceding, p. 134. For Jefferson's version see Selections preceding, p. 316, and note 120. See also Chinard, *Jefferson,* p. 261.

29. Compare Jefferson's letter to Madison, Selections preceding, p. 278; to Hopkinson, p. 293; and *Autobiography,* p. 283.

30. In answer to a letter from Washington stating objections to his financial policy made in Virginia by George Mason, doubtless at the prompting of Jefferson, Hamilton sent a memorandum of some forty pages, answering the objections *seriatim;* this forms, in effect, a defense of his funding system (*Works,* II, 237–279). Objection 14 was one constantly urged by Jefferson. Compare "Catullus," Selections preceding, p. 134. One notes here that Hamilton's defense touches the practicability, not the desirability of a monarchy. The question of his "monarchical tendencies" is difficult, partly from the vagueness of the evidence, partly from the ambiguity of the terms (monarchy, republic, democracy). On the whole, however, it appears that in the Convention of 1787 he advocated as near an approach to monarchy as possible, and that, though he supported the government as adopted and considered any monarchical subversions of it impracticable, he continued to the end of his life to regard it as experimental and at least theoretically less desirable than that he had originally proposed. Compare Hamilton's letters to Bayard, Selections preceding, p. 170, and to Pickering, p. 175; and Jefferson's *Anas,* p. 304. Hamilton's friend, Gouverneur Morris, supports Jefferson's view: "He was in principle opposed to republican and attached to monarchical government, but then his opinions were generally known and have been long and loudly proclaimed. . . . He knew that a limited monarchy, even if established, could not preserve itself in this country." (A. C. Morris, *Diary of Morris,* II, 456.) "A government," Hamilton said, "must be fitted to a nation as much as a coat to an individual." (See Selections preceding, p. 164.) See also the work by L. B. Dunbar, in bibliography.

31. The reference is probably to Aaron Burr.

32. Compare "Catullus," III, Selections preceding, p. 141.

33. The quarrel between Hamilton and Jefferson increased Washington's difficulties, and he remonstrated with both. Hamilton replies here: Jefferson in a letter of the same date, which may be compared; see Selections preceding, p. 312.

34. See note 38.

35. "Catullus" (Hamilton), continuing the newspaper war begun in "An American," writes four papers against "Aristides," attacking Jefferson as "the instigator and patron of a certain Gazette," and as the early enemy of the Constitution.

36. Epithets Hamilton later applied to Burr.

37. "Discourses on Davila," by John Adams, advocating an aristo-

cratical government, had recently appeared in Fenno's *United States Gazette*.

38. For Jefferson's connection with the American publication of Paine's *Rights of Man* see his letters to Adams and Washington, in his *Writings*, VIII, 192, 212, 242. Though involuntarily connected with this publication, he was probably pleased that American readers should find in it an antidote, not only to Burke, but to Adams's reactionary "Discourses on Davila," and to Hamilton's "monarchical" tendencies.

39. In 1793 Hamilton's development of his domestic policies was interrupted by the outbreak of war between England and France (Feb. 11), and its becoming an American party issue. Washington issued his famous proclamation of neutrality on April 22. Hamilton's purpose in a series of seven papers, signed "Pacificus," was to justify this proclamation and stem the tide of French sympathy.

40. The "Pacificus" papers were soon followed by a second series, "No Jacobin;" and on "fresh appearances of a covert design to embark the United States in the war," by a third, "Americanus." Only a part of the first of the latter series is reprinted here; the remainder discusses the second of the two questions it propounds (numbered II).

41. Hamilton's anticipation in 1794 of the victorious Napoleon and the failure of French liberty is striking.

42. Hamilton is now forced to return to domestic politics. His excise on whiskey had provoked the "Whiskey Rebellion," threatening not only his financial programme, but the authority of government. In August, 1794, in a report on "Opposition to Internal Duties," he gave a history of the rebellion, which had been going on for two years. Two days later he drafted for Washington a proclamation declaring "that the very existence of the government and the fundamental principles of social order are involved in the issue." In four papers signed "Tully" he enlightens the people in this crisis.

43. Having given up his secretaryship (January, 1795), but still continuing to influence the government as "minister without portfolio," Hamilton supported the famous Jay Treaty against a popular storm in a series of thirty-eight papers by "Camillus." These are more serious, dignified, and thorough in treatment of their subject than some earlier papers with similar titles. Covering nearly 500 pages in the Lodge edition, they form an exhaustive treatise. As this subject has now only historic interest they lack the permanent value of the *Federalist*, but they are equally admirable in their closeness of reasoning, wide knowledge, and moderation. Only a very small sample can be given here.

44. One of the very few letters of a personal nature preserved.

45. At the date of "The Stand," relations with France were strained. The failure of Adams's special mission to France, with the X. Y. Z. affair, aroused in America indignation and warlike feeling. Though he had

hitherto favored peace, Hamilton now took advantage of this feeling to urge vigorous preparation for war.

46. To this letter Washington replied that the expedient of the Southern "circuit" would not, in his opinion, "answer the end that is proposed;" and that he was not yet in "the expectation of open war."—*Works*, ed. J. C. Hamilton, VI, 291.

47. Lear had been Washington's secretary.

48. In the election of 1800–1801, Jefferson and Burr being tied and the election thrown into the House of Representatives, some Federalists saw the opportunity of thwarting the Jeffersonians by supporting Burr. This Hamilton opposed—because Jefferson was the lesser of two evils, and because the Federalist party would eventually be held responsible for Burr's elevation.

49. This rather enigmatical paragraph should be weighed carefully in connection with the charge that Hamilton aimed at shifting the government toward a monarchy. Compare note 30.

50. From at least as early as 1792 Hamilton had represented Burr as dangerous; see letter "To ———," September 26, 1792: "If we have an embryo Cæsar in the United States, 'tis Burr." (*Works*, VIII, 285.) In a letter to Wolcott, December 16, 1800, Burr "is truly the Catiline of America." (VIII, 566.)

51. In 1801 Hamilton's eldest son, Philip, was shot in a duel occasioned by a political quarrel in a theatre.

52. In a letter of G. Morris, to which Hamilton is here replying, Morris regrets that Hamilton has "opposed sending a petition to Congress against the repeal of the law of last session for amending the judicial system. . . . It will enable your personal enemies to say, that you wished the repeal to take effect, so as to overturn the Constitution."—*Works*, ed. J. C. Hamilton, VI, 528.

53. The parts of the two great antagonists are now ironically reversed. Jefferson being in and Hamilton out of power, it is Hamilton's role to turn farmer and comment from retirement on the errors of administration.

54. Probably refers to Jefferson's second Annual Message, December 15, 1802, which continued the "lullaby" of his First Inaugural.

55. This statement of Hamilton's position in the Convention, sixteen years earlier, seems to be substantially borne out by the contemporary evidence. See, however, note 30 and discussion in the Introduction.

56. This letter, written the day before the fatal duel, expressing Hamilton's anxiety for the Union and his fear of democracy, "may be regarded," Sumner thinks, "as his political testament." (*Hamilton*, p. 243.) Compare Jefferson's last letter, Selections preceding, p. 402, and note thereon.

THOMAS JEFFERSON

(References are to Jefferson's *Writings*, Memorial Edition, 20 vols., 1903.)

57. Compare Shelley, *Defense of Poetry:* "Poetry strengthens the faculty which is the organ of the moral nature of man, in the same manner as exercise strengthens a limb."

58. Compare Sidney, *Defense of Poesy:* "Then certainly is more doctrinable the feigned Cyrus in Xenophon than the true Cyrus in Justin," etc. Later in life Jefferson thought "a great obstacle to good education is the inordinate passion prevalent for novels," resulting in "a bloated imagination, sickly judgment, and disgust towards all the real businesses of life."—*Writings*, XV, 166.

59. Of this paper Jefferson gives in an appendix to his *Autobiography* the following particulars (*Writings*, I, 183): Before leaving to attend the Virginia State Convention of 1774 he prepared a draft of proposed instructions to the delegates to Congress. Taken sick on the road, he sent on two copies, one of which was laid before the Convention. "Tamer sentiments," he says, "were preferred, and I believe, wisely preferred; the leap I proposed being too long, as yet, for the mass of our citizens. The distance between these, and the instructions actually adopted, is of some curiosity, however, as it shows the inequality of pace with which we moved, and the prudence required to keep front and rear together. My creed had been formed on unsheathing the sword at Lexington. They printed the paper, however, and gave it the title of 'A summary view of the rights of British America.'" It was published in Williamsburg, 1774, and reprinted in Philadelphia and London. A copy of the Williamsburg edition, with Jefferson's MS. notes, is preserved in the Library of Congress.

60. For discussion of the natural rights here claimed see Chinard, *Jefferson*, pp. 45–53, and *Commonplace Book*, pp. 56–63. The right of expatriation had already been asserted by Richard Bland, in *An Inquiry into the Rights of the British Colonies*, Williamsburg, 1766: "When subjects are deprived of their civil rights . . . they have a natural right to quit the society of which they are members, and to retire into another country," etc.

61. The principle of the present federated British Commonwealths.

62. Randolph, who had been attorney-general, withdrew from Virginia with the royal governor. In a letter to Randolph, three months later, Jefferson goes a little farther toward independence: "We want neither inducement nor power to declare and assert a separation."

63. Of the composition of the *Autobiography*, nothing is known beyond what is told in its first paragraph as follows: "January 6, 1821. At the age of 77, I begin to make some memoranda, and state some recollections of dates and facts concerning myself," etc. It was first published in

Memoirs, edited by T. J. Randolph, Charlottesville, 1829. It begins with an account of Jefferson's family and early life and extends to his arrival in New York, March 21, 1790. It is most important for his share in the Revolution.

64. In this portion of the *Autobiography* Jefferson is utilizing notes "I took in my place while these things were going on." This extract therefore was written in 1776. The reference is to debates in Congress, June 8, 1776, on the motion, (referred to a little farther on as "the original motion") of the delegates from Virginia of June 7, "that the Congress should declare that these United Colonies are, and of right ought to be, free and independent states," etc. A second motion was made June 10, to appoint a committee to "prepare a declaration to the effect of the said first resolution." Thus, as Jefferson notes elsewhere (*Writings*, I, 178), there were two questions: "1st, the Virginia motion of June the 7th, to declare Independence; and 2d, the actual Declaration, its matter and form." Affirmative action having been taken on both, the first actually declared our independence; the second vindicated it to the world.

65. The composition of the Declaration, its revision by Adams and Franklin, the changes made in committee and by Congress, and its sources —matters too complicated to be discussed here—are fully treated in Hazelton, *Declaration of Independence*, Becker, *Declaration of Independence*, and Chinard, *Jefferson*, pp. 69–78. Becker (p. 141) gives the "Rough Draft as it probably read when Jefferson first submitted it to Franklin." The form here given incorporates subsequent revisions by Jefferson, and slight changes suggested by Adams and Franklin; and it also indicates the changes made by Congress. The credit for both conception and expression belongs substantially to Jefferson.

66. The substitution of "happiness" for the Lockian "property," which might have been expected, is characteristic. As has been often noted, however, the "happiness" idea is not original with Jefferson. To the many other sources that have been suggested may be added Blackstone, *Commentaries* (Sec. I, "Of Laws in General"): "The Creator . . . has graciously reduced the rules of obedience to this one paternal precept, 'that man should pursue his own true and substantial happiness.'" Curiously, it occurs also in Hamilton's *Farmer Refuted* (1775).

67. Jefferson is probably wrong in stating that the Declaration was signed July 4; see *Writings*, ed. Ford, I, 28, note.

68. Jefferson refers to the Virginia delegation in Congress and the new state government in Virginia.

69. Ford questions Jefferson's authorship of this bill; *Writings*, ed. Ford, I, 51. Compare Selections preceding, p. 242, and note 80.

70. Compare Selections preceding, p. 238, and note 80.

71. Compare Selections preceding, p. 232, and note 80.

72. This paragraph refers to Congress in 1783, under the Confederation.

73. After his treason Arnold, as a major-general in the British army, was conducting a campaign against Virginia.

74. *Notes on Virginia* was written in the winter of 1781–2 in answer to a set of queries propounded to Jefferson by the Marquis de Barbé-Marbois, Secretary of the French Legation in Philadelphia. Corrected and enlarged, it was privately printed by Jefferson in Paris in 1784 (dated 1782). See Selections preceding, p. 255, "Introductory Notes" to the work in the Memorial and Ford Editions, and also Jefferson's account in the *Autobiography* (*Writings*, I, 90). Though an English edition was authorized by Jefferson (1787), it should be noted that the work, though carefully done, was casual and not originally intended for the public. In 1814, however, he writes of it: "Nearly forty years of additional experience in the affairs of mankind . . . has not altered a single principle." (*Writings*, XIV, 220.)

75. "The first map of Virginia which had ever been made" (*Autobiography*, *Writings*, I, 2),—by Joshua Fry, Professor of Mathematics at William and Mary, and Jefferson's father.

76. "I sometimes think of building a little hermitage at the Natural Bridge (for it is my property)," etc.—*Writings*, VI, 29.

77. On an earlier page Jefferson had questioned the opinion advanced by the Count de Buffon, "that the animals common both to the old and the new world are smaller in the latter."

78. According to later letters, Jefferson himself collected some forty Indian vocabularies, which were unfortunately lost; see *Writings*, XV, 153; XVI, 109.

79. "All the controversy with the Federalists already exists in germ, in this declaration."—Chinard, *Jefferson*, p. 129.

80. The Virginia Assembly having voted, after the Revolution, to revise the Code, Jefferson notes "the most remarkable alterations proposed." The two included here originated with Jefferson, and though neither was adopted, both had his support throughout his life. As early as 1769, as a member of the Virginia legislature, he proposed negro emancipation (*Writings*, I, 4). At this later time (1776) he found "that the public mind would not bear the proposition" (see Selections preceding, p. 212). Two years before his death he reverted to the plan of emancipation and colonization, as "it was sketched in the *Notes on Virginia*." (*Writings*, XVI, 8. See also Selections preceding, p. 212.) The bill "for the Diffusion of Knowledge," here outlined, became, with some modification, the basis for his later "Plan for Elementary Schools," 1817 (*Writings*, XVII, 417), which provided also for the establishment of the University of Virginia. "No system [of education] so complete, so logically constructed, and so well articulated had ever been proposed in any country in the world." (Chinard, *Jefferson*, p. 99.) Compare letter to Wythe, Selections preceding, p. 256.

81. Jefferson's bill "for Establishing Religious Freedom" did not pass

until 1786; see Selections preceding, p. 253, and note 87. See also Chinard, *Jefferson*, p. 100; and *Commonplace Book*, pp. 57, 291, and 359, showing influences in this matter from Locke and Montesquieu.

82. See note 80.

83. Though Jefferson recognized that sometimes "war may become a less losing business than unresisted depredation" (*Writings*, XII, 267), his writings contain countless expressions against it. "I abhor war and view it as the greatest scourge of mankind"; "War is as much a punishment to the punisher as to the sufferer."—*Writings*, IX, 385, 285.

84. Jefferson, more than a quarter of a century later, adopted this policy of "withdrawing a while from the ocean" in his Embargo.

85. In a letter to Adams, November 1, 1822, Jefferson reviews his opinions on the Navy (*Writings*, XV, 400).

86. Ezra Stiles was president of Yale from 1778 to 1795.

87. This act, in Jefferson's opinion, stood with the Declaration of Independence among his services to mankind. Compare his letters to Wythe and Madison, Selections preceding, pp. 256, 260.

88. The *Notes on Virginia;* see note 74.

89. The Convention at Annapolis, September, 1786, which was attended by representatives of but five states, Hamilton representing New York, and which recommended the Constitutional Convention, Philadelphia, 1787.

90. From this letter, originally partly in cipher, and imperfectly deciphered by editors, unimportant imperfect passages are omitted. The paragraph about John Adams is not included in this letter in the Ford edition, and is perhaps not properly a part of it, but in any case is probably Jefferson's.

91. Shays's Rebellion, against the Massachusetts state government, in 1786–7. Jefferson's letters of 1786–7 contain numerous passages palliating this, and rebellion in general. "They are a proof that the people have liberty enough, and I could not wish them less than they have." (*Writings*, VI, 25.) "The way to prevent these irregular interpositions of the people is to give them full information of their affairs through the channels of the public papers," etc. (VI, 57. Compare Selections preceding, p. 280.)

92. Jefferson's friendship with Adams, though broken by political and even personal differences, was "coeval with our government" and extended to their deaths occurring on the same day. His opinion of Adams is fairly represented by this passage. It is most succinctly stated in another letter to Madison, July, 1789: "Always an honest man, often a great one, but sometimes absolutely mad." See notes 90 and 138.

93. Carmichael, at this time American minister to Spain.

94. Vergennes, minister of foreign affairs from 1774 and negotiator of the Treaty of 1783, died within a fortnight.

95. Madame de Tesse, a cousin of Lafayette, whom Jefferson saw much of in Paris.

96. The Assemblée des Notables, called to consult "on the general good," met February 22, 1787. Feeling that France was not yet ready for democratic government, Jefferson advises as a model the English Constitution (the "best guide" mentioned below). Compare his letter to Lafayette, Feb. 28, 1787: "Keeping the good model of your neighboring country before your eyes," etc.

97. To Peter Carr, his nephew, Jefferson addressed another interesting letter of advice; in *Writings*, V, 82.

98. Referring to one of the several varieties of foreign rice with which Jefferson hoped to improve the culture in South Carolina. Numerous letters refer to this subject.

99. Compare Selections preceding, p. 263, and note 91.

100. For other references, in letters, to the provisions of the Constitution, see Selections preceding, pp. 278, 293, 316. These letters bear on the charge, repeatedly made by Hamilton, that Jefferson was opposed to the Constitution; see, for example, p. 127.

101. See note 100.

102. The amendment proposed in this paragraph, for controlling the judiciary, was suggested to Jefferson by his experience as president. The election of 1800 left the judiciary alone still in Federalist hands. In 1801, in the celebrated case of "Marbury vs. Madison," the Federalist Chief-Justice, Marshall, held that the power of passing on questions of constitutionality rested with the Supreme Court. Jefferson believed that it belonged equally to the federal executive; and also to the States, and finally to the people (compare the statement of his position in his letter to Mrs. Adams, *Writings*, XI, 50). Marshall's decisions, along with other judicial "usurpations," led him to think the Constitution defective at this point.

103. In 1784 Jefferson was sent as minister to France, and occupied this position until September, 1789. During the last months of his stay he witnessed, with great interest, the events of the early Revolution. The account in this text begins with the 12th of July, 1789.

104. Note that the term "federalist" is now applied merely to one who has supported federation under the new Constitution; and that it was only later applied (often with capital letter) to a definite political party. Jefferson objected to its appropriation by the "self-styled Federalists."

105. At his death Jefferson left "three volumes bound in marbled paper," with an "Explanation" of their contents, according to which they originally contained: 1) copies of his official opinions, while Secretary of State, with relevant documents; 2) "memorandums on loose scraps of paper" made during the same period as an aid to memory. He had these all bound together, and long afterward, in 1818, he gave "to the whole a calm revisal," cutting out what now seemed "incorrect, or doubtful, or merely personal or private." He had felt, during his secretaryship, that since "the contests of that day were contests of principle," these records

should be preserved; and he now saw their value as "testimony" against Marshall's *Life of Washington*, "which pretends to have been compiled from authentic and unpublished documents." After his death the 1) official opinions were separated from the 2) loose scraps; and the latter were published separately—first in Vol. IV of T. J. Randolph's *Memoirs*, 1829— under the none too appropriate title of "Anas." This title now includes the memoranda for the years 1791 to 1806, with the "Explanation," dated 1818. The publication brought from his opponents indignant charges of violation of private confidence and of "hate and bitterness surviving the tomb." These are convincingly met by Randall in his *Jefferson* (II, 26 ff.). Though there is some question as to the extent of Jefferson's "calm revisal," there is none as to the value of the *Anas* for the history of their period. The first extract in this text is from the "Explanation."

106. Jefferson's communication on this point may be found in *Writings*, XVII, 80.

107. Ford's note (*Writings*, I, 161), pointing out "curious errors" in Jefferson's account, is itself erroneous, misinterpreting the text. There are, however, some minor errors at other points.

108. Even Bowers, along with less favorable critics, finds this "attempt of Jefferson . . . to explain his part in the bargain over Assumption, with the assertion that he had been deceived by Hamilton . . . in the nature of an alibi created after the crime. He was no simple-minded rustic," etc. (*Jefferson and Hamilton*, p. 67.) The "bargain" and the explanation, which seem to have thrown some shadow on Jefferson's character, deserve examination. Bowers argues that Jefferson knew perfectly well the merits of assumption and could not have been duped, citing a letter to Monroe, June 20, 1790. This may be granted, though in a letter to Morris a week earlier, he has said: "My duties preventing me from mingling in these questions [assumption and seat of government], I do not pretend to be very competent to their decision." "In general," he continues, "I think it necessary to give as well as take in a government like ours." Though he prefers "letting the states raise money in their own way," he sees the necessity of yielding, "for the sake of the union and to save us from . . . the total extinction of our credit in Europe." His give and take was therefore not a "crime," or a "bargain" in a corrupt sense. After all, however, what in the *Anas* he really professes he was "ignorant and innocent" of was not assumption, but Hamilton's larger conception of a despotic government based upon it. This he did not realize until the next year, when he broke with Hamilton. This is the "game" to which he was unwittingly "holding the candle." Compare his defence addressed to Washington, (Selections preceding, p. 314): "The first and only instance of [my intermeddling with the Legislature] I was duped into by the Secretary of the Treasury, and made a tool for forwarding his schemes, not then sufficiently understood by me." Of Hamilton's larger "schemes" he was still "innocent."

109. Compare Hamilton's defence, Selections preceding, p. 130. It should be noted that Hamilton there shows a monarchy not undesirable, but merely impracticable in America; see note 30. Jefferson's whole treatment of Hamilton here should be read in the light of Hamilton's "Objections and Answers." (*Works of Hamilton*, II, 237.)

110. Adams's *Defence of the Constitution of the United States* (London, 1787) and *Discourses on Davila* (1791) were interpreted as favoring monarchy.

111. The "Publicola" papers, attacking the principles of Paine's *Rights of Man*, at first thought to be by John Adams, were by his son, John Quincy Adams.

112. On Hamilton's proposing his National Bank in 1790, Washington asked opinions on its constitutionality from members of his cabinet; Jefferson here replies. Hamilton answered in an "Opinion" (see Selections preceding, p. 103, and note 24), with the advantage of having Jefferson's in hand.

113. After serving as member of the Assembly of Notables, 1787, and of the States General, 1789, Lafayette was now commanding an army against the Austrians.

114. Jefferson and Hamilton falling out, Washington remonstrated with both. For Hamilton's reply, of the same date, see Selections preceding, p. 132.

115. Compare note 108.

116. Compare Selections preceding, p. 127.

117. Compare letter to Madison, Selections preceding, p. 278.

118. A few days after the publication of the "American" letters and before replying to Washington, Hamilton made public a statement showing the great progress he had made "towards extinguishing the debts;" see *Works of Hamilton*, II, 305.

119. For Freneau's *National Gazette* see note 28.

120. No doubt Jefferson makes this asseveration honestly. He must, however, have had at least tacit understanding with Freneau and given him tacit approval. And unquestionably he was highly gratified that the people should hear something besides "the hymns and lauds chanted by Fenno." In the *Anas*, entry for May 23, 1792, he tells of a conversation with Washington about Freneau's paper. "He was evidently sore and warm, and I took his intention to be that I should interfere in some way with Freneau. . . . But I will not do it. His paper has saved our Constitution, which was fast galloping into monarchy," etc. (*Writings*, I, 353.) Washington later referred to "that rascal Freneau" (I, 382).

121. John Adams's "Discourses on Davila," inculcating "aristocratical and monarchical principles," appeared in Fenno's *United States Gazette.* On the publication of the Philadelphia edition of Paine's *Rights of Man*, prefaced by Jefferson's note (see note 38), a series of articles signed "Publicola" appeared in the Boston *Centinel*, denouncing both Paine and

Jefferson; see *Writings*, VIII, 212, 242. The "Publicola" papers were by John Quincy Adams; see note 111.

122. Compare the *Anas*, November 19, 1792 (more than two months after this letter to Washington): "Beckley brings me the pamphlet, written by Hamilton before the war, in answer to [Paine's] Common Sense. It is entitled 'Plain Truth' " (*Writings*, I, 324). M. C. Tyler (*Literary History of the American Revolution*, I, 479) thinks the ascription of this feeble work to Hamilton an "immeasurable absurdity." Evidently Jefferson had been seeking the pamphlet as party ammunition.

123. If he does not actually threaten, Jefferson at least reserves his rights.

124. This letter to Mazzei, formerly Jefferson's neighbor in Albemarle County, now in Italy, was by him given to an Italian paper. Finding its way back to America in a garbled form, it was construed as an attack on Washington and made "the burden of federal calumny." Jefferson thought best to defend himself only in private; see letters to Madison, August 3, 1797, and to Van Buren, June 29, 1824.

125. Jefferson sends his "Essay on the Anglo-Saxon Language," for which see *Writings*, XVIII, 365, and compare XVI, 130. "Jefferson was one of the first, if not the pioneer, in this country to advocate the study of Anglo-Saxon and incorporate it in the college curriculum."

126. Gerry, a political friend of long standing, had just returned from serving as commissioner to France.

127. "The most luminous exposition of the Jeffersonian doctrine ever made."—Chinard, *Jefferson*, p. 351.

128. Republicans ridiculed Hamilton's phrase: "A national debt, if not excessive, will be to us a national blessing. It will be a powerful cement of our Union."—Letter to R. Morris, April 30, 1781.

129. See note 140.

130. Granger, of Connecticut, was later Postmaster-General in Jefferson's administration.

131. Adams and Pinckney, Federalist candidates for president in 1800.

132. "The Federalist newspapers never ceased laughing at the 'spasms' so suddenly converted into 'billows,' and at the orthodoxy of Jefferson's Federalism,"—H. Adams, *History*, I, 200. See note 133.

133. The meaning of this "key-note" is slightly diverted, if as has been done by Henry Adams and others, it be printed with capitals; though he is of course playing upon words, Jefferson is talking not of parties but of principles. Temperamentally a harmonizer, he is trying to continue Washington's policies, unite parties, and usher in an "era of good feeling."

134. Knox, as Secretary of War in Washington's cabinet, had generally supported Hamilton against Jefferson. This letter aims at conciliation.

135. Jefferson's removals were not actually so limited; and he soon professed a different principle. Washington and Adams having appointed none but Federalists, he felt that Republicans should have their due share. But "if a due participation of office is a matter of right, how are vacancies

to be obtained? Those by death are few; by resignation none. Can any other mode than that of removal be proposed? This is a painful office; but it is made my duty." (*Writings*, X, 272.) After the balance has been redressed the only question concerning a candidate will be, is he competent? "He contented himself with claiming that to the victors belonged half the spoils." (H. Adams, *History*, I, 226.) Considering the "revolution" which had taken place, his removals, however, were moderate.

136. To his "old and able friend," Rush, a physician in Philadelphia and a signer of the Declaration, Jefferson addressed many letters. For Jefferson's religion, compare Selections preceding, pp. 273, 339, 350, 393, 396. The following contain some important and frequently reiterated points: "I am of a sect by myself, as far as I know." (Selections preceding, p. 393.) "Dispute as long as we will on religious tenets, our reason at last must ultimately decide, as it is the only oracle which God has given us." (XIV, 197.) "Our particular principles of religion are a subject of accountability to our God alone." (XIV, 198.) "Freedom of religion I deem [one of the] essential principles of our government." (First Inaugural.) "We are not in a world ungoverned by the laws and power of a Superior Agent. Our efforts are in His hand, and directed by it; and He will give them their effect in His own time." (XIV, 297.) "I am a Christian in the only sense in which he [Christ] wished anyone to be, sincerely attached to His doctrines." (Selections preceding, p. 340.) "I have ever judged of the religion of others by their lives. . . . For it is in our lives, and not in our words, that our religion must be read." (XV, 60.) Such views, not unusual at present, but advanced at that period, naturally led to charges of irreligion. See also photographic reproduction of the "Jefferson Bible" in *Writings*, vol. XX; and Chinard, *Jefferson*, pp. 519–528.

137. In this message, Jefferson announces the acquisition of Louisiana, and on the renewal of European war, following the truce of Amiens, urges a policy of American non-participation and peace. This text includes only the last paragraph.

138. The correspondence between Jefferson and Adams, dating from 1777, ceases in 1796 with a letter in which Jefferson wishes Adams success in his presidency. At the time of Jefferson's inauguration (1801) Adams left Washington without welcoming his successor, and estrangement became complete. In this letter to Mrs. Adams Jefferson makes overtures which were not accepted. The reconciliation occurred in 1811; see the letter to Rush, Selections preceding, p. 357, and note 143.

139. Jefferson and Hamilton agreed in applying morality to international relations. "The established rules of morality and justice," Hamilton says, "are applicable to nations as well as to individuals," (*Works*, II, 295.)

140. New England orthodoxy identified Jefferson's philosophy with irreligion; Jefferson its "anti-philosophy" with superstition. "I still dare use the word philosophy, notwithstanding the war waged against it by bigotry and despotism." (*Writings*, X, 191.)

141. Nearly thirty years before (1776), Jefferson had proposed, as a device for the seal of the United States, "the children of Israel in the wilderness led by a cloud by day, and a pillar by night." Early American history, indeed, is filled with this comparison.

142. Jefferson gives his grandson, now in Philadelphia for his education, some rules which had evidently guided his own conduct.

143. Rush's kindly offices (see letter, Selections preceding, p. 357) effected a reconciliation between Jefferson and Adams. Adams, remembering one of Jefferson's interests, sent him fine specimens of Massachusetts homespuns, which are here acknowledged. The correspondence thus begun, and continued until the death of the two friends, is probably the most interesting in American history.

144. Melish, an Englishman, had published his American travels and an American atlas.

145. "Ἴδαν," etc.: Theocritus, *Idyll* xvii, lines 9–11.

146. Jefferson refers to a letter to Priestley (*Writings*, X, 228) in which, reprehending "bigotry in politics and religion," he cites an address of Adams. In a letter of June 10, 1813, Adams has called for chapter and verse.

147. In letters of 1813 Jefferson and Adams apply leisurely scholarship to a question which, in earlier years, had been one of practical politics. In two letters, beginning with "epigraphs" from Theognis, Adams maintains that aristocracy is ineradicable from society, as may be demonstrated "by examples drawn from your own Virginia, and from every other state in the Union, and from the history of every nation." No society "can pretend to establish a free government without attention to it." "The five pillars of aristocracy are beauty, wealth, birth, genius, and virtue. Any one of the three first can . . . overbear any or both of the two last," (Adams, *Works*, 1856, X, 52, 59, 65). Jefferson, in answer, here propounds his theory of the "aristoi."

For the passage from Theognis see Bergk edition, lines 184 ff.; and for that from Ocellus, *Fragmenta Philosophorum Græcorum*, ed. Mullach, I, 402.

148. Pickering, an old political opponent, had sent Jefferson one of the discourses of William Ellery Channing, possibly the well-known sermon of 1819 on Unitarian Christianity, which expressed many views in consonance with Jefferson's.

149. Jefferson, some six weeks before the Monroe Doctrine was officially promulgated, approves its principle: the exclusion from "this hemisphere" of the "lawless alliance, calling itself Holy."

150. This letter, written ten days before Jefferson's death, may be compared with Hamilton's "political testament;" see Selections preceding, p. 178, and note 56, above.